4TH EDITION

SHOPPING MATTERS

ENGLISCH FÜR EINZELHANDEL UND VERKAUF

von
Michael Benford

unter Mitarbeit der Verlagsredaktion

Cornelsen

SHOPPING MATTERS

Verfasser:	Michael Benford, Bochum
Beraterteam:	Annette Derr, Ulm Marc Engels, Erkelenz Bianca Sonnenschein, Erkelenz
Projektleitung und Verlagsredaktion:	Simone Conrad
Außenredaktion:	Neil Porter
Redaktionelle Mitarbeit:	Oliver Busch (Wörterverzeichnisse), Christine House, Karla Seedorf
Layoutkonzept:	finedesign, Berlin
Layoutanpassung:	graphitecture book & edition
Technische Umsetzung:	Straive
Umschlaggestaltung:	vitaledesign, Berlin
Coverfoto:	Shutterstock.com/zhu difeng
Illustrationen:	D'Avila Illustration Agency

www.cornelsen.de

1. Auflage, 1. Druck 2022

Alle Drucke dieser Ausgabe sind inhaltlich unverändert und können im Unterricht nebeneinander verwendet werden.

Druck: Mohn Media Mohndruck, Gütersloh

ISBN 978-3-06-451982-4

PEFC™
PEFC/04-31-1033

PEFC zertifiziert
Dieses Produkt stammt aus nachhaltig bewirtschafteten Wäldern und kontrollierten Quellen.

www.pefc.de

Vorwort

Shopping Matters 4th edition ist eine Neubearbeitung des bewährten Englisch-Lehrwerks für Verkäuferinnen und Verkäufer sowie Einzelhandelskaufleute und wurde für die Ausbildung in Berufsschulen sowie die innerbetriebliche Aus- und Weiterbildung konzipiert. Das Lehrwerk setzt Englischkenntnisse voraus, die dem Niveau A2 des Europäischen Referenzrahmens (*Common European Framework of Reference*) entsprechen. Es deckt die Themen der aktuellen Lehrpläne der Bundesländer für Englisch in der Berufsschule konsequent ab.

Besonderer Wert wird in diesem Lehrwerk auf **Handlungskompetenz** und direkten Berufsbezug gelegt. Jede Unit beginnt mit einem kapitelübergreifenden, branchenspezifischen **SCENARIO,** das die Unit mit Hilfe einer Input-Seite einleitet und sie mit einer Output-Seite abschließt:

Input: Die offene Aufgabenstellung führt in die Lernsituation ein.

Output: Die Lerninhalte der Unit unterstützen bei der selbstständigen Entwicklung der geforderten Kompetenzen. Der Projektcharakter der Output-Seite lässt vielfache Lern- und Lösungswege seitens der Lernenden zu.

Die *Scenarios* führen über handlungs- und kompetenzorientierte Lernschritte zu einem Handlungsprodukt und ermöglichen so eigenverantwortliches Lernen. Die Lernziele der thematischen Einheiten sind jeweils zu Beginn des Moduls mit einem Pfeil gekennzeichnet und bieten so eine schnelle Orientierung.

Die zwölf Units des Lehrwerks sind flexibel einsetzbar. Jede Unit umfasst vier weitere, modulartige ***Situations,*** die jeweils in einer Doppelstunde bearbeitet werden können und so konzipiert sind, dass sie ausgelassen oder zu einem anderen Zeitpunkt behandelt werden können:

Foundation: Diese Doppelseite bietet Ihnen mit Grundwissen und elementarem Themenvokabular einen Einstieg in das Thema der Unit.

Part A / B: Diese stark berufsbezogenen Module behandeln fachspezifische Schwerpunkte der Unit mithilfe authentischer und aktueller Materialien.

Communication: Berufliche Kommunikation steht im Fokus des abschließenden Communication-Teils. Ein „Das kann ich"-Kästchen – eine Checkliste zur Selbstevaluation – rundet die Unit ab und ermöglicht es den Lernenden, über ihren persönlichen Lernerfolg zu reflektieren.

Um der Heterogenität der Auszubildenden gerecht zu werden, finden sich zahlreiche Aufgaben zur **Binnendifferenzierung** in den Units. Diese sind mit einem Strich unter der Aufgabenziffer gekennzeichnet und verweisen auf editierbare Kopiervorlagen im Unterrichtsmanager Plus, die alternative Bearbeitungsmöglichkeiten für die jeweilige Aufgabe zur Verfügung stellen.

Zur systematischen Vorbereitung auf die **KMK-Prüfung** wird eine komplette Musterprüfung (Stufe II – B1) im Anhang angeboten. Ebenfalls im Anhang finden Sie *Thematic vocabulary* sowie berufsbezogene *Useful phrases* zur Erweiterung des **berufsrelevanten Wortschatzes** und zur Schulung einer effektiven beruflichen Kommunikation. Außerdem steht Ihnen dort eine umfangreiche *A-Z word list* mit allen neuen Wörtern in alphabetischer Reihenfolge zur Verfügung.

Sämtliche **Audio-** und **Videomaterialien** finden Sie im E-Book sowie im Unterrichtsmanager Plus. Die kurzen Videos geben thematisch passende Einblicke in das spätere Berufsleben und vermitteln Fachwissen in motivierender Form. Neben diesen Materialien sind auch die dazugehörigen Arbeitsblätter zur Unterrichtsvorbereitung für Lehrkräfte im Unterrichtsmanager Plus zugänglich.

Die Verlagsredaktion sowie der Verfasser und das Beraterteam wünschen Ihnen viel Erfolg und Freude mit *Shopping Matters 4th edition.*

Table of contents

Unit		Content	Situation	Skills	
1	**My workplace**				6
	Lernsituation: Creating a brochure or flyer about a career in the retail trade				
	FOUNDATION	My background	Presenting yourself to others	Introducing yourself and others Describing your shop Explaining your career choice Introducing people Making small talk	
	PART A	Where I work	Presenting your training shop		
	PART B	Why retail?	Explaining why you chose a career in retail		
	COMMUNICATION	Introductions and small talk	Introducing people and making small talk		
2	**My company**				17
	Lernsituation: Writing a wesbite page about your company				
	FOUNDATION	My company	Creating an organization chart of my company	Creating an organizational chart Discussing roles in your company Examining distribution networks Mediating a text Understanding a website's structure Giving directions	
	PART A	My company's profile	Mediating a text about distribution networks		
	PART B	My company's website	Presenting your company's mobile website		
	COMMUNICATION	Giving directions	Giving directions		
3	**Working conditions**				29
	Lernsituation: Detailing the working conditions in your shop				
	FOUNDATION	Work routine	Describing your duties and responsibilities at work	Describing typical tasks at work Examining working conditions Writing your job profile Giving a presentation	
	PART A	Pay, conditions and equality in the workplace	Presenting information about working conditions in a company		
	PART B	Workwear	Describing the dress code where you work		
	COMMUNICATION	A short presentation	Giving a presentation about your workplace		
4	**Retail in Germany and abroad**				41
	Lernsituation: Producing a dossier about working conditions in Germany for an American retailer				
	FOUNDATION	Career paths in Germany and the USA	Comparing career paths	Writing an email Drawing up a table Presenting a table to class Comparing working conditions in different countries Drawing graphs	
	PART A	Shopping hours and restrictions	Detailing changes you would like to make to opening hours		
	PART B	Working conditions in different countries	Giving a presentation about working conditions in retail		
	COMMUNICATION	Diagrams and statistics	Drawing a chart about popular shopping times in your shop		
5	**Presenting products**				53
	Lernsituation: Redesigning the layout of a supermarket to make it more attractive to customers				
	FOUNDATION	Product groups and labels	Reviewing labelling regulations	Listing product groups Explaining product labels Understanding store layout and product presentation Promoting products through cross-selling and upselling	
	PART A	Displaying products	Discussing the pros and cons of displaying goods		
	PART B	Designing the best store layout	Examining product displays in your shop		
	COMMUNICATION	Cross-selling and upselling	Learning how to cross-sell and upsell		
6	**Advising customers**				65
	Lernsituation: Dealing with an angry customer so that he becomes a loyal customer				
	FOUNDATION	Sales talk	Learning how to structure a sales talk	Analysing the different stages of a sales talk Optimizing your website to help customers Improving services for your customers Using polite and professional language	
	PART A	Understanding customers	Learning about different types of customers and how to sell to them		
	PART B	Customer loyalty	Discussing the pros and cons of loyalty cards		
	COMMUNICATION	Polite language	Practising polite language with customers		

Unit		Content	Situation	Skills	
7	**Online and offline sales**				79
	Lernsituation: Writing a short text with details of your shop's delivery and returns policy				
	FOUNDATION	Online vs offline	Discussing new sales strategies and platforms	Analysing a graph Discussing pros and cons Filling in returns forms Dealing with customers returning goods Creating promotional emails	
	PART A	Distance selling	Examining returns policies for online purchases		
	PART B	Returning goods to a shop	Processing in-shop returns		
	COMMUNICATION	Newsletters	Finding out how to get customers to read newsletters		
8	**Enquiries and terms of delivery**				91
	Lernsituation: Devising enquiry templates for purchasing products from abroad				
	FOUNDATION	The layout of business letters	Practising the layout of letters	Practising the layout of business letters Writing letters of enquiries Learning about Incoterms® 2020 Practising telephone numbers and email addresses Making telephone enquiries	
	PART A	Enquiries	Writing enquiries to suppliers		
	PART B	Terms of delivery	Comparing terms of delivery from different suppliers		
	COMMUNICATION	Telephone enquiries	Making and receiving enquiries		
9	**Terms of payment, offers, orders and acknowledgements**				103
	Lernsituation: Offering more favourable terms of payment to a customer				
	FOUNDATION	Terms of payment	Reviewing terms of payment	Saying and writing prices in English Comparing offers Negotiating terms	
	PART A	Offers	Writing an offer		
	PART B	Orders and acknowledgements	Writing an order		
	COMMUNICATION	Negotiating better terms	Negotiating terms with different styles		
10	**Problems and complaints**				115
	Lernsituation: Preparing yourself for a customer with a complaint				
	FOUNDATION	Customer complaints in retail outlets	Finding solutions to customer complaints	Learning about consumer rights and obligations Writing letters of complaint Making telephone complaints Responding to a written complaint Responding to a telephone complaint Learning how to calm angry customers	
	PART A	Complaining to a supplier	Writing a letter of complaint		
	PART B	Replying to customer complaints	Writing a reply to a complaint		
	COMMUNICATION	Dealing with angry customers	Practising dealing with angry customers		
11	**The future of retail**				127
	Lernsituation: Setting out ideas how to attract young customers				
	FOUNDATION	Future trends	Examining how the future of retail might look	Comparing methods of payment Examining graphs Mediating information Taking part in a meeting	
	PART A	Methods of payment	Identifying future trends in payments		
	PART B	Smart stores	Examining different types of smart stores		
	COMMUNICATION	Business meetings	Taking part in a meeting		
12	**Applying for a job**				137
	Lernsituation: Preparing yourself for a job interview abroad				
	FOUNDATION	Working abroad	Writing a personal profile	Examining job adverts Writing a CV Writing a covering letter Booking a hotel Having a job interview	
	PART A	CV and covering letter	Writing a CV and a covering letter		
	PART B	Travel arrangements	Planning a trip to a job interview		
	COMMUNICATION	Job interviews	Practising for a job interview		

Appendix

KMK mock exam: Stufe II	149
Partner files	154
Grammar files	165
Transcripts	170
Useful phrases	189
Thematic vocabulary	198
A–Z word list	201
Global trade	225
Talking about numbers	227
Irregular verbs	228
Maps	229
Acknowledgements	231

1 My workplace

SCENARIO: Input

The manager of the shop where you are doing your apprenticeship is pleased with your work and asks you to be part of a team representing your company at an international job fair in Frankfurt. Your employer hopes to recruit more staff, so your job at the fair will be to talk to English-speaking visitors to your company's booth about yourself, your background and your training course, and say why you like your job as a retail sales adviser or retail sales assistant.

→ **In this unit you are going to look at your background, your workplace and your reasons for training to work in retail.**

→ **At the end of the unit you will be asked to create a brochure or flyer to be handed out to school-leavers and young people interested in a career in the retail trade.**

FOUNDATION: My background

Situation: You attend a language seminar for retail sales apprentices to improve your English.
→ **You present yourself to other people.**

1 Creating a portrait of yourself

The seminar leader tells you to prepare a short portrait of yourself.

Create a portrait of yourself with the help of the headings (A–D) and the language boxes and your own ideas. Go through each section and write a few sentences about yourself for each heading.

A About me

My name is … (*first name*) … (*family name*). I'm … (*age*, e.g. *18*). I'm single/married. I have a daughter/son aged … (e.g. *2*). I live in … (*town/city*). I was born in … (*town/city/country*).

I'm doing an apprenticeship to become a … (*job*, e.g. retail sales assistant/adviser) at … (*name of employer*). I drive/walk to work / go to work by public transport. At my shop we work five/six days a week. We do / don't do shift work. I prefer morning/day/afternoon/evening shift.

My vocational training college is in … (*town/city*). I go there two days a week on day release / for three weeks at a time on block release. I'm in my first/second/final year of the course. My exams are in … (*month/year*).

B My family

FAMILY TREE

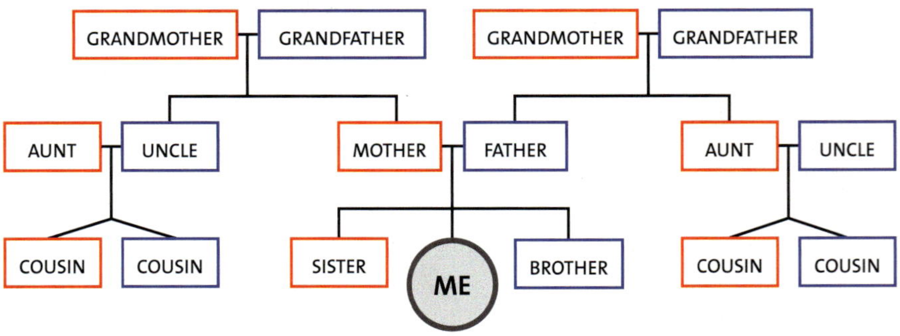

I have 1/2/3 brother(s) and sister(s). / I'm an only child.
My twin/elder/younger brother/sister is called …
He/She is … (e.g. 17). He/She goes to school / works in … (*place*, e.g. Essen).
My mother's/father's called … (*name*). She's/He's … (*age*).
He/She works in … (*place*) / doesn't work.
My mother/father/parents was/were born in … (*place*, e.g. Munich).

C My likes, dislikes and hobbies

		sport	entertainment	helping others	hobbies
I	like enjoy love don't like don't enjoy hate	swimming mountain biking skiing (horse) riding athletics boxing cycling playing football playing volleyball playing chess skateboarding weightlifting in-line/roller skating going to the gym	clubbing going to the pub going to restaurants going to the cinema going to football matches listening to music reading (e.g. novels) streaming films watching music videos travelling watching TV series	babysitting doing charity work helping out at church / the mosque / a food bank / a local care home working for the Red Cross / ambulance service / technical emergency service volunteering at …	dancing acting shopping DIY knitting/sewing playing the drums/ guitar/ piano singing teaching (e.g. swimming)

D My education

I went to a	secondary school comprehensive grammar school	in … (*place*).

Then I did	a one/two-year course at a vocational training college in … (*place*). a placement in an office / at a company/shop.

My favourite subjects	are were	German English maths science sport history *other subject(s)*	because I like	(*e.g.*) languages. numbers. understanding how things work. learning about the past. current affairs. keeping fit. *other reasons*

I didn't like … (*subject*) because	it was too theoretical/abstract. there was too much to remember. *other reasons.*

2 Talking about yourself

The seminar leader asks you to present yourselves.

With a partner take it in turns to present yourselves. Start like this:

Partner A:
Tell me about yourself.
And what about your family?
What are your likes and dislikes?
How about school?

Partner B:
My name's …
I have …
I like …
…

PART A: Where I work

Situation: The leader of your language seminar for retail sales apprentices puts you into teams of apprentices from different shops and gives you the task of describing your workplace to each other.
→ **You present the shop you are doing your training at.**

1 Talking about where my shop is

The seminar leader asks you to talk about the location of your shop.

A **Use expressions from the box below to name and describe the locations shown (A–D). Some expressions can be used more than once.**

at the edge of a town · in the city centre · in the centre of town · mall · narrow streets · near the city centre · pedestrian precinct · retail park · small town

Example: The mall is located at/near/in …

A

B

C

D

B **Explain how to get to each of the four locations in exercise 1A. Use the expressions in the box below.**

best accessed by/on · by bike · by car · by public transport · expensive parking · large free car park · limited parking · on foot · vehicles not allowed

Example: As the shops are in the pedestrian precinct, they're best accessed …

C **Explain where your training shop is and how to access it in a few sentences. Describe the advantages and disadvantages of the location of your training shop.**

2 Describing what my shop sells

The seminar leader asks you to talk about what your shop sells.

VIDEO 1

Watch the video about different types of shops.

A **First match the descriptions (A–F) with the photos (1–6) on page 11.**

A My shop is a self-service chain store selling toiletries, health and beauty products, baby products and cleaning agents. Most people come to us to buy their soap, shampoo, toothpaste, vitamin pills, plasters, cosmetics and washing powder. My branch is always busy because it's at the central station.

B My shop is a big box store that sells a wide range of flat-pack furniture for customers to assemble at home. We also sell kitchen appliances, lighting, soft furnishings, bedding, cutlery, crockery and home decorations. When customers arrive, they walk through our showroom. They can order the things they want from the sales assistants. We also have a restaurant, a café and a supervised children's play area.

C I work in a small, privately owned shop. It has a limited range of very expensive garments with famous brand names. We also stock shoes and accessories, such as jewellery and handbags. We offer a very personal service and take a lot of time with each customer.

D I work for a large chain of self-service food stores with big and small branches everywhere. We sell a limited range of staple goods, basically food and household items, often straight out of the delivery cartons to cut costs and save time. We only advertise in local newspapers and not on TV and there's no background music in our shops.

E My shop is one of a chain of self-service grocery stores with branches everywhere. We sell a wide variety of fresh and packaged food and drinks, including fresh meat and cheese, dairy products and vegetables, soft drinks and alcoholic beverages. Our range includes everyday household products like soap, toilet paper, washing-up liquid and dishwasher tabs. We have a bakery at the entrance to the shop.

F I work in big box store with an inside and outside sales area and a gardening centre. We sell a wide range of hand and power tools, building materials, paint and machinery. We cater for people who want to do work on their homes and gardens themselves. We have a drive-in section for bulky or heavy items.

1 boutique

2 discounter

3 DIY store

4 drugstore

5 furniture retailer

6 supermarket

B Match the German equivalents in the box with the highlighted English words.

Accessoires • alkoholische Getränke • Filialen • großflächiges Kaufhaus • Heimtextilien • Hygieneartikel • Kleidungsstücke • Milchprodukte • Reinigungsmittel • Selbstbaumöbel • sperrig • Waren des täglichen Bedarfs

C Complete the sentences with information from the descriptions.

1 Boutiques don't only sell clothes. They also sell ___ .
2 Discounters only stock staple goods that everyone needs and some cut costs by selling items out of ___.
3 The customers at DIY stores install, replace and repair things themselves, and for this they need to buy ___.
4 In Germany, drugstores aren't allowed to sell drugs and medicines. They sell cleaning agents, baby products, toiletries and ___.
5 A lot of furniture is too big to fit into a car, so some shops sell flat-pack furniture that customers can ___.
6 Supermarkets sell a wide range of food and drinks and also other things that are used every day, such as ___.

Talking about routine actions

- Our shop **sells** clothes. We **stock** all the major brands.
- We **open** six days a week. We **don't open** on Sundays.
- The cashier **speaks** German, Polish and English. She **doesn't speak** Spanish.

› *Grammar: Simple present, page 165*

D Give a short description of your shop to the class. Include details of its location and the goods it sells. Either present your shop in the form of a poster or an infographic.

PART B: Why retail?

Situation: The seminar leader tells each team of apprentices to consider their reasons for wanting to work in the retail trade and why they chose their particular type of shop.
→ **You list your reasons for your choice of job and explain them to your team.**

1 Explaining why I chose retail

The seminar leader asks you about the reasons why you chose your shop.

A **Brainstorm reasons for your choice of shop and write them down. You can use words from the word cloud.**

sales commission · creative · interesting products · challenging · never boring · working with people · smart appearance · flexible working hours · working in the local community · responsibility · secure job · discounts · basic school qualifications · uniform · good promotion prospects · helping people

B 2 **Listen to four apprentices talking about why they chose their shops. Copy the table and complete it with the information you hear.**

	Oskar	Sevda	Niko	Emma
age				
type of shop				
first reason				
second reason				
third reason				

C 2 **Listen again and fill in the gaps with the words you hear.**

Oskar In summer after the early ___[1] I can still go out after work and enjoy the sunshine.
Sevda Window ___[2] is so important because it brings in the customers if it's good.
Niko I also like working at the ___ ___[3] .
Emma Perhaps a shelf is empty and needs ___ ___[4], or a display stand looks wrong. It's my job to fix it.

D **List your own reasons for choosing your training shop in order of importance.**

E **Compare your priorities with a partner and discuss any differences.**

2 Talking to a potential retail sales apprentice

You meet people from other seminars and one person shows interest in working in retail.

A **Work with a partner and use the instructions to have a conversation in English.**

Partner A: You

Stellen Sie sich informell vor. Sagen Sie, dass Sie Auszubildende/r bei (*Name Ihres Ausbildungsbetriebs*) im … (*ersten/zweiten/dritten*) Jahr sind. Fragen Sie nach Ihrer/Ihrem Gesprächspartner/-in.

Beschreiben Sie Ihren Ausbildungsbetrieb (Standort, Produktsortiment, Kundinnen/Kunden).

Beschreiben Sie Ihre Tätigkeiten.

Beschreiben Sie Ihre alte Schule und nennen Sie Ihre Lieblingsfächer dort.

Zählen Sie Ihre Gründe auf.

Beschreiben Sie, was Ihnen am meisten am Job gefällt.

Geben Sie Ihrem/Ihrer Gesprächspartner/-in die Adresse der Firmenwebsite und wünschen Sie ihm/ihr alles Gute bei der Suche nach einem Ausbildungsplatz.

Partner B: Seminar participant

Stellen Sie sich informell vor. Sagen Sie, dass Sie sich für einen Beruf im Einzelhandel interessieren. Bitten Sie um mehr Informationen zur Firma.

Fragen Sie, welche Tätigkeiten Ihr/Ihre Gesprächspartner/-in ausübt.

Fragen Sie Ihren/Ihre Gesprächspartner/-in, welche Schule er/sie besucht hat und was seine/ihre Lieblingsfächer waren.

Fragen Sie, warum Ihr/Ihre Gesprächspartner/-in sich für einen Beruf im Einzelhandel entschieden hat.

Fragen Sie, was Ihr/Ihre Gesprächspartner/-in am meisten am Job gefällt.

Bitten Sie um Informationen über einen Ausbildungsplatz bei der Firma.

Bedanken Sie sich für die hilfreichen Informationen.

B **Now swap roles.**

COMMUNICATION: Introductions and small talk

Situation: The leader of your seminar asks you to introduce yourselves and make small talk.
→ **You practise talking to visitors, introductions and small talk.**

1 Introducing yourself

Four apprentices introduce themselves.

A 3)) **Copy and complete their profiles with the information you hear.**

	1	2	3	4

name	Almira Ibrahim	Paul Fischer	Lena Hoffmann	Kingsley Ekoku
age	[1]	[3]	[6]	20
lives in	[2]	Dortmund	[7]	Cologne
shop	discounter	[4]	[8]	[9]
apprenticehip year	third	[5]	second	[10]

B **Now introduce yourself to at least four other members of your class.**

Hi, I'm … (*first name*).

I'm doing an apprenticeship at a … (*type of shop*).

Most customers come to our shop to buy … (*products*).

I go to a vocational college in … (*place*).

I'm in my … (first/second/third/final) year.

Introducing yourself

I'm 18. / I'm 18 years old.
(NOT: I'm 18 ~~years~~.)
I'm Paul Fischer. I was born in Germany.
(NOT: I ~~am~~ born in Germany.)
I'm doing an apprenticeship at a drugstore.
(NOT: ~~by~~ a drugstore)

C **Work in groups of three. Use the phrases in the box on the right and the information on page 15 to introduce people to each other.**

› *Useful phrases: Making introductions, page 189*

Introducing people to each other

Informal
This is … (*first name*). He's/She's new. He's/She's from …
Formal
Let me introduce you to the (Assistant) Manager.
I'd like you to meet … from … . He's/She's our new apprentice.
May I introduce you to …
Pleased to meet you.

You introduce:	to:
1 Lena Hoffmann · 2nd year apprentice · Dresden	Ben Welz · new apprentice · Dortmund
2 Kingsley Ekoku · final year apprentice · Cologne	Mrs Richter · District Manager
3 Almira Ibrahim · Syria · third year	Dr Haverkamp · Sales Director

Invent two more examples.

2 Making small talk

When you meet people for the first time, you need to know how to make small talk.

What is small talk?
Small talk isn't about information or facts. It's about creating a nice atmosphere. It's about agreeing and saying more than the minimum. You shouldn't use just short answers and you shouldn't disagree about anything. You should only talk about safe topics.

Example: It's warm for this time of year, isn't it?
Bad answer: ~~No, it isn't.~~
Good answer: Yes, it is. Very pleasant!

A **Choose safe small-talk topics from the list below and compare your answers with a partner. Discuss which topics you should avoid, and why.**

cars · celebrities · clothes · computers · culture · entertainment · food and drink · hobbies · holidays · illness · money · music · politics · relationships · religion · sport · the weather · your boss

B **Match the sentences in columns A, B, C and D to make small talk.**

A	B	C	D
1 I love that top you're wearing!	**1** Thanks for reminding me. What time?	**1** Yes, and they do great lattes.	**1** Amazing! Nature is so fascinating!
2 Germany's playing against Poland tonight.	**2** I love animals! Are there any polar bears?	**2** Do you like them? I got them at SuperFash.	**2** I love lattes and latte macchiatos.
3 There's a great new café near here.	**3** Thanks, and I really like your earrings!	**3** No, but there's an anaconda that's 10 metres long.	**3** Yes, I want to see some good goals.
4 There's a big zoo here if you're interested.	**4** Oh really? Can you sit outside?	**4** 9 o'clock. I hope it's a good match.	**4** Yes, that's a great shop.

C **Work with a partner, choose at least two safe topics and practise making small talk. Remember this isn't about showing off or being correct – it's about creating a pleasant atmosphere.**

DAS KANN ICH (Unit 1)

- Mich und meinen Ausbildungshintergrund auf Englisch beschreiben. (Foundation)
- Meinen Ausbildungsbetrieb auf Englisch vorstellen. (Part A)
- Über meine Beweggründe, im Einkauf zu arbeiten, sprechen. (Part B)
- Mich selbst und andere auf Englisch vorstellen. (Communication)

SCENARIO: Output

Now go back to the beginning of the unit (page 7) and study the task again.

→ **Create a brochure or flyer to be handed out at an international job fair to school-leavers and young people interested in a career in the retail trade.**

STEP 1 **Before you work on your task, think about the following:**

1 Your target audience
- What sort of information will encourage them to apply to your company?
- Do you want to include information about yourself?
- Do you want to include information about other employees?

2 The design of the brochure or flyer
- Which of the following do you want to include?
  - a headline that catches the reader's attention
  - text (short or long?)
  - photos
  - bullet points highlighting important aspects
  - contact details (telephone number, email address, website)

STEP 2 **Start by writing down:**

- Information about the shop (goods, location)
- Your reasons for choosing a career in retail

STEP 3 **Think of the vocabulary and phrases you will need.**

- Find exercises in this unit which offer useful vocabulary for your task.
- List vocabulary according to the topic.

2 My company

SCENARIO: Input

Your training shop is now re-thinking its online presence and has decided that it needs a new website. It employs an international consultancy for this project and sets up a website team. You are a member of the team.

→ **In this unit you are going to look at different types of sales outlets and discuss goods, services and distribution networks.**

→ **At the end of the unit you will be asked to write a page for your company's website, explaining what sort of company it is, what it sells, how it sells and how it tries to be an ethical company.**

FOUNDATION: My company

Situation: Your company, Outlet Becker, is updating the English version of its website, including details of its organization.

→ **You create an organization chart of your shop.**

1 Talking about your shop's business organization

You listen to a podcast that explains German retailing to a worldwide audience.

A 4)) **Listen to four people in the retail business describe the firms where they work. Match the statements (a–h) to the people (1–4).**

1 Nathalie Müller	2 Orhan Bayrak	3 Frank Stoppel	4 Angelika Schwan
sole trader *Einzelunternehmerin*	general partnership *offene Handelsgesellschaft*	supermarket manager *Marktleiter*	franchisee *Franchisenehmerin*

a Ich muss die Anweisungen der Geschäftsleitung befolgen.
b Ich muss mich nicht um Werbung kümmern, dafür aber einen Teil meines Umsatzes an die Dachgesellschaft zahlen.
c Ich hafte nicht für die Produkte in meinem Laden.
d Ich muss den Gewinn mit niemandem teilen.
e Ich darf nur bestimmte Produkte verkaufen, weiß aber von vornherein, dass sie beliebt sind.
f Ich muss den Gewinn teilen und hafte mit meinem ganzen Vermögen, sollte etwas schiefgehen.
g Ich habe die absolute Entscheidungsfreiheit.
h Ich muss bereit sein, Kompromisse zu schließen, denn sonst ist der Fortbestand der Firma gefährdet.

B **Use the switchboard to write about the pros and cons of the different types of business organizations.**

Sole traders General partners Franchisees Employees	own don't own	the company and/but	have a lot of don't have much	freedom	to do what they want. to change things.

Sole traders General partners Franchisees	don't share share	their profits with	anyone. their partner(s). the franchisor.

Sole traders General partners Franchisees Employees	are aren't	free to decide what	goods to stock services to offer the prices are times to open	because	they are someone else is	the boss.

Sole traders General partners Franchisees Employees	bear don't bear	the risk if something goes wrong and	could don't	lose everything	if the company fails.

Common forms of business organization in retail

Einzelunternehmer/-in	sole trader
offene Handelsgesellschaft (OHG)	general partnership
Kommanditgesellschaft (KG)	limited partnership
Genossenschaft	cooperative
GmbH (Gesellschaft mit beschränkter Haftung)	Ltd (private limited company)
AG (Aktiengesellschaft)	plc (public limited company)
e. K. (eingetragene/r Kaufmann/-frau)	registered merchant
Franchisegeber/-in	franchisor
Franchisenehmer/-in	franchisee

C **Discuss the pros and cons of the sort of shop you work in first with a partner, then with your class.**

2 Finding out who's who

You find a typical organization chart for a retail sales outlet.

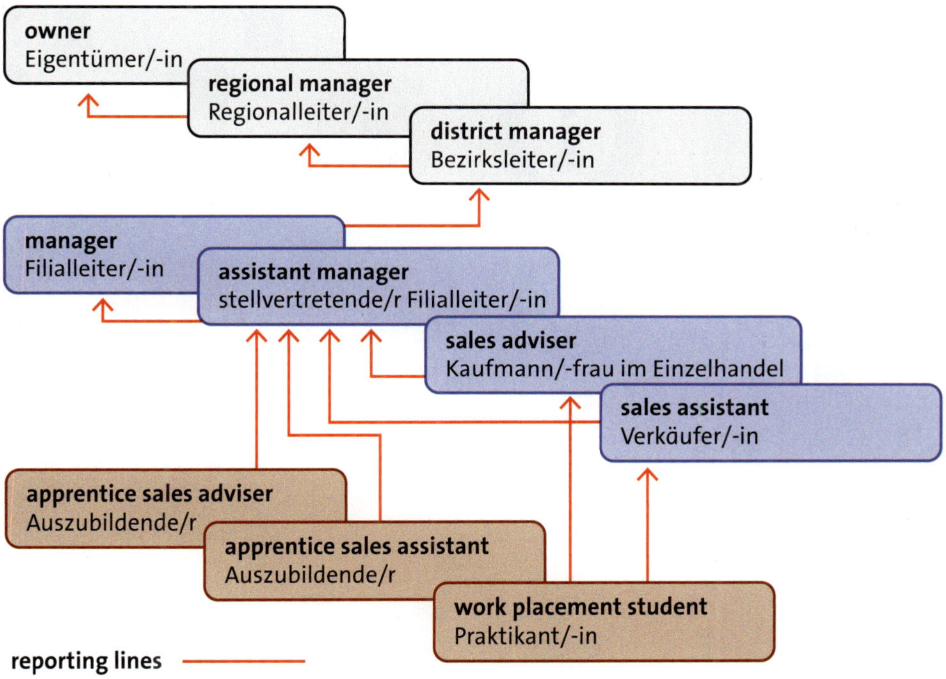

A **Study the organization chart and match the sentence beginnings (1–10) with the endings (a–j).**

1 The owner is responsible for
2 The regional manager reports to
3 The district manager reports to the
4 The district manager is in charge of
5 The manager is responsible for everything
6 The sales advisers and sales assistants report
7 The assistant manager reports
8 The assistant manager supervises
9 The apprentices
10 The sales advisers and sales assistants

a to the assistant manager.
b supervise the work placement students.
c to the manager.
d the owner.
e the whole company.
f a smaller area than the regional manager.
g report to the assistant manager.
h that happens in the shop.
i regional manager.
j the apprentices.

B **Create an organization chart for your shop and describe who does what. Use your answers in 2A.**

PART A: My company's profile

Situation: Outlet Becker's website team is creating a profile of the company's goods, services and sales outlets.
→ **You mediate a text about omnichannel sales to your German colleagues.**

1 Looking at goods and services

Outlet Becker has a wide range of products and services on offer.

A **Label the illustrations with the words in the box below the illustrations.**

apps · bakery · bikes and e-bikes · bottle return machine · café · car park · cash machine · charging station · cleaning agents · click and collect · clothes · confectionery · consumer electronics · contactless payment · cosmetics · dairy products · delivery · drinks · flowers and plants · fresh fish · fresh fruit and vegetables · fresh meat · frozen food · information · packaged foods · preserves · refunds · tableware · toiletries · toys

B **Sort the items shown in 1A into the following categories.**

food	non-food	services

C **Name goods and services that your company offers and add them to the lists.**

2 Examining distribution networks

Outlet Becker uses a variety of sales outlets and describes them on its website.

A Read the text on page 22 and label the diagram (1–16) with the highlighted words.

Outlet Becker and omnichannel sales

The retail sales landscape is changing fast, and with omnichannel sales we at *Outlet Becker* are changing with it to give everyone the best possible service. Wherever our consumers live, we have the perfect shop for them.

1 **Big box stores:** Young families love our big box stores with free parking, cafés, restaurants and play areas for the children. Parents have peace of mind because they know their kids are in safe hands.

2 **Shopping malls:** Shopping is fun and that's why we have stores in all the big shopping malls in the city, with cheap parking and great public transport links. Whatever the weather, you can relax in pleasant surroundings, browse what's on offer in the many different shops and take time out for a coffee, a snack or a meal in the food court.

3 **Pop-up shops:** And if you're hurrying through a station to catch your train, or just walking down the high street, don't be surprised if you suddenly see one of our pop-up shops with Christmas decorations in winter or camping equipment in summer. Seasonal goods and the latest trends are our speciality!

4 **Dark stores:** In this busy world, some people have no time at all to go shopping, but don't worry! You can still shop around the clock thanks to our dark stores. You may not know it, but there are warehouses packed with goods just near where you live. Use the *Outlet Becker* app to upload your shopping list to our online platform and get what you want with our 24-hour delivery or our click-and-collect service.

5 **Convenience stores:** And where do you go if the shops are closed and you suddenly remember you need something for breakfast tomorrow? Our convenience stores at service stations everywhere are the answer. They have a good selection of products and are open 24/7.

B **Work with a partner. Write a short description of your training shop. (Include information on its services, customers, opening hours and the locations it offers its products or services from.)**

› *Useful phrases: Talking about my shop, page 189*

C **Der Marktleiter bittet Sie, die aktuellen Trends in der Ausgestaltung der Vertriebswege stichpunktartig zusammenzufassen und als E-Mail an andere Auszubildende im Betrieb zu verschicken. Schreiben Sie eine Zusammenfassung in deutscher Sprache auf der Grundlage des Textes in Aufgabe 2A.**

Talking about actions in progress

- Our company **is changing** fast.
- The kids **are playing** safely together.
- I can see him. He**'s running** through the mall.
- The pop-up shop **is selling** camping gear this month.

PART B: My company's website

Situation: A consultancy firm is helping Outlet Becker to optimize the company's website, boost sales and show customers its social responsibility.
→ **You present your company's website with details of its goods, services and values.**

1 Examining a mobile website layout

Many customers use a smartphone when they shop.

A **Use the words below to label the various areas (1–8) in the retailer's mobile website.**

changing advertisements · deals · drop-down menu · logo · my account · search box · shopping basket · store locator

B **In small groups, compare the layout with some major retailers' websites and discuss any differences in small groups.**

2 Understanding mobile website structure

The website consultant explains how website content is structured.

A 5 **Listen to what the consultant says and choose the correct answer for each sentence.**

1 Outlet Becker's website needs ___ changes.
   a one or two
   b a large number of
   c a few

2 Most people use ___ to shop online.
   a a laptop
   b a tablet
   c a phone

3 When you tap on the hamburger button of a website, you ___.
   a get a drop-down menu **b** go to the food section **c** order a hamburger

4 Level 1 of the menu contains ___.
   a promotions **b** categories **c** products

5 Electrical is ___ batteries.
   a a smaller category than **b** the same category as **c** a bigger category than

6 Shoes is ___ clothes.
   a a smaller category than **b** the same category as **c** a bigger category than

7 Buffalo women's trekking boots, €74.99, is in a category ___.
   a under clothing and shoes **b** between clothing and shoes **c** over clothing and shoes.

B Work with a partner and sort the items (1–27) into the three categories described by the website consultant.

1 25% off 6 or more red wines!
2 Ambiente charcoal grill
3 Australian red wine
4 BBQs
5 books
6 Cheeky Chappy kids' pyjamas
7 cleaning & household
8 clearance sale!
9 clothes
10 disinfectants
11 Freezi organic Brussels sprouts
12 frozen foods
13 furniture
14 garden
15 Glam Primrose lipstick
16 groceries
17 health & beauty
18 home office
19 Homeline adjustable laptop stand
20 Just a few rucksacks left!
21 nightwear
22 reduced
23 special offers
24 *To Peru and Back*
25 travel books
26 women's toiletries
27 Yes! Antibacterial Spray 750 ml

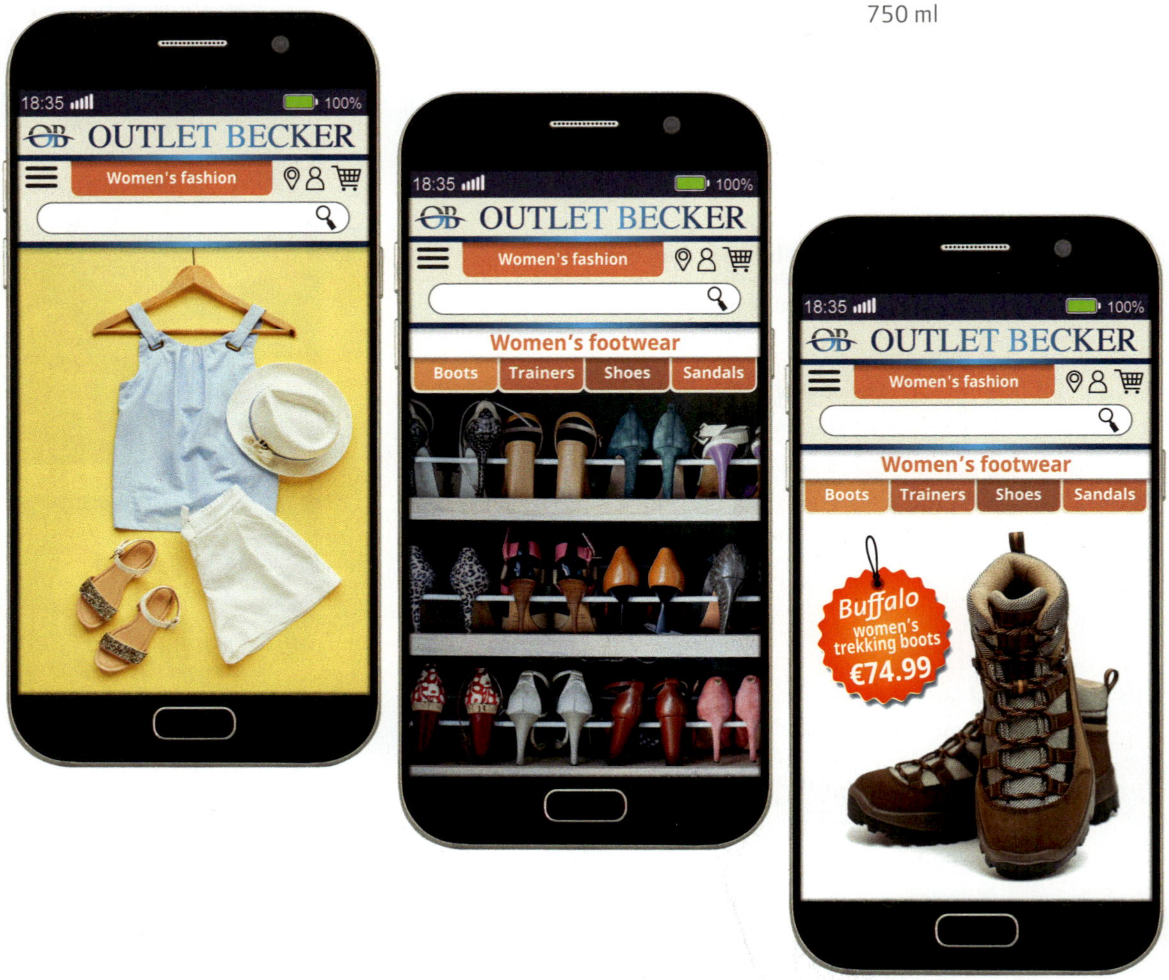

C Examine your own company's product range online and write down:
- the most important general categories
- sub-categories under each general category
- specific products in each sub-category

D Make screenshots of your company's website (or a company you know), describe how it is structured and present it to your class.

3 Examining a company's commitment to sustainability

Outlet Becker outlines its values on its website.

A **Use the expressions in the box to complete the description (1–9) of Outlet Becker's supply chain.**

fair pay · free electric charging points · green energy shops · no battery hens · no child labour · no factory farming · no GM foods · no sweatshops · recyclable packaging

Our values

Like shoppers around the world, customers of Outlet Becker are demanding that our supply chains meet ethical standards such as sustainable sourcing, reducing waste and decent working conditions. We no longer just buy products – we check that they come from ethical suppliers. This means incorporating social and environmental considerations as well as good working conditions into how we do business across the world.

1. respect for nature and animals

ethical sourcing
- not tested on animals
- ___ 1
- ___ 2
- ___ 3

2. ethical suppliers

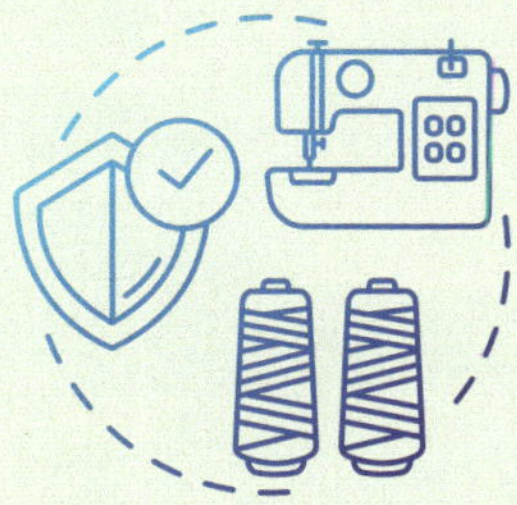

human rights
- safe working conditions
- ___ 4
- ___ 5
- ___ 6

3. ethical retailing

environmentally friendly
- reduced carbon footprint
- ___ 7
- ___ 8
- ___ 9

B **Research your company's policy on sustainability and add a diagram of its supply chain to the screenshots in exercise 2D.**

our supply chain

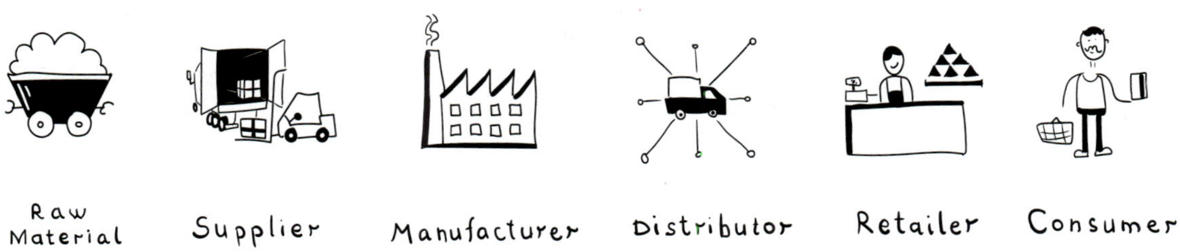

COMMUNICATION: Giving directions

Situation: You help out at the information desk in a busy mall.
→ **You practise giving directions.**

1 Giving directions in a mall

You are working at the information desk on the ground floor of a busy shopping mall and learning to help English-speaking customers find their way.

A **First, study the plan of the mall below and locate the goods or services (1–9). With a partner take turns to name the shop where you can find them and then state which floor the shop is on.**
Start as follows:

You can find ... *(product/service; use the plural form)* in the ... *(type of shop)* on/in the ... *(floor level)*.

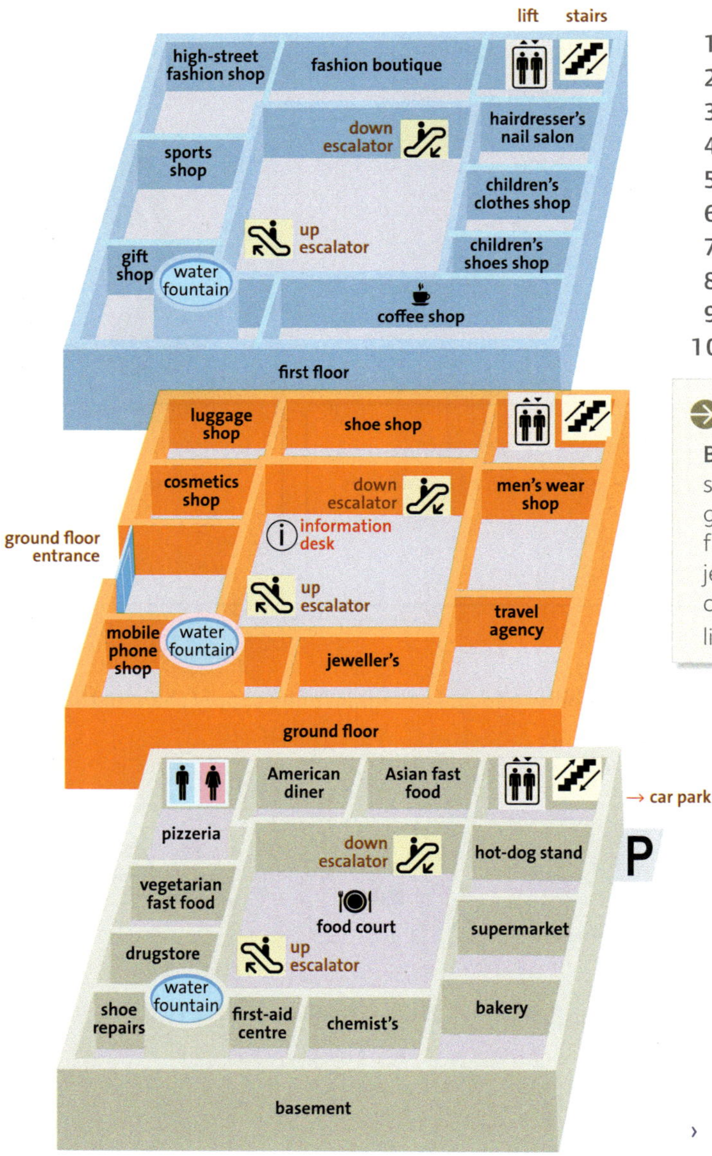

1 a fashionable top
2 a football
3 a hamburger
4 a jeans jacket
5 a phone battery
6 a wristwatch
7 bread
8 mascara
9 medical help
10 a girl's winter jacket

British and American English

British English	=	American English
shop	=	store
ground floor	=	first floor
first floor	=	second floor
jeweller's	=	jeweler's
chemist's	=	pharmacy/drugstore
lift	=	elevator

› *Useful phrases: Giving directions, page 190*

B **Work with a partner. Study the example below, then write and role-play dialogues with customers in the situations listed (1–4). Give each customer a store guide and remember to be polite.**

Example:

Customer	Excuse me. Could you tell me where I can find a child's anorak, please?
You	Certainly, sir/madam. There's a children's clothes shop on the first floor. You can take the escalator from here and when you get to the first floor, turn left and left again and it's on your right just after children's shoes.
Customer	Thanks. I would also like to have a coffee. Is there anywhere where I can get a coffee?
You	Yes, there is. There's a coffee shop on the first floor near children's shoes. In fact, you'll pass it when you go to the children's clothes shop.
Customer	Great! Thanks.
You	You're welcome. Here's a store guide to help you find your way.
Customer	Thanks.

1 An American man wants to buy a wedding ring and a pair of skis.
2 Two teenage girls each want to buy a pair of high heels and then have a snack.
3 An Irishman wants to buy a suitcase and some painkillers.
4 A housewife wants to go to the hairdresser's and then do the food shopping.

2 Giving directions in a supermarket

The diagram below shows the layout of a typical supermarket.

A **With a partner, copy and complete it with items from your local supermarket.**

B **Practise giving each other directions to products.**

› *Useful phrases: Giving directions, page 190*

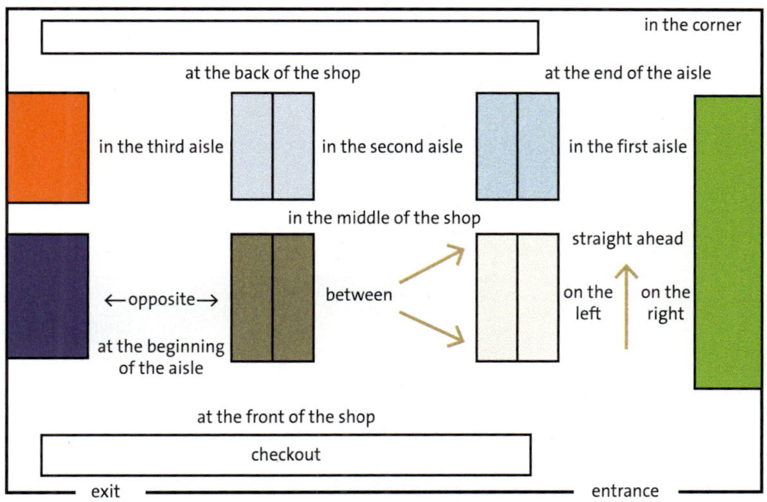

DAS KANN ICH (Unit 2)

- Ein Organigramm meiner Firma erstellen. (Foundation)
- Das Profil einer Firma beschreiben. (Part A)
- Die Webseite einer Firma analysieren. (Part B)
- Wegbeschreibungen auf Englisch geben. (Communication)

SCENARIO: Output

Now go back to the beginning of the unit (page 17) and study the task again.

→ **Write a page for your company's website, explaining what sort of company it is, what it sells, how it sells its products and how it tries to be an ethical company.**

STEP 1 **Before you work on your task, think about the following:**

1 The areas you need to cover:
- what sort of company it is (e.g. small retailer, outlet store, high-street shop)
- what sort of products it sells (e.g. discounted goods, food, furniture)
- what distribution outlets is has (e.g. shop in mall, shop in high street, online)
- its ethics (e.g. source of products, working conditions of manufacturers, natural resources)
- anything else you might think of

2 What makes a good website page
- brief and well-structured information
- thing you may wish to include:
  - a headline that catches the attention of the reader
  - several headlines
  - photos
  - bullet points highlighting important aspects

STEP 2 **Start by doing the following:**

- Make a mind map with information about your shop.
- Select the most important information.

STEP 3 **Think of the vocabulary and phrases you will need.**

- Find exercises in this unit that offer useful vocabulary for your task.
- List vocabulary according to the areas you are covering.

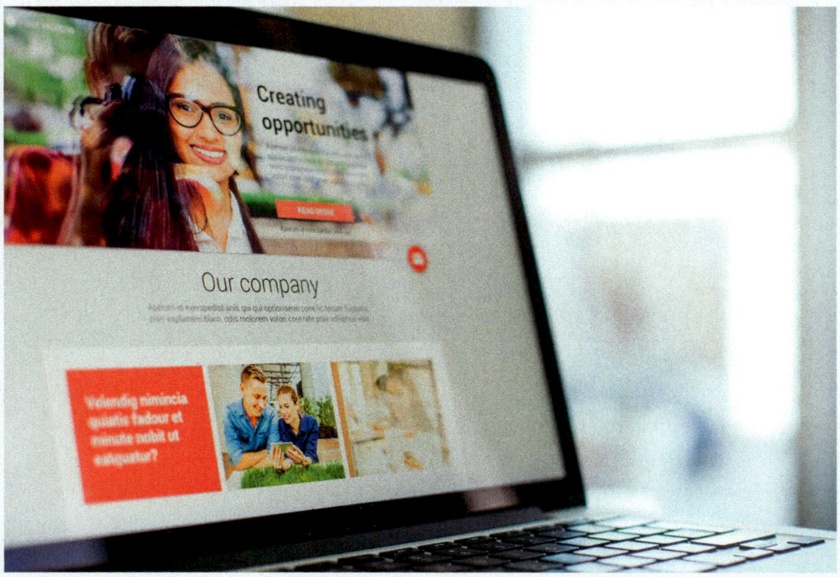

3 Working conditions

SCENARIO: Input

The works council at your shop will soon be meeting the management to discuss the working conditions at the parent company's different branches. Members of the works council need therefore to collect data about working conditions at your shop too. One person from each shop has been chosen to collect all the information. Your colleagues have decided you will be the one to give the works council the information.

→ In this unit you are going to look at working conditions, including the daily routine, pay, hours, workwear and equality.

→ At the end of the unit you will be asked to give your works council details on the working conditions in your workplace.

FOUNDATION: Work routine

Situation: The works council is collecting data in preparation for a meeting with the management.
→ **You and apprentices from other companies describe your duties and responsibilities at work.**

1 Describing typical tasks

The apprentices talk about typical aspects of their work.

A First, match the vocabulary in the box with the photos (1–8).

clothes hanger · clothes tag · dummy · name tag · pallet truck · security tag · shelves · tagging gun

B Study the table below and make positive and negative sentences.

Example: The manager *unlocks* the shop but *doesn't clock in* or *out*.

	work placement student	shop assistant	manager
unlock the shop	✘	✘	✓
clock in/out	✘	✓	✘
wear a uniform	✘	✓	✘
wear a name tag	✓	✓	✓
unpack goods	✓	✓	✘
tag clothes with a tagging gun	✘	✓	✘
label goods with a pricemarker	✘	✓	✘
put clothes on hangers	✓	✓	✘
dress dummies	✓	✓	✘
stock the shelves	✓	✓	✘
check the use-by dates	✘	✓	✓
work on the till	✘	✓	✘
move goods with a pallet truck	✓	✓	✘
order goods	✘	✘	✓
phone suppliers	✘	✘	✓
demonstrate products	✘	✓	✘
count the day's takings	✘	✘	✓
do the inventory	✓	✓	✘

› *Grammar: Simple present, page 165*

C Write down a list of typical activities at your shop.

Example: At my shop I *wear* a uniform but I *don't wear* ... Other assistants *unload* ... and I *unpack* ... but *don't* ...

D With a partner, use the table in 1B to ask each other questions about your daily activities.

Example: *A* *Do* you ... (e.g. clock in and out?).
B Yes, I *do*. How about you?
A I *do* too. / No, I *don't*. *Does* the manager ...?

Questions and short answers in the simple present

Does the manager **unlock** the shop?	Yes, he **does**.
Does he **clock in**?	No, he **doesn't**.
Do you **clock in**?	Yes, I **do**. / No, I **don't**.

Short answers always have three words.

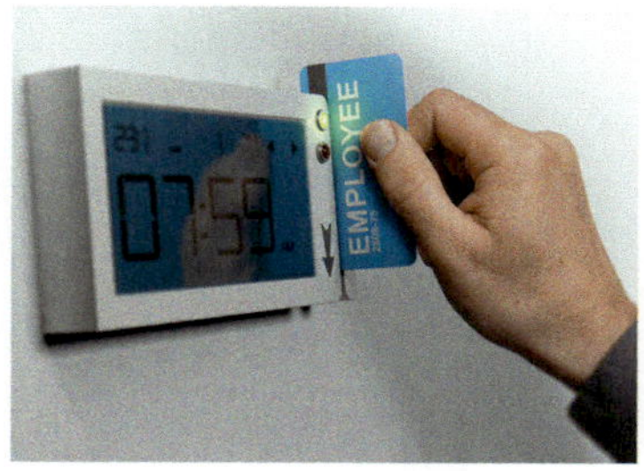

2 Discussing problems and solutions

The works council wants to discuss the problems apprentices have with the management.

A Match the problems of the apprentices (1–8) with the questions for management (a–h).

1 I just do the same task all day long. It's so boring.
2 I never finish a job. I'm always interrupted.
3 They make me carry heavy objects when we get new deliveries.
4 I just sit around with nothing to do.
5 Nobody ever has time to explain things to me.
6 I have to work late on Saturday night. I'm sure that's not allowed!
7 They leave me alone in the shop for hours at a time. Surely that can't be right?
8 My manager sacked another apprentice after three months just because he didn't like her. Can he do that?

a Can you get a pallet truck to help unload vans?
b Could you make sure that there is always a trained assistant in the shop when the apprentice is there?
c Can you give the apprentices a mentor or work buddy to help them understand things?
d Could you put the rules for working hours and overtime on the noticeboard?
e Can apprentices be allowed to finish one task before they start another one?
f Could you give the workers reasons why they can be sacked?
g Who is responsible for the apprentices learning about different areas of the business?
h Who do the apprentices turn to when they want more work?

B Many problems can be solved if they are brought to an employer's attention. Work with a partner and discuss any problems you are having at work. Make a list of the problems and the questions to ask in each case.

Read out your list of problems and questions in class and discuss possible solutions.

PART A: Pay, conditions and equality in the workplace

Situation: The works council is collecting data on working conditions in preparation for a meeting with the management.

→ **You present information about working conditions in a company you are interested in joining.**

1 Looking at pay and working conditions

First, you read some statements from different people describing their pay and working conditions.

A Skim the four statements and find out:

a who earns the most
b who earns the least
c who works the longest hours
d who works the shortest hours

1

Christian, 40

I'm the manager of a large supermarket in the town centre with 30 employees. I'm married with two children. On paper I work 40 hours a week but in reality I work a lot more, because we open from 7 a.m. to 9 p.m six days a week with early and late shifts. I have a good salary: my gross pay is €4,500 plus Christmas and holiday bonus, which means my take-home pay after all deductions is just under €2,250 per month. I have a company car with free fuel that I can use privately and I get six weeks paid holiday a year.

2

Lea, 19

I'm a fully qualified retail sales assistant in a small stationery shop. I work 40 hours a week and my gross monthly pay is €1,800 per month and I get 24 days' paid holiday per year. After deductions for income tax, church tax, health insurance, nursing care insurance, unemployment insurance and my old-age pension contribution, my net monthly pay is just over €1,300. If I do overtime, for example at Christmas when we work up to 48 hours a week, I don't get extra pay. I get time off instead.

3

Max, 18

I'm an apprentice sales adviser at a big clothes shop in the city centre. I'm in the first year of my apprenticeship, so I earn €800 a month plus sales commission. My take-home pay after all deductions is just under €640 per month and I get an employee discount on company products. The shop opening hours are 10 a.m. to 8 p.m. from Monday to Saturday. I work 173 hours a month but I can change to 160 hours for less pay if I want.

4

Julia, 34

I'm a fully trained retail sales adviser with five years' experience. My husband works at a bank and we have a daughter aged 9. I have a part-time job in a furniture shop in a mall. I work 60 hours a month on a flexible basis six days a week and earn €15 an hour. My net monthly pay is just over €720 per month. Later I want to work full-time.

Comparatives and superlatives

Managers earn **most**. Apprentices earn **least**.
Part-time workers earn **less than** full-time workers.
Trained sales advisers earn **more than** untrained shop assistants.
An early shift is **good/better** for some people and **bad/worse** for others.

B Find the English equivalents in the statements in exercise 1A of the German words (1–21).

1 Schicht
2 Gehalt
3 brutto
4 Weihnachts- und Urlaubsgeld
5 Nettolohn
6 Abzüge
7 Firmenwagen
8 Treibstoff
9 Einkommenssteuer
10 Kirchensteuer
11 Krankenversicherung
12 Pflegeversicherung
13 Arbeitslosenversicherung
14 Rentenversicherung
15 netto
16 Überstunden
17 Freizeitausgleich
18 verdienen
19 Provision
20 Personalrabatt
21 Erfahrung

C Read the four statements in detail and write notes for each person about the following points.

- weekly/monthly working hours, including overtime
- gross and net pay, overtime arrangements and commission
- benefits

2 Examining working conditions

The works council now explains some important points about retail in Germany.

A 6 Listen to the discussion and choose the correct option for each sentence.

1 The gender pay gap means that men earn ___ women.
a the same as b more than c less than

2 In the retail trade, the gender pay gap is at least ___
a 10%. b 15%. c 20%.

3 The name over the door of a shop ___ you exactly who the owner is.
a doesn't always tell b never tells c always tells

4 If there is a wage agreement, the employees' pay is normally ___ than average.
a higher b lower c the same

5 Privately owned shops ___ a wage agreement.
a normally have b normally don't have c never have

6 A trade union fights for better conditions for ___
a employers. b employees. c employers and employees.

7 ___ of all shop workers are members of a trade union.
a 10% b 50% c 90%

8 ___ of the workers in retail are part-timers or mini-jobbers.
a Less than half b Half c More than half

B Now write your own job profile with details of your working hours, pay, deductions, holiday and overtime arrangements. Say who owns your shop and if there is a wage agreement and union membership.

› *Thematic vocabulary: Working conditions, page 199*

3 Taking equality into consideration in the workplace

The works council gives you a questionnaire to complete.

A Copy the table and tick off the statements according to how you feel about them.

Questionnaire: What can I expect of my employer?						
		very strongly agree	agree	have no strong opinion	disagree	very strongly disagree
1	All employees must have equal opportunities at work.					
2	The management must do everything possible to help employees with their work-life balance.					
3	Employees doing the same or similar work must be paid the same hourly rate regardless of full- or part-time status, sex, gender, age or ethnic background.					
4	The management must make special allowances for single parents.					
5	All employees must have the right to take paid educational leave every year.					
6	In-house or in-service training courses must take place during normal working hours without loss of pay.					
7	The management is not allowed to contact employees outside normal working hours.					
8	The management must give support and assistance to employees with personal or domestic problems.					

B With a partner, find the points where you agree or disagree and discuss your opinions.

C Have a class discussion about points 1–8 in 3A and any other important matters concerning equality and expectations in the workplace. Decide what employees can reasonably expect of their employers.

4 Researching a future employer

You research a potential employer who you would like to work for.

Find out what they say about working conditions, including equality, in the workplace. Present your findings to your class.

PART B: Workwear

Situation: The works council collects data about clothes that are allowed, expected and not allowed at work.

→ **You review different employers' workwear guidelines and describe the dress code where you work.**

1 Dressing for work

Sales staff are usually expected to wear some sort of regulated outfit at work.

A **In groups of four, choose four photos each and decide which of the clothes items below (a–k) the sales staff are wearing.**

1

2

3

4

5

6

7

8

a apron
b buttoned-up blouse
c cap
d gloves
e jacket
f long-sleeved shirt
g name tag
h overalls
i polo shirt
j short-sleeved shirt
k tie

VIDEO 2

Watch the video about workwear.

B **Discuss in class why some companies give their sales staff uniforms and workwear, while others don't.**

2 Examining food handlers

There are special rules about clothing and personal hygiene for people who handle food.

A Study the illustration above and complete the sentences with *must* (✓) or *mustn't* (✗).

Example: Food handlers *must* always wear clean clothes. They *mustn't* wear dirty clothes.

1 Food handlers ___ have their hair out of their caps.
2 They ___ have their hair tucked into their caps.
3 They ___ wear jewellery like earrings, necklaces and chains.
4 They ___ wear a watch or rings when they're handling food.
5 All wounds ___ be covered with a plaster
6 When they touch food, they ___ wear gloves.

Talking about rules and regulations

- Food handlers **must** wear gloves.
- They **mustn't** have bare feet.
- Some shops assistants **are allowed to** wear T-shirts.
- Others **are expected to** wear suits.
- Shop assistants **aren't allowed to** wear beachwear.

› *Grammar: Modal verbs, page 169*

B Now write your own sentences with *must* and *mustn't*, using the words in the box below.

fingernails · gloves · pockets · shoes

3 Looking at dress code

Dress codes and workwear guidelines vary from shop to shop and are often flexible.

A Study the table below and expand the notes (1–5) into sentences, using *be allowed to, be expected* and *be not allowed to*.

1 at a DIY store / assistants / denim
2 at an antique furniture shop / a female assistant / jacket, skirt and blouse or a trouser suit
3 at some discounters / assistants / jeans / trainers
4 at a bridal wear shop / female assistants / low cut tops
5 at all shops / assistants / clean clothes

WORKWEAR GUIDELINES			
convenience store • discounter • DIY store • drug-store • fast-fashion shop • sports shop • supermarket		jeweller's • antique furniture shop • bridal wear shop • exclusive shoe shop • men's outfitters	
ALLOWED / EXPECTED			
workwear/uniform + own clothes:		**own clothes:**	
✓	T-shirt	jacket, skirt and blouse	✓
✓	denim / jeans	trouser suit	✓
✓	skirt	dress	✓
✓	cloth trousers	cloth trousers	✓
✓	shirt	shirt and tie	✓
✓	blouse	suit	✓
✓	jewellery	jewellery	✓
✓	flat shoes / low-heel shoes	flat shoes / low-heel shoes	✓
✓	trainers	leather shoes / high heels	✓
SOMETIMES ALLOWED			
✓	shorts • piercings • visible tattoos		✓
OFTEN NOT ALLOWED			
✗	unironed clothes • unnatural, coloured hair • low cut tops • short skirts • beachwear • heavy make-up • excessive jewellery • a lot of bare skin • offensive slogans on clothes		✗

B Now use the table to write five more sentences about what is *allowed*, *expected* and *not allowed* at different shops.

4 Writing a dress code

Now think about the dress code in your shop.

Your employer asks you to draw up simple workwear guidelines in English for new employees at your shop. Work with a partner and list what is *allowed*, *expected* and *not allowed*.
Present your guidelines to your class and explain the thinking behind them.

› *Thematic vocabulary: Work clothes, page 199*

COMMUNICATION: A short presentation

Situation: Some employees from branches of your company in other countries are visiting Germany.
→ **You prepare a short presentation to the visitors about your workplace.**

1 Preparing your presentation

Your shop manager asks you to give a presentation to the visitors about your shop and to include the following points.

product range • opening hours • working hours

A **Work with a partner. Make notes on each point in the list. Add more points of your own (e.g. location, typical customers, best-selling product(s), competition with other shops nearby).**

B **Compare your list with other apprentices from your company and decide on the most important points.**

C **Decide on the order in which you will present your points. Make a numbered list. Write the name and date of your talk at the top of the list.**

Presentation to visitors: 08.01.20..
1 *Introduction (self)*
2 *The company's ...*
3

2 Writing the presentation

Now it's time to write your presentation.

A **Use your notes from exercise 1 to write your text. Use the structure below.**

Introduction	– Introduce yourself and your colleague(s).
Welcome	– Welcome the visitors from ... (*country/countries*) to ... (*shop*) in ... (*location*).
Main points	– Write one paragraph about each point. – Use signposts to move from point to point.
Conclusion	– List your main points again. – Invite questions from the audience.

› *Useful phrases: Giving presentations, page 191*

B **Work with a partner. Check your texts together for clarity and correctness as follows:**

- Check that the information in the text is correct. If it isn't, correct it.
- Use a dictionary to check the spelling. Use a grammar book to check the grammar.

3 Making prompt cards

It makes a bad impression if you read out a text to an audience, so you make prompt cards with your main points and important facts.

Follow the steps below.

- Underline the most important points.
- Copy these points onto index cards.
- Write out your first sentence word for word.

product range: we ...
opening hours: during the week, ...
working hours: I work ...

4 Giving a presentation

Your presentation will be a success if you follow the tips below.

Divide the tips (A–L) into *Before/During/After* the presentation. Decide which tips are not relevant for your presentation.

Tips for a great presentation

A Always face your audience!
B Use good visual aids such as photos, graphs, etc.
C Explain what the presentation is about.
D Don't move around too much.
E Give out handouts.
F Keep slides/transparencies clear and simple.
G Make eye contact with members of the audience.
H Offer to answer questions from the audience.
I Speak slowly and freely, using only your prompt cards.
J Thank your audience for listening.
K Use hand-held prompt cards with keywords.
L Welcome the audience and introduce yourself.

5 Giving your presentation

The next step is to give your presentation and then to give each other feedback.

A **When it is your turn, look directly at the audience and smile. Then speak freely and clearly using your prompt cards. Ask for questions at the end.**

B **Use the feedback sheet to give each other feedback. Give points from 1–3 (1 point = OK, 2 points = good, 3 points = very good).**

› *Useful phrases: Giving presentations, page 191*

Presentation feedback		Points
Content	you covered all the necessary points you used examples to support your points	
Structure	your talk was easy to follow you used signposts to structure your talk you summarized the main ideas in your conclusion	
Presentation	you smiled and looked friendly you spoke clearly and freely you looked at the audience when you spoke	
Questions	you dealt with questions in a friendly manner you answered all the questions clearly	
	Total score	/30

DAS KANN ICH (Unit 3)

- Die Arbeit der verschiedenen Abteilungen meiner Firma beschreiben. (Foundation)
- Ein Informationsblatt über meine Firma erstellen. (Part A)
- Unterschiedliche Berufsbilder beschreiben. (Part B)
- Eine kurze Präsentation über meine Arbeit halten. (Communication)

SCENARIO: Output

Now go back to the beginning of the unit (page 29) and study the task again.

→ **Give your works council details on the working conditions in your workplace.**

STEP 1 **Before you work on your task, think about the following:**

1 Which of the areas below do you wish to cover?
- employees' work routines, duties and responsibilities
- pay, conditions and equality in the workplace
- workwear, uniforms and dress code
- benefits
- any issues/problems that employees feel need attention

2 How do you wish to present the information?
- table with information
- individual job profiles
- questions that need to be answered by management

STEP 2 **Start by writing down:**

- All the information you have about the working conditions in your and your colleagues' shops, especially the similarities and differences.
- If you don't know the pay level, you can check the wage agreement or make an educated guess.

STEP 3 **Think of the vocabulary and phrases you will need.**

- Find exercises in this unit which offer useful vocabulary for your task.
- List vocabulary according to the various aspects you wish to cover.

4 Retail in Germany and abroad

SCENARIO: Input

A successful American retail chain wishes to expand into the German market. It sets up a task force to identify important differences between retailing in Germany, the UK and the USA. The task force examines career paths and training, shopping hours, paid holidays and workers' rights, working hours, notice periods and reasons for dismissal, paid holiday entitlement, social security payments and bonuses.

→ **In this unit you are going to look at working conditions in Germany and abroad.**

→ **At the end of the unit you will be asked to produce a dossier to present to the American retailer.**

FOUNDATION: Career paths in Germany and the USA

Situation: Your vocational training college is taking part in a project with colleges in the USA.
→ You compare career paths in retailing.

1 Comparing career paths

As part of your college project, you look at the careers of two successful retailers.

A **Study the two texts, then copy and complete the career ladders on page 43 with details of each retailer's education and training.**

Justin Slater, DIY store manager, Columbus, Ohio

I left high school at 16 without a high school diploma and didn't know what to do with myself, so I enrolled in a business course at my local community college because I didn't need any qualifications. At the same time, I got a part-time job as a shelf-stacker at the local branch of a big chain of DIY stores. At college I got a basic knowledge of business management and at the DIY store they gave me more responsibility and trained me as a cashier. After two years at the community college, I passed my course with a good grade and the DIY store gave me a full-time job as a sales associate. My sales figures were good, and I attended in-house training courses and became a supervisor after three years. Next, I went back to the community college part-time and took a two-year course in business administration. I passed and three years later when the DIY company opened a new store, they offered me the job of manager and I took it. That was two years ago and now I'm doing a distance-learning course to get a Masters in Business Administration (MBA)[1] because my next goal is to become a regional manager.

[1] Master in Betriebswirtschaft

Lea Koch, discount store manager, Frankfurt

I did a work placement at a big discounter in class 9 at school and just filled the shelves and helped out. I left school at 16 and got a two-year apprenticeship at the discounter to train as a sales assistant. I went to vocational training college on day release two days a week. I liked it and got good grades, so I added another year and qualified as a sales adviser after three years. I wanted to work near home but there were no vacancies, so I was unemployed for six months. Then I got a job I applied for at another discounter. They sent me to different branches to get experience and after three years they said I could become head of department if I did a part-time course in business administration and passed a chamber of commerce exam[2]. It was a private distance-learning course with some face-to-face teaching. The course lasted two years, I passed and became head of department. After four years, the store manager retired and I got his job. I found the work really interesting but I'm also very interested in people, so after two years as a manager I decided to do a two-year part-time higher education course to get an MBA in HR (Human Resources). I finished last month and now I hope to get a job at company headquarters.

[2] Handelsfachwirt/-in (IHK)

Justin Slater: career ladder

position	1	shelf-stacker	2		3		4		5		6	
education/ training		high school										MBA in business administration

Lea Koch: career ladder

position	1	work placement as student	2		3		4		5		6	
education/ training		school										MBA in HR

B **Now draw a timeline for each retailer and work out how old they are now. Start like this:**

Justin Slater: timeline
Age 16: 2 years community college ——▸ **Age 18:** 3 years

Lea Koch: timeline
Age 16: 2-year apprenticeship ——▸ **Age 18:**

Talking about the past

I **left** high school at 16.
When **did** she **get** the job?
I **didn't know** what to do. (NOT: I ~~didn't knew~~)
I **didn't start** work until I was 18. (NOT: I ~~didn't started~~)
My sales figures **were** good.

› *Grammar: Simple past, page 165*

2 Describing your career path

You exchange information with students at an American community college about your career paths.

A **Work with a partner. Practise asking and answering the questions below.**

Examples: Ask when your partner left school.
A When did you leave school? *B* I left at 16.

Ask
1 which school your partner went to.
2 if they learned a foreign language.
3 when they started their apprenticeship.
4 if they liked their first day at work.
5 why they liked / didn't like their first day at work.
6 what they did on their first day as an apprentice.
7 if they wore a uniform on their first day at work.
8 what they spent their first pay packet on.

Invent two more questions to ask your partner.

B **Now use your answers to write an email to the American students about how you started your apprenticeship and what you hope to do next. Also ask the American students questions.**

Start like this: *I left school at …*

› *Useful phrases: Describing events and times, page 191*

PART A: Shopping hours and restrictions

Situation: An international retail chain with branches in Germany, the UK and the USA plans to offer customers an app with the opening hours of all of its branches.
→ **You give details of German shopping hours in your region and also discuss what changes you would make to opening hours.**

1 Comparing shopping hours

Traders in Germany, the UK and the USA give details of their opening hours.

A 7)) **Read or listen to what the four traders say and complete the table on page 45 with the information they give.**

Düsseldorf furniture shop manager
Shops in North Rhine-Westphalia can stay open for 24 hours from Monday to Saturday, but we have to close on Sundays and public holidays. The only exception is Christmas Eve everywhere in Germany. If it's on a regular shopping day, everything closes at 2 p.m. If it's on a Sunday, only food and Christmas tree sales are allowed. Some chemist's and service stations are also open 24 hours on Sundays everywhere in Germany because they're essential services. You can buy cakes and flowers in North Rhine-Westphalia on a Sunday because bakers and florists are allowed to open for five hours but not all do. Shops can also open eight Sundays a year, of which two can be Advent Sundays but only for up to five hours and not before 1 p.m.

Munich supermarket assistant
Shopping hours in Bavaria are shorter and stricter than in other parts of Germany. Our regular shopping hours are from 6 a.m. to 8 p.m. On Sundays, bakers are only allowed to open for three hours and florists for two, apart from the first Sunday of Advent when florists are allowed to open for six hours. Sunday trading is allowed on four Sundays per year but only for up to five hours and not when people would normally go to church and only until 6 p.m.

London convenience store employee
In the UK shops can open 24 hours a day from Monday to Saturday. It's a bit different on Sundays because then only small shops are allowed to stay open for 24 hours; large shops can stay open for six hours between 10 a.m. and 6 p.m. All UK shops are closed on Easter Sunday and Christmas Day.

New York liquor store owner
You can shop around the clock all over the United States for almost everything, apart from alcohol. Some religious areas have so-called blue laws banning alcohol on Sundays, but here in New York I'm allowed to sell beer 24/7. On regular shopping days I'm allowed to sell wine and liquor (what Europeans call 'spirits') from 8 a.m. to midnight and on Sundays from midday to 9 p.m. Otherwise, there are no restrictions.

			Sunday trading		
city, state	**Monday – Saturday**	**public holidays**	**chemist's & service stations**	**bakeries & florists**	**all other shops**
OPENING HOURS					
Düsseldorf, North Rhine-Westphalia	___[1] hours	24/12 until ___[2] if normal shopping day; if 24/12 is a Sunday only food and ___[3] sales allowed	___[4] hours	at any time for a maximum of ___[5] hours	___[6] times a year; no more than ___[7] Advent Sundays for a maximum of ___[8] hours from 1 p.m.
Munich, Bavaria	___[9] – 8 p.m.			bakers at any time for a maximum of ___[10] hours, florists ___[11] hours and ___[12] hours on the first Sunday of Advent	four times a year; for a maximum of ___[13] hours; not at same time as with church services; must finish by ___[14]
London, UK	24 hours	___[15] shops: 24 hours large shops: up to ___[16] hours between 10 a.m. and ___[17]		24 hours	closed on ___[18] Sunday and Christmas Day
New York	24 hours beer: 24 hours, wines and spirits: 8 a.m. – ___[19]	24 hours		24 hours	24 hours beer: 24 hours, wines and spirits: midday – ___[20]

B **Work with a partner. Draw up a table of your shop's opening hours under the headings *Monday–Saturday, public holidays* and *Sunday trading*.**

Telling the time

In everyday spoken English the 12-hour clock is used.

Time	Numbers only + a.m. or p.m.	Numbers + words
4.05 / 16.05	four oh five a.m./p.m.	five past four (in the morning/afternoon)
4.15 / 16.15	four fifteen a.m./p.m.	quarter past four (in the morning/afternoon)
7.30 / 19.30	seven thirty a.m./p.m.	half past seven (in the morning/evening)
7.40 / 19.40	seven forty a.m./p.m.	twenty to eight (in the morning/evening)
11.00 / 23.00	eleven a.m./p.m.	eleven o'clock (in the morning / at night)
12:00	12 p.m.	twelve o'clock / twelve noon / midday
00:00	12 a.m.	twelve o'clock (at night) / midnight
7:30	half past seven / half seven (NOT: ~~half eight~~)	

C **Present your table to the class and find out which shops have the longest and shortest opening hours per week.**

2 Limiting shopping hours

There are pros and cons to limiting shopping hours.

A Study the three speech bubbles and list the advantages and disadvantages in each case.

Shopping hours shouldn't be limited. If I could, I'd open seven days a week. Weekends are the time when people go clothes shopping, so why shouldn't they be free to shop on Sundays when they have time and can bring their partner with them for a second opinion?
Madeline, 37, boutique owner

I want shopping hours to be more limited. I finish at 10 p.m. sometimes and I can't wait for Sunday when the shop's closed and no one can make me come to work! I'm on my feet eight hours a day, so Sunday really is a day of rest, and I also go to church. And as for Advent, most people love it because it's cosy and Christmas is coming but it's no fun for me working on two Advent Sundays when other people are free. It's unfair!
Petra, 40, supermarket assistant

I got a shock when I came to Germany. I went to a car dealer one Sunday to buy a car and there were no sales staff, just security guards! On Christmas Eve I wanted to do some last-minute gift shopping, so I went out at 4 p.m. and all the shops were shut! I was invited to *Kaffee und Kuchen* one Sunday afternoon in a small town in Bavaria, but when I went to the florist's to buy some flowers, I couldn't get any because they only opened for *two hours* from 10–12. All these laws are so confusing! Is there a law here to stop people going shopping when they have the time?
Brad, 30, American businessman

B Work with a partner and discuss the pros and cons of your shop's opening hours from the point of view of a customer and a sales assistant.

C Discuss with your class what changes you would like to make to your shop's opening hours if you could and why.

Talking about possibilities

If I **could**, I **would open** seven days a week.
If the shops **closed** earlier, I **would have** more time for my family.
If my shop **didn't stay** open so late on Saturdays, I **wouldn't be** so tired.
If the shops **weren't** closed on Sundays; I **wouldn't need** to stay open so late on other days.

› *Grammar: Conditional sentences, page 167*

PART B: Working conditions in different countries

Situation: A large American retail chain is planning to enter the German and the UK markets, so it consults two retail experts to compare employees' pay, rights and benefits in Germany, the UK and the USA.

→ **You prepare and present a paper with an overview of benefits, rights, pay and deductions for employees in retailing.**

1 Comparing rights and benefits

Mary Anderson, the Head of Human Resources at a firm in Washington, DC, is discussing employee rights and benefits with experts from Germany and the UK in an online meeting.

A 8)) **Copy the table, then listen to the discussion and complete it with the information you hear.**

		Germany	UK	USA
1	Paid annual leave	___	___	___
2	Paid public holidays	___	___	___
3	Minimum wage	___	___	___
4	Notice period	___	___	___
5	Christmas bonus	___	___	___

B 8)) **Listen again and complete the sentences below with the words you hear.**

1 What's the ___ position on vacation in Germany, Julia?
2 In the UK, employees are also ___ to paid annual leave.
3 US workers have no ___ to paid vacation.
4 In Germany we certainly have a lot of public holidays, but the number ___ from region to region.
5 In Austria they get 25 days' paid ___ leave and 13 paid public holidays.
6 Let's now talk about ___ periods if an employer wants to fire someone.
7 Here in Germany, an employer needs an acceptable reason to ___ an employee.
8 We call this at-will ___. It makes the labour market flexible.
9 53% of German workers get a Christmas bonus, in particular at companies with a ___ agreement.
10 In the UK, there is no Christmas ___.

C **Work with a partner. Use the five points listed in A to write a short description of your rights and benefits with your employer.**
Begin like this:

At … (*name of your shop/employer*) apprentices are entitled to … . Full-time shop assistants get …

› *Thematic vocabulary: Working conditions, page 199*

2 Comparing pay packets

Mary Anderson now asks her contacts in Germany and the UK to email her data on pay and deductions in their countries.

A **First copy the table below, then complete it with data from the three emails below and on page 49.**

		Germany	UK	USA (DC)
	Gross pay	€2,000	£2,000	$2,000
	Deductions:			
1	– income tax			
2	– health insurance			
3	– old-age pension			
4	– unemployment insurance			
5	– nursing care insurance			
6	– church tax			
	Total deductions			
	Total deductions %			
	Net pay			

Prices

€1.00 one euro
€0.01 one cent
€1.10 one euro ten
€2.00 two euros
€0.90 ninety cents
€2.10 two euros ten

(English) €10,500.50 = *10.500,50 € (Deutsch)*

To: julia.neumann@eh-consulting.ger; frank.taylor@thinkretail.gbr
Subject: Comparing pay in the US, Germany and the UK
From: mary.anderson@topsell-carter.usa

Dear Julia and Frank

It was great to meet with you online and get so much information.
I now need some more data from you. The payroll department has asked me to find out about gross pay, net pay and deductions in Germany and the UK compared with the USA. Please send me all the details for a gross monthly income of €2,000 in Germany and £2,000 in the UK for an unmarried employee with no children.
Here are the details for $2,000 in Washington, DC:
The total deductions would be $292, which is about 15%. This is made up of $139 in income tax (federal and state), $124 Social Security Tax (old-age pension and unemployment insurance) and $29 for Medicare (for help with healthcare when you're 64 or older). Healthcare may or may not be provided with a job.
Now you know about the USA, please let me have your data on Germany and the UK asap.

Best wishes
Mary Anderson

Good morning Mary

Many thanks for your email. I agree that our online meeting was most informative.
As regards the data you need, I'm pleased to let you have the following details.
The deductions in the UK on a gross monthly income of £2,000 for an unmarried, full-time employee with no children would come to a total of £337, i.e. almost 17%. This figure includes £192 income tax and £145 National Insurance (old-age pension and unemployment insurance). Health insurance is free in the UK. There are no other automatic deductions.
Please don't hesitate to get in touch if you need any more data.

Best regards
Frank Taylor

Dear Mary

Thanks for your email and our great online discussion. It was a pleasure meeting you.
In answer to your request, I'm pleased to let you have the information you need about deductions in Germany.
On €2,000 gross pay, the total deductions would be €584.26, which amounts to just over 29%. This figure contains €164 income tax, €157 health insurance, €186 old-age pension contribution, €24 unemployment insurance, €35.50 nursing care insurance and €17.76 church tax, because many employees are church members. People with a very high income also pay a solidarity surcharge to cover some of the costs of German reunification but €2,000 is too low for that.
I hope you now have all the data you need. Please let me know if there is any other way I can help you.

Regards
Julia Neumann

B **Work with a partner. Study the table and the emails and find out in which of the three countries:**

- **a** deductions are highest and lowest.
- **b** income tax is highest and lowest.
- **c** a 50-year-old employee does not automatically have health insurance.
- **d** health insurance is free.
- **e** there is no nursing care insurance.
- **f** there is church tax.

C **Add a column to the table with data from your own monthly pay packet and calculate**

- your net pay
- the total deductions as a percentage of your gross pay: $\frac{\text{gross pay} - \text{net pay} \times 100}{\text{gross pay}} = \%$ deductions

D **Discuss with a partner and then in class whether it is better to have more money in your pocket at the end of the month to spend as you please or have higher deductions and more benefits.**

3 Giving a presentation

With the data you have, prepare a presentation about deductions from your pay packet.

A **Work with a partner. Prepare a presentation about employees' benefits, rights, pay and deductions in retailing.**

B **Give the presentation and use the feedback sheet like the one on page 39.**

COMMUNICATION: Diagrams and statistics

Situation: Your employer is expecting visitors from abroad and wishes to give them some statistics about the retail trade in Germany.
→ You collect data and use suitable diagrams to present it.

1 Choosing the right diagram

You review different types of diagrams and what information they show best.

Match the three descriptions (1–3) with the three different types of diagram (A–C).

1 A pie chart is a circle cut into parts like the pieces of a pie. It shows how big one piece is compared with the whole pie.
2 A graph is a line. It is used to track changes over periods of time. It has a vertical y-axis and a horizontal x-axis.
3 A bar chart is made up of blocks of different heights (vertical) or lengths (horizontal). It compares particular categories with each other.

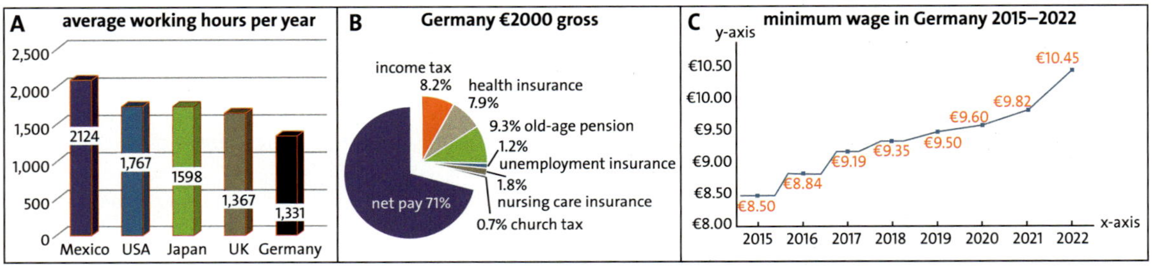

From: Statista.com

From: Statista.com

Comparatives and superlatives

In Germany, medicine is **cheaper than** in the USA.
South Korea is one of **the cheapest** countries for medicine.
Medicine in Egypt is almost **as cheap as** in South Korea.
Which country has the **most/least efficient** healthcare system in the world?
Canada's healthcare system is **more efficient than** the USA's but **less efficient than** Germany's.

2 Talking about data and statistics

You review vocabulary you can use when talking about data.

A **Look at diagrams A and B in exercise 1 and complete the sentences with a form of the words in brackets. Add extra words like *than* or *as … as* if necessary.**

1 Germany has the ___[1] (short) working hours per year of the five countries compared. Working hours in the UK are ___[2] (long) in Germany but a lot ___[3] (short) in Mexico where working hours are the ___[4] (long) of all. In Japan, working hours are almost ___[5] (long) in the USA.

2 Health insurance in Germany is ___[6] (expensive) in the UK, where all citizens have free access to the health service. However, the health insurance system in Germany is ___[7] (expensive) the old age pension system, which takes 9.3% of an employee's gross income, making it one of the ___[8] (expensive) pension systems in the world.

B **Study the graph in diagram C in exercise 1 and complete the text with the simple past form of the verbs in brackets.**

› *Grammar: Simple past, page 165*

Before 2015 many people in Germany ___[1] (work) for less than €8.50 per hour. In 2009, for example, one chain of drugstores ___[2] (pay) its shop assistants only €6.78 per hour. Three years later in 2012, that same drugstore ___[3] (go) bankrupt and 25,000 employees ___[4] (lose) their jobs. Between 2016 and 2017 the minimum wage ___[5] (rise) by 34 cents and then ___[6] (stay) the same for two years. It ___[7] (increase) by 35 cents at the end of 2018 and ___[8] (break) the €10 barrier in 2022.

3 Plotting a graph

One of the visitors gives you some data about popular shopping times in London.

A 9 **Listen to what the visitor says and write down the percentages for the following times of the day.**

- **a** 7–8 a.m.
- **b** 8–10 a.m.
- **c** 10–12 p.m.
- **d** 12–2 p.m.
- **e** 2–4 p.m.
- **f** 4–6 p.m.
- **g** 6–8 p.m.
- **h** 8–10 p.m.

B 9 **Listen again and complete the sentences with the words you hear.**

1. … this figure ___ up to 10% between 10 a.m. and 12 p.m. …
2. … it ___ at 10% for the lunchtime period …
3. It ___ to 13% between 2 and 4 p.m.
4. This figure ___ to 25% between 6 p.m. and 8 p.m. …
5. … and then between 8 and 10 p.m. it ___ to 16%.

C **Copy the empty bar chart below and complete it (a–h) with the percentages you have written down. Label the y-axis *per cent* and the x-axis *time of the day*.**

D **Work with a partner from your shop. Draw a bar chart showing the most popular shopping times at your shop on the busiest day of the week. When you have finished, present the data to your class.**

› *Thematic vocabulary: Charts and graphs, page 199; Useful phrases: Discussing graphs, page 192*

DAS KANN ICH (Unit 4)

- Meine berufliche Laufbahn beschreiben. (Foundation)
- Über Ladenöffnungszeiten reden. (Part A)
- Arbeitsbedingungen in verschiedenen Ländern vergleichen. (Part B)
- Eine Grafik erstellen. (Communication)

SCENARIO: Output

Now go back to the beginning of the unit (page 41) and study the task again.

→ **Produce a dossier to present to the American retailer about working conditions in Germany.**

STEP 1 Before you work on your task, think about the following:

1 Your target audience
- What sort of information do they need about working conditions before they can open a store in Germany?

2 The dossier
- How do you want to present the information?
  – as a text
  – with statistics
  – with graphs
- Do you want to concentrate on the differences that the Americans should be aware of, on similarities, or a mixture of both?

STEP 2 Start your dossier by doing the following:

- Write down all the areas you want to cover in your dossier.
- Make notes using bullet points to separate the areas.
- Then decide how best to present the information.

STEP 3 Think of the vocabulary and phrases you will need.

- Find exercises in this unit which offer useful vocabulary for your task.
- List vocabulary according to the different areas you are going to cover.
- Find vocabulary about comparing and contrasting, about positive aspects and negative aspects.

5 Presenting products

SCENARIO: Input

The supermarket you work at has poor sales figures compared to other supermarkets in the area. In particular, a lot of Y fruit, vegetables and dairy products are being thrown away because they are past their sell-by date. The bakery also has poor sales figures.
Head Office sends a team to the shop to analyse the problems, and they discover that the supermarket is poorly laid out (see diagram below).

→ **In this unit you are going to look at different ways of presenting products.**

→ **At the end of the unit you will be asked to redesign the layout of the supermarket to make it more attractive to customers.**

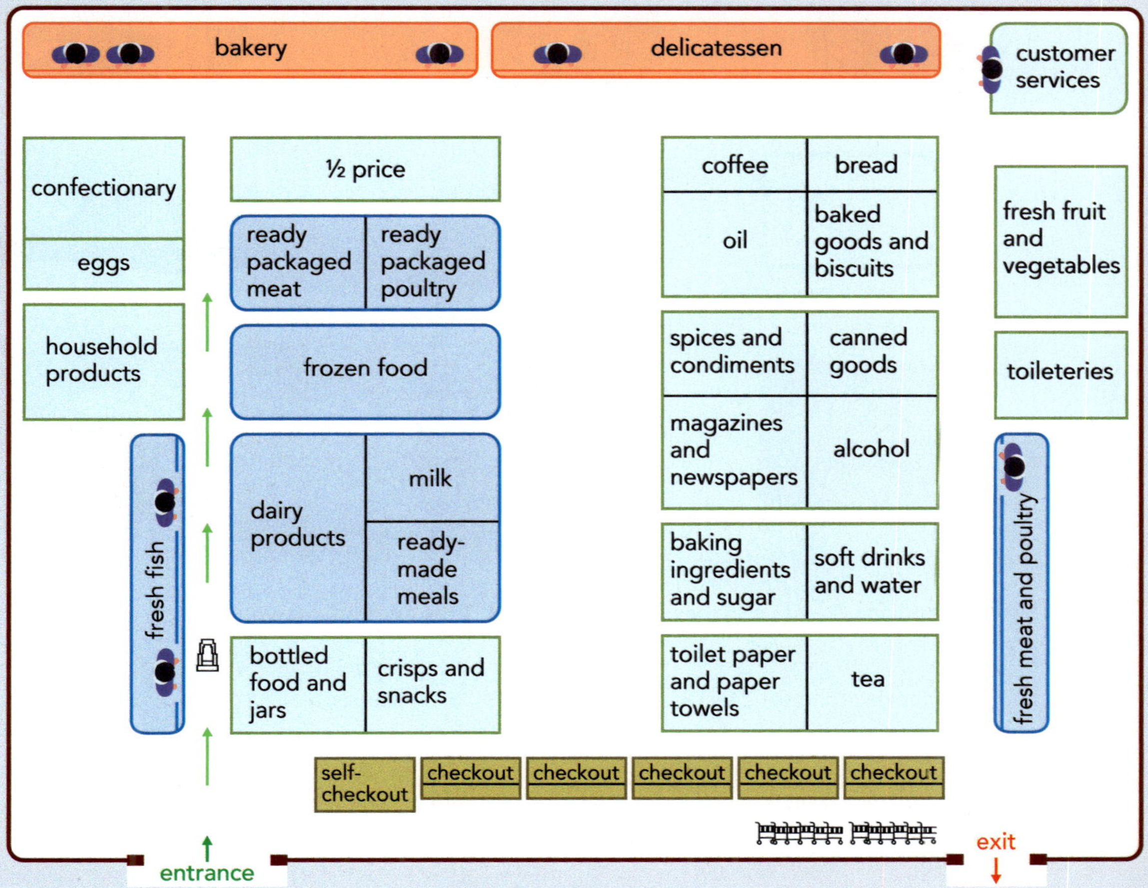

FOUNDATION: Product groups and labels

Situation: You work for a company with a wide range of retail outlets.
→ **You review different product groups and labelling regulations.**

1 Identifying product groups

You look at a cross-sample of the different products sold by your employer's companies.

A Use the words in the box to name the products (1–12).

chest of drawers · comb · crockery · jam · paint · pork chops · skirt · suit · tablet · timber · washing machines · washing-up liquid

B Sort the products (1–12) into these six retail sectors. Then add two more products to each.

a clothing and shoes
b consumer electronics and electrical appliances
c DIY
d furniture, homeware
e groceries
f health, beauty and household

C Talk about which sector you work in and name two of your best-selling products.

2 Understanding labels

You go online and find a podcast explaining some of the labelling regulations in the EU.

A **With a partner, decide if the labels (1–8) are mandatory (*verpflichtend*) or voluntary (*freiwillig*).**

B **Match the labels with the descriptions in the box.**

> best-before date · calories, fat, saturated fat, carbohydrate, sugar, protein and salt · energy efficiency · EU organic food label · Fairtrade certification mark · packaging can be recycled · price per bottle, crate and litre plus deposit · use-by date

C 10 **Listen to the podcast, check your answers and then complete the sentences with the correct option.**

1 The final price of €6.99 for the beer ___.
 a includes value added tax and the deposit
 b includes VAT but not the deposit
 c excludes VAT and the deposit

2 Food that has passed its best-before date ___ be thrown away.
 a must always
 b mustn't ever
 c needn't always

3 Food that has passed its use-by date ___.
 a must always be thrown away
 b is perishable
 c should be sold at a reduced price

4 ___ are good examples of perishable foods.
 a Fresh fish and poultry
 b Rice and pasta
 c Potatoes and carrots

5 Under EU law, the 'Big 7' are nutrition facts that must be displayed on the labels of ___.
 a fresh meat
 b fresh vegetables
 c packaged food.

6 An electrical appliance with a B rating is ___.
 a efficient
 b inefficient
 c old.

7 Food products with label no. 6 are ___.
 a genetically modified
 b made with pesticides
 c organic

8 The Fairtrade label shown means that ___.
 a the product is not too expensive
 b the producer was paid a fair price
 c the quality is better

D **Photograph some of the price and product labels in your shop and explain them to your class.**

PART A: Displaying products

Situation: The store you work for is reviewing how best to display different types of goods.
→ You discuss the pros and cons of the different ways your shop displays goods.

1 Looking at shop interiors

You find the following text about how products can be displayed

Different shops display goods in different ways. A supermarket, for example, has fruit and vegetables near the entrance. Apples can be arranged nicely in a basket, but most fruit and vegetables are displayed in green trays next to each other. Dairy products, such as butter or milk, are kept cold in long refrigerated units along the wall, but a butcher will put fresh meat on a hook and store it in a closed refrigerator. Discounters often stack fast moving goods such as toilet paper on pallets for customers to serve themselves, but a bookseller will arrange books on shelves according to topic. Jewellers keep expensive jewellery in locked glass cases for security reasons, whereas fast fashion shops hang their shirts on hangers because they can be hung up anywhere. Supermarkets and traditional bookshops have aisles lined with shelves everywhere, but a clothes shop will place jeans, for example, on a table or simply hang items like straw hats or summer handbags on pegs on the wall. Displaying goods is an art, so expensive wines, for example, are best presented in decorative wooden boxes, whereas drinks like beer are cheaper and bought in large quantities, so off-licences often sell them in a plastic crates. Shops also sometimes need to react quickly, so last-minute items such as rain ponchos and umbrellas are often displayed in a dump bin by the door for easy access.

Read the text and write a sentence for each photo (1–9) saying how the goods are displayed.

Example: *1. The apples are arranged in a basket.*

› *Grammar: Passive forms, page 166*

1

2

3

4

5

6

7

8

9

2 Discussing pros and cons

Customers and sales staff gives their views on different ways of displaying goods.

A **Read the speech bubbles (1–6), identify the type of shop and say if the speaker is a customer or a shop assistant.**

1 I sometimes ask myself if there are any people working in the shop at all. My local store has more than 65,000 items but almost everything is arranged for self-service; tools on hooks, pegs and rails; power tools on display tables; nuts, bolts, washers and screws in different sizes and qualities in boxes and trays but no one there to help you! If you know exactly what you want, it's fine but if you don't it's a nightmare.

2 I spend all day putting items back in the right place. People, both young and old, try things on and then just throw them down anywhere – sometimes on the floor! They mix up the sizes and colours and then other customers can't find them and think the goods are out of stock! Why can't customers put things back where they found them?

3 I sometimes think that the way we sell fruit and vegetables is extremely unhygienic. People are allowed to pick things up, touch them, squeeze them and sniff them and then put them back again. You can be sure that the apples left in the tray at the end of the day have been touched again and again. That's a good reason for washing fruit before you eat it.

4 The store is so big that I often feel I have to be at two places at the same time. When I'm trying to fill up the shelves with one item, people often queue up to ask me questions about tools, materials and how to make and repair things, especially at the weekend, and I never finish my work. It's important to give advice but it's also important to keep the shelves stocked with goods.

5 I like to touch and smell fruit and vegetables to see if they're ready to eat. Avocados, for example, should be soft to the touch but pears should be firm. You need to sniff a melon to see that it has the right aroma and check that apples aren't bruised before buying them. That's why I prefer self-service.

6 It's a great feeling to go through all the racks and rails with a friend, find some nice things and try them all on in front of the mirror or in the changing rooms. We don't need help. We just take what we want, leave the rest, pay at the till and go.

B **Work with a partner and describe to each other how your shop displays its goods, e.g. in trays for self-service, or in locked display cases to which only the assistants have the key.**

C **First with your partner and then in class, discuss the pros and cons of the shop displays where you work from the point of view of the customer and the sales staff.**

PART B: Designing the best store layout

Situation: Your company organizes regular seminars for its staff on different aspects of retailing.
→ **You learn about customer behaviour, store layout and product display, and review arrangements at your own shop.**

1 Looking at customer behaviour

The seminar leader starts with statistics about how customers behave when they shop.

A 76% of shoppers never speak to a sales assistant.
B 43% browse the entire store if the cash register is further back.
C 33% of shoppers visit the whole store if the cash register is located at the front of the store.
D 74% of purchases made are not planned.
E Shoppers are only willing to wait four minutes at the cash register before becoming dissatisfied.

In small groups, discuss and make notes on the following points concerning your shop.
– how often customers talk to you and what they say or ask
– the position of the till(s)
– how much time a typical customer spends in your shop
– typical waiting time at the till(s)

2 Understanding why people buy

Retail is detail and if the details are right, customers will come back to your store again and again.

A **Read this information about store layout and choose the correct option for each sentence, according to the text.**

Basic principles of store layout
There are many things that customers don't notice in shops, or only notice if the shop is badly designed or managed, so let's start with the basics.

Make time stand still in your shop. There must be no clocks. Stop the stress. Think of pleasant smells like fresh bread, fresh coffee and fresh flowers. What about some background music? Bookshops have chairs and reading tables; fashion shops have comfortable seats outside the fitting rooms; an in-store coffee shop helps customers take their time and relax.

Appearances are everything. Windows, floors, shelves, display stands and sales staff must be clean. Lighting must be bright and easy on the eye. A dead fly in a shop window is a no-no. All clothes on display must be fresh, pressed and wrinkle-free. Any spillage, from, for example, a broken yoghurt carton, must be cleaned up immediately.

Plan **customer flow.** When customers come into a shop, they enter the transition zone. These first few metres after the entrance are where a customer takes in the changed surroundings with new sounds and smells and often a different temperature. Customers don't notice products in the transition zone, so there is no point putting any goods there. Most people are right-handed, which means they automatically turn right when they come in. The right hand is also the buying hand, so goods should be displayed with this in mind. Place destination goods, things like toilet paper that customers need and will look for, at the back of the shop. Create 'perfect partners', e.g. shoes with bags and belts, teapots with cups and saucers. Structure queueing at the cash register carefully because customers hate waiting and get restless after a few minutes. Experiment with one queue leading to multiple tills, or multiple queues leading to multiple tills.

Locate and create **high-selling zones**. Everyone goes to the till, so this is a good place for promotions and impulse buys. Furniture shops sell tables and chairs but also tealights because customers buy them on impulse on their way to the checkout. Customers naturally look at things between eye and knee level, so this is where they will see new products, especially if they are next to popular items. Create end-of-aisle displays that stand out, e.g. champagne at the end of the household products aisle before New Year's Eve. Use moveable display stands, baskets or bins with special offers as flow breakers in the middle of aisles with heavy customer traffic, so everyone sees them. Use identical free-standing product displays at several places in the shop to promote special offers.

Eliminate typical problems, such as half-empty shelves that make goods seem out of stock; aisles too narrow for customers to pass each other; dark areas where customers feel uncomfortable; aisles that come to a dead end and make customers turn back; products out of reach or out of sight; one product blocking another and products *after* the checkout.

Follow these simple guidelines and your customers will enjoy shopping at your store.

1 Why is it recommended not to have a clock in a shop?
  a A clock makes customers feel more stressed.
  b A clock stops customers from enjoying the background music.
  c The staff looks at the clock most of the time.

2 In order to improve customers' sense of well-being, shops could offer ___.
  a comfortable seats, nurseries and coffee bars
  b the smell of fresh bread, coffee and flowers
  c chairs, free coffee and background music

3 A shop's appearance is important, so make sure that ___.
  a there are no spillages from broken products
  b the lighting is as bright as possible
  c the staff are running around looking busy

4 Customers don't ___.
  a notice that the transition zone has different smells and sounds
  b notice the difference in temperature between the transition zone and outdoors
  c buy anything in the transition zone

5 Shops are generally designed for people who ___.
  a know what they want to buy
  b only buy what they want
  c are right-handed

6 The thing customers really hate is ___.
  a not being able to find the cash register
  b standing in a queue for too long
  c going to the back of the shop to get toilet paper

7 The best two places to display goods are ___.
  a at aisle ends and tills
  b in the middle of aisles and at the back of the shop
  c on top shelves and at cash desks

8 Shops should not ___.
  a leave shelves half-empty
  b place products on bottom or top shelves
  c have wide aisles

B In small groups, guess what sort of shops photos 1–4 show. Then discuss whether these shops make a good or a bad impression on the customer.

1

2

3

4

C Draw a plan of your own shop and check to see if it is laid out as suggested in the text.

3 Displaying products: Visual merchandising

The next seminar is about product displays.

A 11 Listen to the different ways products can be arranged. Match the photos with the words in the box.

horizontal • power of one • power of three • props • pyramid • repetition • stacks • vertical

1

2

3

4

5

6

7

8

B **Working in small groups, sketch out on paper how you would arrange the following products. You can either group the product with 'perfect partners' or display it alone.**

- a winter anorak
- a pair of boots
- a box of breakfast cereal
- a frying pan
- men's shirts
- a tent
- a bottle of Italian wine
- garlic

3 Creating great displays

The seminar leader shows you a photo of a display for clothes and accessories and a form to explain how they are displayed.

Type of shop	*clothes shop*							
Product(s)	*clothes and accessories*							
Location of display	shop window	transition zone	near entrance	middle of shop	back of shop	end of aisle	flow breaker	other
	✓							
Type of display	pyramid	horizon-tal	vertical	stack	power of one	power of three	repetition	other
		✓				✓		
Prop(s)	*two dummies wearing fashionable clothes*							
Short description	*Two dummies in a window display. To the right of them are a stack of three: a neat pile of clothes with sunglasses on top; then there are shoes; on the final display are handbags.*							

A **Copy the form above and use it to analyse a new or an existing display in your shop.**

B **Photograph or sketch the display.**

C **Discuss the display with a partner or in small groups. Think what could be changed or improved.**

COMMUNICATION: Cross-selling and upselling

Situation: Your company regularly invites specialists to give workshops on different aspects of retailing.
→ You attend a seminar on cross-selling and upselling.

1 Understanding cross-selling and upselling

The retail specialist first explains the difference between cross-selling and upselling with the help of two examples from his website.

Read the explanations and match the sentence halves.

Cross-selling
To understand cross-selling, imagine a customer who goes into a shoe shop to buy a pair of shoes and is persuaded by the assistant to also buy a pair of matching socks and a tube of shoe cream. The shoes are the primary product, and the socks and shoe cream are accessories. Cross-selling means selling a customer extra products to go with the primary product.

Upselling
Imagine a customer goes into a shop to buy a normal filter coffee machine for €99 and leaves the shop with a bean-to-cup coffee machine that makes ten different sorts of coffee and costs €249. The primary product was a normal coffee machine, but the assistant persuaded the customer to buy a more expensive model. Upselling means persuading the customer to buy a more expensive primary product.

1 In a shoe shop, shoes are
2 Items such as socks and shoe cream
3 A good shoe shop assistant tries to sell
4 A cheap coffee machine is also a
5 A good electrical shop assistant shows the
6 The customer then forgets the cheap model

a typical primary product.
b and buys a more expensive one.
c customer some much better primary products.
d the primary product.
e are accessories.
f the customer more than the primary product.

2 Promoting products

You listen to a dialogue between a sales assistant and a customer in which the assistant successfully uses cross-selling and upselling.

A First study the items for sale (1–10) and identify the primary products and the accessories.

1

trailer

2

pump

3

city bike

4

mirror

5

lock

6

helmet

7

e-bike

8

water bottle

9

mountain bike

10

cape

B Before you listen to the dialogue, guess how many products the assistant sells to the customer and which ones they are.

C 12 Listen to the dialogue. Complete the sentences with the words you hear, and check if your guesses in 2B were correct.

1 … do you have ___ for about five hundred euros?
2 I'm afraid we don't have anything in that price ___.
3 What price do bikes ___ at here?
4 The regular price is nine ninety-nine, but it's on ___ next week.
5 That would make the ___ price eight ninety-nine.
6 … perhaps an e-bike would be the ___.
7 … we can go ___ to the lower price.
8 … you might be ___ in a good lock.

D With a partner, choose a primary product from your shop, match it with some accessories and write a dialogue in which you cross-sell and upsell the product to a customer. Use the expressions in exercise 2C. When you have finished, perform the dialogue to your class.

DAS KANN ICH (Unit 5)

- Die Bedeutung von Etiketten erklären. (Foundation)
- Erklären, wie man Produkte am besten ausstellt. (Part A)
- Die Gestaltung eines Ladens entwerfen. (Part B)
- Den Unterschied zwischen Cross-Selling and Upselling erklären. (Communication)

SCENARIO: Output

Now go back to the beginning of the unit (page 53) and study the task again.

→ **You have been asked to redesign the layout of the supermarket on page 53 to make it more attractive to customers.**

STEP 1 **Before you work on your task to redesign the layout of the supermarket, think about the following:**

1 How best to present the new layout
- Do you just want to draw a new sketch of the new layout?
- Do you just want to combine a new sketch of the new layout with explanations as to why you have changed parts of the layout.

2 Examine the diagram of the supermarket on page 53.
- Note down all the things that you think work in the supermarket.
- Note down all the things that you think are wrong about the design.
- Note down anything you would remove from the supermarket.

STEP 2 **Start by collecting the information you have learned about presenting products in this unit.**

- Which exercises in this unit might be helpful?
- Make notes on relevant information from the unit.

STEP 3 **Think of the vocabulary and phrases you will need.**

- Find exercises in this unit which offer useful vocabulary for your task.
- List vocabulary according to products and presentation.

6 Advising customers

SCENARIO: Input

You work at a specialist camera shop with a lot of regular customers who are members of your shop's loyalty programme and so enjoy many advantages and concessions.
While the manager is away, an angry customer complains about a camera he bought the day before. The camera was his first purchase at your shop but he has now found the same model at a nearby shop for €50 less, so he wants a €50 refund. He points out that he was intending to buy an expensive wide-angle lens but will go elsewhere if he doesn't get the refund.

→ **In this unit you are going to look at how to make customers enjoy their experience in your shop.**

→ **At the end of the unit you will be asked to think of ways of dealing with the customer so that he leaves both happy and certain to return to buy the wide-angle lens.**

FOUNDATION: Sales talk

Situation: As part of your training, you learn how to sell goods to customers.
→ **You review and practise the different stages of a sales dialogue.**

1 Structuring a sales dialogue

The Sales Manager at your shop explains that a sales dialogue has four stages:

1 greetings and general inquiries
2 the customer's needs
3 focusing on the goods
4 selling the goods

A First, sort the typical phrases from a sales dialogue (a–p) into what the shop assistant says and what the customer says.

a All right, I'll take it.
b Can you put it aside for me?
c Do you have it in XS/XL/red/blue?
d Feel free to just look around.
e Hi, just let me know if I can help.
f How would you like to pay?
g I'll order it now, so it should arrive tomorrow.
h I'm looking for a(n) …
i I was wondering if you sell …?
j Is everything in this area reduced?
k Is it for everyday use or a special occasion?
l Is it for work/college/indoors/outdoors?
m Is this the sort of thing you're looking for?
n Thanks, I'm just looking around.
o Where can I try this on?
p Yes, that's the sort of thing I'm looking for.

B Now group the phrases under the four stages of a sales dialogue. There are four phrases for each stage.

greetings and general inquiries	the customer's needs	focusing on the goods	selling the goods

2 Analysing sales talk

As part of your training, you examine some successful and unsuccessful sales dialogues at different shops in your employer's retail organization.

Assistant Hi, just let me know if I can help.
Customer Thanks, I'm just looking around. Is everything in this area reduced?
Assistant Not everything but some of the older models are. Are you looking for anything in particular?
Customer Yes, I'm looking for a new phone. The battery on this one runs out after about six hours.
Assistant Well, today's models can go for up to three days without recharging. Is it for private use or more for work?
Customer Work, mainly. I need it in the office and when I'm on the building site and, of course, in the car and at home. I work for a construction company, and I'm always on the move.
Assistant I see. Do you also use it for entertainment, videos and so on?
Customer Just communication really. Texts, emails for work and some photos. I don't watch many videos, just clips of my kids, that's all.
Assistant Well, texts and emails don't take up much storage space, but what about music and podcasts?
Customer Well, when I'm travelling, I listen to a lot of podcasts that I've downloaded.
Assistant Well, podcasts can take up a lot of storage space. How much storage space do you have on your phone now?
Customer 64 gigabytes. It's pretty full.

Assistant	In that case, I think you'll need at least 128 gigabytes.
Customer	Yes, that makes sense.
Assistant	Here's our latest model. It's light but very tough. It has a great display that doesn't break if you drop the phone, and it's also waterproof to a depth of six metres. Just feel how light it is.
Customer	Yes, it feels good. How many gigabytes storage did you say it has?
Assistant	128 gigabytes.
Customer	And how much is it?
Assistant	The normal price is €949 but this week it's just €849.
Customer	Any extras with it?
Assistant	I'm afraid not. You just get the phone nowadays, but you may want to buy a wireless charger with it. You just lay the phone on it for a couple of hours and it's charged.
Customer	How much are they?
Assistant	€35.
Customer	All right, I'll take the phone and the charger.
Assistant	You've made a good choice, sir! How would you like to pay?
Customer	I'd like to pay by phone.
Assistant	Great. Just tap it against the terminal.

VIDEO 3

Watch the video about sales talks.

much/many/a lot of

Use **much** for questions and negatives with uncountable (*unzählbar*) words.
– **How much** storage space do you have**?** I do**n't** have **much** storage space.
Use **many** for questions and negatives with **countable** (*zählbar*) words.
– **How many** videos do you watch**?** I do**n't** watch **many** videos.
Use **a lot of** with uncountable and countable words.
– I need **a lot of** storage space, as I download **a lot of** podcasts.

A **Look at how the shop assistant structures the sales dialogue by doing the following tasks.**

1 Write down the five questions the assistant asks at the beginning of the dialogue.
2 Write down the five questions the customer asks.
3 Find the sentence in which the assistant says what she thinks the customer needs.
4 List the words and phrases that the assistant uses to describe the model she wants to sell the customer.
5 Explain how the assistant makes a high price sound low.
6 Find the expression that the assistant uses to say 'no'.
7 Find the expression that the assistant uses to praise the customer.

B 13 **Listen to a dialogue in a clothes shop.**
14 **Listen to a dialogue in an electrical shop.**
Make a note in each case of the customer's needs and the presentation of the products.

dialogue	customer's needs	presentation of the products
1 clothes shop		
2 electrical shop		

Explain whether you think the dialogues were successful or not.

C **Now choose a product from your own shop and work with a partner to improvise a successful or unsuccessful sales dialogue in four stages.**

› *Useful phrases: Sales talks, page 192*

PART A: Understanding customers

Situation: The human resources department of your company has training courses to help employees deal with different types of customers, and also with each other.
→ **You attend a training course and practise sales situations.**

1 Understanding yourself

Some personality types work well together while others don't, so the course starts with a personality test to help you find out what sort of person you are.

A **Answer the questions honestly a) for yourself b) for someone you know very well (e.g. brother/sister/parent/partner). Write your answers in your exercise book like this:**
1e, 2a, 3c, etc.

	agree	slightly agree	neutral	slightly disagree	disagree
1 I don't take things seriously and like to have fun.	a	b	c	d	e
2 I always look for ways to make money.	a	b	c	d	e
3 I don't criticize other people's ideas.	a	b	c	d	e
4 I want people to like me when I meet them for the first time.	a	b	c	d	e
5 I like to be in noisy groups of people.	a	b	c	d	e
6 I don't show off.	a	b	c	d	e
7 I need to be in control.	a	b	c	d	e
8 I love it when things are orderly and tidy.	a	b	c	d	e
9 I think cooperation is more important than competition.	a	b	c	d	e
10 I want everyone to be happy and relaxed.	a	b	c	d	e
11 I always try to be better than others.	a	b	c	d	e
12 I always try to find any mistakes in new ideas.	a	b	c	d	e
13 I always make a lot of noise.	a	b	c	d	e
14 I tell people what to do and make sure they do it.	a	b	c	d	e
15 I always check everything in detail before I act.	a	b	c	d	e
16 I don't show my emotions.	a	b	c	d	e

B **The answers are colour-coded in four groups: red, yellow, green, blue. Use the answer sheet in File 16 on page 164 to work out how many points you have for each colour, then move on to task 2.**

2 Understanding your results

The trainer explains that the DISC assessment is a popular tool for identifying four basic personality types.

- D = Dominance *(Dominanz)*
- I = Influence *(Einfluss)*
- S = Steadiness *(Stetigkeit)*
- C = Conscientiousness *(Gewissenhaftigkeit)*

A Read the four descriptions and use your results to identify the one or two colours where a) you b) the person you know well has the highest score(s). Do the descriptions of yourself and the other person ring true? Discuss your results with a partner.

Fiery red (D)	**Sunshine yellow** (I)
– is in control – wants results – decides quickly – doesn't try to be friendly – asks direct questions – no fear of conflict	– needs good relationships – wants to build trust – wants fun – laughs and smiles a lot – centre of attention – not interested in detail
Cool blue (C)	**Earth green** (S)
– loves details – precise – correct – careful – doesn't show emotion – not interested in relationships	– needs harmony – relaxed – patient – caring – needs time to do things – unhappy under pressure

B Match the speech bubbles with the four personality types.

A Can you deliver by next Monday or not?

B How heavy is this table exactly?

C This is a fantastic song! Can you turn it up louder?

D I need time to think about this.

E Is the cotton in this shirt from Turkey, India or China, or is it a mixture of all three?

F You don't seem to know much about DIY. Have you just started work here?

G It's almost closing time. I don't want to make you work overtime, I'll come back another day.

H Hey, don't we know each other? Didn't we go to the same school?

3 Mirroring customers

The trainer tells you the best way to handle customers is to identify what type they are and then give them what they want by mirroring their behaviour. She gives you a list of Dos and Don'ts to help you.

DOs	DON'Ts
Fiery red (D)	
– speak with authority – ask direct questions – recommend a product/service	– try to make small talk – try to build a friendly relationship – give too many details
Sunshine yellow (I)	
– be friendly – build trust – recommend a product/service	– give too many details – be in a hurry – forget to laugh and smile
Earth green (S)	
– take your time – relax – give details	– be in a hurry – expect a quick decision – be too friendly
Cool blue (C)	
– give details – answer every question – expect a long discussion	– try to build a relationship – expect a quick decision – recommend a product/service

A Study the four types and match the sentence halves.

1 'D' customers decide quickly
2 'D' customers don't want to talk about
3 'I' customers aren't
4 'I' customers want a friendly
5 'S' customers are relaxed
6 'S' customers need to feel they
7 'C' customers need all the details before
8 'C' don't want the assistant

a interested in details.
b they can come to a decision.
c to recommend a product.
d have a lot of time to make a decision.
e if they want to buy something or not.
f and not in a hurry.
g things like the weather, sport or children.
h relationship with the assistant.

B 15 Next the trainer gives you a check sheet and plays four sales dialogues at a furniture shop. Copy the check sheet and fill it in for each dialogue.

Check sheet	
The customer wants/needs:	
– product:	
– a nice atmosphere with small talk:	yes/no
– a recommendation:	yes/no
– a lot of details:	yes/no
– time to come to a decision:	yes/no
The assistant makes or will make a sale:	yes/no
Customer type:	red / yellow / green / blue

C **Discuss the four check sheets with a partner and make sentences like this:**

The first customer wanted a nice ... She also wanted a ... but she didn't need ... The assistant made / didn't make a sale because ...

measurements

The table is **a hundred and twenty centimetres long.**
It's **eighty centimetres wide.**
It's **seventy-five centimetres high.**

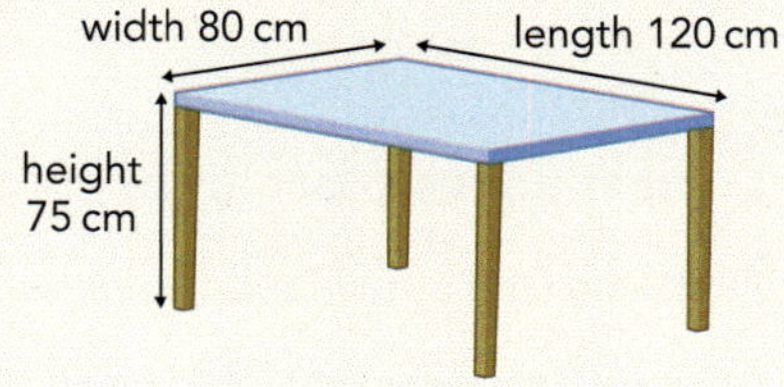

The bed is **two metres / two hundred centimetres long.**
The footboard is **fifteen centimetres high.**
The headboard is **thirty-three point five centimetres high.**
The slats are **eighty centimetres long.**
The **total length** of the bed is **two hundred and twelve centimetres.**

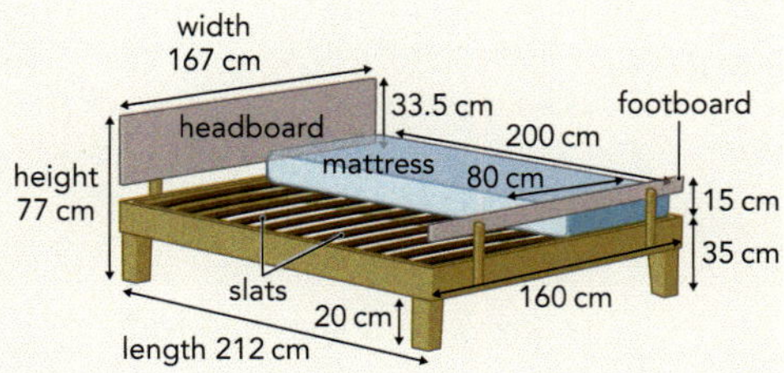

4 Making a sale

Now it's time for you to put your knowledge into practice.

A **Work with a partner. Practise selling the same product(s) to four different types of customer. Select a product from the box below or choose one from your own shop.**
Use the check sheet to structure your dialogue.

a sofa • a single bed • a wardrobe • a pair of jeans • a T-shirt • an anorak • a pair of high heels • a pair of trainers • a pair of shoes for the office • an electric drill • a picture frame • a barbecue

B **Perform two or more of your sales dialogues in front of your class and use the check sheet to evaluate it.**

PART B: Customer loyalty

Situation: You work for an electrical retailer. Your store finds that it has fewer and fewer regular customers.

→ **You examine the pros and cons of introducing a customer loyalty programme and/or improving services offered with products.**

1 Comparing customer loyalty programmes

First, you find out what different customers think about loyalty programmes.

A Read the statements (1–16) by customers and group the statements under the headings 'Pros' and 'Cons'.

1 I can pay with my customer card. It costs a few euros a year, but I get big discounts and a birthday voucher.
2 I cancelled my card because of all the emails and letters. I think they sell your data to other companies.
3 I collect points in different shops and get products and vouchers. My card saves me money!
4 I don't like all that small print on the registration form. I don't want to say yes to something I don't want.
5 I donate my points to people in need and good causes.
6 I get a free drink in the cafeteria, and they even sent me a birthday card last year!
7 I just show my app at the checkout and get a discount of 3% on the regular price. Nice and simple.
8 I got an invitation to a workshop about using power tools safely, and they also have helpful online tutorials.
9 I'm worried about identity theft. They say your data is safe, but they can hack into anything these days.
10 You need so many points before you can get anything. It's just not worth it.
11 It's just too complicated to register for a card or an app. I can't be bothered.
12 The app's fun! It has games and competitions with prizes. I love that!
13 The newsletter tells me when there are special offers on plants or flowers.
14 There are too many cards. I haven't got room for them all in my purse and the apps are confusing.
15 They share your data with 40 other physical shops and 600 shops online. How many people know that?
16 You lose your privacy. They have all your personal details and track your behaviour. No thank you!

B Look at the list (1–16) again and sort the statements under the following headings.

saving money · use of personal data · help and information · entertainment · charity

C List the top three advantages (pros) and disadvantages (cons) of loyalty cards in your opinion and discuss your list with a partner.

2 Explaining a loyalty programme

You go online and find a podcast about different types of customer loyalty programmes.

16)) **Listen to the recording and choose the correct answer for each sentence.**

1 A multi-store loyalty programme ___.
- **a** only works with a smartphone
- **b** only works with a card
- **c** works with a card and a smartphone

2 A multi-store loyalty programme is ___.
- **a** for shopping in physical stores and online
- **b** only for online shopping
- **c** only for physical stores

3 If you activate a premium, you ___.
- **a** get a free drink
- **b** get more points
- **c** have to spend at least €100

4 The premiums ___.
- **a** have no time limit
- **b** have a time limit
- **c** all have a time limit of 24 hour

5 A multi-store loyalty programme is ___.
- **a** for both goods and services
- **b** only for goods
- **c** only for services

6 The points can ___.
- **a** only be used online
- **b** be turned into vouchers for cash
- **c** only be used in a physical store

7 The points ___.
- **a** can only be used by one customer
- **b** cannot be given away
- **c** can be given away

8 Customers' personal data is ___.
- **a** never used by retailers
- **b** used to send customers special offers
- **c** deleted after three months

9 Stand-alone single company loyalty programmes are mainly used by ___.
- **a** big retailers
- **b** small shops
- **c** supermarkets

3 Optimizing your company's internet presence

Ihr Unternehmen möchte seine Website optimieren und sie mit den sozialen Medien verlinken, um mehr Kundinnen und Kunden zu erreichen. Sie finden einen interessanten Artikel im Internet mit Tipps für Firmen, die ihre Produkte online bewerben.

Schreiben Sie eine E-Mail an Ihren Vorgesetzten / Ihre Vorgesetzte, in der Sie die wichtigsten Inhalte des Artikels in deutscher Sprache zusammenfassen. Berücksichtigen Sie dabei folgende Punkte:
- Zielgruppe(n)
- Mobilfreundlichkeit
- einfache Entscheidungswege
- Suchmaschinenoptimierung

How to get the best out of your website

Identify your customers
Begin by defining your target group and their demographics. Is your site geared to professionals, such as software developers, designers and architects or the general public? If it's for the general public, it can't be for 'everyone', so is it, for example, for children, parents, teenagers, 20+, 30+, 40+, homeowners, the working or the retired population? The list is endless so you need to have a clear picture of who your customers are because, put simply, don't try to sell meat to vegans or car accessories to cyclists.

Think mobile
Older websites were designed for desktops and laptops and look great on a big screen but flop on a mobile device because it's too small. Optimize your online presence for mobile users. Make sure your website loads fast because today's users are prepared to wait up to three seconds and no longer. Make the content easy to see and read because if the page is overloaded your customers will lose patience.

Plan your customer's journey
A lot of customer journeys to a retailer's site start on social media, so make sure you advertise on the platforms your target group is naturally drawn to. When a customer lands on your website, the journey begins, so draw a roadmap of where they're supposed to go and how fast you can get them there. One seller was shocked to discover that it took 22 clicks to buy something on their site. Three or four clicks should be enough, and make sure the customer's journey is intuitive. Test it on a variety of users and find out if it leads to a sale or to what online sellers call 'basket abandonment'. Online buyers leave the goods they want to buy in their virtual shopping baskets if they have to do complicated things like produce a lot of data to sign up to a new payment platform or choose from a confusing selection of shipping options.

Optimize for search engines
Search engines send out robotic agents called bots to scan the worldwide web looking for data, which they then collect and index for quick reference. It's important to understand that the bots first go to mobile websites. This is called mobile-first indexing. This means that a company's most important data must be on the mobile version of its website and not on the desktop version. So if your company has all its great stuff on its desktop website and a watered-down version on its mobile site, the watered-down version is all that the bots will find. It's also important to understand that bots don't swipe or click on icons, words or images. This means that your good stuff has to be visible from the start and not only after the user has interacted with your page.

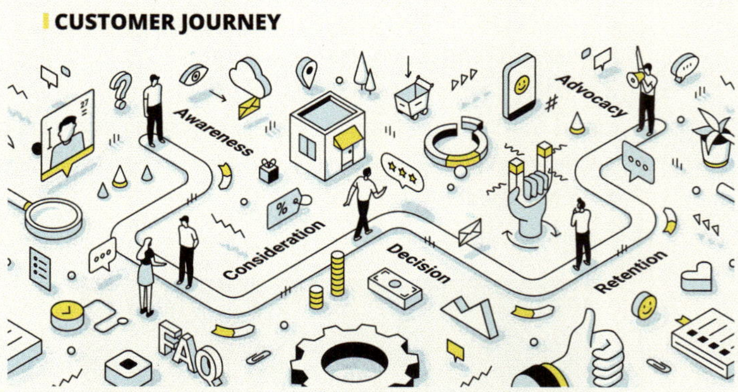

4 Improving services

The electrical retailer you work for sells a wide range of high-quality domestic appliances and home entertainment products.

A Use the words in the box to label the appliances.

air conditioning unit • blender • curling tongs • dishwasher • electric oven • electric shaver • fridge freezer • induction hob • iron • microwave oven • satellite dish • smart TV • toaster • vacuum cleaner • washing machine

1

2

3

4

5

6

7

8

9

10

11

12

13

14

15

B Your shop makes a charge for some services (see table below). List the appliances and products from exercise 3A that customers often cannot transport, install or recycle themselves.

Service charges			
advice	free	installation	charge
estimate	free	repairs under warranty	free
delivery	charge	extra 5-year guarantee	charge
recycle old appliance	charge	exchange or refund	*free

*If the appliance or product is defective.

C Discuss in class if it would make sense to make some or all of these services free (e.g. permanently or for a limited time) to attract more customers.

D Discuss if it would be a good idea to introduce a multi-store or stand-alone customer loyalty programme, so that customers get some or all of the services free if they sign up for the customer card,

COMMUNICATION: Polite language

Situation: More and more English-speaking tourists are coming to your shop, so you need better language skills to speak to them appropriately. The shop invites a trainer to help the staff.
→ You learn polite ways of asking questions and making requests.

1 Direct and indirect questions

Your trainer teaches you how to make polite indirect questions from direct questions. She puts the following information on the board.

Politeness means being indirect!
'Is this your bag?' is a direct question.
'Could you tell me if this is your bag?' is an indirect question.
Indirect questions are more polite.

Direct question	Indirect questions			
		1	2	3
Is this your bag?	Could you tell me	if	this	is your bag?
Are you paying by card?		if	you	are paying by card?
Does your mother need help?		if	your mother	needs help?
What is your address?		what	your address	is?
When did you buy it?		when	you	bought it?

Formula

Introduction	1		2	3
Could/Can you tell me Do you know Do you happen to know Would you mind telling me	if wh-	 (wh-/how) question word	subject	verb

Turn the direct questions (1–10) into polite indirect questions. Use all four introductions in the section 'Formula'.

1 Is this the right colour?
2 Is your husband waiting outside?
3 Does your wife need a bigger size?
4 When is your flight?
5 Are you looking for a particular brand?
6 What size does your husband take?
7 Do you need a taxi?
8 Does your mother need to sit down?
9 How many suitcases do you need?
10 How big does the rucksack need to be?

2 Talking to customers politely

Next you look at some typical situations where polite language is needed.

Read how an impolite shop assistant talks to customers at a big shop and improve the assistant's dialogue by using expressions from the box below.

Could you ...? • Could I possibly ask you to ...? • Do you happen to ...? • Excuse me, but • If you'd just like to ... • I'm afraid ... • I'm extremely sorry, but ... • May I ..., please? • Would you mind ...?

1 Assistant: Customers aren't allowed to use their own bags. Take a trolley or use a basket.
Example: Excuse me, sir, but I'm afraid customers aren't allowed to use their own bags. Could you take a trolley or use a basket, please?
2 Assistant: Show me the receipt.
Customer: Here you are.
3 Assistant: Come with me to the men's department.
4 Assistant: You can't bring that dog into the shop. Only guide dogs are allowed.
5 Customer: Excuse me. Is this 100% cotton or synthetic?
The phone rings.
Assistant: Wait. *(Answers phone)* Schmidt? Okay, ich komme sofort. *(To customer)* I have to go. Ask someone else.
6 Assistant: Your car's blocking the car park exit. Move it.
7 Assistant: This till's closed. Go to another one.
8 Assistant: Do you have a customer card?
Customer: No, I don't have one but I'd like one.
Assistant: Certainly. Fill in this form, sign it and bring it next time.

3 Practising polite language

You work in the Customer Services department of your shop.

Work with a partner and use polite language to role-play conversations with customers in two typical retail situations. When you have finished swap roles and do each role-play again.

Partner A and Partner B: **Go to File 1 on page 154.**

DAS KANN ICH (Unit 6)

- Ein Verkaufsgespräch durchführen. (Foundation)
- Auf unterschiedliche Kundentypen reagieren. (Part A)
- Neue Kundschaft gewinnen und bestehende Kundschaft binden. (Part B)
- Höflich mit Kunden und Kundinnen umgehen. (Communication)

SCENARIO: Output

> Now go back to the beginning of the unit (page 65) and study the task again.
>
> → **Think of ways of dealing with the customer who complained about the price of the camera so that he leaves both happy and certain to return to buy the wide-angle lens.**

STEP 1 **Before you work on your task to give feedback, think about the following:**

1 a method of dealing with the customer
- a conversation that takes place in the shop
- an email which explains what you can offer the customer
- a telephone call from the manager or yourself

2 the sort of person the customer is
- someone who is quick to anger
- someone who feels misunderstood
- someone who feels he has been treated unjustly
- someone who believes shops should know their own business

3 what to offer your customer to keep his business
- your customer loyalty programme
- just giving the customer the reduction he wanted
- incentives to continue shopping at your shop (guarantee of lowest price for all articles, discount on the wide-angle lens – and one further item)
- something else

STEP 2 **Start by writing down:**

- arguments to convince the customer not to take his business elsewhere
- arguments the customer might use not to continue shopping at your shop or not to accept what you offer

STEP 3 **Think of the vocabulary and phrases you will need.**

- Find exercises in this unit which offer useful vocabulary for your task.
- List polite phrases.
- List vocabulary according to your offers.

7 Online and offline sales

SCENARIO: Input

A number of small independent shops in the town centre, including the one you work for, are facing closure due to decreasing sales. They decide to offer their goods and services online on a platform run by a regional provider. Before they can join, the provider sends them a checklist including things such as their policy on delivery and returns.

→ **In this unit you are going to learn about differences between buying goods online and in shops.**
→ **At the end of this unit you will be asked to write a short text for the platform with details of your shop's delivery and returns policy.**

Checklist

- ❐ **delivery**
  - ❐ express
  - ❐ same-day
  - ❐ standard
  - ❐ click and collect
- ❐ **returns**
  - ❐ legal minimum
  - ❐ general right of return and refund
  - ❐ right of return and refund except in certain circumstances

FOUNDATION: Online vs offline

Situation: A retailer that only sells its products from physical shops is losing customers and is therefore rethinking the way it operates.
→ **You examine how customers' buying habits are changing and review new sales strategies.**

1 Examining consumer preferences

You do some research on developments in retailing and find interviews and statistics about shopping habits.

A **Match what the consumers say (A–H) with the categories in the bar chart (1–8).**

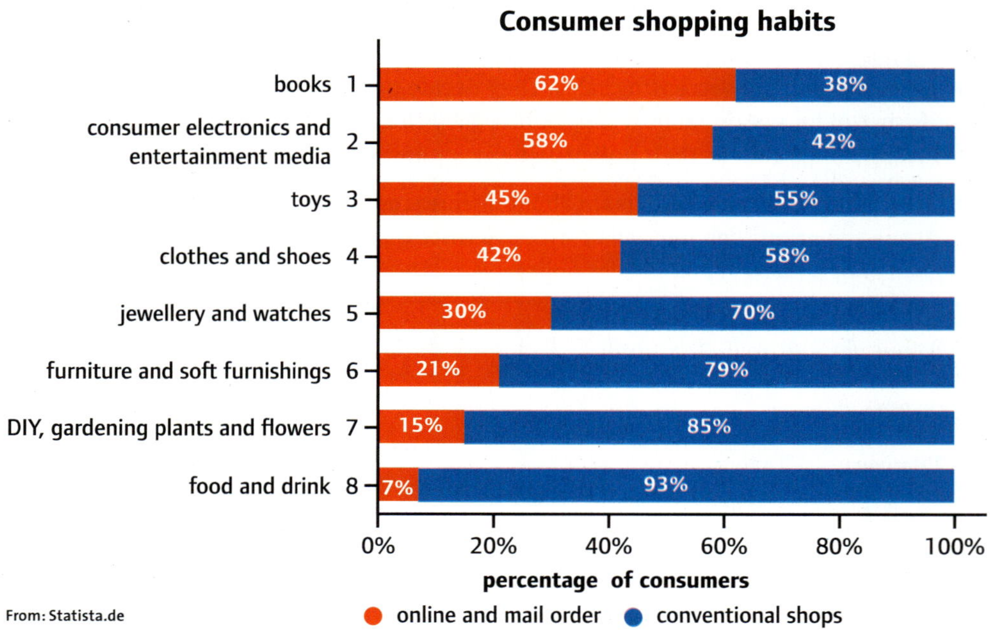

From: Statista.de

A I buy some things online, like games and so on, but young children grow so fast and lose interest in things so quickly that I often need advice from the assistant about what to buy them next and you can't get that online or from a catalogue.

B I do a lot of work on the house and in the garden, so before I buy tools, building materials and gardening equipment, I need real face-to-face advice. You can only get that in a shop.

C I love reading thrillers and detective stories and when I've finished one, I go online, look at the recommendations and order another one immediately without needing to leave the house.

D I often try on four or five dresses before I find one that looks and feels right and then, of course, I need the accessories. Some people find things that they can wear online but for me it's much better to go to a shop and try them on.

E I wouldn't dream of buying groceries on the internet! I need to see, touch and smell something before I'm prepared to eat it.

F I buy all my digital media and anything to do with communication and entertainment online. I also think that the advice and product reviews you get on the internet are far more objective than what a shop assistant will tell you because they just want to sell you stuff.

G No matter how good your screen is, you can't get a feeling for something like a table or a sofa until you can actually see, feel and test it. The same goes for rugs, carpets, lampshades and any kind of home decorations. I always go to a shop for these things.

H You can buy a cheap bracelet, a necklace, or an ankle chain online but if you want something really good, like a wedding ring that fits your finger perfectly or a pair of solid gold earrings, you need the advice of an expert and you certainly don't want it to be sent in the post.

B **Study the graph and say which types of shop are most and least at risk of losing customers to the internet.**

C **State how many of the consumers say that they want advice, help or recommendations before buying something, and say where they prefer to get them from.**

D **List the products that most consumers want to see, touch or feel before buying them.**

2 Opening an online sales channel

Some shops that are losing customers hope to survive by opening an online sales channel.

A 17 **Copy the table, then listen to the three interviews with small shop owners and complete it with the information you hear.**

	type of shop	online platform	delivery	advantages	disadvantages
1					
2					
3					

B **If the shop where you are doing your apprenticeship also sells online, add its details to the table.**

C **More than 64,000 German retailers sell their goods on the same huge internet platform that is used by more than 44 million German consumers. Discuss with a partner and then in class whether it is better for internet sellers to use this platform or set up their own platform.**

PART A: Distance selling

Situation: Your employer is planning to open an online sales channel, so it organizes a seminar to prepare its employees for distance selling.
→ **You learn about the buyer's and seller's rights and obligations in distance sales contracts and discuss the pros and cons.**

1 Returning goods

The seminar trainer examines the issues concerning returning goods.

The trainer puts up the following two scenarios on the board. In small groups, discuss the three questions.

Two scenarios

A customer goes into a shop, tries on a dress, pays for it, takes it home, but the next day decides that she actually doesn't like it.

A customer sees a dress online. She orders it in her size and pays for it. A few days later the dress arrives by post. When she examines the dress, she finds that she doesn't like it.

What cancellation rights do they have?

1 Do they both have the same right to return the article with no questions asked and to get a full refund of the money they have paid?
2 Can the seller refuse a refund for any reason?
3 Can the seller make a deduction from the refund if goods show signs of use?

2 Distance selling

As part of the seminar, the trainer gives you a handout with information about returning goods.

Consumer guarantees

According to EU law, a seller must give a consumer a **two-year legal guarantee** as a protection against faulty goods or goods that are not as advertised. During this time, the seller must rectify any defects, e.g. by repairing or replacing the goods, or, if the defect cannot be rectified, refund the purchase price plus expenses, e.g. transport costs.
A seller may offer the consumer an **additional commercial guarantee**. In such cases, the customer must be informed that the commercial guarantee does not replace the 2-year legal guarantee.
Physical shops: If a product is bought from a physical shop, the consumer is not entitled to return it to the retailer and receive a refund of the purchase price just because the consumer doesn't like it or has decided he or she doesn't need it. The product must be faulty.
Distance sales: With distance sales the situation is different. Distance sales are those that are made online, on the phone, by mail order or through a TV shopping channel. The most important characteristic of distance sales is that the consumer is not able to physically examine the goods before buying them. The consumer therefore has 14 days after receipt of the goods to return them and is entitled to cancel the order with a full refund of the purchase price without giving any reason.
Online sellers have different obligations from offline retailers in physical shops. The following is a list of the most important information that online sellers must give to the consumer before accepting an order:

- the consumer's cancellation rights
- a description of the main characteristics of the goods
- the seller's identity, contact details and phone number (if available)
- the total price, including all taxes and charges
- the terms of delivery and payment
- methods of payment
- the legal guarantee period
- the customer's obligation to pay for returning the goods
- a copy of the sales contract

It is not enough for this information to be on the seller's website. It must be sent to the consumer in writing, e.g. on paper or by email. If the seller does not do this, the consumer has one year and 14 days to cancel the order and receive a full refund of the purchase price, including transport costs.
The seller is obliged to refund the purchase price even if the customer has opened the packaging and, for example, tried on clothes or tested equipment. The seller has the right to refuse to refund the purchase price for some items, such as perishable goods (e.g. food or flowers) or sealed items that have been unwrapped (e.g. computer software). The seller may also reduce the amount refunded if the goods have clearly been used (e.g. shoes that have been worn in the street).
The seller must refund the purchase price within 14 days after the goods have been returned. The seller must refund the purchase price using the same payment method used by the consumer unless the seller and consumer agree on a different method.
Some traders may not charge you the cost of returning your goods. However, they must tell you before you order if you have to pay for postage costs. Otherwise, the trader must pay for the return postage.

A Choose the correct answer for each sentence.

1 The EU's distance selling laws cover only goods ___.
 a bought online
 b ordered from a catalogue or from a TV shopping channel
 c ordered without the customer being able to physically examine them

2 If a customer has bought goods in a physical store but doesn't like them, he or she has ___.
 a 14 days to take them back in order to get their money back
 b 30 days to return them but they won't get the full purchase price refunded
 c no right to take the goods back and get a refund

3 If a customer has bought goods online but doesn't like them, they have ___.
 a 14 days to send them back in order to get their money back
 b 30 days to return them but they won't get the full purchase price refunded
 c no right to take the goods back and get a refund

4 An online seller must give the following to a customer: ___.
 a their full name, their physical and email addresses
 b their physical and email addresses and phone number
 c their full name, their physical and email addresses, and their phone number

5 If a consumer buys a shirt online, opens the packaging, removes the pins, tries the shirt on, doesn't like it and sends it back, the online seller ___.
 a has the right to make a deduction from the refund because the shirt is no longer new
 b has no right to make a deduction from the refund because a customer could do this in a shop
 c can refuse to refund the customer any money at all because the shirt is no longer new

6 If a customer buys fresh flowers online and doesn't like them, the online seller ___.
  a needn't refund the purchase price
  b must refund the purchase price
  c isn't allowed to refund the purchase price

7 If a customer returns goods bought online to the seller, ___.
  a the customer pays the cost of returning the goods
  b the seller pays the cost of returning the goods
  c the seller and the customer share the cost of returning the goods

3 Deciding on a returns policy

Your company is deciding if it is better to allow customers to return goods bought online free of charge or make them pay. You find a podcast on the internet with a range of different opinions.

A **18))) Copy the table, then listen to the podcast and complete columns A–G with the information you hear for Melissa, Tom, Sebastian and Laura. Then complete line 5 of the table (*You*) with information about your own shopping habits.**

	A	B	C	D	E	F	G
	spends most money on:	buys online	buys offline	wants express delivery	wants free returns	wants advice	environ-mental concerns
	product(s)	*never, seldom, some-times, often, always*		*yes/no*	*yes/no*	*yes/no*	*yes/no*
1 Melissa							
2 Tom							
3 Sebastian							
4 Laura							
5 You							

B **Summarize each line of the table (1–5) like this:**

1 *Melissa spends most money on … She (e.g. always/often …) buys things online and … (e.g. sometimes/seldom) … offline. She wants/doesn't want … and is/isn't worried …*

C **Discuss the pros and cons of free online returns.**

- First find out how many members of your class want (D) express delivery, (E) free returns and/or (G) are worried about the environment.
- Write the numbers for D, E and G on the board and discuss whether companies should take responsibility for the environment by never offering free returns or if it should be left to the customer to act responsibly and reduce returns to a minimum.
- Take a vote at the end of the discussion to find out if your class is for or against free returns.

> **Adverbs of frequency**
>
> **How often** do you buy clothes online?
> I **always/often/sometimes/seldom/never** buy clothes online.
> Adverbs of frequency go *before* the verb.

› *Grammar: Adverbs of frequency, page 169*

PART B: Returning goods to a shop

Situation: Outlet Becker's exchanges and refunds policy allows customers to return products bought in its shops within 30 days as long as they meet the company's terms and conditions.
→ **You practise how to process customers' requests for in-shop exchanges and refunds.**

1 Understanding an in-shop returns form

Outlet Becker uses the same returns form for all its branches.

A Study the form and match the highlighted English expressions on the form with the German words (1–20).

1 abgelehnt
2 Beschreibung
3 EC-Karte
4 Erstattung
5 fehlerhaft
6 Gebrauchsspuren
7 genehmigt
8 Gutschrift
9 Hersteller
10 Kaufbeleg
11 Kaufdatum
12 Kundenkarte
13 maßgeschneidert
14 nicht umtauschbar
15 Originalverpackung
16 persönliche Pflege
17 Postleitzahl
18 reduzierte Ware
19 Überweisung
20 Umtausch

IN-SHOP RETURNS FORM

This form to be completed and signed by the customer and countersigned by the employee.

Customer details

First name	*Henrietta*	Family name	*Vogel*
Street & house no.	*Kleinstraße 649*	Postcode	*43400*
Town/City	*Neustadt*	Phone no.	*01622090503*
Email	*henrietta.vogel@linkall.ger*	Customer loyalty card	*no*

1 Product details

Description	Make/Brand/Manufacturer	Size/Dimensions	Colour	Purchase price
women's trainers	*TopSpeed*	*39*	*pink*	*€119.95*

2 Reason(s) for return

Faulty		Wrong size		Wrong colour		Don't like it	*x*
Additional information							

3 Customer's preference

Refund	*x*	Exchange		Repair		Credit note	

4 Checklist

Date of purchase	Proof of purchase		Original packaging		Labels		Signs of use		Seal	
	yes	no	yes	no	yes	no	yes	no	unbroken	broken
(14 days ago)	*x*			*x*		*x*	*x*			

5 Method of payment

Cash	Debit card	Credit card	Bank transfer	Other
	x			

6 Non-returnable items

All sale or reduced items.

The following items if they show signs of use, have been personalized or the seal has been broken: bedding • cosmetics • made-to-measure clothing • personal care products (e.g. electric shaver) • pierced earrings • software • swimwear • underwear

Town/City	Date (dd/mm/yyyy)	Employee's full name	Employee's signature	Customer's signature

7 For internal use only

Refund approved		Refund refused		Replacement		Repair	
Cash refund		Credit/debit card refund		Bank transfer refund		Credit note	

B **Study the entries on the form and say if the customer's request should be approved or refused. Give reasons for your answer.**

2 Processing in-shop returns

You work in the Customer Services Department of Outlet Becker in Frankfurt.

A 19 **Listen to the two dialogues and write down the information for sections 1–7 of the in-shop returns form for each customer.**

B **Now summarize what happened in each case. Start like this:**

1 *A customer called Mark Taylor brought back a black …*

2 *A customer called Chantal Clark brought back a blue …*

3 Handling in-shop returns

You deal with customers wanting to return purchases.

A **Work with a partner and role-play the situations (1–4) on page 87. In each case an English-speaking customer brings back the product because they are dissatisfied with it.**

Partner A: In situations 1 and 3, you are the employee. In situations 2 and 4, you are the customer.
Partner B: In situations 1 and 3 you are the customer. In situations 2 and 4, you are the employee.

When you are the employee, decide what the best solution is in each case, but don't tell your partner until the end of the role-play. Fill in a returns form if necessary. You must always remain polite and respectful.
When you are the customer, invent any extra details.

1 a faulty hairdryer

- looks brand new but produces a bad smell when switched on for longer
- purchase price €19.99 (debit card)
- purchased seven days ago
- customer loyalty card
- no receipt but bank statement and original packaging
- customer wants a replacement or exchange

2 2.5 kilos of apples in a plastic bag

- looked all right in the shop but at home one apple found to be rotten
- purchase price €4.99 (cash)
- purchased yesterday
- has receipt and original packaging
- customer wants a refund

3 a man's shirt

- customer doesn't like the shirt
- looks clean but has traces of lipstick on the collar
- purchase price €49.95 (credit card)
- purchased four days ago
- no loyalty card
- receipt
- customer wants a refund

4 a wooden shelving unit for self-assembly

- shelving unit doesn't go with furniture in customer's flat
- has been assembled and dismantled, plastic bag of screws has been opened
- purchase price €150 (debit card)
- purchased two weeks ago
- customer loyalty card
- receipt and original packaging
- customer wants to look in the store for a more suitable unit
- refund if they can't find anything suitable

B **Now role-play a situation in your own shop in which a customer brings back goods and requests an exchange, refund, repair or credit note. It can be a situation that you have experienced yourself or heard about. Prepare a role card for your partner with all the details. Your role is the employee. Practise the situation with your partner and then perform it to your class.**

› *Thematic vocabulary: Returns, page 199*

COMMUNICATION: Newsletters

Situation: Your company regularly emails newsletters to its registered customers with updates on new products and promotions, but customers often don't open them or unsubscribe from the mailing list.
→ You find out how to get customers to read your newsletters.

1 Landing in the primary inbox

Email providers use artificial intelligence (AI) to categorize emails such as newsletters before they reach the addressee. Many never make it to the inbox.

A **Look at the content of the three emails sent out to customers below (A–C) and sort them according to whether they would reach your primary inbox, your promotions folder or your spam folder.**

A

B

C
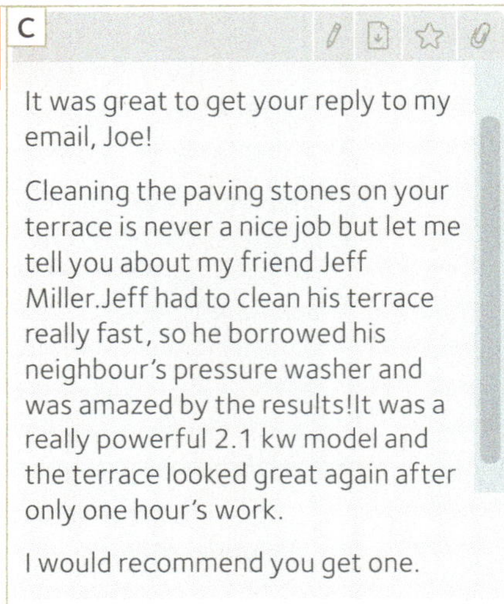

B **Check your own email and see if any newsletters have made it into your primary inbox or if they have all been saved under *promotions or spam*.**

2 Making sure your newsletters get read

You do some research on the best way to send newsletters to subscribers on a mailing list and find a podcast explaining what to do.

A 20)) **Hören Sie dem Podcast zu und vervollständigen Sie die unten stehenden Sätze auf Deutsch.**

1 Die meisten Newsletter enthalten ___.
2 Leider werden solche Newsletter ___.
3 Das intelligente Postfach der E-Mail-Provider erkennt Newsletter und ___.
4 Damit Newsletter gelesen werden, müssen sie aussehen wie ___.
5 Die Betreffzeile sollte nicht Informationen enthalten, sondern ___.
6 Viel besser als ein Bild ist ein ___.
7 Anstatt über Fakten zu schreiben, sollte man lieber ___.
8 E-Mails sollten immer kurz sein, denn sie werden nicht richtig gelesen, sondern ___.
9 Man sollte nie die gleiche E-Mail an ___.
10 Die „three-to-one"-Regel besagt, dass man zuerst drei ___.

B **Working with a partner or in small groups, decide if this is a successful newsletter or not. Examine the following aspects:**

- headlines
- images
- text
- subject line

Subject: 70 things you need to know about wedding dresses

NEWSLETTER

GREAT OFFERS FOR BRIDAL GOWNS!

SUMMER SALE NOW ON!

Some girls have been dreaming about the perfect wedding dress since they were five and know exactly what it's going to look like right down to the last sequin.
Others never give it a moment's thought until, a few months before the Great Day, their future mother-in-law says: 'You still haven't bought the dress!'
No matter what type of future bride you are, we are the experts when it comes to choosing the best dress for you. We'll help you understand how to choose between organza, A-line, fit-and-flare, sheath, chiffon and charmeuse, and when that's done, we'll help you with accessorizing, so your Great Day will be a great success!

C **Make changes to the newsletter in exercise 2B so that it will be more successful. The following suggestions may help you:**

- Avoid banner headlines.
- Write short one-sentence paragraphs.
- Offer a story of interest to the reader.
- Use one image only or a short video clip.

3 Sending out promotional emails

The speaker in the podcast explained the three-to-one rule: you send three emails with helpful tips, advice and information before you send a fourth email with a link to a product or service.

Devise a three-to-one series of four emails to promote a product or sales event, e.g. a summer/winter sale, Black Friday, or an event at your shop. Choose or take a suitable photo for the second email and make a video with a smartphone for the third. Make sure your emails are short and simple.

DAS KANN ICH (Unit 7)

- Die Rolle von Onlineplattformen erklären. (Foundation)
- Kunden und Kundinnen über ihr Rückgaberecht informieren. (Part A)
- Rückgaben verarbeiten. (Part B)
- Erfolgreiche Werbe-E-Mails gestalten. (Communication)

SCENARIO: Output

Now go back to the beginning of the unit (page 79) and study the task again.

→ **Write a short text for the provider's website with details of your shop's delivery and returns policy.**

STEP 1 **Before you work on your task, think about the following:**

1 what sort of shop you work in

2 what sort of products you offer
- how this affects the returns policy

3 what delivery policies you can offer

4 what returns policy you offer (for different products)
- deductions made for signs of use
- reasons to refuse refund
- time limit for refunds
- anything else you might think of

STEP 2 **Start by writing down:**

- description of your shop and products
- information about your delivery options
- information about your returns policy

STEP 3 **Think of the vocabulary and phrases you will need.**

- Find exercises in this unit which offer useful vocabulary for your task.
- List vocabulary concerning delivery.
- List vocabulary concerning returns.

8 Enquiries and terms of delivery

SCENARIO: Input

Your retail company normally gets its consumer electronics supplies from a Polish manufacturer, but due to unexpected circumstances it has gone bankrupt. It is just three months until Black Friday and Cyber Monday, and immediately afterwards the Christmas season starts. This has put you under a lot of pressure, as you need to place larger orders to satisfy customer demand.
You search the market for suitable suppliers and find some both inside and outside the EU. At first sight, the offers from the companies outside the EU seem more favourable but, on closer examination, you see that some of them quote Incoterms® 2020 rules that do not cover the main carriage and/or import clearance.

→ **In this unit you are going to deal with business correspondence, enquiries and terms of delivery in order for you to be able to help business customers more effectively.**

→ **At the end of this unit you will devise two standard enquiry templates for purchasing products from abroad. You should include your company's preferred Incoterms®2020 rules. One template is for suppliers inside the EU, while the other is for suppliers outside the EU.**

FOUNDATION: The layout of business letters

Situation: You start work in the purchasing department of a large retail organization which orders products from suppliers around the world.
→ **You learn how to do the layout of business letters.**

1 Looking at business letter layout

The head of department gives you an example of a business letter.

Outlet Becker AG 1
Kleinstrasse 400
60315 Frankfurt am Main
Germany

Tel. +49 69 24445830-0
Fax +49 69 24445830-4
Email: info@outlet-becker.ger
www.outlet-becker.ger
•
LS/BK 2
24 March 20.. 3
•
AIRMAIL 4
•
UK Trading Ltd 5
275 Jason Street
LIVERPOOL
L5 5DY
VEREINIGTES KÖNIGREICH
•
Attn Ms Megan Desmond, Purchasing Department 6
•
Dear Ms Desmond 7
•
Sales contract 8
•
We are pleased to send you your copy of Sales Contract No. 89WV as requested. 9
•
Please do not hesitate to contact us should you have any queries.
•
Yours sincerely 10
Outlet Becker AG
•
•
 11
•
•
Lea Schmidt (Ms)
Purchasing Department
•
Enc. 12

Match the sections of the letter (1–12) with the labels below (a–m).

	labels	guidelines
a	**attention line**	Place it *under* the inside address, so it can be seen in a window envelope.
b	**body of the letter**	Always start with a capital letter.
c	**complimentary close**	This is linked with the salutation. (See Infobox below) Write the name of the sender's company under the complimentary close.
d	**date**	Always write the month as a word to avoid confusion. Write the year with four digits (e.g. 2025).
e	**enclosure**	Use 'Enc.' when something has been added to an envelope.
f	**inside address**	Write the town or city in capital letters and the postcode on a separate line in a letter to the UK. Include the country of destination in capital letters.
g	**letterhead**	Include 'Germany' in letters sent abroad.
i	**reference initials**	The initials of the person who signs the letter are followed by initials of the person who wrote the letter LS = signatory's initials; BK = secretary's initials
J	**salutation**	This is linked with the complimentary close. (See Infobox)
k	**signature**	Write the signatory's name under the signature because signatures can be hard to read. Women can add their preferred title in brackets, e.g. (Mrs), after their name if they wish.
l	**special markings**	These include URGENT / PRIVATE AND CONFIDENTIAL / PERSONAL / AIRMAIL / REGISTERED, RECORDED DELIVERY. Place them *over* the inside address, so they can be seen in a window envelope.
m	**subject line**	This should be underlined or **bold.**

salutation and complimentary close

Letter/Email to a named business partner	Dear Ms Desmond →	Yours sincerely
Letter/Email to an unnamed business partner	Dear Sir or Madam →	Yours faithfully

2 Practising the layout of a letter

The head of department asks you to draft a business letter using the correct layout.

Use the information below to write the business letter.

Luisa Klein, the purchasing director at Möbel Schmidt GmbH, Hohenzollernstraße 400, 65400 Neustadt, Germany, dictates an airmail letter to her secretary, Frank Trautmann, and encloses a sales contract. She is writing to Mr Ronan Doyle in the sales department of Murphy Furniture Makers Ltd in Ireland (175 Long Street, Cork T12 HA21), about order no. 99K. The date is 3 July of this year. She starts the letter by thanking him for his offer. Just write the first few words of the body of the letter.

VIDEO 4

Watch the video about business letters.

PART A: Enquiries

Situation: Outlet Becker is currently looking for new suppliers of garden furniture.
→ **You send enquiries to several companies.**

1 Enquiring about a product

You line manager sends an enquiry to Lotus Manufacturing, a Chinese company in Shenzhen.

To: enquiries@lotus-manu.chn
Subject: Enquiry about garden furniture
From: lea.schmidt@outlet-becker.ger

Dear Sir or Madam

We note from your company's website that you sell a wide range of indoor and outdoor furniture.

As a major German retailer of DIY and home and garden products with many long-standing customers all over Europe, we are particularly interested in garden furniture, as we need to stock up before the beginning of spring.

Please send us a favourable quotation for your *Summer Relax* garden furniture set, including all discounts granted and details of your terms of delivery and payment.

We would require delivery within six weeks at the latest.

References are available on request.

We look forward to hearing from you soon.

Yours faithfully

Lea Schmidt (Ms)
Purchasing Department
Outlet Becker AG

Study the email and match the sentence halves.

1 Lotus Manufacturing sells a wide range
2 Lea Schmidt works for
3 The German company sells
4 Lea Schmidt wants Lotus Manufacturing
5 She also needs details of all discounts
6 Delivery must be made

a DIY and home and garden products.
b granted and the terms of delivery and payment.
c to send her a quotation.
d within six weeks at the latest.
e of indoor and outdoor furniture.
f Outlet Becker AG.

2 Structuring an enquiry

Most enquiries have a similar structure.

A Match the words in the box (1–14) from an enquiries checklist with the German translations (a–n).

ENQUIRIES CHECKLIST ✓

1 Source of address
2 Description of your company
3 Reason for your enquiry
4 Your requirements
5 – quotation
6 – sales material
7 – price list
8 – discounts
9 – samples
10 – terms of delivery and payment
11 – delivery
12 – representative's visit
13 References
14 Polite ending

a (Preis-)angebot
b Beschreibung Ihres Unternehmens
c Grund für Ihre Anfrage
d höfliche Schlussformel
e Ihr Bedarf
f Liefer- und Zahlungsbedingungen
g Lieferung
h Muster/Probe(n)
i Preisliste
j Quelle der Anschrift
k Rabatte
l Referenzen
m Verkaufsmaterial
n Vertreterbesuch

B You send an enquiry about a patio swing chair to an Italian supplier, but your computer crashes and the email gets mixed up. Use the checklist to put the sentences (a–h) in the right order.

a Delivery would need to be made within six weeks at the latest.
b We look forward to your early reply with interest.
c My company is a well-known retailer of home and garden products both in Germany and abroad.
d Please send us a quotation for 100 units, including your terms of delivery and payment and all discounts granted.
e References are available on request.
f We are looking for a supplier of garden furniture and are particularly interested in your Hampton patio swing chair.
g I was very impressed by the garden furniture I saw at your stand at the trade fair in Cologne.

C Match the sentences (a–h) with the terms in the enquiries checklist above.

D Use words from the email in exercise 1 and the sentences in exercise 2B to complete this enquiry to a Finnish company. Use one word for each gap.

Dear Mr Häkkinen

We note from your company's ___ 1 that you sell a wide ___ 2 of home and garden furniture and would like more information on your ___ 3.

We are a ___ 4 German retailer of DIY supplies with many ___ 5 customers both in Germany and ___ 6. Please send us a favourable ___ 7 for your Helsinki sunbeds, including your ___ 8 of delivery and payment and details of all ___ 9 granted.

We look forward to ___ 10 from you soon.

Yours ___ 11

Lea Schmidt (Ms)
___ 12 Department
Outlet Becker AG

3 Writing an enquiry

You send an enquiry to a British firm.

Using the information in German below, write an enquiry to the firm either as an email or as a letter.

Situation:
Sie (Ihr Name, E-Mail: vorname.nachname@outlet-becker.ger) sind im Einkauf bei der Firma Outlet Becker AG, Kleinstraße 400, 60315 Frankfurt am Main, Germany, tätig. In der aktuellen Ausgabe von *House and Design Weekly* haben Sie eine Anzeige für Sonnenschirme (*patio umbrellas*) gesehen, die vom englischen Unternehmens Patio Mania Ltd, 250 Sackville Road, Ashford TN23 1AC, England, vertrieben werden, und möchten Näheres über dieses Produkt erfahren.

Aufgabe:
Schreiben Sie die Anfrage unter Berücksichtigung folgender Punkte:
- heutiges Datum (bei einem Brief)
- Ansprechpartnerin: Ms Olivia Parker, Export Sales Director (E-Mail: olivia.parker@patio-mania.gbr)
- Bezug auf Anzeige
- Beschreibung Ihrer Firma: bedeutender deutscher Einzelhändler für Gartenmöbel u.a. mit vielen langjährigen Kundinnen und Kunden im In- und Ausland
- Sie interessieren sich insbesondere für den Sonnenschirm Casablanca und hätten gerne ein günstiges Preisangebot for 100 Stück einschl. aller gewährten Rabatte.
- Lieferung bis spätestens Ende des Monats erforderlich
- Referenz auf Wunsch erhältlich
- Aussicht auf größeren Auftrag, wenn die Produkte Ihren Anforderungen entsprechen
- höflicher Schluss

PART B: Terms of delivery

Situation: Your company receives offers for goods from suppliers both inside and outside the EU with terms of delivery using Incoterms® 2020 rules.

→ **You examine the Incoterms® 2020 rules in order to compare the terms of delivery offered by several suppliers.**

1 Understanding Incoterms® 2020 rules

You find an explanation of the Incoterms® 2020 rules in your company's information pack.

Incoterms® 2020 rules: information sheet
The Incoterms® 2020 rules are used by importers and exporters to define the costs and risks of international trade.

Transport costs
If an **F term** is used, the seller is only responsible for the pre-carriage part of the goods' journey to their destination. In practice, this means that the seller only loads the goods on the first carrier's vehicle, e.g. at the seller's premises, or pays for transporting the goods to a convenient location not too far away from the seller's premises, e.g. a nearby port, airport or train station, and loading the goods at that location, e.g. at the port of shipment. The buyer is then responsible for arranging a contract of carriage to transport the goods to their destination and for unloading them when they arrive.

If a **C term** is used, the seller pays the costs of the main carriage to the destination but not of unloading at the destination. Post-carriage is the buyer's responsibility.

If a **D term** is used, the seller pays all transport costs until the goods have reached the premises of the buyer.

Risks
With an **F term**, the seller bears the risk until the goods have been handed over to the first carrier, e.g. at the seller's premises, or in the case of FOB until the goods are on board a ship at the port of shipment.

With **CPT** and **CIP**, the risk to the seller is the same because it passes to the buyer when the goods have been collected by the first carrier. In the case of CIP, the seller also insures the goods for the main carriage but no longer bears any risk when they have been handed over to the first carrier.

D terms cover all risks until the goods have reached the premises of the buyer.

Import and export clearance
Export clearance (e.g. export licences, documentation) is arranged and paid for by the seller. Import clearance (e.g. customs duty, import licences and documentation) is arranged and paid for by the buyer.

Erklären Sie auf Deutsch mithilfe des Texts, …

1 welche Transportkosten der Verkäufer bei einer F-Incoterms®-Klausel übernimmt. Geben Sie zwei Beispiele an.
2 wer bei einer C-Incoterms®-Klausel die Kosten für den Haupttransport trägt.
3 wer bei einer C-Incoterms®-Klausel die Entladungskosten trägt.
4 welche Transportkosten der Käufer bei einer D-Incoterms®-Klausel trägt.
5 bis zu welchem Punkt der Verkäufer bei FOB das Risiko trägt.
6 bis zu welchem Punkt der Verkäufer bei CPT und CIP das Risiko trägt.
7 wer das Risiko bei einer D-Incoterms®-Klausel trägt.
8 wer für die Besorgung einer Importlizenz zuständig ist.
9 wer die Kosten einer Ausfuhrgenehmigung trägt.

2 Comparing four Incoterms® 2020 rules

You look at offers for garden furniture made to your company made by four different suppliers.

Supplier	Terms of delivery	Transport costs paid by supplier paid by buyer
1. Lotus Manufacturing, Shenzhen, China	FOB Port of Shanghai Incoterms® 2020 free on board (named port of shipment) *frei an Bord (benannter Verschiffungshafen)*	
2. NLPA Ltd, Canterbury, UK	CIF Rotterdam Incoterms® 2020 cost, insurance and freight (named port of destination) *Kosten, Versicherung und Fracht (benannter Bestimmungshafen)*	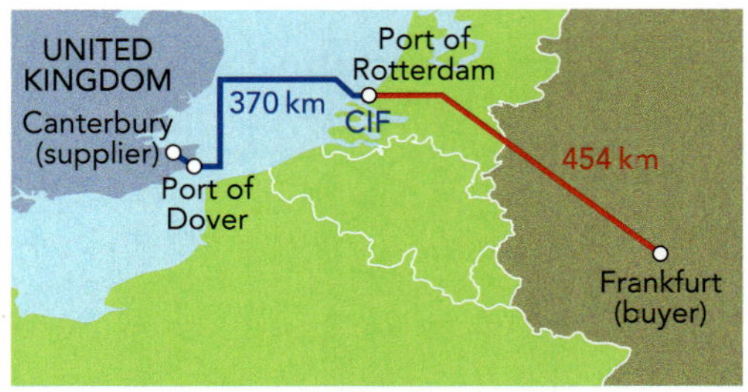
3. Intramobili, Naples, Italy	CIP buyer's premises Frankfurt Incoterms® 2020 carriage and insurance paid to (named place of destination) *frachtfrei versichert bis (benannter Bestimmungsort)*	
4. Gundersun SA, Oslo, Norway	DPU buyer's premises Frankfurt Incoterms® 2020 delivered at place unloaded (named place of destination) *geliefert benannter Ort entladen (benannter Bestimmungsort)*	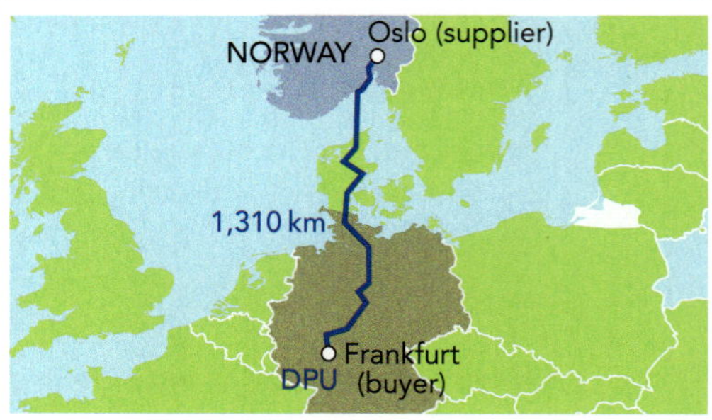

A Study the maps illustrating the Chinese, British, Italian and Norwegian offers, and find out the following:

1 Who pays for the main carriage in each case?
2 In which offer does the supplier pay to transport the goods to a destination in their own country.
3 In which case(s) does the German buyer in Frankfurt need to arrange for some part of the transport?
4 Which seller pays all the transport costs from the supplier to the buyer?
5 Which supplier or suppliers are outside the EU? How does this affect the payment of customs duties?

B **Next you study the definitions of the four Incoterms® 2020 rules quoted by the suppliers in more detail.**

FOB – free on board (named port of shipment)
frei an Bord (benannter Verschiffungshafen)
The seller delivers the goods at his own expense and risk, cleared for export, on board the vessel selected by the buyer unless otherwise agreed, at the named port of shipment. Thereafter, the buyer bears all the costs and risks of transporting the goods to their destination.

CIF – cost, insurance and freight (named port of destination)
Kosten, Versicherung und Fracht (benannter Bestimmungshafen)
The seller delivers the goods at his own expense and risk, cleared for export, on board the vessel selected by the buyer, at the named port of shipment. The seller pays the transport costs for the goods, including transport insurance, up to the named port of destination. The buyer pays all import duties and taxes and transportation to their destination.

CIP – carriage and insurance paid to (named place of destination)
frachtfrei versichert bis (benannter Bestimmungsort)
The seller delivers the goods cleared for export to the carrier, which he selects. The seller bears the risk until the goods have been delivered into the custody of the first carrier. The seller pays the transport costs for the goods, including transport insurance, up to the named destination. The buyer pays all import duties and taxes and the unloading of the goods.

DPU – delivered at place unloaded (named place of destination)
geliefert benannter Ort entladen (benannter Bestimmungsort)
The seller is responsible for the carriage of the goods, cleared for export to the named place at the destination by the carrier, which he selects. He bears the risk until the goods have been delivered to the destination. The seller is responsible for unloading the goods at the place of destination. The buyer pays all import duties and taxes.

Copy and complete the table below with data from the four definitions.

B = buyer | S = seller

	Main carriage		Seller bears risk		Seller insures for main carriage	Export clearance		Loading		Import clearance		Unloading	
	paid	unpaid	including main carriage	excluding main carriage		B	S	B	S	B	S	B	S
FOB		✓											
CIF													
CIP													
DPU													

C **Write a memo to your boss suggesting which supplier offers you the best delivery deal.**

COMMUNICATION: Telephone enquiries

Situation: Your company trades in a wide range of goods both at home and abroad.
→ **You make and receive enquiries about several different articles.**

1 Dealing with a telephone enquiry

A Swedish company calls about fashionwear.

A 21)) **Übertragen Sie den Vordruck für eine Telefonnotiz und füllen Sie ihn mithilfe der Informationen aus dem Telefongespräch aus.**

TELEFONNOTIZ

Anrufer/in Vor- und Nachname / Unternehmen / Land / Telefonnummer / E-Mail	*Peter* ___
Nachricht für Vor- und Nachname des Mitarbeiters / der Mitarbeiterin und Abteilung	___
Bedarf Ware / Menge / Lieferbedingungen / Lieferzeit	___
Sonstiges: z. B. Quelle unserer Anschrift / Beschreibung des Unternehmens / Referenzen	___

B 21)) **Listen again and write down the missing words.**

1 Could you put me ___ to him, please?
2 Can I take a ___?
3 Is that all in small letters or are there any ___?
4 Everything in lower ___.
5 Right, I've made a ___ of that.
6 Could you ___ that for me, please?
7 Right, so ___ pass on your message to Mr Steinmeier.

2 Giving your telephone number and email over the phone

Study the two infoboxes.

Saying telephone numbers

0 is 'oh' or 'zero'.
Say each number separately, except for double digits, e.g. 0218 55329 is 'oh (or zero) – two – one – eight – double five – three – two – nine'
00 is 'double oh' or 'zero, zero'. +49 is 'plus four nine'.

Saying email addresses

@	at
.	dot
+	plus
-	hyphen
_	underscore
A	capital A / upper case A
a	small a / lower case a

Work with a partner and practise dictating telephone numbers and email addresses to each other.

Partner A: **Look at File 17 on page 164.**
Partner B: **Look at File 6 on page 158.**

3 Asking to be contacted by phone or email

Your company has found a potential supplier of webcams in Japan.

Work with a partner. Use the notes below to role-play a telephone conversation.

Partner A
Vertriebsmitarbeiter/-in bei Yokohama Electrics

Nehmen Sie das Gespräch entgegen, indem Sie „Moshi, moshi" sagen.

Partner B
Sie (Ihr Name), Outlet Becker, Germany

Stellen Sie sich auf Englisch (Vor- und Nachname, Unternehmen, Land) vor. Sagen Sie, dass Sie mit Herrn Miyamoto aus der Exportabteilung sprechen möchten.

A: Sagen Sie, dass er heute nicht im Hause ist. Fragen Sie, ob Ihr Gesprächspartner / Ihre Gesprächspartnerin eine Nachricht hinterlassen möchte.

B: Sagen Sie, dass Sie folgende Nachricht hinterlassen möchten: Sie hätten gerne ein Angebot für 100 Webcams vom Typ JT4K; DPU Incoterms 2020 Ihre Geschäftsräume in Frankfurt; Lieferung binnen sechs Wochen; Referenzen auf Wunsch; bedeutendes Unternehmen in Deutschland.

A: Wiederholen Sie alle Einzelheiten. Fragen Sie anschließend, ob der Gesprächspartner / die Gesprächspartnerin sonst noch etwas braucht.

B: Sagen Sie, dass Herr Miyamoto Sie bitte kontaktieren möge.

A: Fragen Sie nach den Kontaktdaten des Anrufers / der Anruferin.

B: Geben Sie Ihre Handynummer (+49 162 2083640) und E-Mail-Adresse (vorname_nachname@outlet-becker.ger) an.

A: Fragen Sie, ob es sonst noch etwas gibt.

B: Sagen Sie, dass Sie keine weiteren Wünsche haben.

A: Kommen Sie zu einem freundlichen Ende des Gesprächs.

B: Beenden auch Sie das Gespräch freundlich.

DAS KANN ICH (Unit 8)

- Einen Geschäftsbrief richtig gestalten. (Foundation)
- Eine schriftliche Anfrage auf Englisch erstellen. (Part A)
- Die passenden Zahlungs- und Lieferbedingungen für internationale Geschäfte auswählen (Part B)
- Telefonische Anfragen auf Englisch durchführen (Communication)

SCENARIO: Output

Now go back to the beginning of the unit (page 91) and study the task again.

→ You devise two standard enquiry templates for purchasing products from abroad. You should include your company's preferred Incoterms®2020 rules. One template is for suppliers inside the EU, while the other is for suppliers outside the EU.

STEP 1 **Before you work on your task, think about the following:**

1 Incoterms®2020 rules
- Which are best for your company?
- Which might be accepted by a supplier?
- What difference might there be between carriage between an EU country and Germany and a non-EU country and Germany?

2 Delivery time
- What is a reasonable period of time between ordering goods and their arrival?
- How might the delivery time vary between an EU and a non-EU country?

STEP 2 **Check the following:**

- The layout and structure of an email or a letter

STEP 3 **Think of the vocabulary and phrases you will need.**

- Find exercises in this unit which offer useful vocabulary for your task.
- List vocabulary concerning delivery.

9 Terms of payment, offers, orders and acknowledgements

SCENARIO: Input

The sales director of your company receives an email (see extract below) from Shane Doyle, purchasing director of Killarkey Trading in Ireland. She asks you to formulate a reply based on your company's guidelines regarding terms of payment (see below: *Einkaufsgrundlagen*).

→ **In this unit you are going to learn about payments and writing offers and orders.**
→ **At the end of this unit you will write a reply to the Irish customer detailing more favourable terms of payment in the shorter and the longer term on the basis of your company's guidelines.**

Our company has been trading with you for almost two years now and our volume of business has doubled in the last year, currently standing at €10,000 per quarter. We therefore think it is time to review our terms of payment, which are CWO. In view of our history of punctual payment and the increasing volume of business, we would like to request a change to our terms of payment to 10 days 2%, 30 days net with immediate effect, with a view to trading on open account terms with quarterly settlement in the longer term.

Einkaufsgrundlagen

Dauer der Geschäftsbeziehung

Bei **Neukunden** wird prinzipiell Vorauszahlung bzw. Barzahlung bei Auftragserteilung verlangt.
Bei **Stammkunden** können je nach Auftragsvolumen verschiedene Arten von Kreditkauf gewährt werden, u. a. 14 Tage 2/3 % Skonto, 30 Tage netto, offenes Zahlungsziel mit vierteljährlicher Abrechnung.

Auftragsart und -volumen

Beträgt das monatliche Auftragsvolumen **weniger als 1.000 €**, wird Vorauszahlung bei Auftragserteilung verlangt. Beträgt das monatliche Auftragsvolumen **mehr als 1.000 €** über einen Zeitraum von **mindestens 12 Monaten**, kann Kreditkauf gewährt werden.

Zahlungsmoral

Stammkunden **mit guter Zahlungsmoral** kann Kreditkauf gewährt werden. Bei Zahlungsverzug oder -ausfall **aus nicht berechtigtem Grunde** wird der gesamte Schuldbetrag sofort fällig und bei künftigen Aufträgen Vorauszahlung bei Auftragserteilung verlangt.

Preisnachlässe

Diese beziehen sich auf den Listenpreis und können aus verschiedenen Anlässen gewährt werden u. a. Erstauftragsrabatt (5–10 %); Treuerabatt (5–10 %); Mengenrabatt (5–10 %).

FOUNDATION: Terms of payment

Situation: As your company is increasingly looking abroad for cheaper deals, you have been asked to help formulate terms of payment with foreign suppliers.
→ You review the terms of payment used with suppliers.

1 Saying prices

You make sure you know how to say prices in different currencies.

A First, study the examples in the box and then say the following prices.

a €57.75	**c** €395.50	**e** $2,500.00
b €1.99	**d** £850.00	**f** $3,275,000.00

Saying prices

€1.00	a/one euro
€100.00	a/one hundred euros
€150.00	a/one hundred and fifty euros
€1,000.00	a/one thousand euros
€1,000,000.00	a/one million euros
€1,250.00	a/one thousand two hundred and fifty euros
€0.01	a/one (euro) cent
€0.02	two cents
€250.75	two hundred and fifty euros and seventy-five cents

Don't forget to pronounce the final '**s**' and to say '**and**' after '**hundred**'.

B Work with a partner and practise saying prices to each other.
Partner A: Turn to File 2 on page 156. Partner B: Turn to File 11 on page 162.

2 Writing prices

There has sometimes been confusion about prices in written communication between your company and foreign trading partners, so you check how prices are written in English.

A First, study the examples in the box, then write out the following prices in figures.

1 a million euros
2 ninety-nine euros and seventy-five cents
3 thirty-two (euro) cents
4 20 pence
5 forty-five dollars and fifty-four cents
6 a hundred and eighty-four euros and sixty-nine cents
7 three hundred and sixteen pounds and seven pence
8 five thousand five hundred dollars
9 five thousand five hundred and fifty-five pounds
10 nine thousand eight hundred and seventy-six euros

Writing prices

- currency sign first
- no space
- comma where there is a point in German
- point where there is a comma in German

€10,500.00

B 22 Now listen to the recording and write down the prices you hear in the way shown in the box.

3 Understanding terms of payment

You study an explanation of the terms of payment most frequently used by your company.

A Lesen Sie den Text und die Tabelle und vervollständigen Sie die untenstehenden Sätze auf Deutsch.

Terms of payment

Before the buyer and seller sign a contract of sale, they must first agree when and how payment will be made. Ideally, the seller would like payment in advance before starting work on the order while the buyer would like a long time to pay for the goods, so that they can be sold before they are paid for. In practice, if the seller trusts the customer, the seller will usually give a credit period of 30, 60 or 90 days. Some trusted customers get open account terms, which means that they pay for the goods at the end of the month or quarter. If the seller doesn't know or doesn't trust the customer, the terms of payment will be payment in advance, cash with order (CWO).

The table shows typical terms of payment and whether they are good or bad for the buyer and seller.

Importer / Buyer			Exporter / Seller
	payment in advance (TT) cash with order (CWO)	*Vorauszahlung/Vorkasse*	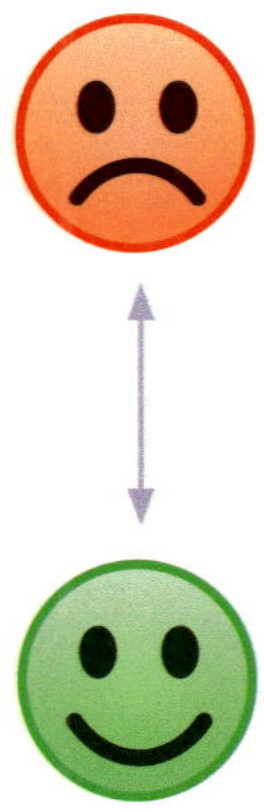
	30% with order, 70% before loading	*30 % bei Auftragserteilung, 70 % vor Verladung*	
	⅓ with order, ⅓ on delivery, ⅓ 30/60/90 days after delivery	*⅓ bei Auftragserteilung, ⅓ bei Lieferung, ⅓ 30/60/90 Tage nach Lieferung*	
	10 days 2%	*2 % Skonto Zahlung innerhalb 10 Tagen*	
	30 days net	*30 Tage netto*	
	open account terms with monthly/quarterly settlement	*offenes Zahlungsziel mit monatlicher/vierteljährlicher Abrechnung*	

1 Einzelheiten über die Zahlungsbedingungen stehen im ___.
2 Der Käufer möchte möglichst viel Zeit, bevor er die Ware bezahlt, damit er sie ___.
3 Vertrauenswürdige Kundinnen und Kunden bekommen ein Zahlungsziel von ___.
4 Ein Kunde, dem ein offenes Zahlungsziel eingeräumt wurde, bezahlt erst am Ende des ___ oder des ___.
5 Unbekannte oder nicht vertrauenswürdige Kundinnen und Kunden müssen im ___.
6 Die günstigste Zahlungsbedingung für den Verkäufer ist ___.
7 Manchmal verlangt der Verkäufer 30 % bei Auftragserteilung und den Rest ___.
8 Um zu erreichen, dass der Käufer zeitnah nach Erhalt der Ware zahlt, gewähren einige Händler 2 % ___.

B With a partner study the table above and find suitable terms of payment for the following situations. There is sometimes more than one answer.

1 A new customer in Asia contacts your company and is interested in buying goods worth € 25,000.
2 A new customer places four orders worth a total of € 30,000 over three months and pays CWO each time. The customer now asks you for better terms of payment.
3 A regular customer with open account terms and quarterly settlement starts paying your invoices late.

PART A: Offers

Situation: Outlet Becker has received an enquiry about hotel beds from a large hotel chain in Ireland.
→ You send an offer to the customer.

1 Making an offer

Your line manager sends an offer to the hotel chain's headquarters in Dublin.

To:	Orla Keane, Purchasing Director <orla.keane@dfh-ltd.irl>
Subject:	Enquiry about *Bodymatch* beds
Attachment(s):	hotelbeds.pdf

Dear Ms Keane

We were delighted to receive your enquiry and feel sure we can supply Doyle's Family Hospitality Ltd with the goods you need. As a major distributor of furniture with an excellent reputation both at home and abroad, we have many satisfied customers throughout the EU and beyond.

A brochure on a variety of hotel beds is attached for your information.

As regards the items requested, we are pleased to submit the following quotation:

Bodymatch standard single bed (80 x 200 cm)	€650.00
Bodymatch standard double bed (140 x 200 cm)	€950.00

Our prices are quoted FCA our premises in Frankfurt Incoterms 2020.
A quantity discount of 10% is granted on orders for 10 or more items.
Our usual terms of payment for an initial order are CWO by bank transfer. If regular orders are placed with our company, open account terms may be granted.

Delivery can be made immediately from stock.

We feel sure that a trial order will convince you of the quality of our products.

Please do not hesitate to contact us if you require further details.

Yours sincerely

Philipp Jung
Sales Department
Outlet Becker AG

A Study the email and complete the following sentences.

1 Outlet Becker AG has received an enquiry from an Irish company called ___.
2 The purchasing director at the Irish company is called ___.
3 The Irish company is interested in buying ___.
4 Outlet Becker sells furniture to customers in Germany and ___.
5 The Incoterms 2020 rule quoted means that the buyer will have to collect the goods at the seller's ___.
6 The price per bed will be lower if the customer buys ___.
7 Outlet Becker may grant open account terms to a customer if they place ___.
8 Delivery to the customer won't take long because Outlet Becker has the goods in ___.
9 Philipp Jung suggests the Irish company test the quality of the beds by placing a ___.

B Match the words in the box (1–8) from an offers checklist with the German translations (a–h).

OFFERS CHECKLIST ✓

1 reference to enquiry
2 description of your company/goods/services
3 sales material
4 price
5 terms and discounts
6 delivery
7 polite ending
8 enclosure(s) *(letters)* / attachment(s) *(emails)*

a Anlage(n)
b Beschreibung Ihrer Firma/Waren/Dienstleistungen
c Bezugnahme auf Anfrage
d Geschäftsbedingungen und Rabatte
e höflicher Schluss
f Lieferung
g Preis
h Verkaufsmaterial

C With a partner go through the email to the hotel chain and decide which sentences or paragraphs belong to each item on the checklist.

D You draft an offer for furniture but the sentences get mixed up. Match the sentence halves.

1 As agreed in our telephone conversation,
2 We are a major distributor of furniture
3 Our current catalogue is
4 To download our export price list, please
5 Delivery will be made FCA our
6 Wholesalers are granted
7 Our terms of payment are 10 days 2%,
8 Regular customers may be granted
9 Delivery is made within
10 We hope our offer is to your liking

a open account terms.
b approx. 30 days after receipt of order.
c and look forward to receiving your order.
d 30 days net with favourable references.
e a trade discount of 30%.
f visit our website at www.outlet-becker.ger.
g I am pleased let you have details of our products.
h attached for your information.
i premises in Frankfurt Incoterms 2020.
j with many high-quality products.

› *Useful phrases: Writing offers, page 194*

E **The predictive text function on your computer inserts some strange words into your email to a customer. Spot the mistakes and correct them.**

1 As agreed in our unpleasant telephone conversation, we are sending you our offer.
2 We were depressed to receive your enquiry this morning.
3 We are a minor distributor of furniture.
4 We have many dissatisfied customers throughout Western Europe and North America.
5 Our company manufactures a wide range of low-quality products.
6 Our old catalogue and price list are attached.
7 Our terms of payment for a final order are CWO.
8 Regular customers may be granted closed account terms.

2 Writing an offer

Your line manager asks you to write an offer.

A **Using the information in German below, write an offer as an email or letter.**

Situation:
Sie (Ihr Name, E-Mail: vorname.nachname@outlet-becker.ger) sind in der Exportabteilung von Outlet Becker AG, Kleinstraße 400, 60315 Frankfurt am Main, Deutschland, tätig. Gestern erhielten Sie eine E-Mail von der Firma Norwood Tableware Pty Ltd, 80 Industry Street, 7109 Cape Town, Südafrika. Das südafrikanische Unternehmen interessiert sich für Besteck der Serie „Parma“, und zwar für die 30-teiligen *(30-piece)* und die 66-teiligen Bestecksets *(cutlery sets)*.

Aufgabe:
Schreiben Sie ein Angebot unter Berücksichtigung folgender Punkte:
- heutiges Datum (Brief)
- Ansprechpartner: Mr Julius Esterhuizen, Purchasing Director (E-Mail: julius.esterhuizen@ntw.saf)
- Bezug auf Anfrage
- Beschreibung Ihres Unternehmens: ein bedeutender Großhändler für Haushaltswaren mit vielen zufriedenen Kundinnen und Kunden im In- und Ausland
- Sie fügen eine Broschüre über Besteck der Serie „Parma“ bei (bei E-Mail-Angebot: parma.pdf) mit Verweis auf Ihre gesamte Produktpalette und Exportpreisliste unter www.outlet-becker.ger.
- Sie unterbreiten der südafrikanischen Firma folgendes Angebot:
  Besteckset Parma, 30-tlg. *(30-piece)*: 175,00 €
  Besteckset Parma, 66-tlg. *(66-piece)*: 350,00 €
- Ihre Preise verstehen sich FOB Hamburg Incoterms® 2020, einschl. eines 10-prozentigen Erstauftragsrabatts.
- übliche Zahlungsbedingungen Kasse bei Auftragserteilung per Überweisung
- Lieferung ca. 14 Tage nach Auftragseingang
- Empfehlung, einen Probeauftrag zu erteilen
- höflicher Schluss

PART B: Orders and acknowledgements

Situation: You have just started work in the purchasing department of Outlet Becker, which has suppliers all around the world.
→ **You learn how to compare offers, place orders and check acknowledgements.**

1 Comparing offers

Your company has buying agents in several countries. It is currently looking for a good source of men's suits. Its buying agents in Italy, France and Sweden have located potential suppliers. Purchasing director Anna Klein first shows you the product comparison sheet and points system used to evaluate offers and then you listen in when she calls the agents.

A 23)) **Copy the table below and fill it in using the information your hear and adding points according to what is said with the information you hear. The suppliers are:**

1 Massimo Milano SRL
2 Paris Confection SARL
3 Stockholm Style AB

Product comparison sheet				
	supplier	1	2	3
1 unit price				
			points	
2 quality/workmanship	very good (10) good (5) average (0)			
3 sustainability / EU Ecolabel	yes (10) no (0)			
4 terms of delivery	D term (10) C term (5) F term (0)			
5 delivery period	1–2 weeks (10) 2–3 weeks (5) 4 or more weeks (0)			
6 terms of payment	30 days net or ⅓, ⅓, ⅓ (10) early payment discount (5) in advance / with order (0)			
7 free advertising material	yes (10) no (0)			
8 credit rating	low risk (10) average risk (5) high risk (0)			

B **Now work out the total number of points for each company to find out who should get the order.**

C **How could the company with the second highest score improve its offer to get the order?**

2 Analysing an order

Next, you learn how to place an order and start by studying an order recently placed with an Indian supplier.

To: daljit.singh@bhopal-garments.ind
Subject: Order for fashionwear

Dear Mr Singh

Having seen your offer on the internet and spoken to you on the telephone, we now wish to place an order for the following goods:

Quantity	Description	Article no.	Unit price	Total
50	New Style denim jeans	MDJ-96	US$30.00	US$1,500.00
50	New Style denim shorts	MDS-90	US$25.00	US$1,250.00
50	New Style informal suit	LDJ-76	US$25.00	US$1,250.00
50	New Style informal jacket	LDS-70	US$20.00	US$1,000.00
			Total price	**US$5,000.00**

Terms of delivery: CIF Port of Bremen, Germany, Incoterms 2020 within 30 days after receipt of order
Terms of payment: 30% with order, 70% before loading by transfer to your account at Indian International Bank Ltd
Packing: Container, palletized in sturdy cartons

Transport and insurance of the goods from Bremen to Frankfurt will be arranged by us.

We look forward to receiving your confirmation of order and advice of dispatch in the near future and trust the goods will arrive punctually and in good condition.

Yours sincerely

Lea Neumann (Mrs)
Purchasing Department
Outlet Becker AG

A First, match the words in the box (1–13) from an orders checklist with the German equivalents (a–m).

OFFERS CHECKLIST ✓

1 reference to offer
2 details of goods ordered
3 price(s) and discount(s)
4 delivery
5 – Incoterms® rule 2020
6 – delivery date/period
7 – transport
8 – packing
9 – insurance
10 payment
11 acknowledgement / advice of dispatch
12 polite ending
13 enclosure(s) *(letter)* / attachment(s) *(email)*

a Angaben über die bestellten Waren
b Anlage(n)/Anhang/Anhänge
c Bezugnahme auf Angebot
d Eingangsbestätigung/Versandanzeige
e höfliche Schlussformel
f Internationale Handelsklausel
g Liefertermin/-zeit
h Lieferung
i Preis(e) und Rabatt(e)
j Verpackung
k Versand
l Versicherung
m Zahlung

B **Look at the email on page 110 and discuss where each point in the orders checklist in 2A can be found. Some may not be in the email.**

C **Study the order and say if the following statements are true or false. Correct the false statements.**

1 Daljit Singh at Bhopal Garments in India orders fashionwear from Outlet Becker in Germany.
2 Lea Becker and Daljit Singh first discussed the order on the telephone.
3 Payment is to be made in euros.
4 The buyer will pay the costs of the main carriage.
5 The buyer will be able to take delivery of the goods after paying 30% of the total price.
6 Payment is to be made by bank transfer.
7 The goods will be flown from Mumbai to Bremen.
8 The buyer will pay for the transport and insurance of the goods in Germany.

3 Writing an order

You have to send off an order.

Use the information below and the phrases in the email in exercise 2 to write an order as an email.

Situation:
Sie (Ihr Name) sind im Einkauf bei der Firma Steinmeier Haus- und Küchengeräte GmbH tätig, E-Mail: vorname.nachname@shk-gmbh.ger. Ihr Unternehmen importiert Haushaltsgroß- und Elektrokleingeräte u. a. aus China. Sie haben im Internet ein Angebot der chinesischen Firma Hunan Kitchen Factory gesehen und die Firma daraufhin angerufen.

Aufgabe:
Erteilen Sie der chinesischen Firma einen Probeauftrag unter Berücksichtigung folgender Punkte:
- an Ms Ammy Liu (E-Mail: ammy.liu@123.chn), Verkaufsabteilung.
- Bezugnahme auf Angebot im Internet und Telefongespräch
- Sie bestellen mit Auftrags-Nr. GBT98 10 Küchengeräte *(food processors)* vom Typ Blendy zu je 100,00 US-$, Katalog-Nr. CPPP10 und 10 Kaffeemühlen *(coffee grinders)* vom Typ CoolNow Xtra zu je 30,00 US-$, Katalog-Nr. CNX5.
- Lieferung FOB Hong Kong Incoterms® 2020 innerhalb von 30 Tagen nach Auftragserhalt
- Versand und Versicherung der Ware von Hongkong nach Deutschland über Bremen werden von Ihnen übernommen.
- Zahlungsbedingungen: 30 % im Voraus, 70 % bei Fertigstellung per Banküberweisung
- Bitte um Auftragsbestätigung und Versandanzeige
- Hoffnung auf pünktliche Lieferung der Ware in gutem Zustand
- Aussicht auf weitere Aufträge, wenn sich die Ware gut verkauft
- höflicher Schluss

COMMUNICATION: Negotiating better terms

Situation: Your company has been doing regular business with a new supplier for over a year now and now wishes to negotiate more favourable terms.
→ **You review your current terms and negotiate better ones.**

1 Reviewing current terms

Study the last order your colleague, Sven Maier, placed with A.P. Leather International in Lahore, Pakistan.

To: Nasir.Mahmood@AP.L.pak
Subject: Order for fashionwear

Dear Mr Mahmood

Having seen your offer on the internet and spoken to you on the telephone, we now wish to place an order for the following goods:

Quantity	Description	Article no.	Unit price	Total
100	Men's fashion jacket	MFJ-303	US$30.00	US$3,000.00
100	Men's fashion pants	MFP-304	US$25.00	US$2,500.00
100	Ladies' fashion jacket	LFJ-603	US$25.00	US$2,500.00
100	Ladies' fashion pants	LFP-604	US$20.00	US$2,000.00
			Total price	**US$10,000.00**

Terms of delivery: EXW Lahore, Pakistan Incoterms 2020 within 30 days after receipt of order
Terms of payment: 25% with order, 75% before loading by transfer to your account at Allied Bank Limited
Packing: Container, palletized

Transport and insurance of the goods from Lahore to Frankfurt via the ports of Karachi and Bremen will be arranged by us.

We look forward to receiving your confirmation of order and advice of dispatch in the near future and trust the goods will arrive punctually and in good condition.

Yours sincerely

Sven Maier
Purchasing Department
Outlet Becker AG

Work with a partner and discuss how the terms of delivery and payment could be improved and any other changes that could be made in Outlet Becker's favour. Then discuss your ideas with your class.

2 Negotiating better terms

Your colleague, Sven Maier, phones Nasir Mahmood at A.P. Fashion International to negotiate better terms and place an order.

24 **Read the email on page 112, then listen to the dialogue and note down the following information.**

1 the terms of delivery and payment of the last order
2 the terms of delivery and payment that Outlet Becker wants
3 the terms of delivery and payment agreed
4 the validity of the new agreement

3 Using different negotiating styles

Some people prefer a direct approach and others an indirect one when negotiating. Study these examples.

Direct approach	Indirect approach
Introduction	
There's a problem with … *(the price, terms of delivery/payment, delivery period, quality, etc.)*	Do you have a few moments to talk about … *(the price, terms of delivery/payment, delivery period, quality, etc.)*?
Price	
The price is too high. You need to reduce it by 20%.	We need to talk about the price.
Terms of delivery	
Ex works is no good. We need better terms of delivery.	Other companies are offering C and even D terms of delivery for a similar product.
Terms of payment	
We don't want CWO anymore. We want open account terms now.	We're regular customers now. Can we review our terms of payment?
Delivery period	
We need delivery within 10 days, or we'll cancel.	Delivery in 30 days could be a problem in the future because some customers aren't prepared to wait.
Quality	
The quality of your last order was terrible.	Some customers have contacted us with quality issues.
If the quality is not up to our standards next time, we'll cancel.	It will be hard to sell the goods if we can't find a solution to the quality issue.

Now work with a partner and practise using both approaches.
Look at File 3 on page 156.

Making promises

We **will deliver** the goods within 14 days.
They **will not (won't)** arrive late.
Use the 'will-future' to make promises.

DAS KANN ICH (Unit 9)

- Passende Zahlungsbedingungen für internationale Geschäfte auswählen. (Foundation)
- Schriftliche Angebote auf Englisch erstellen. (Part A)
- Schriftliche Aufträge auf Englisch erteilen. (Part B)
- Gute Konditionen mit Lieferanten aushandeln. (Communication)

SCENARIO: Output

Now go back to the beginning of the unit (page 103) and study the task again.

→ **You write a suitable reply to the Irish customer detailing more favourable terms of payment in the shorter and the longer term on the basis of your company's guidelines.**

STEP 1 **Before you work on your task, make notes about the following:**

1 What the terms with Killarkey Trading currently are.
2 What terms Killarkey Trading wants.
3 What your company guidelines are concerning the request of Killarkey Trading.

STEP 2 **Decide on the following:**

How to react to the terms requested by Killarkey Trading:

- Accept them
- Reject them
- Try to reach a compromise

STEP 3 **Write down your terms precisely**

- Which elements in this unit could help you?
- If you accept their terms, repeat them exactly so there is no misinterpretation.
- If you reject them, explain why you wish to stick to the original terms.
- If you wish to offer other terms, write them down clearly.

STEP 4 **Using polite language**

- Whatever your decision, start by telling your customer how valuable they are.
- If you accept the terms, do so in a way that shows that trade between you and your partner is valuable.
- If you reject the terms, do so in a way that shows that the rejection is not a reflection of the good relationship you have.
- If you want to negotiate terms, consider how to negotiate so that your trading partner feels that they will also get a good deal.

STEP 5 **Think of the vocabulary and phrases you will need.**

- Find exercises in this unit which offer useful vocabulary.
- List vocabulary concerning terms of payment, negotiating and politeness

10 Problems and complaints

SCENARIO: Input

A young couple with two children recently came to your shop and you sold them a 1,500 litre paddling pool. They put it in their garden, filled it with water and invited some other children over to play in it the following day. However, when the children arrived, the paddling pool was only three quarters full and the grass around it was wet because it had leaked during the night. The husband topped up the pool and the children played in and around it for several hours. During that time, the grass turned into mud, the mud got into the pool, making the water dirty and the children then brought mud into the house, making a mess everywhere they went. That evening the children's father phoned your shop and left an angry voicemail message, saying that he was coming in the next day to complain.

→ In this unit you are going to look at how to deal with customer complaints by earning about consumer rights and how to talk to customers.

→ You listen to the voicemail message the next morning. At the end of this unit, you will prepare yourself for the arrival of the angry customer.

FOUNDATION: Customer complaints in retail outlets

Situation: Your company has regular training courses about consumer rights and customer complaints in its shops.
→ You attend a seminar and learn about the buyer and seller's rights and obligations.

1 Managing customer expectations

First, the seminar leader describes a typical problem in a shop.

With a partner write down notes on the following:

- the customer's and retailer's rights and obligations in this situation with the toaster.
- the same problem with an oven (*Backofen*).

2 Understanding consumer rights and obligations

Next you receive a handout outlining the basic legal situation.

Legal and commercial guarantee
Goods bought in the EU have a mandatory two-year legal guarantee. Some manufacturers also offer an additional voluntary commercial guarantee covering the costs of repair or replacement, either free of charge or at an extra cost for two years or longer.

Faulty goods
During the legal guarantee period, the retailer must repair or replace faulty goods, for example if they have a technical defect (e.g. a machine breaks down) or are not as advertised (e.g. waterproof shoes that let in water). If this is not possible, the customer is entitled to a reduction in price or a full refund and even compensation in some cases, e.g. for spoiled food in a defective freezer. Lost data on computers and smartphones is excluded because the customer is responsible for backups.
If goods are returned during the first six months after purchase, the retailer must prove that the goods were not faulty when sold. As from the seventh month, the customer must prove that the goods were faulty when purchased, which is often impossible.

In-shop returns
The customer must provide proof of purchase, e.g. the receipt or a credit card or bank statement, but the goods do not have to be in the original packaging.

The customer does not like the goods
A retailer does not have to take back goods bought in a shop if the customer decides he or she does not like them. Some shops refund the purchase price or give a voucher as a gesture of goodwill.

Repair, replacement or refund
A customer has no right to an immediate refund if goods are faulty but can choose between repair or replacement, whichever is more reasonable. In all cases, the retailer bears the costs, including a technician's visit and/or transport for bulky items. As a rule, the customer must give the retailer two chances to repair the product or one chance to replace it. After that, the customer is entitled to a refund.

Wrongly priced goods
Under German law, the price on an article in a shop is not binding. If the price on the article is lower than the price at the till, the shop does not have to sell the product at the lower price.

A Match the highlighted words in the text with their German equivalents (a–r).

a	Auszug	**g**	gesetzliche Gewährleistung	**m**	tragen
b	berechtigt	**h**	Kaufnachweis	**n**	verantwortlich
c	beweisen	**i**	Kulanz	**o**	verbindlich
d	ersetzen	**j**	mangelhaft	**p**	verdorben
e	Erstattung	**k**	Schadenersatz	**q**	verpflichtend
f	freiwillig	**l**	sperrig	**r**	zumutbar

B Beantworten Sie folgende Fragen auf Deutsch mit den Informationen im Handout.

1 Was ist der wesentliche Unterschied zwischen gesetzlicher Gewährleistung und Garantie?
2 Wie wird der Begriff „mangelhaft" definiert?
3 In welcher Reihenfolge wird vorgegangen, wenn ein Kunde einen Mangel bei einem Produkt feststellt?
4 Wann tritt die Beweislastumkehr in Kraft, wenn ein Produkt sich als fehlerhaft erweist?
5 Was muss der Kunde dem Verkäufer bei einer Reklamation vorlegen, was braucht er nicht vorzulegen?
6 Wann kann der Verkäufer dem Kunden einen Gutschein geben?
7 Wie viele Versuche sind dem Verkäufer erlaubt, eine mangelhafte Ware zu reparieren oder zu ersetzen?
8 Wo wird dem Kunden der endgültige Preis einer Ware im Laden mitgeteilt?

C Look at the notes you made in exercise 1. Would you change anything?

3 Finding the best solution

You are now given some problems to solve.

Work in small groups and for each situation below discuss the following.

- the retailer and customer's rights and obligations
- the best practical solution

not have to (= nicht müssen)

The shop **does not have to** sell the product at the lower price.
= The shop is *free* to choose the lower price or not.
The goods **do not have to** be in the original packaging.
= The customer is *free* to bring back the goods in the original packaging or not.

1 'I bought a solid oak dining-room table here for €2,000 and had it delivered to my house but when I unpacked it, I discovered that one leg was scratched. I want a new table or my money back.'

2 'The price tag on this dress says €49 but now at the till you tell me it costs €99. By law, you must sell it to me at the lower price.'

3 'I bought this computer in your shop for €1,000 eight months ago but yesterday the hard drive failed and I lost all my data. All new computers have a two-year legal guarantee, you must now replace the hard drive and recover my data for free.'

4 'I bought this watch here at your shop four months ago and now it doesn't work. I want my money back. I paid by credit card, here's my credit card statement. I no longer have the box.'

5 'I bought this hat here last week but now I don't like the colour. I have 14 days to bring it back, so want a full refund. It's in perfect condition but it just doesn't suit me. Here's the receipt and the box.'

PART A: Complaining to a supplier

Situation: You work in the purchasing department of Outlet Becker AG. Several months ago, you bought a consignment of smoke alarms from Safety First Ltd in Ireland but have since received complaints from a number of customers who bought them.
→ **You complain to the supplier.**

1 Writing a complaint

Your colleague, Tamara Meier, complains to the sales director at Safety First in Dublin.

To: fiona.murphy@safety-first-ltd.irl
Subject: Order no. VBF900 for 5,000 EW1 smoke alarms
From: tamara.meier@outlet-becker.ger
Attachment(s): photos_smoke_alarm.zip

Dear Ms Murphy

I'm afraid we have to complain about the EW1 smoke alarms which were delivered on 12 June 20... On their arrival, we forwarded them to various customers throughout Europe. When they opened the boxes, our customers discovered that some were without batteries and mounting screws and others were discoloured and did not work when tested.

We enclose photographs of these items for your information.

Please explain why our order was so poorly executed.

Whatever the case may be, you will appreciate that we cannot sell these articles and must therefore ask you to replace the entire consignment as soon as possible, as these goods are needed urgently.

We feel sure you will appreciate that our future business relationship will depend on how this matter is dealt with.

We expect to hear from you in the very near future.

Yours sincerely

Tamara Meier
Purchasing Department
Outlet Becker AG

Read Outlet Becker's complaint and match the sentence halves.

1 Outlet Becker bought the smoke alarms from	a had also changed.
2 Outlet Becker sold the smoke alarms to	b an explanation from the supplier.
3 The customers discovered that	c customers in different European countries.
4 The colour of some of the alarms	d if a satisfactory solution is found.
5 Tamara Meier wants	e some alarms were incomplete and/or faulty.
6 Outlet Becker wants the supplier to	f to deal with the matter immediately.
7 Outlet Becker will only place further orders	g replace all the smoke alarms.
8 Tamara Meier expects the supplier	h an Irish supplier called Safety First Ltd.

2 Structuring a complaint

Most complaints have a similar structure.

Match the terms in the complaints checklist (1–7) with their German equivalents (a–g).

COMPLAINTS CHECKLIST ✓

1 Reference to goods
2 Description of problem
3 Request for explanation
4 Consequences for the buyer and seller
5 Request for action
6 Polite ending
7 Enclosure(s)/Attachment(s)

a Anlage(n)/Anhang/Anhänge
b Bezug auf Waren
c Bitte um Ergreifung geeigneter Maßnahmen
d Bitte um Erklärung
e Darstellung des Problems
f Folgen für Käufer/-in und Verkäufer/-in
g höfliche Schlussformel

3 Describing problems

You acquaint yourself with language dealing with products or services that are not good.

example	meaning	comment
poor quality/service	not good	more polite than 'bad'; can also mean disappointing (*enttäuschend)*
substandard goods/service	not as good as normal	used to describe goods or services that are not good enough
a faulty light switch	describes a minor problem	can probably be repaired
a defective alarm	describes a major problem	probably cannot be repaired and needs to be replaced
The car was damaged in the accident.	partly but not totally broken	can probably be repaired
a broken mirror	no longer in one piece	cannot be repaired and needs to be replaced
The product/repair/service/explanation is unsatisfactory.	not good enough, unacceptable	describes the quality of a product, service or an action
I am dissatisfied with your work.	not pleased with something	describes an emotion

Use seven of the eight highlighted words from the table above to complete this excerpt from an email.

I am writing to inform you that we are ___[1] with the consignment of kitchen furniture and equipment ordered on 25 April 20.. .

Some of the microwave ovens have ___[2] on/off switches that don't always work. The glass in three of the wall cupboards is ___[3]. Ten of the electric cookers have ___[4] heating elements because they do not warm up when switched on. Most of the equipment arrived dirty as a result of ___[5] packing. One kitchen table was ___[6] in transit, probably due to rough handling.

As our company has a reputation for high quality products, I am sure you will appreciate that we cannot accept ___[7] goods.

4 Making a telephone complaint

Tamara Meier deals with problems concerning a consignment of air conditioners supplied by a Danish company. She phones Gunner Kristoffersen, the sales director at Dansk Electrics in Copenhagen.

A 25)) **Hören Sie sich das Telefonat an und machen Sie sich Notizen zu folgenden Punkten:**

1 gesetzliche Gewährleistung
2 Garantie
3 Zahlungsbedingungen
4 was Outlet Becker vom Lieferanten verlangt
5 mögliche Konsequenzen für den Lieferanten
6 wie lange Outlet Becker noch bereit ist, auf eine Lösung zu warten

B Listen to the dialogue again and complete the sentences with the words you hear.

1 We're extremely ▭ with the air conditioners you sent us.
2 Some of the air conditioners are ▭.
3 … and let me point out that the air conditioners are still ▭ guarantee.
4 … we can't sell ▭ quality goods.
5 We expect you to replace the whole consignment free of ▭.
6 And we won't be paying for the air conditioners until we are completely ▭.

C Work with a partner and create a telephone dialogue in which you complain to a supplier about a consignment of furniture.

Partner A: **Look at File 4 on page 157.** Partner B: **Look at File 5 on page 158.**

5 Making a written complaint

Tamara Meier has asked you to write a letter of complaint to a Swedish supplier.

Write an email based on the following information.

Situation:
Sie (Ihr Name, E-Mail: vorname.nachname@outlet-becker.ger) sind im Einkauf der Firma Outlet Becker AG tätig. Ihr Unternehmen hat gerade eine Lieferung T-Shirts des schwedischen Lieferanten Svenska Fashion AB erhalten, die Anlass zu Beanstandungen gibt.

Aufgabe:
Verfassen Sie eine Beschwerde an die schwedische Firma unter Berücksichtigung folgender Punkte:
- heutiges Datum
- Ansprechpartnerin: Ms Lilly Berglund, Exportleiterin (E-Mail: lilly.berglund@s-fashion-ab.swe)
- Bezug auf Auftrag Nr. GBST12 über 1.000 T-Shirts vom Typ *Summer Style* von vor 14 Tagen
- Ware bei Ankunft nass wegen mangelhafter Verpackung
- Farbe und Qualität weichen erheblich von dem Muster ab (Fotos beigefügt)
- Bitte um Erklärung des Schadens
- Bitte um umgehenden Ersatz, da T-Shirts dringend benötigt werden
- ohne beträchtliche Ermäßigung keine Bereitschaft, die minderwertige Ware zu behalten
- Bitte um Stellungnahme
- Fortsetzung der Geschäftsbeziehung von der Regelung der Beschwerde abhängig
- höfliche Schlussformel

PART B: Replying to customer complaints

Situation: Your apprenticeship at Outlet Becker includes some time in the customer service department.
→ **You learn how to deal with customer complaints.**

1 Analysing a complaint

A customer leaves a message on the English-language page of the company's website with a complaint.

Outlet Becker Customer Services

What is your email about?

Problem with a product	Return	Refund	Change order	Cancel order	Delivery
✓					

Where did you buy your item?

Online		Shop	✓	Shop location:	An der Mühle 99 44626 Herne
Original packaging:		Yes		No	

Proof of purchase

Receipt	✓	Bank/card statement		Date of purchase	19 April 20..

Your details

First name	Kenneth	Surname	Clark
Postcode	44620	Town/City	Herne
Email	k.clark@linkall.ger	Phone number	0162 2082682

Your message

I bought a pair of size 42 Alltrek DL walking shoes seven months ago. I used them over the summer to go hiking and they were fine. However, now the weather is wetter and when it rains, my feet get wet. The product information sheet clearly states, 'When it rains, your feet stay dry'. As this is not the case, I request a replacement pair of shoes in the very near future or a refund of my money.

A **Lesen Sie die Reklamation und beantworten Sie die anschließenden Fragen stichwortartig auf Deutsch.**

1 Um welche Ware handelt es sich?
2 Wo wurde die Ware gekauft?
3 Wann wurde die Ware gekauft?
4 Welchen Kaufnachweis hat der Kunde?
5 Warum reklamiert der Kunde die Ware?
6 Mit welcher Regelung wäre der Kunde zufrieden?

VIDEO 5

Watch the video about dealing with complaints.

B **First, review the text on page 116, then, with a partner, discuss the complaint from the retailer's point of view with regard to the following points**

1 legal guarantee
2 commercial guarantee
3 original packaging
4 importance of where and when the goods were bought
5 importance of the description of the goods in this case
6 best next step for the retailer in your opinion

2 Replying to a complaint

Your colleague responds to the complaint with an email.

A Use words from the box to match the checklist of a response to a complaint (1–6) to their German equivalents.

RESPONSE TO A COMPLAINT CHECKLIST ✓	
1 Confirmation of receipt	a Bedauern ausdrücken
2 Express regret	b erneute Entschuldigung
3 Action taken	c höflicher Schluss
4 Suggested solution	d Lösungsvorschlag
5 Second apology	e Empfangsbestätigung
6 Polite ending	f unternommene Schritte

B Note down which sentences in the email correspond to the terms (1–6) in the checklist in 2A.

To: k.clark@linkall.ger
Subject: Alltrek DL walking shoes
Attachment(s): OB-return.pdf

Dear Mr Clark

Thank you for your email regarding your *Alltrek DL* walking shoes.

We are sorry to hear about your experience with them. We have contacted the manufacturer and discovered that this model is no longer available.

We would therefore ask you to send back the shoes with the attached free return label to be tested by our quality control department. If they do not pass our waterproofing test, we will refund the full purchase price of €139.95.

In the meantime, please accept our apologies for the inconvenience caused. We are sure that the matter will be settled to your satisfaction. We will contact you again in the very near future.

Yours sincerely

Jana Brandt (Mrs)
Customer Service Department
Outlet Becker AG

C Ergänzen Sie die unten stehenden Sätze mit Informationen aus der E-Mail.

1 Nach Erhalt der E-Mail hat Ihr Unternehmen an den Käufer zurückgeschrieben und ___.
2 Alltrek DL Wanderschuhe werden nicht ___.
3 Der Käufer möchte jetzt ___.
4 Outlet Becker wird prüfen, ob ___.
5 Wenn die Schuhe den Test nicht bestehen, wird Outlet Becker ___.
6 Outlet Becker wird den Käufer zeitnah ___.

3 Responding to a telephone complaint

A customer phones in with a complaint about goods bought using 'click and collect'.

A 26 **Hören Sie das Telefonat an und ergänzen Sie das Reklamationsformular (einschl. Beschreibung des Mangels und vereinbarter Regelung unter Sonstiges). Schreiben Sie die Antworten in Ihr Arbeitsheft.**

Reklamationsformular				
Reklamationsdaten			***Abwicklung** (bitte ankreuzen)	
*zu reklamierendes Produkt			Gewährleistungs-, Garantiefall	
*Kaufdatum				
*Kaufbeleg (bitte ankreuzen)	vorhanden		kostenlose Reparatur	
	verloren			
*Auftragsnummer			kostenloser Ersatz	
*Beschreibung des Mangels			Erstattung	
			Gutschrift	
			Sonstiges (nähere Angaben unten)	
Sonstiges				
				*Pflichtfelder

B **Schreiben Sie die E-Mail mit der vereinbarten Regelung an Mr Paige (eric.paige@ruhrnet.ger) auf Englisch. Nutzen Sie die E-Mail in Aufgabe 2 als Muster und berücksichtigen Sie folgende Punkte:**

- Betreff und Anrede
- Bezug auf Anruf
- Bedauern über den Vorfall
- Sie haben inzwischen den Hersteller kontaktiert und um Stellungnahme gebeten.
- Ersatz kostenlos zur Abholung bereitgestellt
- Bitte, den mangelhaften Artikel zeitnah zurückzubringen
- erneute Entschuldigung
- höflicher Schluss

COMMUNICATION: Dealing with angry customers

Situation: Your company has regular training courses about dealing with complaints from customers.
→ **You learn how to deal with angry customers.**

1 Keeping cool

First you get a handout on how to calm down angry customers.

DOs	DON'Ts
Be a good listener Let the customer talk, listen and accept the customer's anger.	**Interrupt** – '~~Calm down!~~' – '~~You're shouting!~~'
Show sympathy – 'I understand that you're upset.' – 'I can understand why you're dissatisfied.' – 'I'm sorry to hear that.'	**Take it personally** – '~~This isn't my fault.~~' – '~~You've come to the wrong person.~~' – '~~There's nothing I can do about it.~~'
Show you understand the problem Summarize the problem in your own words: – 'So if I've understood you correctly, when you switched on the …, it … .'	**Take as little time as possible** – '~~I don't need to know all the details.~~' – '~~There are other customers waiting.~~' – '~~We're closing in a few minutes.~~'
Ask what the customer wants Sometimes the customer wants less than you think, so it's best to ask: – 'What would you like us to do?' – 'How can we solve this problem for you?'	**Start with a negative statement** – '~~We can't give you a refund.~~' – '~~We can't give you a new one.~~' – '~~There's not much we can do about it.~~'
Look for the best solution You want the customer to come back, so say: – 'Leave this with us and we'll phone you back.' – 'It's out of guarantee but as a gesture of goodwill we can contact the manufacturer for you.' – 'We can repair it for … *(price)*.' – 'We can offer you a discount of …% on a new one.' – 'We can give you a voucher for … *(amount)* on your next purchase.'	**Offer the minimum** It's easy to lose a customer by saying: – '~~This isn't our problem. Contact the manufacturer.~~' – '~~It's out of guarantee. We can't help you.~~' – '~~It's over six months old, so you have to prove it was faulty when you bought it.~~' – '~~There will be a charge if our technician finds that you broke it yourself.~~'

Match the English words (1–10) from the handout with their German equivalents (a–j).

1 anger
2 charge
3 dissatisfied
4 faulty
5 goodwill
6 manufacturer
7 refund
8 to solve
9 to summarize
10 sympathy

a (Rück-)Erstattung
b fehlerhaft
c Gebühr
d Hersteller
e Kulanz
f lösen
g unzufrieden
h Verständnis
i Wut
j zusammenfassen

2 Learning how to de-escalate

A customer comes into a branch of a chain of cycle shops with a problem but the assistant reacts incorrectly, making everything worse.

A **Work with a partner and identify seven things the assistant should not have said to the customer. Count the negative statements.**

Customer:	Excuse me. I bought this bike here last week and there's a problem with the brakes.
Assistant:	You've come to the wrong person, sir. This is the sales section. You need to talk to the workshop and it's their lunchbreak now. Come back in an hour.
Customer:	But look, it's my lunchbreak too and I have to be back at work in half an hour. As I said, there's a problem with the brakes on this bike. I bought it here last month. I think they're faulty. Every time it rains, ...
Assistant:	Look, I don't need to know all the details and there are other customers waiting.
Customer:	Can I just leave the bike here for the workshop to look at? I have the receipt.
Assistant:	As I said, there's nothing I can do about it. Come back tomorrow before 1 o'clock or after 2 and speak to the workshop.
Customer:	This is really no good! I paid over a thousand euros for the bike, it's only one month old and now there's a problem with the brakes. I want to see someone now!
Assistant:	Calm down! You're shouting!
Customer:	I have every reason to shout! This bike has a two-year legal guarantee and it's unsafe after one month! I want my money back!
Assistant:	We can't give you a refund. Come back tomorrow and talk to the workshop before 1 or after 2.
Customer:	This is outrageous! I'm going to make a written complaint!

B **Now re-write the dialogue with your partner without any negative statements. If possible, use phrases from the handout.**

C 27 **Listen to the recording of the corrected version of the dialogue and compare it with yours. Make changes to your dialogue if necessary.**

3 Explaining how to deal with customers

The customer complains to the bicycle retail chain's head office about the behaviour of the employee.

Die Personalleitung schreibt eine E-Mail an den Verkäufer mit Hinweisen, worauf er künftig achten soll. Schreiben Sie die E-Mail auf der Grundlage des Dialogs in Aufgabe 2 unter Einbezug der Informationen aus Aufgabe 1.

4 Dealing an angry customer

You now practise dealing with angry customers.

Look at File 8 on page 159. Work with a partner and practise a dialogue between a customer and a retail assistant. Swap roles when you have finished.

DAS KANN ICH (Unit 10)

- Kunden und Kundinnen über ihre Rechte aufklären. (Foundation)
- Sich bei einem Lieferanten beschweren. (Part A)
- Mit Kundenbeschwerden auf Englisch richtig umgehen. (Part B)
- Höflich mit Beschwerden umgehen. (Communication)

SCENARIO: Output

Now go back to the beginning of the unit (page 115) and study the task again.

→ **You prepare yourself for the arrival of the angry customer who bought the pool that leaked.**

STEP 1 **Before you work on your task, think about the following:**

- What rights does the customer have in this situation?
- What responsibility do the sellers have in this situation?

STEP 2 **Make a checklist of all the factors to remember when dealing with an angry customer.**

STEP 3 **Consider how you want to present the situation in class:**

- a written dialogue
- a role-play
- anything else

STEP 4 **Write down words and phrases from this unit that will help you deal with the customers.**

11 The future of retail

SCENARIO: Input

Your shop, a traditional retailer with several outlets in small towns, is losing customers because more and more people are shopping online or going to big city malls. The management therefore asks its apprentices for suggestions as to how young people might be attracted to its shops.

→ **In this unit you are going to look at possible future developments in the retail industry.**

→ **At the end of the unit you will be asked to set out ideas to the management how the retailer might attract young customers.**

FOUNDATION: Future trends

Situation: Outlet Becker is losing younger customers, so the management sets up a task force to review how it can adapt to future trends.
→ **You examine how the world of retailing might look in the future.**

1 Making your store future-ready

The company's management team talks to retail expert Julie Fernandez about the future of retail.

A **28))) Listen and label the bar chart (1–4) with the four types of retail outlets in the box.**

internet-only retailing · omnichannel retailing · online marketplaces · physical shops

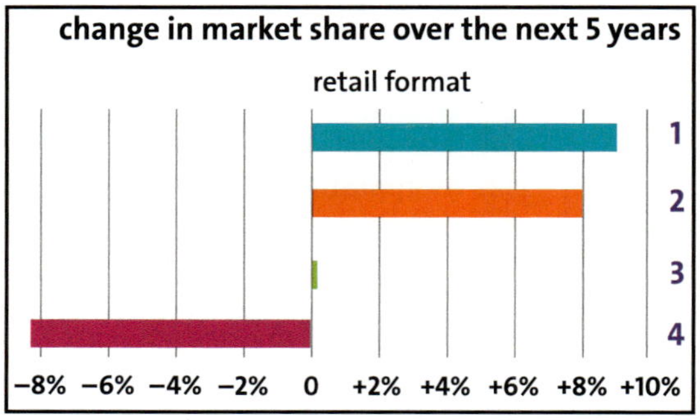

B **28))) Hören Sie sich die Diskussion wieder an und schreiben Sie kurze Definitionen folgender englischer Begriffe: *omnichannel, online marketplace* und *retail theatre*.**

2 Following the fashion

Julie Fernandez expects huge changes in the retail clothing industry and gives your company's management team a handout describing how retailers will need to adapt.

A **Before your read the texts, use the words in the box to label the three images.**

smartphone avatars · crypto fashion · smart mirror

1

2

3

B **Now skim the three texts (A–C) and match them with the images (1–3).**

A Some people love clothes shopping and others hate it. One way to make it easier is to install smart mirrors. This device scans you and creates a 3D digital image, so you can simply choose a garment, hold it up to the mirror and see yourself wearing it. You can then change the sizes, colours and styles instantly, using a virtual on-screen menu controlled by hand movements. The digital image can be edited, e.g. to make you look fatter or thinner, and customers who want more privacy can scan themselves in a fitting room.

B No matter how great your fashion store's live retail theatre is, with its beautiful scenery, music and events, some people still prefer to shop online – and return up to 60% of their purchases. All they need to do is take a selfie of themselves with a smartphone, upload it to a website and create an avatar – a perfect 3D digital image of their body shape. They can now dress the avatar with items from your online shop anytime, anywhere and for as long as it takes. This cuts down on returns, boosts sales and protects the environment.

C Parallel to the physical world there is another dimension – the metaverse, a virtual world populated by avatars. Here people interact with each other via their avatars and can be anyone or anything they want. Just like real people, avatars need clothes, so now a crypto clothing market is evolving, which enables people to design, buy and sell garments for their avatars. Wearables for avatars are bought as NFTs (non-fungible tokens). Just like an article of physical clothing, NFTs are unique, i.e. they cannot be copied, and the prices for virtual clothes are very real, e.g. $140 for a virtual kimono. Major fashion brands now sell NFT wearables.

C **Study the texts above carefully and match the sentence halves.**

1. A smart mirror enables customers to
2. The customer operates an on-screen
3. A lot of clothes bought online are returned,
4. Customers are not under time pressure
5. The metaverse is a virtual world, inhabited by
6. Avatars wear virtual garments, which are

a. which is bad for the environment.
b. avatars controlled by people in the real world.
c. see an image of themselves in different clothes.
d. designed, bought and sold like real clothes.
e. menu to choose matching styles and colours.
f. when they try out clothes on an avatar.

D **Pair each word in A with a word in B to form collocations that are used in the texts.**

A	B
smart • digital • fitting • retail • body • online • crypto • fashion	brands • clothing • image • mirrors • rooms • shape • shop • theatre

E **Use collocations from 2D to complete the following text. Make any necessary changes.**

The boutique where I work recently installed a ___[1] to help customers see themselves in different outfits. We scanned them in the ___[2] to guarantee privacy and also helped them correct their ___[3], e.g. to make it fatter or thinner, and they loved it! We then told them that they could also make a perfect 3D copy of their ___[4] by creating an avatar with their smartphone and then buy clothes either in the boutique or in our ___[5]. We sell a mixture of our own lines and clothes made by major ___[6] and now the manager wants to sell ___[7] for people to put on their avatars in the metaverse.

3 Looking at the future of your retail organization

Now think about your own retail organization.

Work with a partner or in small groups and discuss how your retail organization is preparing for the future, or what, in your opinion, it should be doing.

PART A: Methods of payment

Situation: The retail organization you work for is reviewing its payment procedures, so it can be future-ready.
→ **You compare the different methods of payment used by your customers and identify future trends.**

1 Comparing methods of payment

First, you collect data on customers' payment habits and preferences in the retail trade.

A **With a partner, study graph 1 and do the following:**

- Identify the most popular means of payment.
- Describe the trend for each of the four means of payment.
- Find the trend that is changing fastest.

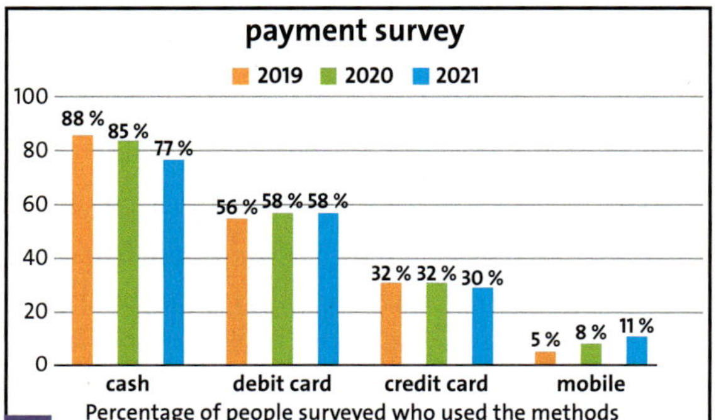

1 Percentage of people surveyed who used the methods of payment shown in retail, etc. over the last 12 months

From: Statista.com

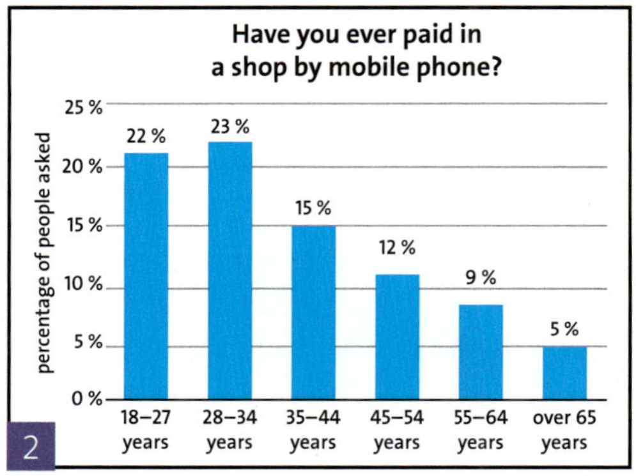

2

B **Now study graph 2 and do the following:**

- Identify the two age groups that use mobile payment a) the most b) the least.
- Discuss possible reasons for this with your partner, including the prerequisites for mobile phone payment.

2 Moving towards seamless shopping

Retail expert Kate Livingstone is interviewed by a radio reporter at a trade fair and describes how Generation Z and Millennials will shop in the future.

A **Look at the diagram below and explain what is meant by 'Generation Z' and 'Millennials'.**

B **State which generation you belong to.**

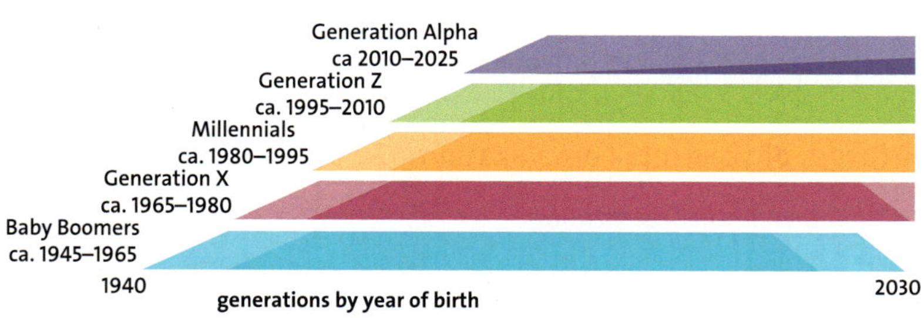

C 29 **Listen to the interview and complete the sentences with the information you hear.**

1 In future, consumers will shop for anything and everything several times a ___.
2 Delivery will be same-day or even within one or two ___.
3 Millennials and Generation Z want ___.
4 When young people go out, they always take their ___.
5 Open banking means that consumers give third parties permission to ___.
6 Young people already share their data with ___.
7 A consumer's financial data belongs to ___.
8 Open banking makes it possible for retailers to send consumers instant ___.
9 Payment by QR code takes less than ten ___.
10 Crypto is a form of ___.
11 Cash has already disappeared in ___.
12 In Germany, payment by QR code is already possible at ___.

Making predictions

Use the **will-future** to make predictions about the future:
- In future, consumers **will snack** on retail.
- They'**ll shop** for anything and everything online.
- They **won't go** on shopping trips to their favourite shops.

D **Combine words from columns A, B and C to make Kate Livingstone's predictions. Invent two more sentences of your own.**

A	B	C
People Delivery Payment Cash	will won't	be by drone or robot. take longer than a few hours. be by face ID or QR code. be used any more. buy goods at any time of the day or night. take longer than a few seconds. disappear. go on big weekly shopping trips.

› *Grammar: Future with* will *and* going to, *page 166*

3 Discussing the future of cash

You consider whether cash will still exist in ten years' time.

A **Discuss with a partner whether all payments should be cashless. Examine this from the point of view of a) the customer and b) the retailer.**

B **In class, discuss whether we will still be paying with cash in ten years' time.**

PART B: Smart stores

Situation: The retail organization you work for is planning to launch a range of digitally operated smart stores for maximum customer convenience.
→ **You examine different types of smart stores.**

1 Frictionless shopping

You find an article about smart stores in the online magazine *Retail Today*.

A Read the article and then label the diagram with information about the vending machine store (1–14).

Grab and go is here to stay

The problem with shopping is that (unless you're a shoplifter) you can't just walk into a shop at any time of the day or night, pick up what you want and walk out. You have to come during opening hours, look for a place to park, queue up at the cash desk and wait while people look for the right money at the till. All this is highly inconvenient but there is a solution: frictionless shopping in smart stores. There are basically two types of smart store: walk-in and vending machine stores.

A **walk-in store** is basically a shop with no checkouts or cashiers but with staff to help customers and fill up the shelves. Customers first identify themselves at the entrance, e.g. by smartphone with a QR code and are then free to walk around. Cameras and sensors are placed throughout the shop to track the customers' movements. When a customer picks up an article, this is registered by weight-sensitive shelves with cameras and depth-sensors. They also register if an article is put back. After shopping, customers simply walk out and are billed later for everything they have taken.

There are different types of **vending machine stores** but they are normally completely unstaffed. The products are stored in a warehouse operated by robots and include, for example, fresh goods (fruit and vegetables), frozen goods and refrigerated goods and many others. Customers order goods in advance, e.g. from home by app, and then pick them up in the store whenever they want. When they arrive, they use the scanner at the entrance to verify their identity, e.g. by credit or debit card, QR code, fingerprint or palm print. If they haven't ordered in advance, they can use the in-store terminal to select what they want. The warehouse robots then place the goods in a collection compartment, which the customer opens by touchscreen or remotely by app.

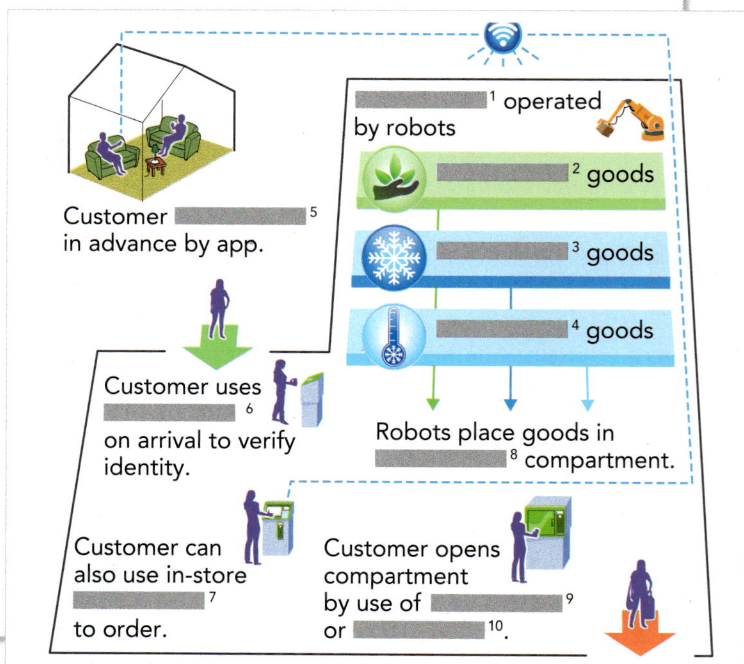

B **List the similarities and differences between walk-in and vending machine stores.**

C **With a partner discuss what sort of products are most and least suitable for smart stores.**

2 Creating a digital village

Your company hears about a new smart retailing project in Germany, so you attend an international webinar on it and take notes.

A 30 **Listen to the guest speaker's presentation and write your notes under the following headings:**

Location · Ownership · Suppliers · Opening hours · Sales staff · Product range · Entry · Extras

B 30 **Listen again and fill in the gaps with the words you hear.**

1 … the store is ___ by the community and not by a big retail chain.
2 … our store isn't ___.
3 The shelves are ___ up regularly by our suppliers.
4 … the store is ___ every day.
5 … just about everything you need is ___ there.
6 The shop is ___ by indoor and outdoor cameras.
7 … the data is ___ for a number of things.
8 Footfall data is ___ to help us get an overview of customer numbers.
9 The goods are ___ by the customers themselves.
10 … parcels can be ___ at our store.

The passive

A sentence in the passive focuses on the action (*verb*) and not on the person or thing doing it (*agent*), often because this is unimportant or obvious.
Active sentence: Cleaners clean / cleaned / will clean the store every day.
Passive sentence: The store **is cleaned / was cleaned / will be cleaned** every day.

Use 'by' if you wish to name the agent:
The goods **are scanned by** the customers (*agent* = the customers).

C **Study the language box and then make the following sentences passive.**

1 Local people own the shop.
2 The shop doesn't deliver goods.
3 Big retail chains supply some goods.
4 The shop sells over a thousand articles.
5 The villagers opened the shop a few years ago.
6 The local TV station showed the shop on the news.
7 Many people will use it in the years to come.
8 More people will join the co-operative.

› *Grammar: Passive forms, page 167*

3 Mediating information

Ihr/e Vorgesetzte/r braucht eine Tischvorlage über Smart Shops für die nächste Vorstandssitzung, also bittet er/sie Sie, die wichtigsten Inhalte des Webinars stichpunktartig auf Deutsch zusammenzufassen.

Erstellen Sie die Tischvorlage mit Hilfe Ihrer Notizen zu Aufgabe 2A.

COMMUNICATION: Business meetings

Situation: The retail organization you work for plans to open smart stores in different locations.
→ **You attend a three-day conference in Dublin, Ireland, to discuss the details.**

1 Receiving an invitation

Everyone going to the conference first receives an email with details of the arrangements.

A Match the highlighted words with the definitions (1–12) below.

From: sarah.schmidt@outlet-becker.ger
Subject: Smart store project
Attachment(s): conference programme.pdf
smart store kick-off meeting agenda.pdf

Dear attendees

I hope you are all well.
The programme for our three-day conference on smart stores from 15–17 November 20.. is attached, together with the agenda for our kick-off meeting on the first day.
The venue is the Doyle Hotel in Dublin (www.doylehoteldublin.irl).
If you are flying in from abroad, please book economy class air fares to and from Dublin Airport and transfer to the city centre by public transport. Taxi fares will be refunded if shared with one or two other attendees.
Single en-suite rooms with half board have been booked for all attendees. Please let us know in advance if you have and special dietary requirements.
As always, the minutes of all meetings will be emailed to you at the end of the conference.

Best regards
Jessica König

Human Resources Department

1 a record of everything decided at a meeting
2 all the activities planned for the conference
3 breakfast and an evening meal
4 first
5 food, e.g. vegetarian, gluten-free
6 location
7 personnel
8 the cheapest seats on a plane
9 the money paid to travel by plane, bus, taxi, etc.
10 the people who go to a meeting
11 the points to be discussed at a meeting
12 with its own bathroom

B Verwenden Sie folgende Überschriften, um eine E-Mail auf Deutsch mit den wichtigsten Informationen an weitere Kollegen und Kolleginnen zu verfassen, die ebenfalls eingeladen sind.

1 Tagungsthema
2 Tagungsort
3 Tagungsbeginn u. -ende
4 erstattungsfähige Reisekosten
5 Unterbringung und Mahlzeiten
6 Sitzungsprotokolle

C **A colleague writes an email to a guest speaker with details of the arrangements for the conference and asks you to check it for mistakes. Read and correct the following text.**

Dear Dr O'Toole

Thank you for agreeing to lead a workshop.
Please check out at the Doyle Hotel when you arrive in Dublin. We have reserved a single room for you and your partner and, as lunch is provided at the conference centre, your room includes full board.
Please let us know after the conference if you have any dietary requirements.
I have attached the minutes of the first meeting with a list of all the points to be discussed for your information. The agenda will be sent to all attendees after the meeting. Taxi fares will be refunded if the taxi is not shared with other attendees. Please remember to collect your name tag and information pack before the kick-off meeting on the last day of the conference.
We look forward to seeing you in Dublin.

Best regards

Kevin Hase

2 Attending a meeting

The kick-off meeting takes place as planned, but some changes have been made to the agenda.

31 **Listen to the meeting and write down the new items on the agenda in the correct order. Which point is not discussed?**

Agenda

Item 1: Presentation (Liam O'Reilly, Dublin, Ireland)
Item 2: Unstaffed walk-in stores
Item 3: Digital vending machines
Item 4: Security and shoplifting
Item 5: AOB (any other business)

VIDEO 6

Watch the video about business meetings.

3 Taking part in a meeting

Now you take part in a meeting to discuss opening a smart store in a rural community.

Work in groups of four. Conduct a meeting and agree a date for the next one.
Partner A: **Look at File 10 on page 161.**
Partner B: **Look at File 14 on page 163.**
Partner C: **Look at File 12 on page 162.**
Partner D: **Look at File 13 on page 162.**

› *Thematic vocabulary: Taking part in meetings, page 197*

DAS KANN ICH (Unit 11)

- Überlegungen zur Zukunft des Einkaufens anstellen. (Communication)
- Über künftige Zahlungsarten sprechen. (Part A)
- Das Konzept von Smart Stores erklären. (Part B)
- An Geschäftsreisen und -treffen teilnehmen. (Communication)

SCENARIO: Output

Now go back to the beginning of the unit (page 127) and study the task again.

→ Set out ideas to management how the retailer might retain younger customers.

STEP 1 **Before you work on your task, think about the following:**

1 Your target audience
- What sort of information does the management want?

2 The presentation of the information
- How do you want to set out your ideas?
  - an info-sheet
  - a text
  - a presentation

STEP 2 **Start by going through the exercises and writing down:**

- young people's shopping habits and expectations
- current and future methods of payment
- future trends and products
- your own ideas

STEP 3 **Think of the vocabulary and phrases you will need.**

- Find exercises in this unit which offer useful vocabulary for your task.
- List vocabulary according to the various topics above.

12 Applying for a job

You have decided that you want to work abroad to gain more experience.

→ In this unit you are going to look at job adverts in English, learn how to write a CV and a covering letter, and prepare yourself for job interviews.

→ At the end of the unit you will prepare yourself for a job interview abroad.

FOUNDATION: Working abroad

Situation: You are considering working in an English-speaking country after completing your apprenticeship so you look at job advertisements.
→ **You create a personal profile with details of your skills and abilities and what you expect from an employer.**

1 Understanding job adverts

First, you surf the internet and find some examples in English posted by a recruitment agency.

A Study the headings in the job descriptions and find the English equivalents of the German terms below.

1 Stellenangebot	5 Schichtarbeit	9 Einstiegs(gehalt)
2 Standort	6 Gehalt	10 Praktikum
3 Arbeitgeber	7 wettbewerbsfähig	11 Zusatzleistungen
4 Branche	8 Mindestlohn	12 Mitarbeiterrabatt

Vacancy no. 1								
Job description	Retail sales adviser		**Location**	London, UK	**Reference**	RSA-LO		
Minimum qualifications	Secondary school leaving certificate or higher							
Employer	EverTalkNow		**Contact**	Ms Trish Brewer, Human Resources (trish.brewer@etn.bxt), EverTalkNow, 400 Oakway, London SW30 4JJ, England				
Sector	food and household		clothing		footwear			
	furniture and homeware		DIY		telecommunications	✓		
Working hours	full-time	✓	part-time		shift work	✓	Sundays	
Salary	minimum wage		entry level		competitive	✓	unpaid	
Contract	permanent	✓	temporary		apprenticeship		work placement	
Benefits	uniform / work clothes	✓	canteen	✓	employee discount	✓		

We:
- provide in-service training.
- organize exciting team-building activities.
- have a generous bonus scheme.
- offer good promotion prospects.
- give you 28 days' paid holiday per year.
- have a company pension scheme.

You:
- are good at explaining how things work.
- are a polite, friendly and hard-working team player.
- have good spoken and written language skills.
- are passionate about giving good service.
- are flexible and prepared to do overtime.
- can work well without supervision.

EverTalkNow is an Equal Opportunities Employer.

➔ Equal opportunities employer
Equal opportunities (*Chancengleichheit*) means that people of any age, sex, gender, race, religion, sexual orientation, with or without disabilities have the same chance of getting the job advertised.

B **Work with a partner and list what the employer and candidate have to offer (1–10) under the right headings. The first one has been done for you.**

Employer: We offer ...	Candidate: You are ...
28 days' paid holiday per year	

1 28 days' paid holiday per year
2 a good communicator
3 a generous bonus scheme
4 a good team player
5 a pension scheme
6 able to work without supervision
7 hard-working and flexible
8 in-service training
9 team-building activities
10 passionate about good customer service

good/well

Adjective
She's a **good** worker.
She's **good** at explaining things.

Adverb
She works **well.**
She explains things **well.**

2 Describing your skills and abilities

Before creating your personal profile, you review what you can offer an employer.

With a partner, use the table below to list your skills and abilities. Add your own ideas.

I'm good at ... I'm not (so) good at ...	arranging products attractively being friendly to customers dealing with children dealing with younger/older customers demonstrating products encouraging customers to buy things English and other languages explaining things hair styling and cosmetics handling breakable objects handling difficult customers	helping foreign customers listening patiently making phone calls matching clothes and colours mental arithmetic remembering faces remembering where things are understanding technology up-selling and cross-selling using computers working under pressure

3 Writing your personal profile

Before applying for jobs, you create your own personal profile.

Draw up a list of your skills and abilities and what you expect from an employer.

PART A: CV and covering letter

Situation: You see an advertisement for a job in an English-speaking country.
→ **You research English CVs and covering letters and write a job application.**

1 Preparing to write your CV

First, you go to a recruitment agency website to get some tips on how to write a CV. You download the information sheet below.

With a partner, read the tips (1–9) and match them with the headings (a–i).

a Work experience
b References
c Personal statement
d Personal details
e Key skills
f Hobbies and interests
g Further skills
h Education and training
i Contact details

Tips for writing your CV

A CV (curriculum vitae; American English: résumé) is a short summary of your abilities, education, training and work experience in tabular form. There is no set format for a CV but it should be no longer than two pages, use headings to make it easy to follow and be tailor-made to the job advertised. It should not be a universal CV to be used for any job.

1 Start your CV with your name, address, telephone number(s) and email address in the header. Don't label your CV 'CV' or 'Curriculum vitae' because it's clear to the reader what the document is, so an extra heading is a waste of space.
2 This section is the first thing a recruiter reads. It explains who you are, what you can offer a company and what you're looking for. Make sure this paragraph catches the reader's attention and shows why you're suitable.
3 This is a list of the skills you have that make you a suitable candidate for the job advertised.
4 List all relevant work experience here, starting in the present and working backwards. Include job titles, names and locations of organizations and your responsibilities and achievements in each case.
5 Starting in the present and working backwards, list the colleges and/or secondary schools you attended and the qualifications and grades you achieved.

6 This is where you can list general, work-related skills of interest to an employer, such as foreign languages, computer skills, driving licence, first aid etc.
7 Not all CVs include this section, but what you do in your spare time shows something about your personality and might make you a more interesting candidate. Include information that is relevant to the job, or makes you stand out, e.g. community work (helpful, caring person); swimming instructor (can take responsibility); song-writing (artistic, creative). Leave out trivial activities, such as eating out with friends (everyone does this) and dangerous pastimes, e.g. BASE jumping (irresponsible).
8 This is where you can state your date of birth and nationality.
9 The safest option in this section is to find professionals who are willing to describe your skills, character and work performance favourably and then state that references are available on request. This saves space in your CV that can be used elsewhere for other more important information.

2 Analysing a CV

You find some sample CVs on the recruitment agency's website, including the one on page 141, which was sent to a British company.

Work with a partner and make a list of the differences between this CV and a German CV.

LAURA GRAF
Klingerstraße 275, 60313 Frankfurt am Main, Germany
+49 (69) 24445830
+49 162 2082784
laura.graf@bignetz.ger

PERSONAL STATEMENT	Highly motivated and hard-working apprentice retail sales adviser in a busy city centre consumer electronics store, currently seeking a position in an English-speaking sales environment. A friendly, well-mannered and engaging individual with a passion for customer service and an excellent track record for up-selling and cross-selling.
KEY SKILLS	Excellent communication skills Polite and professional manner Natural ability to understand electronic products Able to explain and demonstrate digital devices
WORK EXPERIENCE	
August 20... to date	Apprentice retail sales assistant at Outlet-Becker Elektronik, Frankfurt.
Responsibilities:	Advising customers; demonstrating products; handling deliveries and payments
Achievements:	Best sales figures of all apprentice sales staff in January sales; offered permanent post by employer
March–April 20 ...	Temporary sales assistant at Mercury Consumer electronics store, Frankfurt, Germany. Gained experience of dealing with a wide range of customers.
EDUCATION	
August 20.. to date	Two-year dual system apprenticeship with day release at Frankfurt Vocational Training College
Main subjects:	Business Studies, Business Processes, Accounting, IT, Commercial English
Achievements:	Good grades in all subjects
June 20.. – August 20..	Secondary education at Bernd Meier Schule, Frankfurt Obtained German higher education entrance qualifications (*Abitur*) Main subjects: Information Technology, English
FURTHER SKILLS	Excellent command of standard office software and open source operating systems Driving licence First-aid certificate Languages: German (native speaker), English (fluent), Spanish (conversational)
HOBBIES AND INTERESTS	Travel Tae kwon do (junior tae kwon do instructor)
PERSONAL DETAILS	Date of birth: 04 July 20.. Nationality: German
REFERENCES	Available on request

3 Writing a covering letter

The recruitment agency shows a sample covering letter with advice about the most important things to remember, so you make a checklist for yourself.

Match the checklist (a–h) with the numbered parts of the sample covering letter (1–8).

a Check that the complimentary close matches the salutation.
b Describe the skills you have that match the job advertised.
c Don't forget the polite ending.
d Explain why you are the right person for the job and say when you are available for an interview.
e Include the source of the job advertisement.
f Make sure the salutation is to a named person.
g Remember to include a subject line.
h Say what you can give to the company and describe your career goal.

Klingerstraße 275
60313 Frankfurt am Main
Germany

15 May 20..

1 Dear Ms Brewer

2 Application for post as retail sales adviser, reference RSA-LO

3 I saw your advertisement for a retail sales adviser on the Retail Vacancies Forum website and would like to apply for the post.

4 Having almost completed a two-year traineeship in retailing at Outlet-Becker in Frankfurt am Main, Germany, I already have some retail experience and also achieved the best sales figures of all apprentice sales staff in the January sales. I have a passion for customer service and an excellent track record of up-selling and cross-selling.

5 For this reason, I would be delighted to work at your company and help boost sales. I am sure that the position would also improve my chances of a career in retailing.

6 Since I have the skills and qualifications advertised, I feel I would be ideally suited for this post. I can fly to the UK for interview at a week's notice and am available for a telephone or video interview at any time.

7 I look forward to hearing from you at your earliest convenience.

8 Yours sincerely

Laura Graf

4 Applying for a job

You decide to gain work experience in an English-speaking country and apply for jobs abroad.

Write your CV and covering letter to apply for one or more of the following positions:

- one of the job advertisements in File 9 on pages 160 and 161.
- a job in an English-speaking company currently posted on the internet

PART B: Travel arrangements

Situation: You and a colleague are shortlisted for two jobs, one in England and one in Scotland.
→ You plan trip to the UK for the interviews.

1 Comparing means of transport

First you draw up your itinerary and research different transport options.

A **Study the table below and find the lowest basic price for the round trip from Cologne.**

B **Now work out how long the round trip takes by each means of transport.**

Itinerary				
days and date	**journey**	**plane**	**train**	**coach**
04/07 Monday	Cologne → London	€73 1 h 35m 536 km	€162 5 h 15m 589 km	€93 9 h 40m 589 km
05/07 Tuesday	job interview in London			
06/07 Wednesday	London → Edinburgh	€27 1 h 30m 534 km	€54 4 h 45m 666 km	€14 10 h 40m 666 km
07/07 Thursday	job interview in Edinburgh			
08/07 Friday	Edinburgh → Cologne	€119 1 h 45m 898 km	€216 9 h 45m 1,255 km	€66 20 h 1,255 km

2 Calculating carbon emissions

You are concerned about your carbon emissions for the trip and find the following graph on the internet.

A **Use the table above and the graph to calculate the carbon emissions per person for the three transport options.**

Average carbon emissions per passenger per km travelled

Source: German Federal Environment Agency

B **Now put the following factors in your personal order of priority for the entire trip.**
– carbon emissions – comfort – price – travel time

C **Discuss your personal choice with the rest of the class and find out which means of transport most people would choose, and why.**

3 Booking an overnight stay in London

You and your colleague find a website offering a range of accommodation at hotels and youth hostels.

A **Use the words in the box to label the accommodation types (1–4).**

bunk beds · double bed · single bed · twin beds

1

2

3

4
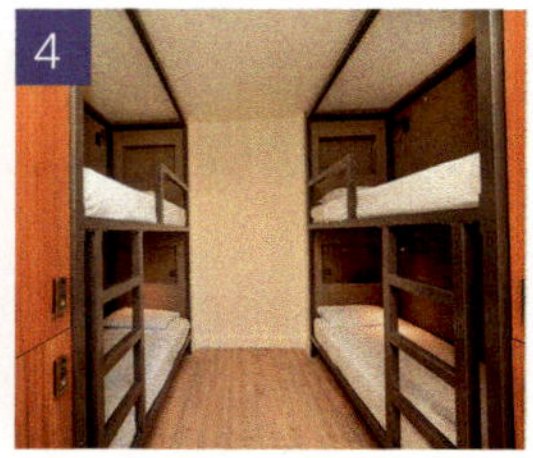

B **Match the highlighted words on the website with their German equivalents (1–12).**

1 abschließbarer Schrank
2 Anzahlung
3 Bettwäsche
4 Erstattung
5 Gebühren
6 Handtücher
7 Heizung
8 Jugendherberge
9 Mehrbettzimmer
10 Selbstversorgerküche
11 Wasserkocher
12 mit eigenem Bad

Go!London Best Price Search Engine

Check-in:	Monday, 4 July 20..	Check-out:	Wednesday, 6 July 20..	Guests:	2 adults

BEST HOTEL DEAL — **CAMDEN HOTEL** (see map for location)

Room type	Sleeps	Price per room per night	Good to know
Basic twin room 2 single beds ✓ shared bathroom ✓ towels ✓ heating ✓ free Wi-Fi ✓ flat-screen TV ✓ tea/coffee maker ✓ electric kettle	2	€70	– Price includes all taxes and charges – Free cancellation until 23:59, 2 days before day of arrival – No deposit required – Pay on arrival – Check-in: 2–11 p.m. – Check-out: until 11 a.m. – Continental breakfast: €15 p.p. – Central location with excellent bus and underground train links – All rooms non-smoking – No parking available
Superior twin room 2 single beds ✓ en-suite bathroom ✓ towels ✓ hairdryer ✓ heating ✓ free Wi-Fi ✓ flat-screen TV ✓ room safe ✓ tea/coffee maker ✓ electric kettle	2	€99	

BEST YOUTH HOSTEL DEAL		**City Centre Youth Hostel** (see map for location)	
Room type	**Sleeps**	**Price per bed per night**	**Good to know**
Dormitory bunk beds in same-gender dormitory ✓ shared bathroom ✓ shared toilet ✓ heating ✓ bed linen ✓ lock on doors ✓ reading light ✓ lockable storage cupboard ✓ smoke alarms	4	€30	– Check-in: from 5 p.m. – Check-out: before 10 a.m. – Payment in advance – 10% discount for Youth Hostel Association members – 90% refund if cancelled 24 hours before noon of arrival day – 24-hour access – Continental breakfast €6.50 p.p. – Self-catering kitchen – TV room

C **Study the website and say if the following statements about the three types of accommodation listed are true or false. Correct the false statements.**

1. All three offers are for en-suite rooms.
2. All three offers are for rooms with double beds.
3. Two offers include tea- and coffee-making facilities.
4. All three offers include a full refund for early cancellation.
5. The prices quoted exclude breakfast.
6. The check-out time for all three offers is 11 a.m.
7. All three types of accommodation include self-catering.
8. A Youth Hostel Association member pays €25.50 per night for a bunk bed.

D **With a partner, choose one of the three offers in 3B. Then copy and complete the booking form below. Calculate the final price for two nights.**

Arrival date			Departure date			
Number of rooms		Number of guests		Number of guests under 18		
I/We wish to stay at (please tick (✓))	Camden Hotel		City Centre Youth Hostel			
Main guest's details						
First name			Last name			
Address	street name		house number			
	town/city		postcode			
Email address			Phone number			
Your room(s)						
Room type (and number)	basic room		superior room		dormitory bed	

E **Research accommodation in Edinburgh, find a suitable hotel or guest house for yourself and another apprentice for two nights and present your findings to your class.**

COMMUNICATION: Job interviews

Situation: Before leaving for the UK, you get ready for your job interviews.
→ You prepare for and practise face-to-face, video/online and telephone interviews.

1 Preparing for the interview

You download an interview checklist from a recruitment website and add advice from colleagues, family and friends to it.

Add the advice (a–h) to the checklist at the points indicated (1–8).

- **a** Check your hair. Go to the hairdresser's a few days earlier if necessary.
- **b** Don't wear strong perfume or aftershave, as the interviewers may not like it.
- **c** If you're going by car, find out where you can park.
- **d** Wear the clothes you would wear for a face-to-face interview. This will make you feel more professional.
- **e** Ask questions about the job to show you are well prepared.
- **f** Practise online with a friend to make sure the camera angle, volume and lighting are right.
- **g** Switch on your computer an hour before the interview to make sure any updates are complete.

<table>
<tr><th colspan="3">Interview checklist</th></tr>
<tr><th colspan="3">WELL BEFORE THE INTERVIEW</th></tr>
<tr><th>Face-to-face interview</th><th>Video/Online interview</th><th>Telephone interview</th></tr>
<tr><th colspan="3">Location</th></tr>
<tr><td>– Check how to get there.
1 ___</td><td colspan="2">– Find a place at home a table and good signal strength.
– Make sure the battery of your phone/tablet/laptop is fully charged.</td></tr>
<tr><td></td><td>2 ___</td><td></td></tr>
<tr><th colspan="3">Clothes</th></tr>
<tr><td colspan="2">– Make sure you have clean, pressed clothes in darker colours and neutral tones. Women need a good-quality top. Men need a good shirt.
3 ___</td><td></td></tr>
<tr><th colspan="3">ON THE DAY OF THE INTERVIEW</th></tr>
<tr><th colspan="3">Appearance and clothes</th></tr>
<tr><td colspan="2">– Don't wear too much jewellery.</td><td>4 ___</td></tr>
<tr><td>5 ___</td><td></td><td></td></tr>
<tr><th colspan="3">AN HOUR BEFORE THE INTERVIEW</th></tr>
<tr><td>– Enter the building 15 minutes early, ask to use the bathroom and check your appearance.
– Turn off your mobile!</td><td colspan="2">– Tell everyone you have an interview and put up a 'Do not disturb' sign.
– Arrange your notes, note pad and pens on your table or desk.
– Turn off and remove all devices that could ring, vibrate or disturb you.
– Have some water nearby in case you get a dry throat.
– Imagine exactly what you will say when the phone rings.</td></tr>
<tr><td></td><td>6 ___</td><td></td></tr>
<tr><th colspan="3">DURING THE INTERVIEW</th></tr>
<tr><td colspan="3">– Sit up straight and smile! This will make you sound and look positive and enthusiastic.
7 ___
– Thank the interviewer(s) at the end of the interview, so that you leave a good final impression.</td></tr>
</table>

2 Handling typical interview questions

Most candidates are asked some or all of the questions below.

Write answers to the questions. Practise asking and answering them with a partner.

1 Can you take us through your CV?
2 Are you a team player?
3 What are your strengths?
4 What are your weaknesses?
5 Why did you decide to become a …?
6 Why should we employ you and not someone else?
7 What are your plans for the future?
8 Do you have any questions you'd like to ask?

3 Choosing the right candidate

Jennifer Winters, the Head of Human Resources at Outlet Becker UK in London, is conducting telephone interviews with candidates who have applied for the job of sales adviser.

A 32 **Copy the table below, then listen to the interviews and complete it with the information you hear.**

	Interview 1	Interview 2	Interview 3
Name			
Present employer			
Strengths			
Weaknesses			
Why they applied for the job			
Future plans			
Own questions			

B **Discuss the interviews in small groups and say which of them were good and which were bad and give examples of what they did right or wrong.**

4 Practising a video or telephone interview

You have been short-listed for a position as sales adviser at Outlet Becker UK and will have a video interview.

Work with a partner and take turns playing the roles of interviewer and candidate using the notes below. Have a copy of your CV in English in front of you.
Partner A: Go to File 7 on page 158.
Partner B: Go to File 15 on page 163.

VIDEO 8
Watch the video about job interviews.

DAS KANN ICH (Unit 12)
– Meine Fertigkeiten für die Jobsuche auflisten. (Foundation)
– Meinen Lebenslauf samt Begleitschreiben verfassen. (Part A)
– Reisen organisieren. (Part B)
– Mich auf Vorstellungsgespräche vorbereiten. (Communication)

SCENARIO: Output

Now go back to the beginning of the unit (page 137) and study the task again.

→ **Prepare yourself for one job interview abroad.**

STEP 1 **Draw up a personal profile with details of your own abilities and skills, as well as your expectations of a job in an English-speaking country.**

STEP 2 **Find a job advertisement that you would respond to.**

- Look for advertisements on the internet.

STEP 3 **Write a covering letter to accompany your CV.**

- Use the covering letter you wrote in this unit, but adapt it for the job you are applying for now.

STEP 4 **Write a CV.**

- Use the CV you wrote in this unit, but adapt it for the job you are applying for now.

STEP 5 **Write down a list of questions for the interview.**

- In every interview there are standard questions you can ask any employer.
- Write down some questions that are particular to this company. This means finding out more about the company.

STEP 6 **In class, form interview panels with three to four members.**

- Look at the covering letters and CVs and the jobs applied for, and interview each person according to the job they applied for.
- Give feedback about which areas the candidates were strong in and which areas they could improve.

KMK

Mock Exam: Stufe II

Schriftliche Prüfung

Zeit: . . . . .90 Minuten
Hilfsmittel: . . . . .allgemeines zweisprachiges Wörterbuch
Maximale Punktzahl: . .100 Punkte

Im Rahmen der schriftlichen Prüfung werden die Aufgabenanteile für die drei Kompetenzbereiche wie folgt gewichtet:

- **Rezeption. . . . . 40 %**
- **Produktion. . . . . . . 30 %**
- **Mediation. . . . . 30 %.**

Im Folgenden werden vier Aufgaben vorgelegt, die Sie bearbeiten sollen. Die erste und die zweite Aufgabe beziehen sich auf Ihre Fähigkeit, englische Texte (gesprochene und geschriebene) zu verstehen = **Rezeption**. In der dritten Aufgabe sollen Sie ein Schriftstück erstellen = **Produktion** eines englischen Textes. Bei der vierten Aufgabe wird von Ihnen erwartet, dass Sie Texte von der deutschen oder englischen in die jeweils andere Sprache übertragen = **Mediation**.
Die Prüfung beginnt mit der Hörverständnisaufgabe. Alle weiteren Aufgaben können in beliebiger Reihenfolge bearbeitet werden.

Rezeption I: Hörverstehen — 20 Punkte

Situation: Sie sind Assistent/-in der Geschäftsleitung bei der Outlet Becker AG in Frankfurt. Ihre Chefin, Verkaufsleiterin Frau Lea Schmidt, besucht nächste Woche die zweitägige *Seamless* Handelsmesse in Singapur und übernachtet im Hotel Mandarin in der Nähe des Messezentrums. Sie entschließt sich spontan, ihren Ehemann zunehmen und bittet Sie, im Hotel anzurufen, um ihre Reservierung entsprechend zu ändern.

33 **Aufgabe: Kopieren Sie die beiliegende Telefonnotiz und füllen Sie sie auf Deutsch aus, indem Sie Einzelheiten über die Zimmertypen und Reservierungsfrist festhalten.**

Outlet Becker AG	
Telefonnotiz	
Für:	
Gespräch mit:	
Mitteilung:	

Situation: Frau Schmidt bittet Sie, für ihren Ehemann herauszufinden, welche Sehenswürdigkeiten von ihrem Hotel aus an der Marina Promenade bequem zu erreichen sind. Sie kontaktieren die Touristinformation in Singapur und erhalten eine Broschüre mit Vorschlägen für eintägige Touren im Stadtkern.

Aufgabe: Lesen Sie die unten stehende Tourbeschreibung, benennen Sie die neun Attraktionen auf der Karte und beschreiben Sie sie kurz in Stichworten auf Deutsch.

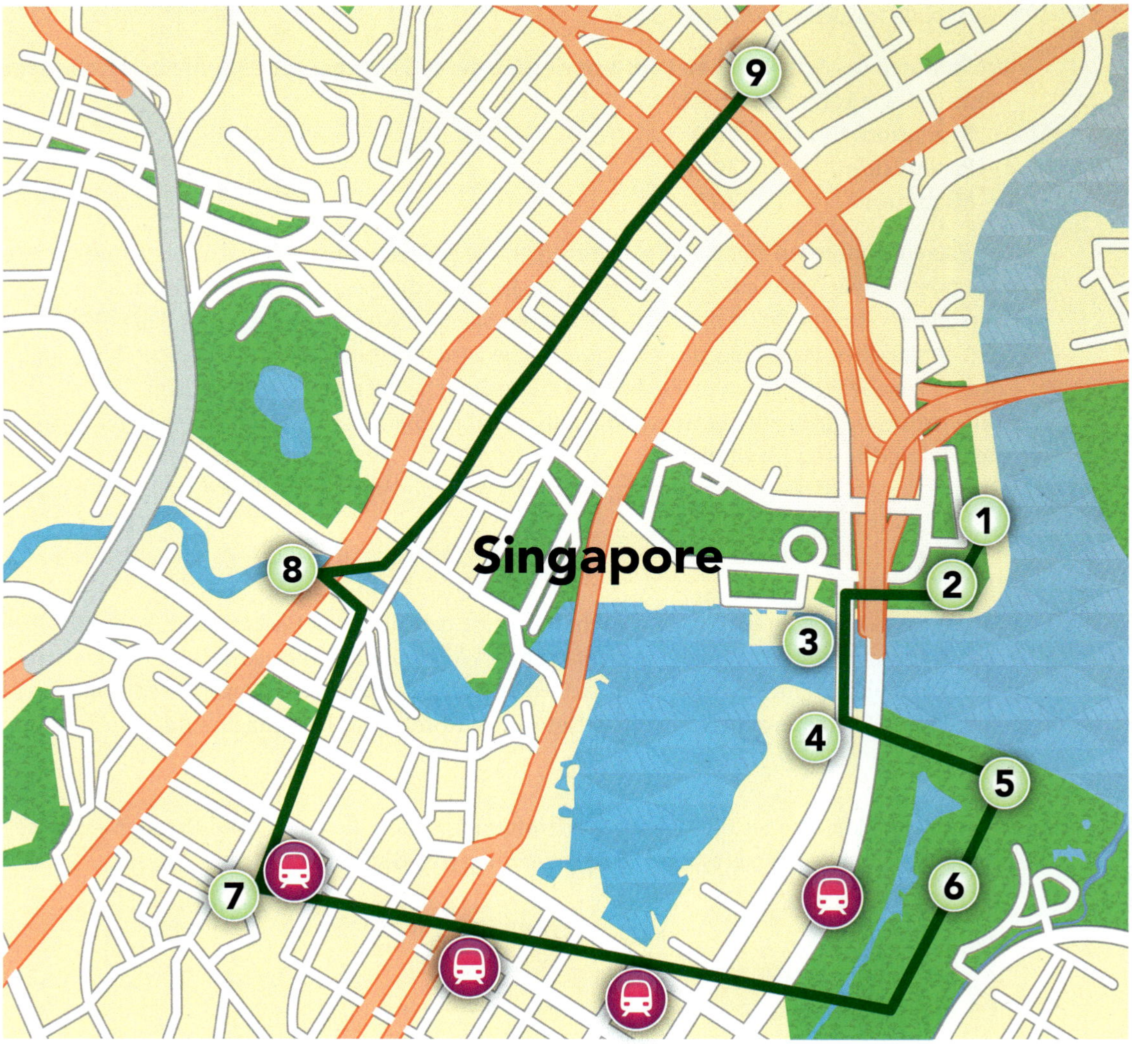

One-day Singapore tour

Singapore has so much to offer and we recommend spending three or four days here to see the sights but if you're pressed for time and prepared to do some walking, this is how we suggest you discover the city in one day.

Starting at the Marina Promenade, famous for its Formula 1 Grand Prix grandstand, walk south to the Singapore Flyer. This is Singapore's big wheel. It's 165 m tall and one rotation takes 30 minutes. It's a must for any tourist and gives you a panoramic view of the city. Next, walk over Helix Bridge, which is a uniquely designed pedestrian bridge showing the double helixes of a DNA molecule. After the bridge, you arrive at Singapore's most famous hotel in the shape of a giant ship, the Marina Bay Sands Hotel. It offers pure luxury, including the world's biggest rooftop pool. Room prices here start at US$400 a night but you still need to book well in advance. Your next stop is Cloud Forest, a forest in a dome-shaped greenhouse with a 35-metre mountain featuring the world's largest indoor waterfall. Make sure you take a jacket or sweater with you because when the outdoor temperature is up in the 30s, here it's a constant 23°C. Now take a short walk to Supertree Grove with its 12 amazing, tree-shaped structures made of concrete and steel between 25 and 50 metres in height. These huge man-made trees are, in fact, vertical gardens and are home to more than 158,000 plants. They use environmentally friendly solar energy to sustain a unique ecosystem and power a breathtaking light show every evening.

Now it's time for lunch, so why not hop on the underground and get off three stops later in Chinatown? It has street markets, museums and temples and, of course, very many affordable restaurants and eateries for every palate. Now, it's time to sit back and see the sights of the city in style by taking a boat trip from Clarke Quay. This extremely popular 40-minute river cruise comes with a commentary in English or Chinese and be sure to book in advance. By now you'll be thinking about how to spend the evening, so we recommend having dinner in Arab Street. You're sure to find a great restaurant there and later you can go for a drink in one of the many bars or browse the boutiques for some late-night shopping.

(402 words)

Produktion — 30 Punkte

Situation: Sie (Ihr Name) arbeiten im Einkauf bei der Outlet Becker Möbel AG in Frankfurt, E-Mail: vorname.nachname@outlet-becker.ger. Ihre Firma hat ein Angebot über Balkonmöbel von der Firma *The Sing-Furniture People* in Singapur erhalten und möchte jetzt mehrere Artikel bestellen.

Aufgabe: Erteilen Sie der Firma in Singapur folgenden Auftrag per E-Mail:

- Heutiges Datum
- Ansprechpartnerin: Ms Hoe Hong, Exportleiterin, E-Mail: hoe.hong@tfp.spr
- Bezug auf Angebot von (datiert vor einer Woche)
- Tisch „Furano", Artikel-Nr. FR42, zu 100,00 €, 20 Stück; Stuhl „Wally", Artikel-Nr. WY38, zu 50,00 €, 80 Stück
- Abzgl. 10 % Mengenrabatt: 600,00 €
- Gesamtbetrag: 5.400,00 €
- Lieferung: CIP Flughafen Frankfurt Incoterms 2020, innerhalb 4 Wochen nach Auftragserhalt
- Verpackung: Container
- Zahlung: 10 Tage 2 %, 30 Tage netto
- Bitte um zeitnahe Auftragsbestätigung und Versandanzeige
- Höflicher Schluss

Mediation — 30 Punkte

Situation: Frau Schmidt möchte, dass die Outlet Becker AG auf der nächsten *Seamless* Handelsmesse in Singapur mit einem Stand vertreten ist, und erfährt, dass Kunden und Geschäftspartner auch virtuell teilnehmen können, wenn man sich für ein hybrides Format entscheidet. Da diese Option in Singapur auch möglich ist, bittet sie Sie, mehr darüber herauszufinden. Sie finden einen Artikel im Internet und senden eine E-Mail an Frau Schmidt, in der Sie die im Text genannten Vor- und Nachteile der zwei Formate gegenüberstellen.

Aufgabe: Lesen Sie den Artikel auf Seite 152 und fassen Sie die Vor- und Nachteile der zwei Formate als E-Mail auf Deutsch zusammen.

Face-to-face vs virtual participation

Most companies think that trade fairs and exhibitions with face-to-face contact are the perfect way of finding new customers, staying in touch with regular customers and networking with business partners. They know that real physical interaction, like a handshake, a cup of coffee and a chat, tells you far more than an email.

But now hybrid events are here to stay, so what are they and what makes them so special?

A hybrid event is a live event with a virtual component. For example, if you have a booth at a trade fair in Leipzig and make it hybrid, you also give people all over the world real-time online access by tablet, smartphone, laptop or PC. Virtual participants can interact with you digitally and stream presentations, talks and discussions as they happen.

Physical distances are no longer a barrier, so you can be at your booth in Berlin and interact with a participant in Perth for as long as you want.

Virtual participation also cuts CO_2 emissions because there is no need to travel for hours and hours over long distances using environmentally unfriendly means of transport and then pay for expensive hotels and business dinners.

Hybrid events are recorded, so contributions can be downloaded later by anyone who missed them or wants to see something again. Recordings can be uploaded to social media channels for marketing purposes.

Valuable customer data is also generated by hybrid events because participants register online, so you can see which events they were interested in, how long they attended them and what they found unimportant.

But there are downsides to remote, non-physical participation. If you attend an event in person, you fully concentrate on what is happening around you but if you're sitting in front of a screen in the office, the phone can ring at any time, or you can be called away by a colleague. For home office participants the chances are even greater that something will happen to distract them. And there are no chance encounters at booths or coffee bars leading to a big order.

Studies have also shown that people's attention span is far shorter online than offline, so all contributions need to be more compact and entertaining to stop people from switching off.

And finally you need state-of-the art equipment, trained staff and stable internet to get your hybrid event up and running. People expect perfection and your image will suffer if they don't get it.

(408 words)

Mündliche Prüfung

Die Prüfung ist eine Gruppenprüfung, bei der Sie Gespräche persönlichen und fachlichen Inhalts in der Fremdsprache führen sollen. Es wird von Ihnen erwartet, dass Sie der vorgegebenen Situation entsprechend sprachlich agieren und reagieren. Es kommt dabei vor allem darauf an, dass Sie sich spontan äußern, dass Sie versuchen, sich verständlich zu machen, und dass Sie gut zuhören.

Die Prüfung besteht aus zwei Teilen und dauert insgesamt ca. 20 Minuten. Zur Vorbereitung haben Sie 15–20 Minuten Zeit.

Phase I: Sie werden gebeten, sich zu persönlichen oder beruflichen Themen (z. B. Vorstellung des eigenen Werdegangs, des Ausbildungsbetriebs und des Aufgabengebietes) zu äußern. Die Kandidatinnen und Kandidaten werden im Wechsel befragt.

Phase II: Im zweiten Teil sollen Sie zusammen mit einem/einer anderen Kandidaten/Kandidatin ein Rollenspiel durchführen. Dazu erhalten Sie von der Prüfungsleitung Rollenkarten, auf denen eine Situation beschrieben ist, die Sie vorspielen sollen. Sie dürfen sich nicht mit der anderen zu prüfenden Person gemeinsam vorbereiten.

Hilfsmittel: allgemeines zweisprachiges Wörterbuch

Interaktion 30 Punkte

Übernehmen Sie entweder die Rolle des Verkäufers / der Verkäuferin oder des Kunden / der Kundin und führen Sie ein Gespräch mit Ihrem Partner / Ihrer Partnerin.

Kandidat/-in A

Situation: Sie sind Verkäufer/-in in einer Filiale eines großen Möbelgeschäfts in Frankfurt. Heute kommt ein englischsprachiger Kunde / eine englischsprachige Kundin zu Ihnen und fragt nach Balkonmöbeln. Führen Sie mit ihm / ihr ein Gespräch mithilfe folgender Angaben.

- Begrüßen Sie den Kunden / die Kundin auf Deutsch.
- Reagieren Sie höflich und setzen Sie das Gespräch auf Englisch fort.
- Bitten Sie den Kunden / die Kundin, Ihnen zu folgen, und fragen Sie, ob er/sie lieber einen Tisch aus Kunststoff oder Holz hätte.
- Ihr Geschäft hat gerade sehr schöne leichte Balkonmöbel aus Holz erhalten.
- Versichern Sie dem Kunden / der Kundin, dass die Möbel winterfest sind.
- Gehen Sie mit dem Kunden / der Kundin zu den Balkonmöbeln und zeigen Sie ihm/ihr den Tisch „Furano".
- Zeigen Sie ihm/ihr den Stuhl „Wally", der perfekt zum Tisch passt.
- Fragen Sie, ob der Stuhl dem Kunden / der Kundin auch gefällt.
- Tisch: 150,00 €, Stühle einzeln: 75,00 €, vier Stück: 250,00 €
- Fragen Sie, ob er/sie sonst noch etwas möchte.
- Ab einem Warenwert von 29 € werden alle Möbel bis in die Wohnung kostenlos geliefert.
- Fragen Sie, ob der Kunde / die Kundin eine Kundenkarte hat.
- Kundenkartenbesitzer/-innen bekommen am Jahresende einen Rabatt und können auch Preise gewinnen.
- Geben Sie dem Kunden / der Kundin einen Prospekt.
- Erklären Sie dem Kunden / der Kundin den Weg zur Kasse und schließen Sie das Gespräch freundlich ab.

Kandidat/-in B

Situation: Sie sind Software-Ingenieur/-in aus Kalifornien. Sie haben gerade eine neue Wohnung in Frankfurt bezogen und möchten jetzt Möbel für den Balkon kaufen. Sie gehen in ein großes Möbelgeschäft und finden nicht, was Sie suchen, also wenden Sie sich an einen Verkäufer / eine Verkäuferin. Führen Sie mit ihm/ihr ein Gespräch mithilfe folgender Angaben.

- Sagen Sie auf Englisch, dass Sie leider kein Deutsch sprechen.
- Erklären Sie, dass Sie einen Balkontisch suchen.
- Fragen Sie, wo die Balkonmöbel sind.
- Sie möchten lieber Holz.
- Fragen Sie, ob sie winterfest (*winterproof*) sind.
- Sie mögen den Tisch und fragen nach Stühlen.
- Probieren Sie den Stuhl aus.
- Der Stuhl gefällt Ihnen. Fragen Sie nach dem Preis.
- Sie haben leider nur Platz für zwei Stühle auf dem Balkon.
- Sie kaufen zwei Stück.
- Fragen Sie, ob die Ware geliefert werden kann.
- Sie haben keine Kundenkarte und fragen nach den Vorteilen.
- Bedanken Sie sich für den Prospekt.
- Sie haben jetzt alles und fragen nach dem Weg zur Kasse.
- Sie danken dem Verkäufer / der Verkäuferin und schließen das Gespräch freundlich ab.

PF Partner Files

FILE 1: Unit 6, Communication, exercise 3, page 77

Partner A:
You are the retail assistant. You must use polite language when talking with the customer. Decide which of the three options in the dialogues is the most appropriate one (some might be too polite), and translate the parts in German.

Partner B:
Use the German information as a basis for your dialogue with the retail assistant.
Go through the dialogue twice to make sure it sounds good. When you have finished swap roles and do the role-play again.
Then do Dialogue 2 along the same lines.

Situation 1: Wardrobe

Assistant	Customer
Guten Tag. 1 *How can I help?* 2 *How may I help you?* 3 *What do you want?*	
	Sie haben eben einen Kleiderschrank gekauft und möchten ihn nach Hause liefern lassen.
1 *May I see the receipt, please?* 2 *Show me the receipt!* 3 *Would it be possible for you to be so kind as to show me the receipt?*	
	Zeigen Sie den Beleg.
1 *Could you tell me your address please, sir/madam?* 2 *Tell me your address.* 3 *What's your address, sir/madam?*	
	Ihre Adresse lautet Bahnhofstraße 20. Fragen Sie, ob er noch heute geliefert werden könnte.
1 *I'm afraid we can't deliver the wardrobe tomorrow.* 2 *No, that's impossible. We can't deliver tomorrow.* 3 *Sorry, but we can't manage that.* Wir können ihn erst übermorgen liefern.	
	Sagen Sie, dass die Verkäuferin Ihnen versichert hat, dass man morgen liefern könne.
1 *Could you tell me the assistant's name?* 2 *Do you happen to remember the name of the assistant who served you?* 3 *Which assistant was that?* Ich rufe sie/ihn gleich an.	
	Sagen Sie, dass es Frau Meyer war.

(Nachdem Sie mit Frau Meyer telefoniert haben:)
1 *Could you please forgive me for my mistake?*
2 *I must apologize for the misunderstanding.*
3 *It seems she was right.*
Der Kleiderschrank wird morgen geliefert.

Danken Sie dem Verkäufer / der Verkäuferin.

Gern geschehen.
1 *Is that it, or do you want anything else?*
2 *Is there anything else I can do for you?*
3 *Would you mind telling me if there is anything else I can do for you?*

Sagen Sie, dass alles in Ordnung ist und schließen Sie das Gespräch höflich ab.

1 *It was great serving you today. Thank you!*
2 *Thanks for shopping with us. Have a nice day.*
3 *We really look forward to seeing you again very soon!*

Situation 2: Electric drill

Partner B: **You are the assistant.**

- Greet the customer politely.
- Ask to see the receipt.
- Ask if the customer has a customer card.
- Ask to see the card.
- Thank the customer for the card and ask them when they bought the drill.
- Ask the customer to wait while you check on the computer.
- The purchase is on the computer.
- Ask the customer to fill in a form.
- Give the customer a pen and tell them to choose a new drill and take the form and the drill to the checkout.
- Finish the dialogue politely. .

Partner A: **You are the customer.**

- Explain that you'd like to exchange an electric drill for a more powerful model. You haven't used it yet. The box is unopened.
- You can't find the receipt.
- You have a customer card.
- Give the assistant the card.
- You bought the drill a week ago.
- Ask for a pen to fill in the form.
- Thank the assistant.
- Finish the dialogue politely.

FILE 2: Unit 9, Foundation, exercise 1B, page 104

Partner A
Take it in turns with your partner to dictate prices to each other. The partner listening should write the prices down.

a $1.00
b $0.01
c $2.50
d $1,535.49
e $789.16
f £0.01
g £67.72
h £15.33
i £50.33
j £2,283.39
k €2,429,927.43
l €0.01
m €49.99
n €17.77
o €70.77

FILE 3: Unit 9, Communication, exercise 3, page 113

Practise the following dialogue using a direct approach.

Partner A
Mr/Ms Alex Marinescu,
Verkaufsleiter/-in Barna Clothing SA, Rumänien

Partner B
Sie (Ihr Name), Einkaufsleiter/-in
MegaKauf Trading GmbH, Deutschland

A: Nehmen Sie das Gespräch entgegen (Begrüßung, Firma, Name).

B: Stellen Sie sich vor (Vor- und Nachname, Unternehmen, Land). Fragen Sie, ob Ihr Gesprächspartner / Ihre Gesprächspartnerin ein paar Minuten Zeit hat, um über den letzten Auftrag zusprechen.

A: Sagen Sie, dass Sie natürlich Zeit hätten, und fragen Sie, ob es ein Problem mit dem letzten Auftrag gab.

B: Sagen Sie, dass die Kleidung in Ordnung war, aber dass einige Kunden und Kundinnen wegen der Lieferzeit Ihre Bestellungen storniert haben.

A: Bedauern Sie das sehr (*I'm so sorry!*), und versprechen, dass Sie sich bemühen werden (*do your best to keep to*), die Lieferzeit von 30 Tagen einzuhalten.

B: Sagen Sie, dass auch eine Lieferzeit von 30 Tagen in der Zukunft problematisch sein könnte, und ob Herr/Frau Marinescu einen Vorschlag hätte.

A: Sagen Sie, dass Sie sich bemühen werden, in der Zukunft innerhalb von 14 Tagen zu liefern, aber Sie können dies erst ab dem nächsten Quartal realisieren.

B: Sagen Sie, dass Sie sehr dankbar (*grateful*) sind, dass er/sie eine zufriedenstellende Lösung finden konnte und bitten Sie um eine Bestätigungs-E-Mail.

A: Sagen Sie, dass Sie sich freuen, dem Kunden / der Kundin geholfen zu haben.

B: Bedanken Sie sich und wünschen Sie einen schönen Tag.

A: Beenden Sie das Gespräch höflich.

Now practise the same dialogue using an indirect approach.

Partner A
Mr/Ms Alex Marinescu,
Verkaufsleiter/-in Barna Clothing SA, Rumänien

Nehmen Sie das Gespräch entgegen (Begrüßung, Firma, Name).

Äußern Sie sich überrascht und fragen Sie, was das Problem ist.

Sagen Sie, dass es nicht einfach sein wird, auf einmal so schnell zu liefern.

Sie sagen, dass Sie alles tun werden, um in der Zukunft innerhalb 14 Tagen liefern zu können.

Sie bestätigen, dass Sie dem Kunden / der Kundin sofort eine E-Mail schicken werden.

Sie beenden das Gespräch.

Partner B
Sie (Ihr Name), Einkaufsleiter/-in
MegaKauf Trading GmbH, Deutschland

Stellen Sie sich vor (Vor- und Nachname, Unternehmen, Land). Sagen Sie, dass es ein Problem mit der Lieferzeit gibt.

Sagen Sie, dass 30 Tage zu lang sind und Sie eine Lieferzeit von 14 Tagen brauchen.

Beharren Sie darauf, dass alle künftigen Aufträge storniert werden, wenn er/sie dies nicht könne.

Sagen Sie, dass Sie dies schriftlich brauchen. Der Lieferant / Die Lieferantin soll Ihnen eine E-Mail schicken.

Sie beenden das Gespräch.

FILE 4: Unit 10, Part A, exercise 4C, page 120

Partner A

Sie sind Juho/Emilia Heikkinen, Exportleiter/-in bei der Firma Interiors OK in Finnland

- Nehmen Sie das Gespräch auf Englisch entgegen (Firma, Vor- und Nachname)
- Drücken Sie Ihr Bedauern aus und bitten Sie um Angabe der Auftragsnummer und des Bestelldatums.
- Der Kunde / Die Kundin hat 100 Küchentische vom Typ *Kensington* zu je 200,00 € bestellt; Zahlungsbedingungen: 30 Tage netto. Bitten Sie ihn/sie, das Problem näher zu beschreiben.
- Bitten Sie um Fotos des Schadens.
- Bedanken Sie sich für die Fotos und sagen Sie, dass die Ware Ihre Geschäftsräume in einwandfreiem Zustand verlassen hat, also kann der Schaden nur während des Transports passiert sein.
- Bieten Sie einen 10%igen Rabatt auf die zerkratzten Tische an.
- Verhandeln Sie mit dem Kunden / der Kundin, bis Sie sich einig sind.
- Versprechen Sie, eine E-Mail zu schicken und entschuldigen Sie sich erneut für den Vorfall. Sie werden den Spediteur kontaktieren, um herauszufinden, was schiefgelaufen ist.
- Schließen Sie das Gespräch höflich ab.

FILE 5: Unit 10, Part A, exercise 4C, page 120

Partner B

Sie (Ihr Name) sind Exportleiter/-in bei der Firma Interiors OK in Finnland
- Vorstellung (Vor- und Nachname, Unternehmen, Land). Sie rufen wegen einer Sendung Holztische an, die gestern angekommen ist. Einige Tische sind zerkratzt.
- Der Auftragsnummer ist FGFB3826 vom (*vor einem Monat*)
- Bei zwölf der Tische sind Kratzer an der Tischplatte (*tabletop*); bei fünf sind die Beine zerkratzt.
- Schicken Sie ihm/ihr sofort 17 Fotos per E-Mail.
- Sie stimmen der Meinung des/der Exportleiter/-in zu, aber wie dem auch sei, können Sie die Tische nicht zum normalen Preis verkaufen.
- 10% sind leider in diesem Falle nicht genug. Handeln Sie einen besseren Rabatt aus.
- Bitten Sie um schriftliche Bestätigung des reduzierten Preises.
- Bedanken Sie sich und schließen Sie das Gespräch höflich ab.

FILE 6: Unit 8, Communication, exercise 2, page 101

Partner B

Take it in turns to dictate the telephone numbers and email addresses below to your partner.

Telephone numbers

a 069 24445830
b 040 32519967
c 0621 39158707
d 0162 2090503
e +49 8421 6899769
f +44 020 7946 9966
g +1 499 5550288
h +353 20 922 3300

Email addresses

a jon-schulz@netlink.eur
b Osman_Demir@chatchat.bxt
c ludoslaw.garczynski@mekon.sci
d Jadwiga-Budziszewski@linkall.ger
e Ryzard_Andrzejewski@prattler.pln
f Khalil-Naaji@netlink.eur
g KCzelusniak@allnet.for
h zima_drzewiecki@chinwag.gbr

FILE 7: Unit 12, Communication, exercise 4, page 147

Partner A

Sie sind Ms Jennifer Winters, Personalleiterin der Firma Outlook-Becker UK
- Vorstellung
- Passender Zeitpunkt für Videoanruf/Telefonat?
- Bitte, etwas zum Lebenslauf zu erzählen
- Wie würde er/sie sich beschreiben?
- Wie würden seine/ihre Kollegen ihn/sie beschreiben?
- Ob er/sie gerne im Team arbeitet? Wenn ja, Beispiel(e)?
- Hobbys?
- Stärken und Schwächen?
- Grund für Entscheidung, Einzelhandelskauffrau/-mann zu werden?
- Erwartungen an die ausgeschriebene Stelle?
- Warum ausgerechnet ihn/sie einstellen?
- Fragen?

FILE 8: Unit 10, Communication, exercise 4, page 125

Partner A
Verkäufer/-in im Bekleidungsgeschäft

Grüßen Sie den Kunden / die Kundin freundlich.

Bitten Sie um den Kaufbeleg.

Bitten Sie den Kunde / die Kundin, das Problem zu beschreiben.

Zeigen Sie Verständnis für das Problem. Fragen Sie, was der Kunde / die Kundin möchte.

Finden Sie eine geeignete Lösung für beide Parteien.

Partner B
Englischsprachiger Kunde / Englischsprachige Kundin

Grüßen Sie den/die Verkäufer/-in freundlich. Sagen Sie, dass Sie eine Hose zurückbringen.

Zeigen Sie den Kaufbeleg. Sagen Sie, dass die Hose zu einem (Hosen)Anzug *([trouser] suit)* gehört, der €400 gekostet hat.

Sagen Sie, dass Sie wütend sind. Sie haben den (Hosen)Anzug auf der Hochzeit Ihres Bruders getragen, aber als Sie sich hingesetzt haben, ist eine Naht geplatzt (*a seam split*), und Sie mussten mit einem Taxi schnell nach Hause, um sich umzuziehen (*to change*). Die Taxifahrt hat €100 gekostet, und Sie haben die Trauung (*ceremony*) verpasst.

Entscheiden Sie, welche Forderungen Sie an den Verkäufer haben, etwa:
- neue Hose
- Geld zurück
- Erstattung der Taxifahrten
- eigene Ideen

Verhandeln Sie mit dem Verkäufer / der Verkäuferin, bis Sie eine geeignete Lösung finden.

FILE 9: Unit 12, Part A, exercise 4, page 142

Vacancy A							
Job description	Retail sales adviser		Location	Malta		Reference	RSA-VMA
Minimum qualifications	School-leaving certificate						
Employer	Valletta Star Fashions		Contact	joseph.silva@v-s-f.mal Mr Joseph Silva, Human Resources Director, 500 West Street, Il-Belt Valletta, Malta			

Sector	food and household		clothing	✓	footwear	✓
	furniture and homeware		DIY		telecommunications	

Working hours	full-time	✓	part-time		shift work	✓	Sundays	
Salary	minimum wage		entry level		competitive	✓	unpaid	
Contract	permanent	✓	temporary		apprenticeship		work placement	

Benefits	uniform / work clothes		canteen		employee discount	✓

We:	You:
– are a chain of up-market fashion boutiques. – have new retail outlets in Valletta and Sliema. – require temporary, English and German-speaking staff for the summer season. – are known for our great working conditions. – reward our staff well with a good salary and performance bonuses. – will help you find temporary accommodation. – promise to contact you as soon as we have your CV and cover letter.	– are friendly, flexible, highly motivated and love fashion. – are confident and speak English well. – are a good team player. – have an eye for detail. – are willing to do overtime when necessary. – will go the extra mile to please the customer. – are available for a video interview.

Valletta Star Fashions is an Equal Opportunities Employer.

Vacancy B							
Job description	Retail sales assistant		Location	Wilmslow, England		Reference	RSA-WUK
Minimum qualifications	School-leaving certificate						
Employer	Wilmslow Foods Ltd		Contact	betty.eccleshare@w-f-ltd.bxt Mrs Betty Eccleshare, Human Resources Department, Wilmslow Foods, 350 Manchester Road, Wilmslow, SL6 3WW, England			
Sector	food and household	✓	clothing		footwear		
	furniture and homeware		DIY		telecommunications		
Working hours	full-time	✓	part-time		shift work	✓	Sundays ✓
Salary	minimum wage		entry level	✓	competitive	✓	unpaid
Contract	permanent	✓	temporary		apprenticeship		work placement
Benefits	uniform / work clothes	✓	canteen	✓	employee discount	✓	

We:	You:
– are a household name for food and household products in the north of England. – have vacancies for entry level staff at several of our stores in the Manchester area. – offer a wide range of benefits and above-average pay rates to the right candidate. – will get back to you within 48 hours after receiving your application (CV + cover letter).	– are highly motivated and enthusiastic. – have good communication skills and a friendly, cheerful manner. – are punctual, reliable and hard-working. – work well under pressure and without supervision. – are a team player and get on well with colleagues.
Wilmslow Foods Ltd is an Equal Opportunities Employer.	

FILE 10: Unit 11, Communication, exercise 3, page 137

Partner A

Mareike/Martin Link

Outlet Becker's smart store project leader

Your company is planning to introduce smart stores in Ireland. The mayoress/mayor of a small village called Ballygort that no longer has a supermarket has contacted you and arranged a meeting to talk about a smart store.

- Introduce yourself (full name, position).
- Choice between unstaffed stores and vending machine stores.
- Ask the mayoress/mayor to describe Ballygort.
- Explain you need a guarantee at least 300 customers for an unstaffed store.
- Outlet Becker will supply all packaged foods and household products.
- Ask if local producers can supply fresh products.
- Answer any questions.
- Agree date of next meeting (in three months' time).

FILE 11: Unit 9, Foundation, exercise 1B, page 104

Partner B

Work with a partner and take it in turns to dictate prices (a–o) to each other and write them down.

a	€10.99	f	$75.57	k	£1.01
b	€0.01	g	$912.23	l	£0.50
c	€80.43	h	$163.36	m	£15.50
d	€18.34	i	$13.30	n	£50.15
e	€9,352,623.11	j	$30.13	o	£439.93

FILE 12: Unit 11, Communication, exercise 3, page 137

Partner C

Claire/Craig O'Sullivan

Mayoress/Mayor of (village of) Ballygort

Your village is dying because the last local supermarket recently closed and people now have to travel at least 10 km to get to a shop. You want Outlet Becker to open a smart shop in Ballygort.

- Introduce yourself (full name, position).
- Ask for information about different types of smart store.
- Describe your local community: rural, 3,000 inhabitants, nearest supermarket is 10 km away, lots of older people with limited mobility, families are moving away, one bus every three hours.
- You need a store with a full range of goods; you want it to be a natural meeting point for the community.
- Ask about suppliers.
- You will form a co-operative with at least 300 members.
- You will bring details about the new co-operative and its members to the next meeting.
- Ask other questions.

FILE 13: Unit 11, Communication, exercise 3, page 137

Partner D

Amy/Adam Murphy

Local suppliers' representative

You represent the bakers, farmers and market gardeners in the local area. You and your colleagues supply fresh food to local supermarkets, including the one in Ballygort until it closed.

- Introduce yourself (full name, position).
- Ask if a smart store can stock fresh bread and local meat, fruit and vegetables.
- Describe the fresh produce that local suppliers can provide:
  - fresh bread (bakers)
  - fresh meat (farmers)
  - seasonal fruit and vegetables (market gardens)
- Ask about payment and when to supply.
- Ask other questions.

FILE 14: Unit 11, Communication, exercise 3, page 137

Partner B

Jens/Julia Müller

Technology consultant at Smartech Müller GmbH

Your company is a high-tech start-up providing the technology for smart stores. You have been called to a meeting in Ireland to discuss what equipment is suitable for a small rural community.

- Introduce yourself (full name, position).
- Describe unstaffed stores and vending machine stores.
- Explain that unstaffed stores can stock fresh local produce.
- Explain the different modes of payment:
  - walk in, walk out and get a bill later by email (expensive technology)
  - self-scanning at the exit with card payment only (less expensive technology)
  - pay online in advance or in the store and pick up the goods from a collection compartment
- Answer any questions.

FILE 15: Unit 12, Communication, exercise 4, page 147

Partner B

Sie (eigener Name), Bewerber/-in

- Vorstellung
- Günstiger Zeitpunkt für Videoanruf/Telefonat
- Sie gehen Ihren Lebenslauf durch.
- Sie beschreiben sich aus Ihrer Sicht und aus der Ihrer Kollegen.
- Sie geben ein oder mehrere Beispiele für Ihre Teamfähigkeit an.
- Sie beschreiben Ihre Hobbys.
- Sie beschreiben Ihre Stärken und Schwächen.
- Sie begründen Ihre Berufswahl.
- Sie beschreiben Ihre Erwartungen an die Stelle.
- Sie begründen, warum man Sie einstellen sollte.
- Sie stellen eigene Fragen.

FILE 16: Unit 6, Part A, exercise 1B, page 68

Points	Points	Points	Points
Question 1 Points for yellow: a: 4 b: 3 c: 2 d: 1 e: 0	Question 2 Points for red: a: 4 b: 3 c: 2 d: 1 e: 0	Question 3 Points for green: a: 4 b: 3 c: 2 d: 1 e: 0	Question 4 Points for yellow: a: 4 b: 3 c: 2 d: 1 e: 0
Question 5 Points for yellow: a: 4 b: 3 c: 2 d: 1 e: 0	Question 6 Points for green: a: 4 b: 3 c: 2 d: 1 e: 0	Question 7 Points for red: a: 4 b: 3 c: 2 d: 1 e: 0	Question 8 Points for blue: a: 4 b: 3 c: 2 d: 1 e: 0
Question 9 Points for green: a: 4 b: 3 c: 2 d: 1 e: 0	Question 10 Points for green: a: 4 b: 3 c: 2 d: 1 e: 0	Question 11 Points for red: a: 4 b: 3 c: 2 d: 1 e: 0	Question 12 Points for blue: a: 4 b: 3 c: 2 d: 1 e: 0
Question 13 Points for yellow: a: 4 b: 3 c: 2 d: 1 e: 0	Question 14 Points for red: a: 4 b: 3 c: 2 d: 1 e: 0	Question 15 Points for blue: a: 4 b: 3 c: 2 d: 1 e: 0	Question 16 Points for blue: a: 4 b: 3 c: 2 d: 1 e: 0

FILE 17: Unit 8, Communication, exercise 2, page 101

Partner A

Take it in turns to dictate the telephone numbers and email addresses below to your partner.

Telephone numbers

- **a** 0211 87547827
- **b** 0162 2081430
- **c** 0208 69699918
- **d** 030 68831748
- **e** +49 221 846595
- **f** +44 1632 960122
- **g** +1 399 5550199
- **h** +353 20 911 6616

Email addresses

- **a** lara.mayer@linkall.ger
- **b** Olesia-Banaszewski@allnet.for
- **c** Yousef.karim@netlink.eur
- **d** Zeynep-Aydin@chatchat.bxt
- **e** tekli_golebiewski@chinwag.gbr
- **f** Walentyna.Bartosiewicz@prattler.ger
- **g** WJaroszewski@nagnag.all
- **h** woytek.zyskowski@mekon.sci

G Grammar

Simple present

1 I **work** in a shop on the high street. I **advise** customers about our range of products.
2 The store **sells** DIY products.
3 The shop **doesn't deliver** its goods on Sundays.

- Das *simple present* wird für wiederholte, oft regelmäßige Handlungen in der Gegenwart verwendet.
- Signalwörter: *regularly, sometimes, often, always, normally* usw.
- Manche Verben, die keine Handlung, sondern einen Zustand ausdrücken (*need, like, want, hate, love, know, believe*), stehen (fast) ausschließlich im *simple present*.
- In der 3. Person (*he, she, it, Peter, the firm* usw.) wird ein -s angefügt (2).
- Verneinungen werden mit *doesn't/don't* gebildet (3).

Present progressive

1 Our shop is currently **trying** to find a new supplier.
2 The managers **are negotiating** with a company from Poland right now.

- Das *present progressive* wird gebraucht, wenn man gerade ablaufende oder noch nicht abgeschlossene Handlungen beschreibt.
- Signalwörter: *at the moment, (right) now, just, currently* usw.

Questions and short answers

1 **Do** you **write** a lot of enquiries? – Yes, I **do**. / No, I **don't**.
2 **Did** you **reply** to her email? – Yes, I **did**. / No, I **didn't**.
3 **Can** you **book** the hotel online? – Yes, you **can**. / No, you **can't**.
4 **Is** it easy to use? – Yes, it **is**. / No, it **isn't**.
5 **When/Why/How did** you **find** a new supplier?

- Fragen im *simple present* werden mit *do/does* gebildet (1).
- Fragen im *simple past* werden mit *did* gebildet (2).
- In Sätzen mit Hilfsverben (*is/have/can/will/should/…*) bildet man Fragen, indem man das Hilfsverb des Aussagesatzes vor das Subjekt stellt (3, 4).
- Kurzantworten bestehen aus *yes/no* + Personalpronomen + Hilfsverb *(+ n't)* (1–4).
- Fragewörter stehen immer am Anfang des Fragesatzes (5).

Simple past

1 I **talked** to my line manager about the complaint last week.
2 I **ordered** the supplies yesterday.
3 What time **did** you start **work**?
4 My first day at work **was** a disaster.

Eine Liste der unregelmäßigen Verben befindet sich auf S. 228.

- Das *simple past* verwendet man, um zu sagen, wann etwas geschehen ist (1, 2), oder um über Vergangenes zu berichten (4).
- Signalwörter: *yesterday, last week, two days ago, in 1998, When …?* usw.
- Bei den regelmäßigen Verben wird im *simple past* in allen Personen meist *-ed* angehängt.
- Verneinungen und Fragen werden in allen Personen mit *did/didn't* gebildet.

Past progressive

1 I **was working** in another shop last week.
2 I **was talking** to a customer when a colleague **bumped** into me and I **dropped** the product.

- Mit dem *past progressive* drückt man aus, dass eine Handlung oder ein Vorgang zu einer bestimmten Zeit in der Vergangenheit gerade im Verlauf war (1).
- Es beschreibt oft eine Handlung, die gerade im Verlauf war, als eine zweite Handlung einsetzte. Die zweite Handlung steht im *simple past* (2).

Present perfect

1 We**'ve** just **updated** the organigram on our website.
2 We**'ve** recently **reviewed** our terms and conditions.
3 We **haven't found** out why the delivery was late yet.
4 **Have** you **been able** to decide which marketing strategy is best?

Eine Liste der unregelmäßigen Verben befindet sich auf S. 250.

- Mit dem *present perfect* sagt man, dass (nicht: wann!) etwas geschehen ist.
- Signalwörter (Zeitadverbien): *this week, already, just, recently, yet* usw.
- Mit for (z. B. for *two years*) and since (z. B. *since 2015*) drückt man auch aus, wie lange oder seit wann ein Zustand schon andauert.

Future with *will* and *going* to

1 I think the meeting **will take** about two hours.
2 We've run out of the new range of dresses. – OK. I**'ll (will) contact** the supplier.
3 We **won't (will not) need** the order until next week.
4 We**'re going to decorate** the shop for Christmas next week.
5 This old computer **is going to break down** soon.

- *Will* wird verwendet, um Vorhersagen zu machen oder Vermutungen über die Zukunft auszudrücken (1).
- *Will* wird für spontane Entscheidungen, Angebote und Versprechen verwendet (2).
- Im gesprochenen Englisch lautet die Verneinung *won't*, ansonsten *will* not (3).
- *Be going* to (+ Infinitiv des Verbs) wird verwendet, um über Pläne oder Absichten zu sprechen (4), oder wenn die Gewissheit (oder ein Anzeichen dafür) besteht, dass etwas geschehen wird (5).

Passive forms

1 The goods **are stored** in our new modern warehouse.
2 The order **was delivered** on Tuesday morning.
3 The shipment **has** already **been dispatched**.
4 The new materials **could be bought** from a local supplier.
5 The equipment **will be installed by** them as part of their customer service.

- Das Passiv wird oft verwendet, wenn man auf eher unpersönliche Art und Weise über Fakten, Vorgänge und Zahlen berichtet.
- Das Passiv wird mit der entsprechenden Form von be + Partizip Perfekt (3. Verbform) gebildet. Es können alle Zeiten gebildet werden.
- Passivsätze mit modalen Hilfsverben werden mit einem modalen Hilfsverb + *be* + Partizip Perfekt (3. Verbform) gebildet (4).
- „Von" und „durch" werden in Passivsätzen durch by ausgedrückt (5).

Conditional sentences

1 Type 1: **If** you **buy** goods worth more than €150, you'**ll receive** a 5% discount.
2 Type 2: If there **was** a delay, we **would inform** you immediately.
3 Type 2: I **wouldn't** do that if I **was/were** you.
4 Type 3: If we **had advertised** the product in the right places, we **would have sold** more.

- Ein *if*-Satz des Typs 1 drückt eine Bedingung aus, die der Sprecher für durchaus möglich oder wahrscheinlich hält. Der damit verbundene Hauptsatz drückt eine Vorhersage aus, die je nach Situation als Warnung, Versprechen o. ä. zu verstehen ist (1).
- Durch einen *if*-Satz des Typs 2 gibt der Sprecher seinem Gesprächspartner einen Ratschlag oder teilt ihm mit, dass er die Erfüllung der Bedingung für unmöglich, unwahrscheinlich (2) oder nicht wünschenswert (3) hält.
- Ein *if*-Satz des Typs 3 drückt eine nicht mehr erfüllbare Bedingung aus. Die Bedinging bezieht sich auf die Vergangenheit (4).
- Steht der *if*-Nebensatz an erster Stelle, wird er durch ein Komma vom Hauptsatz abgetrennt (1, 2, 4).

Relative clauses

1 Our customer service agents are the people **who/that deal with customer complaints**.
2 The supplier **(which/that) our company uses** is based in Berlin.
3 MegaKauf, **which is our biggest competitor**, offers a similar product for a lower price.

- Relativpronomen leiten Relativsätze ein.
- Es gibt den notwendigen und den nicht notwendigen Relativsatz. Notwendige Relativsätze sind für das Verständnis des Satzes unbedingt erforderlich (1, 2) und stehen ohne Komma. Nicht notwendige geben lediglich Zusatzinformationen und werden durch Kommata getrennt (3).
- In notwendigen Relativsätzen kann das Relativpronomen wegfallen, wenn es Objekt ist, d. h. wenn im Relativsatz ein Subjekt steht (2).

Verb + infinitive or *-ing* form

1 I enjoy **working** in a team.
2 I expect **to qualify** as an retail assistant in June.
3 I began **working / to work** for the store last year.
4 I'd prefer **to work** late shifts home more often.
5 I'm interested in **getting** some work experience abroad.

- Auf eine Gruppe von Verben folgt immer die *-ing*-Form (1). Zu diesen Verben gehören *dislike, enjoy, finish, give up, imagine, involve, keep, mind, miss, practise, recommend, risk, stop, suggest.*
- Auf eine zweite Gruppe von Verben folgt immer ein *to*-Infinitiv (2). Zu diesen Verben gehören *afford, agree, arrange, choose, decide, expect, hope, learn, manage, offer, plan, promise, want.*
- Auf eine dritte Gruppe von Verben kann sowohl die *-ing*-Form als auch ein *to*-Infinitiv folgen (3). Zu diesen Verben gehören *begin, continue, hate, like, love, prefer, start.*
- Nach *would hate, would like, would love* and *would prefer* (Kurzform *'d like* usw.) steht nur der *to*-Infinitiv (4).
- Nach einer Präposition kommt immer die *-ing*-Form (5).

Gerunds

1 **Assisting** customers is one of my main responsibilities.
2 Do you like **working** in this shop?
3 My work consists of **dealing** with suppliers from abroad.

- Das Gerundium (= *-ing*-Form des Verbs) kann die Rolle eines Nomens übernehmen.
- Das Gerundium kann als Subjekt (1), Objekt (2) oder nach Präpositionen (3) verwendet werden.

Comparatives and superlatives

1 The new system is **harder/easier** to use.
2 It's **more expensive than shipping** the goods by rail.
3 It's the **simplest** and **cheapest** offer, but not the best.
4 The early morning shift **most enjoyable** one for me.
5 The shop spent **less** money on advertising last year.
6 The new system isn**'t as easy** to update **as** the old one.

- Einsilbige Adjektive und zweisilbige Adjektive, die auf *-y* enden, steigert man mit *-er/-est* (1).
- Zweisilbige Adjektive, die nicht auf *-y* enden, und alle Adjektive mit mehr als zwei Silben steigert man mit *more/most* (2).
- Unregelmäßig sind: *good – better – best, bad – worse – worst, little* (wenig) *– less – least, far – farther/ further – farthest/furthest* (3, 5).
- Vergleiche bildet man mit *than* und (*not*) as ... as (2, 6).

Reported speech

1 The manager **said** that sales **had risen** since last year.
2 The intern **asked** if she **could take part** in the meeting.
3 My line manager **told** me that the trade fair is always **held** in Frankfurt.

- Man verwendet die indirekte Rede, um zu berichten, was jemand gesagt hat.
- Steht das einleitende Verb (*ask, say* usw.) in der Vergangenheit, verschieben sich die Verben im Satz entsprechend (1, 2).
- Wenn das Berichtete immer oder immer noch gültig ist, muss keine Zeitverschiebung erfolgen (3).

Zeitverschiebung bei einleitenden Verben in der Vergangenheit

direkte Rede	**indirekte Rede**
simple present	simple past
present progressive	past progressive
simple past	past perfect
present perfect	past perfect
will	*would*
can	*could*

Adverbs of frequency

1 The trainees **sometimes** attend trade fairs during their training.
2 We've **often** had to work overtime this year.
3 The manager is **frequently** away on business.
4 We deliver goods to our customers **daily**.

- Häufigkeitsadverbien der unbestimmten Zeit stehen vor dem ersten Hauptverb (1), nach dem ersten Hilfsverb (2), und nach *to be* (3). Zu ihnen gehören: *already, always, ever, frequently, mostly, never, soon* usw.
- Häufigkeitsadverbien der bestimmten Zeit stehen meistens am Satzende, z. B. *annually, daily, monthly, once, twice, weekly, yearly* (4). Dies gilt auch für *a lot, before, very much, yet.*

Modal verbs

1 I **can** work shifts in my shop.
2 I **could** work longer hours if I lived closer to the store.
3 The manufacturing costs **must** be covered by the retail price.
4 You **will be able to** order the new product line from May onwards.
5 We **won't be allowed to** install the new software on our own.
6 We **should** compare the costs of the different methods of transport.
7 Some items in the consignment were broken and **had to** be replaced.
8 You **mustn't** accept an offer before talking to your line manager.
9 You **needn't** ring the supplier. I'll do it in a minute.
10 I **would** like to gain some work experience abroad.

- Modale Hilfsverben wie *can, could, may, would* usw. drücken eine Fähigkeit, eine Erlaubnis, eine Empfehlung, ein Verbot oder einen Wunsch aus.
- Modale Hilfsverben haben in allen Personen die gleiche Form; bei der Verneinung gibt es zusammengezogene Kurzformen.
- Modale Hilfsverben stehen normalerweise in der Gegenwartsform, manche auch in der Vergangenheit. Ersatzverben (*substitutes)* werden benutzt, um alle übrigen Zeiten zu bilden.

Hilfsverb	Ersatzverb
can	*be able to*
could	
may	*be allowed to*
might	
must	*have to*
need not	*don't have to*
shall	
should/ought to	
must not	*not be allowed to*

T Transcripts

Track 2: Unit 1, Part B, exercise 1B, page 12

Oskar Hi, I'm Oskar. I'm 17 and I'm doing an apprenticeship at a big discounter. The first thing I like about my job is that I'm never bored. It's such a big shop with so many different things to do all day that I never check the time. The next good thing is the flexible working hours. We have shift work, so in summer after the early shift I can still go out after work and enjoy the sunshine. And finally, it's a secure job. I always have money in my account.

Sevda Hi, I'm Sevda. I'm 19 and I'm really enjoying my apprenticeship because I work in a boutique and I love clothes and fashion. Fashion is so interesting because it changes all the time, there's always something new and I like that. Another reason for liking my job is that it's creative. I help the window dresser and I love that. Window dressing is so important because it brings in the customers if it's good. And finally, I'm interested in people. I ask myself, 'What looks good on this person?' I always try to find the best clothes for every customer.

Niko I'm Niko. I'm 18 and I work in a big sports shop. My first reason for liking my job is simple – sport is my passion. I love all sorts of sport. I play in a football team, go to the gym three evenings a week, go in-line skating and run marathons. The next reason for liking my job is the wide variety of tasks. By wide variety I mean serving customers, unpacking new deliveries of goods, sorting and labelling them, contacting suppliers and so on. And I also like working at the cash desk. My third reason is the good promotion prospects here. I'm 18 but at this company there are shop managers aged 22 earning good money. That's what I want to do.

Emma Hi. My name's Emma and I'm 24, which makes me a bit older than everyone else. I'm doing an apprenticeship in a supermarket and I'm very pleased because I'm able to train part-time. I'm a young mother, so I have to divide my time between my daughter and my apprenticeship, and this employer lets me do this. Another thing I really like about my job is working with people. I couldn't sit at a desk in an office all day. I need people around me and the supermarket gives me this. And thirdly, my boss gives me responsibility. That means that one of my jobs is to walk around the shop, notice what needs doing and do it. Perhaps a shelf is empty and needs filling up, or a display stand looks wrong. It's my job to fix it.

Track 3: Unit 1, Communication, exercise 1A, page 14

Almira Hi. I'm Almira Ibrahim. I'm 22 and I was born in Syria. I live in Stuttgart. I'm doing an apprenticeship at a big discounter. I'm in my third year.

Paul Hello. My name's Paul Fischer. I'm 17 years old and I'm from Dortmund. I'm doing my apprenticeship at a big furniture shop. I'm in my first year.

Lena Hi everyone. I'm Lena Hoffmann. I'm 18 and I'm originally from Dresden, but I now live in Berlin. I'm doing my apprenticeship at a fast-fashion store and I'm in my second year.

Kingsley Hi. I'm Kingsley Ekoku. I'm 20 years old. My parents come from Nigeria, but I was born in Cologne and I'm an apprentice at a big DIY store just outside Cologne. I'm in my final year now.

Track 4: Unit 2, Foundation, exercise 1A, page 18

Nathalie I have my own bike shop in the town centre with a mechanic and an apprentice. As I'm my own boss, I run the business exactly as I please. I only stock good products, open and close when I want, and I keep all the profits. I bear all the risk and could lose everything if something goes wrong, but I'm willing to pay that price for my freedom.

Orhan My brother and I have a jewellery business. I know a lot about jewellery, and he has a good head for figures, so we make a good team. Sometimes we disagree, but it's important to compromise for the good of the business. We have four shops with eight employees in good locations and they're all doing well. My brother and I share the profits and, of course, the risk if anything goes wrong, but so far, so good and that's how we want it stay.

Frank I'm a supermarket manager. My shop has a well-known logo and is one of a chain of shops owned by a private limited company. All our profits go to that company. I do my job and get good pay, and the company makes the big decisions and bears the risk if something goes wrong. I like it like that.

Angelika I sell pet food on a franchise basis. I bought the franchise and now I have my own shop. Pet owners everywhere like the brand, so I can be sure my goods will sell, but as the franchisee I can only sell the brand's products and have to keep to their guidelines. I'm free to decide how to organize my shop, but I share my profits with the franchisor and also bear the risk. The good thing is that the franchisor does all the advertising for the chain.

Track 5: Unit 2, Part B, exercise 2A, page 23

Anna Good morning everyone. Most of you know me but for those who don't, I'm Anna Lang, Outlet Becker's Marketing Director. Thank you all for coming to this very important seminar about our company's online presence. We have a team of website experts here today from Image Boosters Incorporated in New York, headed up by the man of a thousand makeovers, Mike Slater. Welcome to Outlet Becker, Mike!

Mike Thank you.

Anna It's a pleasure to have you here, Mike. I'll now hand over to you, so you can work your magic on our website.

Mike Thanks for your kind words, Anna. Hi, everyone. It's great to be here in Germany and I'm really looking forward to working with you all on Outlet Becker's website. A website can make or break a company – and from what we can see, your website needs a lot of changes to make it more up to date.
But before we look at the details, let's look at the basics. And please ask me questions if something isn't clear. The

world is digital and nowadays most people look online before they buy something. And how do they do that? On a desktop? Before I answer, how many people here have a desktop at home? ... Let's have a show of hands ... Just as I thought, nobody! How about a laptop at home? ... One, two ... three ... four people. A tablet? ... One, two, three, four ... ten people. And a smartphone ... everyone!
So, we don't have desktops, some of us have laptops, more of us have tablets but we all have smartphones and that's why we're going to look at the best website layout for a smartphone, because that's what most people will use to shop online. Now here's a picture of page two of a website. You get to this via the hamburger button on the first page.

Anna Sorry, Mike but what's a hamburger button?

Mike The hamburger button is one of the things we all know and use but never think about. It's three lines in the top corner of a webpage. The three lines look like the three layers of a hamburger. You touch or click on it to get a drop-down menu, and that's what we're looking at now.
OK, so let's call what we see after the hamburger button level 1. What sort of things do we expect to see at level 1? Please don't look at your phones now!

Voice 1 Products?

Mike OK, any more suggestions?

Voice 2 Promotions?

Mike So, we have products and promotions. Any more suggestions?

Voice 1 Perhaps categories?

Mike Now we're getting somewhere! Categories. Yes, and what sort of categories? What about batteries? Batteries is a category, but can you think of a bigger category that includes batteries and lamps, lights, light bulbs and so on?

Anna Electrical?

Mike Fantastic! You got it in one! Electrical is the big category that covers all these things and that's what we want to see at level 1. Big, general categories. Can anyone think of more general categories?

Voice 2 Shoes?

Mike Shoes is big but it's a sub-category. Let's call that level 2. There's a category over shoes. What's the category over shoes?

Voice 1 Clothes?

Mike Perfect! So, we have clothes and shoes, so what's the category under shoes? Let's call that level 3.

Anna A product?

Mike Right again! When the customer taps on shoes, they can then scroll through all shoes offered by the company with all the details, something 'Buffalo women's trekking boots, €74.99'. Products are level 3. They're last in the chain and they're what we want our customers to buy.
OK, so now I want you to work in groups, one for each department and put your products into three categories: general categories, level 1, sub-categories, level 2 and specific products, level 3. Have we all got that?

Track 6: Unit 3, Part A, exercise 2A, page 33

Tim Hi everyone and thank you so much for coming. The works council wants to give you information about retail in Germany so you can make informed decisions before joining a retail company. Before we start, could you just tell me your names, please?

Leonie I'm Leonie.

Latifa My name's Latifa.

Vlad And I'm Vlad.

Tim Thanks. So one big issue in every company is the gender pay gap. Do we all understand what that is?

Leonie Something about how much men and women earn?

Tim Exactly! Pay gap means there's a difference, so who earns more, men or women?

Latifa Men! Everyone knows that.

Tim Yes, but how much more? Let's think about the retail trade, not factory workers or the public sector. What's the difference in per cent?

Vlad 10%?

Latifa No, more. 15% at least.

Tim The answer is 20%, sometimes even more.

Leonie But why is that? It's so unfair!

Tim We can't answer that question for you, but we can tell you not to be surprised when you find out that men are earning more than women. So, if you are a woman, find out about a company's policy on equal pay before signing a contract.
OK, so let's now move on to our next question: who owns the shop where you work?

Latifa In Germany all the shops belong to about twenty big companies. Their names are everywhere.

Tim Well, yes and no. You're right that there are about twenty big names, but they don't always own the shops that have their names over the door. You need to need to know if the shop where *you* want to work is privately owned or belongs to a big private limited or public limited company.

Vlad Why is that important?

Tim A big private or public limited company with a large number of employees will pay them more because there will be a wage agreement. If the shop is privately owned, there's a good chance that there will be no wage agreement and the pay will be lower.

Latifa But who makes the wage agreement?

Tim Wage agreements are made between employers and trade unions. A trade union is an organization for workers who all do the same job, in this case shop workers. It fights for better conditions for its members, meaning better pay, less overtime, more paid holiday and so on but only about 10% of all the workers in the retail trade are in unions.

Vlad Why is that?

Tim There are lots of reasons but one of them is that 60% of all shop workers are part-timers or mini-jobbers.

Latifa And women work part-time because they work so hard at home! They shop, cook, clean, look after the children and then go to work.

Leonie And earn less!

Tim I'm afraid so.

Vlad OK, but you said only 10% are in unions and have wage agreements. How much do the other 90% earn?

Tim They earn the minimum wage plus what the shopowner offers them on top for their gender, age, qualifications and experience.

Track 7: Unit 4, Part A, exercise 1A, see page 44

The presentations are in the unit.

Track 8: Unit 4, Part B, exercise 1A, page 47

Mary Hi, everybody and thank you for taking part in this online meeting. My name is Mary Anderson and I'm Head of HR at the TopSell Carter Corporation in Washington, DC. As you know, TopSell is planning to open some stores in Germany and the UK next year, so we're getting as much information as we can before we start. Today, we're pleased to welcome Ms Julia Neumann. She's a retail expert in Frankfurt, Germany. Thanks for joining us, Julia.

Julia My pleasure.

Mary And a warm welcome to Frank Taylor, a retail consultant in London, England. Glad to see you here at this meeting, Frank.

Frank Delighted to be here.

Mary Now the first point on the agenda today is vacation. What's the legal position on vacation in Germany, Julia?

Julia Well, if we're talking about paid vacation, what we call paid annual leave here, then German workers are entitled to 20 working days paid annual leave per year. That's if they have a full-time job.

Mary Wow, that's a lot! What about the UK, Frank?

Frank In the UK, employees are also entitled to paid annual leave. The law says that full-time workers have a right to 28 days per year.

Mary 28 days! Well, I really am surprised because in the USA it's zero. US workers have no right to paid vacation. It's that simple. OK, let's move on to public holidays. I mean Thanksgiving and so on. Julia?

Julia Well, we don't celebrate Thanksgiving in Germany, but we certainly have a lot of public holidays here, but the number varies from region to region. The minimum is 10 public holidays a year.

Mary Ten's a lot. So workers can take that time off, but do they get paid?

Julia Yes, they get paid as well.

Mary I don't believe this! So German workers get 20 days' paid vacation and at least ten paid public holidays per year! That's 30 days!

Julia In Austria they get 25 days' paid annual leave and 13 paid public holidays. That makes a total of 38 days off per year.

Mary Well, thanks for warning me about Austria, Julia. How about the UK, Frank? How many paid public holidays do you get there?

Frank It's zero in the UK.

Mary And it's zero in the US, too. My next point on the agenda is minimum wage. How about Germany? Do you have a minimum wage?

Julia Yes, we have a minimum wage in Germany. It goes up every year. In 2022 it went up to 12 euros per hour.

Mary Frank?

Frank Yes, we have a minimum wage in the UK, too. In 2022 it went up to nine pounds fifty per hour and it also goes up every year. What about the States, Mary? I expect there isn't one. Am I right?

Mary Actually, you're wrong, Frank! We do have a minimum wage, or should I say minimum wages because it varies from state to state. Washington, DC, has the highest at about fifteen dollars and Wyoming has the lowest at just over five dollars. Now we only have two more points on the agenda and then we're done, so let's now talk about notice periods if an employer wants to fire someone. If an employer wishes to fire an employee, or an employee wishes to leave their job, I believe there are notice periods in Europe. Is that right, Julia?

Julia Yes, that's right, Mary. Here in Germany, an employer needs an acceptable reason to fire an employee and the employer must give the employee at least one month's notice, and the notice period goes up with the number of years the employee has worked at the company. After ten years, for example, it's four months but the minimum notice period is one month.

Mary How about the UK, Frank?

Frank In the UK the minimum notice period is one week.

Mary And after a few years?

Frank It's longer, so after two years it's two weeks, after three years it's three weeks, and so on.

Julia And what about the States, Mary? Is it really hire and fire?

Mary It's not just hire and fire, Julia. It's simpler than that. In general, in the States, employers can fire employees when they want to for any reason, and employees can leave any time they please. We call this 'at-will employment'. It makes the labour market flexible.

Julia But does at-will employment really mean you can fire someone for any reason at all?

Mary The reason cannot be race, gender, ethnicity, disability, religion or because they're aged over 40, but otherwise, any reason.

Julia Amazing!

Mary Amazing for Europeans, but this arrangement has its pros and cons on both sides. Right, now for my last point, Christmas bonus or thirteenth salary. I've heard this exists in Germany. Is that really true, Julia?

Julia It's true. 53% of German workers get a Christmas bonus, in particular at companies with a wage agreement.

Mary A wage agreement between the trade union and the management?

Julia That's right. It isn't a full salary, so we don't call it a thirteenth salary. It's 60–80% of a month's salary, but a lot of workers get it.

Mary Thanks for that, Julia. How about the UK, Frank?

Frank In the UK, there is no Christmas bonus.

Mary And nothing like that in the States, either. Perhaps we should all go and work in Germany! Well, that's it for today. Thank you both for attending this meeting. There's still a lot to talk about before we can open the first stores in Germany and the UK,

Track 9: Unit 4, Communication, exercise 3A, page 51

Good morning everyone. My name's Amy Thomson and I'm the regional manager for 15 supermarkets in London. You asked me to give you some data on the most popular shopping times in London, so here are the figures. We open at 7 a.m. and we get 1% of our customers between 7 and 8 a.m. It's a bit busier after 8 a.m. with 5% between 8 a.m. and 10 a.m. and this figure goes up to 10% between 10 a.m. and 12 p.m. but that time of the day is still quiet. It stays at 10% for the lunchtime period from 12 to 2 p.m. but then it increases to 13% between 2 and 4 p.m. People start going home from work at about 4 p.m. in London, so this is when the peak period starts because 20% of our customer come to the shop between 4 and 6 p.m. This figure rises to 25% between 6 and 8 p.m., and then between 8 and 10 p.m. it falls to 16%. London is a city of late-night shoppers. What's it like in Germany?

Track 10: Unit 5, Foundation, exercise 2C, page 55

Labels, stickers, price tags, call them what you will, they're on every item in every shop everywhere. There are some we always look at, some we sometimes look at and some we try not to look at, but of the eight examples shown here, the first five are mandatory, meaning the seller must display this information and the last three are voluntary, meaning the seller needn't give this information but may if they wish. The EU has strict regulations about labels so let's take a closer look at them.
The first thing we all look at, of course, is the price, but we need to know the final price including value added tax, so this is the price we must see, and we must see it clearly in big print. Our first example is an offer for 11 bottles of beer, each containing half a litre, for €6.99. Perhaps there's another offer next to it, with 12 bottles of beer, each containing a third of a litre, for €7.99. How do we compare the two offers? EU law says the *unit price* must be displayed. The unit price here is the price of one litre of beer. In this case it's €1.27 per litre and in the other case it would be €2.00 per litre. As soon as we know the unit price, we can compare the offers easily. And as beer comes in bottles and bottles come in crates, we need to pay a deposit. The deposit for this offer is €2.38 and this amount must also be clearly displayed.
The next label shows the best-before date. Some foods, such as pasta and rice, can still be eaten after this date, so consumers needn't throw them away, but they should check them before eating them.
Label number three has a very different message, however. This is the use-by date. The use-by date is the date after which the goods must be thrown away because it would be dangerous to eat them. The use-by date is on perishable goods. Perishable means that the goods go off in a short time, start to smell and are dangerous for us. Fresh fish, meat and poultry in particular are good examples of perishable foods.
Label number four is about the 'Big 7'. The big seven are the seven important nutrition facts. Nutrition means food, so these are food facts, that must be on the labels of packaged foods by EU law. The 'Big 7' are energy value, fat, saturated fat, carbohydrate, sugar, protein and salt. The 'Big 7' are important because experts agree that we mustn't eat too much of them, in particular saturated fats, sugar and salt.
Label number five is the energy efficiency label on electrical appliances, like washing machines. It shows you, among other things, that this washing machine consumes 69 kilowatt hours of electricity to wash 100 loads of washing. This label was introduced in 2021 to replace the old label which gave almost every electrical appliance an A rating. Now all appliances and lamps sold must have an energy efficiency label and are efficient if they have a B rating.
Number six is a voluntary label used by organic farmers to show that their products are not genetically modified and were produced without pesticides or factory farming. A lot of producers write 'bio' on their products, but this label is the one to look for because the farmers are checked by the EU.
Label seven is the Green Dot (or Grüner Punkt in German) – the license symbol of a European network of industry-funded systems for recycling the packaging material of consumer goods. All the packaging with this logo can be recycled. Although the use of the Green Dot is not mandatory, almost all products will indicate through the use of the Green Dot that the packaging is recyclable.
The last label is also voluntary and means that a fair price was paid to the producers of this product, which is normally food or textiles. There are many fair trade labels, so it's best to check out the organization to see if it does what it says and is not just telling us what we want to hear.

Track 11: Unit 5, Part B, exercise 3A, page 60

Good morning, everyone. I'm Vanessa Allen from Allen's School of Retail and today we're looking at visual merchandising.
We have five senses: taste, touch, sound, smell and sight but, of all the senses, sight is the most important in retailing.
We all know the customer who comes into the shop, looks around, says nothing and leaves. We don't want them to leave! We need to give them something great to look at that makes them stay, and that's where visual merchandising comes in. I have some slides to show you now and soon you'll never look at goods on display the same way again.
This first slide is a typical shop window with some mannequins. But look how they're arranged. The five to the right are arranged as a pyramid, but the arrangement is not boring, as one of them is sitting while the others are standing. This arrangement tells the eye where to look and we feel comfortable with it. Be sure to use pyramids in your displays.
The next two slides also tell the eye where to look. This one has towels in different colours in a vertical arrangement, so our eyes go from top to bottom, colour by colour. The shoes in the next slide are arranged horizontally, so our eyes are led from left to right.
The display is easy to navigate because we understand how it works, so we quickly find what we want, for example the right size of shoe.
Another simple technique is stacks. Fill your display space with stacks of the same product on top of each other like these red saucepans. You get a wall of colour that looks great. You can also stack boxes of products on top of each other, or wine glasses and beer mugs on sheets of plastic or wood. Fill your display with products!
Repetition is another great way to make customers take notice. Look at these red chairs. They're all exactly the same but they're in the air at eye level. First the eye sees chairs in a strange place and then checks to see if they really are all the same. Simple repetition has attracted the customer's attention.
Now think of the power of one. Just one item in a shop window. If your special promotion this month is a black coat, put one on a mannequin and put it in the window of your shop. Here the mannequin has been given a touch of lipstick to make it stick out even more. The eye has no choice, and the coat gets all the attention.
Now think of the power of three. Three's a great number. We use it again and again in stories, jokes and so on. Here you can see the same handbag in three different colours. Your eye starts checking to see if the goods are all the same or different. And then we decide which of the three we like best.
And finally, use props. Props are the things used by actors in films and plays on stage. A prop can be a hat, a box, an umbrella and so on. Here the prop is a bike, a nice old bike with a basket, but in a bathroom. The prop catches your eye because not many people have a bike in the bathroom – I certainly don't!
OK, so you've seen how to help customers look at what we want them to see, so now it's your turn to go back to your shops and get to work on some great displays!

Track 12: Unit 5, Communication, exercise 2C, page 63

Assistant Hi, let me know if you need any help.
Customer Well, actually there is one thing I'd like to know. My bike was stolen, and I got some money back on the insurance and basically, I'd like to use that to get another one, so do you have anything for about five hundred euros?
Assistant I'm afraid we don't have anything in that price range. Perhaps you should look for a second-hand bike.
Customer I see. What price do bikes start at here?
Assistant We have a city bike for just over eight hundred euros. Eight hundred and thirty-nine euros to be exact. It's a good bike for the price, eight gears, which is enough for getting around town.
Customer Eight gears ... my old bike had 27 and I went everywhere on it until it was stolen. I used it in town and also for longer trips in the countryside.
Assistant So it was a trekking bike then, like this one here. This one has 30 gears and it's very popular with our customers.
Customer Yes, it looks good. Is it light?
Assistant Just pick it up while I look at the details ...
Customer Well, it isn't very light, really. How much does it weigh?
Assistant 17.6 kilos. We have a lighter one, though. This model here is also a trekking bike but it only weighs 15 kilos, which makes all the difference if you're riding uphill, or pulling a trailer.
Customer Yes, it's hard work uphill with a trailer. What's the price of this lighter trekking bike?
Assistant The regular price is nine ninety-nine, but it's on offer next week, so I can let you have it for the lower price now. That would make the final price eight ninety-nine.
Customer I see ...
Assistant You say you use a trailer, so perhaps an e-bike would be the answer.
Customer An e-bike ... at my age? I'm only 30.
Assistant Everyone rides e-bikes these days, especially young families with children.
Customer Well, that's me. Our daughter's two and she loves the trailer, especially when we go camping. How much would an e-bike be?
Assistant One strong enough to pull a trailer would cost about two and a half thousand.
Customer I'm afraid that's out of my price range at the moment.
Assistant No problem. We've got plenty of other bikes. Would you like to test ride the trekking bike?
Customer Yes, if that's all right.
Assistant Most certainly. We always advise customers to test the bikes first. OK, here's a helmet. Take the bike out for a spin and tell me what you think.

Assistant How was it?
Customer Very smooth. What did you say the price was?
Assistant 8.99. The price tag says 9.99 but, as I said, it's on offer next week, so we can go down to the lower price.
Customer OK, it's a deal.
Assistant Excellent! You've chosen a really good model at a really good price. You say your old bike was stolen, so you might be interested in a good lock. We have some heavy-duty ones here, and by the way, do you want to keep the helmet?
Customer Yes, I'll keep the helmet.
Assistant Good. So here are the locks ... this one just snaps onto the frame and is almost impossible to break open. Just one question, when they stole your bike, did you lose just the bike or anything else?
Customer Everything. The pump, my cycling cape and my water bottle, which I had on my luggage rack.
Assistant We can replace those for you.
Customer OK, fine. I don't need a pump. I have a spare one at home. But I do need a mirror.

Assistant So we've got the trekking bike (899), the lock (85), the helmet (129.95), the cape (52), the mirror (19.95) – and the water bottle's on the house.
Customer Great! Thanks.
Assistant You're welcome. So that all comes to one thousand one hundred and eighty-five euros and ninety cents. How would you like to pay?

Track 13: Unit 6, Foundation, exercise 2B, page 67

Assistant Can I help you, sir?
Customer Yes, I'm looking for a suit.
Assistant Very good, sir. Is it for everyday use or a special occasion?
Customer It's for a wedding. My son's getting married.
Assistant Yes, that's a very special occasion indeed, sir! Will it be mainly indoors or outdoors?
Customer Outdoors for most of the time. There will be a lunch outside in the afternoon.
Assistant Sounds marvellous!
Customer Yes, my wife and I are really looking forward to it.
Assistant And are you looking for just a suit or a whole outfit?
Customer Well, I've got the shoes but that's all, so I'll need the whole outfit.
Assistant No problem, sir. We have everything you need. Now for a summer wedding I think you'll need a light suit. What do you think of this one? It's light grey and very fashionable.
Customer Yes, that's the sort of thing I need.
Assistant Good. What size are you, sir?
Customer 50.
Assistant Right, here's a size 50. Would you like to try on the jacket? There's a full-length mirror over there.
...
How does it feel?
Customer Very comfortable.
Assistant Not too tight across the shoulders or under the arms?
Customer No, it's fine. Not too tight, not too loose.
Assistant And how about the colour?
Customer Just right.
Assistant In that case, I would suggest you try on the trousers. Please come this way to the fitting rooms.

Assistant How are the trousers, sir?
Customer A bit long.
Assistant We can have them taken up for you, sir. It'll only take a day or so.
Customer In that case, I'll take the suit.
Assistant Yes, it's just right for you, sir. You've made a good choice. Let me just pin the trousers for you ... There we are.

	Now you said you need the whole outfit, so let's find a shirt to go with it. What's your collar size, sir?
Customer	41.
Assistant	Right, so here's a very nice light blue shirt in 41 to go with it and a matching tie. Would you like to try them on?
Assistant	So how does that feel, sir?
Customer	Great. I'll take the shirt and tie too.
Assistant	Excellent! You can't go wrong with a light summer suit with a matching shirt and tie. How would you like to pay, sir? Cash or card?
Customer	By credit card, please.
Assistant	Very good, sir. Do you have an account with us?
Customer	No, I don't actually.
Assistant	Well, in that case you may be interested in our loyalty card. It gives you a 3% discount on all purchases. Here's a brochure with the details …

Track 14: Unit 6, Foundation, exercise 2B, page 67

Assistant	Good morning, madam. Can I help you?
Customer	Good morning. I've come in to look at your TVs. Mine's a bit small. I also don't like the remote control. The buttons are too small for my fingers now. And there are too many buttons – I have no idea what they are for.
Assistant	Well, this is our latest smart TV, madam. It has a 55 inch screen with 4K resolution and USB and HDMI connectivity and, of course, built-in apps for all the streaming services.
Customer	Well, the screen's nice and big.
Assistant	Yes, it uses the latest LED technology with Dolby vision.
Customer	What about the remote control?
Assistant	The remote control has all the functions you need, and the batteries last for up to six months.
Customer	It looks very complicated. All I really want to do is watch the news and the cooking programmes. That's all.
Assistant	Well, a button on the remote control can be programmed to do that for you, madam. And this one's on offer at the moment. It normally costs €459 euros but we're selling it for €399 until the end of the month.
Customer	Haven't you got anything simpler?
Assistant	We only stock smart TVs, madam. This one over here has simpler technology but as you can see the resolution is only one thousand and eighty pixels and not 4K.
Customer	What about the remote control? Is it easy to use?
Assistant	It has fewer functions than the 4K TV, so it's easier to use.
Customer	It still looks complicated.
Assistant	This is last year's model, madam, so we're selling it for €299. We can also deliver and install it for you.
Customer	Well, I'm not sure at the moment. I'll think about it …

Track 15: Unit 6, Part A, exercise 3B, page 70

Dialogue 1

Assistant	Hi, just let me know if I can help.
Customer	Thanks. Is it all right if I bring my dog in?
Assistant	No problem at all. He's a lovely dog, isn't he? Look, he's wagging his tail.
Customer	Yes, he's very friendly.
Assistant	It's a hot day, so does he need some water? I can get him some if you want.
Customer	Thanks, but he's all right. Anyway, I'm here because we need a new double bed. The old one's falling apart.
Assistant	Well, we have a number of beds on offer at the moment. Do you have any preferences? Wood, metal, upholstered?
Customer	Wood. Light wood looks good in our bedroom.
Assistant	This *Bodymatch* double bed is very popular with our customers.
Customer	Yes, I like the colour. Can I try it out?
Assistant	Yes, certainly. Shall I take the dog's lead while you lie on it?
Customer	Yes, please! Charlie, be a good boy while mummy lies on the bed! Mmm, it feels great. I could fall asleep. How much is it?
Assistant	Well, it normally costs €499, but this month we're selling it for 399.
Customer	Is that for everything – frame, slats and mattress?
Assistant	Yes, and free delivery.
Customer	Great! I'll take it. Charlie, we've got a new bed …

Dialogue 2

Assistant	Hi, just let me know if I can help.
Customer	Yes, I'm looking for a double bed.
Assistant	Well, you've come to the right place, sir. Just come this way. It's a really hot day today, isn't it? But at least we've got air conditioning here. That makes a real difference.
Customer	Are these all the double beds you have?
Assistant	Yes, and some are on offer. This one, for example, the *Bodymatch* model, is on offer …
Customer	I know what I want, but I don't yet know if you have it. I'm looking for a double bed in light wood, preferably pine, two metres long and 160 cm wide with two mattresses and adjustable slats. Do you have that?
Assistant	Yes, just a moment … I think this one is two metres long …
Customer	It says 190 on the label.
Assistant	Ah, yes that's right, but here's one that's two metres long … and 160 wide with two mattresses.
Customer	Is it made of pine?
Assistant	I believe so, just let me check … er no, this one's made of oak.
Customer	Oak is all right as long as I know it's sustainable oak. Where is this oak from? I don't want Spanish or Portuguese oak.
Assistant	Well, I can check that for you, sir, but it will take some time.
Customer	Time isn't the problem. I need to know where the wood comes from. Can you get me the information on the wood?
Assistant	Yes, just one moment please, sir … Here are some brochures on our beds with all the background information.
Customer	Thanks. I'll study them at home. Goodbye.
Assistant	Goodbye, sir, and have a nice day.

Dialogue 3

Assistant	Hi, just let me know if I can help.
Customer	Yes, I'm looking for a double bed two metres by 160 cm, complete with slats and mattress. Can you show me one in that size?
Assistant	Yes, just a moment, madam. Just come this way and I'll show you. We're giving the shop a makeover at the moment. There'll be a new café on the top floor with a fabulous view over the city centre. It'll be great place to sit back and relax.
Customer	Is this the bed?
Assistant	Yes, this is the one. It's our new *Bodymatch* double bed.
Customer	Is it two metres by 160 cm, complete with slats and mattress?
Assistant	Yes, and the headboard height is 92 centimetres and the footboard is …
Customer	Thanks, but I can see that. How much is it?
Assistant	Well, it normally costs €499, but this month we're selling it for 399.
Customer	All right, but can you deliver it by the weekend?
Assistant	Well, deliveries normally take three to five days, so you should be all right.
Customer	Can you *guarantee* delivery by Saturday at the latest? It can be any time until 6 p.m.
Assistant	I don't see why it shouldn't come by Saturday.

Dialogue 4

Assistant	Hi, just let me know if I can help.
Customer	Thanks. I just want to look around for a while.
Assistant	Take your time, sir.
Customer	Thanks, it's been a long day.
Assistant	Yes, I know what you mean. Some days are like that.
Customer	Exactly. Now what I'm looking for, among other things, is a new double bed.
Assistant	Well, you've come to the right place because we have a very wide range. Do you have any particular size or style in mind?
Customer	A double bed, light wood with slats and two mattresses.
Assistant	Well, I can recommend our new *Bodymatch* model. It's two metres by 160 cm, complete with slats and mattresses and it's on offer at the moment.
Customer	That sounds just about right.
Assistant	Good. Just come this way and I'll show you. We're giving the shop a makeover at the moment. There'll be a new café on the top floor with a fabulous view over the city centre. It'll be great place to sit back and relax.
Customer	Sounds like the perfect place for me. Sorry, I have to take this call.
Assistant	No problem, sir.
Customer	I'm at the furniture shop … yes, I'll get some milk … No, I won't forget. Sorry about that.
Assistant	No worries. Here's the bed. Would you like to try it?
Customer	Good idea. Mmm, it feels good. How much is it?
Assistant	Well, it normally costs €499, but this month we're selling it for 399.
Customer	Does that include delivery?
Assistant	Yes, delivery is free and normally takes about three days.
Customer	Look, I have to do some shopping before the shops shut, so do you have a brochure on this bed, so I can think about it?
Assistant	Certainly, sir. Here's a brochure on this one and some other beds. Take a look at them when you get the time and call by or phone me if you're interested. Here's my card.
Customer	Thanks, I'll do that.

Track 16: Unit 6, Part B, exercise 3B, page 73

With a multi-store loyalty programme, a customer has just one card or an app on their phone. For customers without a smartphone there is a terminal in the shop. With the card or app customers collect points for everything they buy in different physical shops and also online.

They always get points when they show the app or the card at the checkout, but if they activate a premium in the app for a particular chain of shops, for example a chain of supermarkets or fashion stores, the next time they shop there, they get five, ten or fifteen times more points than usual. Another type of premium can be activated to give the customer bonus points if they spend over a certain sum in a shop or online, for example 1,000 points for spending €100 or more. The premiums have a deadline, so customers need to activate them again and again, which makes them look at the app again and again.

The multi-store app directs customers to shops that give them points, and there is now a really wide range of retailers: supermarkets, discounters, fast fashion stores, bookshops, petrol stations, travel agents, phone companies, financial services companies – the list is endless.

When the customer has saved up enough points, they can use them to get products online for points or for points plus cash, or for vouchers to use as cash at the checkout of a physical store. And, of course, they can also give their points away as gifts to friends and family, or donate them to charity.

The fun factor is also important. Many people like gaming, so the app also entertains customers with games, competitions, lotteries and special events.

With data from the app and card, retailers can analyse their customers' likes and dislikes and send them personalized offers for goods and services.

Multi-store loyalty programmes are now used by most chain stores and hundreds of retailers online.

There are also stand-alone single company loyalty programmes. They are also popular but, apart from the 'buy ten get one free' cards offered in bakeries and cafés, they are expensive to operate, so only big retailers, like discounters, furniture shops, DIY stores and consumer electronics stores, have them. Stand-alone cards are less complicated than multi-store loyalty programmes and mainly offer discounts at the checkout, free drinks, birthday vouchers and newsletters with information about special offers, sales and events.

Track 17: Unit 7, Foundation, exercise 2A, page 81

Reporter	Hi and welcome to *Retailing Today*. This week we're talking to three retailers who all decided to go online. Thanks to all of you for agreeing to be interviewed about your shops and also for helping listeners who might be thinking of selling online. Let's start with you, Tom. What sort of shop do you have?
Tom	I have a very small one-man shop in the town centre selling shaving products. I sell traditional safety razors, razor blades, shaving cream and so on, and I also sell electric razors and spare parts, and I do repairs.

Reporter And do you have many customers?

Tom That's the problem. I have very few walk-in customers, so that's why I chose to open an online sales channel.

Reporter Could you describe how you did that?

Tom Well, I signed up with, well, I'm not going to mention any names, but it's the world's biggest online platform, if you know who I mean, and they told me exactly what to do. Their customers expect express delivery, so I store my goods in the platform's warehouse and they pack them and ship them to the customers for me. I just need to make sure that they have enough of my goods.

Reporter I see. And has that helped your sales figures?

Tom Yes, business is booming! It's made a huge difference, and now I don't have to worry about closing down my shop.

Reporter Sounds great, but are there any disadvantages?

Tom Well, I pay to store my goods in the platform's warehouse. And I also pay 15% commission on every sale.

Reporter Could you explain that for our listeners, Tom?

Tom Yes, certainly. Every time the platform ships an order from its warehouse to one of my customers, it takes 15% of the sales price as its share of the profit. The platform's commission is sometimes more and sometimes less depending on the product, but it's about 15% on average.

Reporter Thanks for that, Tom. Now let's hear from Daniel. Tell us about your shop.

Daniel I have a wine shop in the city centre. It's a family business.

Reporter And do you have many customers?

Daniel Well, we still have enough to survive but the number of walk-in customers is going down.

Reporter Is that why you decided to go online?

Daniel Exactly. We realized that in a few years' time, we would probably have to close the shop.

Reporter So, tell us about your online sales channel.

Daniel Well, we also signed up with the same platform as Tom, and they also told us exactly what to do.

Reporter So, do you store your wines in their warehouse for them to sell and deliver?

Daniel Well, that's the difference to Tom's shop because we don't want to store our wines in their warehouse as wine needs to be stored in special conditions.

Reporter So, what about delivery?

Daniel We offer express delivery too, but it's express delivery by the seller, meaning us. In Tom's case it's express delivery by the platform.

Reporter So, what does that mean for you?

Daniel It means a lot of work! But seriously we have a lot of online customers now and we can offer more wines too. We can display up to 50 different sorts of wine in the shop but we can offer 300 different sorts online and that's good for business.

Reporter Any disadvantages?

Daniel As I said, it's a lot of work because the platform offers express delivery, so we *must* and I mean *must* ship all orders to the customer within two days. That means we work seven days a week getting orders ready. We can never take a day off. If we deliver late, the platform will freeze our account.

Reporter That sounds pretty extreme.

Daniel It is, and I also think the platform is undercutting us.

Reporter How do you mean?

Daniel The platform doesn't only have third-party sellers. It also sells products in its own name. It knows which of our wines are bestsellers and now it's selling our bestsellers at a lower price.

Reporter Is that legal?

Daniel I don't know, but there's not much I can do about it because I need the online sales and I don't want them to freeze our account.

Reporter Thanks for that, Daniel. Now let's talk to Paula. Tell us about your shop, Paula.

Paula I have a wool shop in the town centre. I run it with a friend of mine and we sell wool, knitting supplies, natural fabrics and some clothes.

Reporter And did you go online because you were losing customers?

Paula Yes, that's right but we didn't sign up with the big online sales platform that Tom and Daniel use. We got together with 25 other retailers in the area and set up our own online sales platform.

Reporter That's a very different way of doing things. So how does that work? What about delivery, for example?

Paula We offer express local delivery six days a week and also click and collect.

Reporter And has that helped sales?

Paula Yes. And we also get more walk-in customers. People go online to look for something and find our shop and as it's local, they come in and look at the goods. And, of course, we don't have the sort of problems that Daniel has.

Reporter How do you mean?

Paula Well, Daniel's big platform can freeze his account at any time and undercut him if they want to and even drive him out of business and he's powerless to stop them. We share our platform with local retailers and we all help each other. No one can freeze the platform.

Reporter Sounds good! Any disadvantages?

Paula Well, we only operate locally and regionally. That limits our market area and sales to a small number of customers, but it's saved our shop from closure.

Reporter Well, thanks to all three of you for sharing your experiences. If you have stories you'd like to share, please post them on our website. And don't forget to tune in next week when our topic will be …

Track 18: Unit 7, Part A, exercise 3A, page 84

Interviewer Hi, we're asking people about their shopping habits. Would you mind answering a few questions?

Melissa Yes, fine.

Interviewer So could I have your first name and age, please?

Melissa My name's Melissa and I'm 20.

Interviewer Thanks, Melissa. Now what sort of things do you spend most money on?

Melissa I would say clothes and shoes.

Interviewer And how do you buy them, online or offline?

Melissa Online.

Interviewer And is that *often* or *always* online?

Melissa Often. Sometimes in shops but often online.

Interviewer So, you often buy clothes and shoes online. Why is that?

Melissa Well, first of all, you can get express delivery, which is great because I hate waiting, and if you don't like something you can get a refund with no questions asked. And when I buy things online, I make sure I can send them back for free. I don't want to pay to send things back because I send a lot back, at least half of what I order and you can't really do that with shops. Some shops take goods back once, or even twice but you can't go back again and again.

Interviewer How about advice from a shop assistant before you buy something? Is that important?

Melissa No, not really. I mean. I order the clothes and shoes, invite my friends round to look at them and if something doesn't suit me, I send it back.

Interviewer What about the environment? Sending things back causes a lot of CO_2.

Melissa Look, I'm just one person, so what I do doesn't really make much difference. I'm not worried about the environment.

Interviewer Right, that's all I need to know, so thanks for your help, Melissa ...

Tom My name's Tom and I'm 42.

Interviewer Thanks, Tom. Now what sort of things do you spend most money on?

Tom DIY. I do a lot of work in the house and garden, so I spend a lot of money on DIY products.

Interviewer And how do you buy them, online or offline?

Tom Well, I seldom buy anything for the house online. I almost always buy things at our local DIY shop.

Interviewer All right, but you know that with online sales you can get express delivery and have 14 days to return the goods and get your money back with no questions asked? Many online sellers also offer free returns, so you pay nothing at all. Isn't that attractive?

Tom I don't need express delivery. I can go and buy something immediately and check it out in the shop. The DIY shop takes back things I decide I don't need. That's much easier than sending back a heavy package. What I also want is advice, face-to-face advice. DIY can be tricky, so you often need advice.

Interviewer Right, that's all I need to know, so thanks for your help, Tom ...

Sebastian My name's Sebastian and I'm 26.

Interviewer Thanks, Sebastian. Now what sort of things do you spend most money on?

Sebastian Well, at the moment it's furniture. I have an old flat. It's pretty big, so I need a lot of furniture for it.

Interviewer And how do you buy the furniture, online or offline?

Sebastian I never buy anything online! I always buy offline. That's the best way to buy furniture and, in fact, anything at all, in my opinion.

Interviewer Yes, but I'm sure you know that many online shops offer express delivery and if you don't like something, you have 14 days to return it and get your money back. A lot of online sellers also offer free returns, so you pay nothing at all. Isn't that attractive?

Sebastian Look, I don't think you understand. I don't believe in online shopping with express delivery and free returns or anything like that at all. Transporting goods from one corner of the earth to another is really bad for the environment. We all have to do our bit to solve the problem of global warming, so I'm totally against online sales with delivery and returns by vans producing lots of CO_2. Shops are great places. You can see and feel the goods on display and you can get advice from the shop assistant. You can't do that on the internet.

Interviewer Right, that's all I need to know, so thanks for your help, Sebastian ...

Laura My name's Laura and I'm 32.

Interviewer Thanks, Laura. Now what sort of things do you spend most money on?

Laura Children's clothes. I've got two young children and I have a full-time job. The children grow out of their clothes and shoes every few months, so that's what I spend a lot of money on.

Interviewer And how do you buy the clothes and shoes, online or offline?

Laura Online.

Interviewer And is that *often* or *always* online?

Laura Almost always. I seldom buy them offline.

Interviewer Seldom offline, almost always online. Why is that?

Laura I work all day at the office and when I get home at night, I work all evening and at weekends I'm with my family. I just don't have time to go out and buy kids' clothes and shoes, so I order everything online with express delivery. I always tick that box because it normally comes the next day. It's so much easier than shopping with the kids.

Interviewer How about returns? Should they be free?

Laura Most certainly. When I return something, I don't want to pay. I want returns to be free.

Interviewer OK, almost finished. Now how about advice? Wouldn't you prefer to get advice about goods from a shop assistant?

Laura They just put pressure on you to buy. They're friendly until they know you don't want to buy anything. Then they stop smiling. I don't need advice from assistants. I read the customer reviews online.

Interviewer OK, last question. How about the environment? Does it worry you that online sales cause a lot of CO_2 because of all the deliveries by van?

Laura Well, to be honest, yes. I *am* worried about the environment but I have no alternative while my kids are young.

Interviewer Right, that's all I need to know, so thanks for your help, Laura ...

Track 19: Unit 7, Part B, exercise 2A, page 86

Dialogue 1

Assistant Guten Tag. Was kann ich für Sie tun?

Mark Hi, I hope you speak English.

Assistant Yes, I do, sir. How can I help?

Mark Well, I bought a coffee table here the day before yesterday but it's too small for my apartment, so I'd like to exchange it for a bigger one. Here's the receipt and here's the table.

Assistant No problem. Could you just fill in this form for me, Mr ...?

Mark Taylor, Mark Taylor.

Assistant Do you happen to have a customer loyalty card, Mr Taylor?
Mark Yes, I do.
Assistant May, I see it, please?
Mark Yes, here you are.
Assistant Thanks. I'll just scan your card. Ah yes, here we are. OK, Mr Taylor, I have all your details now. So it's a coffee table and it's too big. Just let me look, ah yes, it's an Oslo coffee table, and the size is 45 by 62 by 60 in black for €249. And it's too small, you say?
Mark Yes, I need the next size up. It's too short. I need a longer one.
Assistant Just a moment, sir. I'll check our stock records on the computer … Yes, we have the larger Oslo model in stock. It's 90 centimetres long and costs €365.
Mark Perfect. I'll get that one instead.
Assistant OK, so just let me complete the returns form for you. So the reason for the return is 'wrong size'. For additional information I'll just write 'too small'. I'll just put a cross in the 'exchange' box … May I see the receipt, please, sir?
Mark Here you are.
Assistant Thanks. So the date of purchase was the day before yesterday … you have proof of purchase … you have the original packaging and labels … there are no signs of use and you paid by credit card. Just let me print out the form for you … Here you are. I've given you a credit note. Please sign here, Mr Taylor … Thanks. Now you can collect the bigger Oslo table, take it to the checkout and show them this form. The cashier will do the rest.
Mark Great! Thanks.
Assistant Happy to help, Mr Taylor. Have a nice day.
Mark You, too.

Dialogue 2
Assistant Guten Tag, was kann ich für Sie tun?
Chantal Hi, is it all right if I speak English?
Assistant Yes, fine. How can I help?
Chantal Well, I bought a swimming costume here a few days ago and I don't like it, so I'd like to return it and get a refund.
Assistant I see. Could I see the receipt please, madam?
Chantal Yes, here you are.
Assistant Thanks. Do you have a customer loyalty card, madam?
Chantal No, I'm afraid not.
Assistant No problem, madam. If you'd just like to fill in your personal details on this form for me, please.
Chantal Yes, certainly …
Here you are.
Assistant Thanks, Mrs Dark.
Chantal No, that's Clark, Chantal Clark.
Assistant I must apologize. I misread your name, Mrs Clark. I'll just fill in the rest of the form for you … The product category is 'clothing' … and the make is … just let me look at the packaging … Watersplash, the size is M, the colour is blue and the purchase price was €49.
Chantal Yes, that's right. I paid cash, so can I have a cash refund?
Assistant We always refund with the method of payment used to purchase the goods, but we first need to complete this form. I have to give a reason on the form, so it isn't the size … Is it the colour perhaps?
Chantal No, I just don't like the swimming costume. My friends say it doesn't suit me.
Assistant All right, I'll put a cross under 'don't like' … and you would like a refund. So just let me complete the checklist … The date of purchase was ten days ago … you have proof of purchase … you have the original packaging … but I can't see the labels. Do you have the labels?
Chantal I'm sorry but I can't find them any more.
Assistant That's all right but I have to take a closer look at the swimming costume. You say you haven't worn it?
Chantal Just to try it on.
Assistant But it smells of chlorine. Are you sure you haven't worn this in the water, in a swimming pool, for example?
Chantal No, just to try it on.
Assistant And the hygiene seal is broken. Look.
Chantal I didn't do that! The swimming costume is in perfect condition. I just don't like it, that's all! I'm entitled to a refund!
Assistant I'm afraid I'll have to call the manager. Would you like to wait, please, madam?

Manager How can I help?
Assistant This customer wishes to have a refund for a swimming costume, but the costume smells of chlorine and the hygiene seal is broken.
Manager I'm afraid we can't refund the purchase price if there are signs of use and the hygiene seal is broken.
Chantal That's unfair! I'm entitled to a refund!
Manager We refund goods for 30 days as a gesture of good will, madam. By law retailers are not required to take goods back at all if they were bought in a shop. I'm afraid we can't refund the purchase price in this case.
Chantal Well, that's the last time I shop here!

Track 20: Unit 7, Communication, exercise 2A, page 88

Hi, I'm Richard Baker. Welcome to this week's podcast on the secrets of writing good newsletters.
When we think of the newsletters retailers send out, we probably think of big headlines like 'sale, sale, sale' or 'prices slashed' and a screen covered in high-quality pictures of products taken by professional photographers. And there's great software out there that will help you plan these newsletters and structure them in columns with slots for images, headlines and text and so on. So is that the way to do it?
Forget it. These are the newsletters that never get read, and I'll tell you why.
The major email providers use AI to scan all incoming mail, and, as soon as they see one with banners, headlines and images, they send it straight to the promotions folders, where it's forgotten. And it gets worse, because if the provider notices that someone never looks at emails in the promotions folder, those mails will be rerouted to the spam filter and deleted forever.
Email providers use AI as a gatekeeper, just like bosses have a gatekeeper to read their mail and only pass on important letters. You need to get past that gatekeeper and get your email sent to the primary folder and this is how to do it.
Tip number one, your newsletter should have no design. It should look like an email from a friend or family, so don't begin 'Dear Customer', begin with the customer's first name 'Hi Hannah'.

Tip number two, it needs a good subject line. Subscribers don't want information. There's too much of that all around us, so you need to awaken their interest. You can do this with a question, for example: 'Will your car still be legal in five years' time?' Or a challenge, for example: 'How to start a balcony garden.'
Tip number three, it shouldn't have images. Allow yourself one image, like you would in an email to a friend or family, or even better, one link to a short video clip. And you don't need a professional video. Make a short, selfie-style video with a smartphone, put the link in your newsletter and the subscribers will see the thumbnail and click on it. And remember, everyone clicks on videos.
Tip number four, tell a story. People love stories. Don't write: 'There's a new pressure washer on the market that can clean an average terrace in one hour'. Instead, write: 'Jeff Miller was planning a big garden party for his 50th birthday but his terrace was dirty after a long winter. He had to clean it fast and this is what he did.'
Tip number five, keep it short and simple. People don't *read* emails. They skim them, so write one-sentence paragraphs and have lots of white space. No one reads long blocks of text, no matter how carefully you have written them.
Tip number six, segment your subscribers. By this I mean don't write a one-size-fits-all email with all of your products, special offers and discounts. So if you're selling clothes, split your emails into men's, women's and children's clothes. To do this you need to analyse your customer base and find out which customers have responded to your newsletters and what they have bought. For example, if they bought children's clothes, send them offers for children's shoes and so on.
And finally, tip number seven is the three-to-one rule. This means that you send three emails with helpful tips, advice and information before you send a fourth email with a link to a product or service. So, if you're selling carpets, the subject line of email number one could be: 'Did you know that each new American president changes the carpet in the Oval Office?'. The next one could be: 'When and where were the first carpets made?' followed by: 'What are the seven basic styles of carpet?' In your fourth email the subject line could be: 'Finding the best solution for your home'. The email can then include a button with: 'Click here for a personal consultation.'
Follow these tips and your newsletters will reach your subscribers and not end up in the spam filter.

Track 21: Unit 8, Communication, exercise 1A, page 100

Vanessa	Outlet Becker, good morning. You're through to Vanessa Kaiser. How can I help?
Peter	Good morning, it's Peter Norgaard from SPN Fashion in Sweden speaking. I'd like to speak to Mr Marc Steinmeier in the sales department about placing an order for T-shirts. Could you put me through to him, please?
Vanessa	Yes, certainly, Mr ... er ...
Peter	Norgaard. That's N – O – R – G – double A – R – D and my first name's Peter, P – E – T – E – R from SPN Fashion.
Vanessa	Thanks, Mr Norgaard. I'll just see if he's in ... I'm afraid Mr Steinmeier's out at the moment. Can I take a message?
Peter	Yes, please. I'd like him to get back to me as soon as possible, either by phone or email because my company is interested in placing an order for a thousand T-shirts.
Vanessa	Right, so in that case could I first have your phone number please, Mr Norgaard?
Peter	Yes, it's 00 46 16 920 4646.
Vanessa	00 46 16 920 4646. OK, I've got that. And your email?
Peter	My email address is peter.norgaard@spn-fashion.swe.
Vanessa	Is that all in small letters or are there any capitals?
Peter	No capitals. Everything in lower case.
Vanessa	So, I'll just read that back to you P – E – T – E – R dot N – O – R – G – double A – R – D at S – P – N hyphen fashion dot S – W – E, all in small letters.
Peter	Exactly.
Vanessa	And what message would you like me to pass on to Mr Marc Steinmeier?
Peter	My company would like a quotation for a thousand men's and women's *New Look* T-shirts.
Vanessa	... a quotation for a thousand men's and women's *New Look* T-shirts. Right, I've made a note of that. Is there anything else you would like me to tell him?
Peter	Yes, delivery. That's very important. We want delivery CIP Incoterms 2020 our premises.
Vanessa	... Delivery CIP Incoterms 2020 buyer's premises. And could you just tell me where your premises are?
Peter	In Stockholm. We have a big central warehouse in Stockholm.
Vanessa	So it's delivery CIP Incoterms 2020 buyer's premises in Stockholm. Right. I've got that. Is there anything else you'd like me to tell him?
Peter	Yes, the delivery period. We need delivery of the goods within six weeks.
Vanessa	So that's delivery within six weeks. Anything else?
Peter	Yes, Please tell him that we met at your company's booth at the Pitto fashion show in Florence last month.
Vanessa	I'm sorry, but could you spell that for me, please?
Peter	Yes, certainly. It's spelt P- I – T – T – O.
Vanessa	P – I – T – T – O, Pitto fashion show ... in Florence last month. OK, I've got that.
Peter	And I'm sure he's heard about SPN Fashion because we're a major Swedish retailer of fashionwear with branches all over Europe.
Vanessa	... major Swedish retailer of fashionwear with branches all over Europe.
Peter	And if he wants references, we can give him a bank reference and a trade reference.
Vanessa	Just let me get that down ... a bank reference and a trade reference.
Peter	The trade reference is from Lady Blomberg Fashion AB.
Vanessa	Ah yes, Lady Blomberg Fashion AB is big name in fashion here!
Peter	Yes, they're very big.
Vanessa	Anything else you'd like me to tell him?
Peter	That's it, thanks.
Vanessa	Right, so I'll pass on your message to Mr Steinmeier and he'll get back to you as soon as possible.
Peter	Thanks.
Vanessa	Thanks for calling and have a nice day.
Peter	You, too. Bye.
Vanessa	Goodbye.

Track 22: Unit 9, Communication, exercise 1A, page 104

1	ten million dollars
2	seventy-five pounds and ninety-nine pence
3	twenty-three euro cents
4	seven thousand eight hundred and sixty euros
5	fifty pence
6	fifty-four euros and forty-five cents
7	nine hundred and thirteen pounds and eleven pence
8	three thousand four hundred and fifty-six dollars and sixteen cents
9	eight thousand seven hundred and sixty-five euros
10	a hundred and forty-eight euros and ninety-six cents

Track 23: Unit 9, Part B, exercise 1A, page 109

Dialogue 1

Luigi Hello, Anna. How are things?
Anna All good here. How about you?
Luigi It's another sunny day here in Milan.
Anna Lucky you! I wish I could say the same. Have you got a moment to talk about Massimo Milano's offer?
Luigi Yes, fine. I have all the details here. What would you like to know first?
Anna Let's start with the unit price.
Luigi It's a hundred euros per suit.
Anna Good. Now I believe you've looked at a sample, so how about the quality and workmanship?
Luigi Very good, Anna! This is Italy. We know about clothes, so the standard is very high.
Anna Excellent! The next point's sustainability. Does the product have the EU Ecolabel?
Luigi Yes, all of this company's products have it.
Anna Excellent, and now delivery. What delivery terms are they offering and how long is the delivery period?
Luigi Their terms of delivery are FCA Milan Incoterms 2020 and the delivery period is 10–14 days.
Anna ... so that's FCA Milan Incoterms 2020 ... delivery period 10–14 days. Right. I've got that. And the terms of payment?
Luigi CWO, I'm afraid.
Anna OK, so it's CWO.
Luigi But they're offering free advertising material with their products, brochures, QR codes and so on.
Anna Thanks, that's an important point. Now I believe you've done some research on their creditworthiness. So, can we trust them with our money?
Luigi Most certainly. Massimo Milano SRL is classified as a low-risk company.
Anna So credit rating ... low risk. Thanks for that, Luigi. I'll get back to you with our decision very soon.
Luigi Thanks, Anna. Bye.
Anna Bye.

Dialogue 2

Isabelle Bonjour, Anna. Nice to hear from you again.
Anna Hi, Isabelle. Yes, we haven't talk in a while. Do have a few moments to talk about Paris Confection's offer for men's suits?
Isabelle Yes, I've got all the data now, and a sample, too.
Anna Great, so let's start with the unit price.
Isabelle A hundred euros for all sizes.
Anna OK, and the quality?
Isabelle Very good. I showed the sample to my husband and he wants a suit like that!
Anna Well, I can't think of a better recommendation than that, but how about sustainability? Does the product have the EU Ecolabel?
Isabelle Not yet, but they've applied for it and I'm sure they'll get it.
Anna So that's no EU Ecolabel yet. Now let's look at the terms. What terms of delivery are they offering?
Isabelle They're pretty good. CPT buyer's premises in Frankfurt Incoterms 2020.
Anna Let me just get that down ... CPT buyer's premises in Frankfurt Incoterms 2020. Yes, not bad but that's without insurance, of course ... and how about the delivery period?
Isabelle 30 days. They said it's sometimes shorter but they can guarantee 30 days.
Anna All right, I've got that. And payment?
Isabelle They're offering 10 days 2%, 30 days net.
Anna So that's 10 days 2%, 30 days net. Any free advertising material?
Isabelle No, I'm afraid not.
Anna Right, I've made a note of all that but what about their credit rating? Have you run a check on them?
Isabelle Yes, they're fine. Their credit rating is low risk. I think they're a pretty good company.
Anna OK, thanks, Isabelle. I've got all the information I need now and I'll get back to you very soon. Bye.
Isabelle Bye.

Dialogue 3

Ebba Hi, Anna. I was just thinking about you.
Anna And I hope it was nice things!
Ebba Yes, only ever nice things, and I'm sure you're phoning about Stockholm Style's offer for men's suits.
Anna You've read my mind again, Ebba.
Ebba Beginner's luck. What would you like to know first?
Anna Let's start with the price, shall we?
Ebba OK, it's a hundred euros per suit.
Anna A hundred euros ... and the quality and workmanship?
Ebba They gave me a sample and it's good. Good workmanship and good quality.
Anna OK, so quality and workmanship are good ... and how about sustainability? Do their products have the EU Ecolabel?
Ebba Yes, this company's very environmentally aware and all their garments have the EU Ecolabel.
Anna Good, now I need to know about their terms of delivery, delivery period and terms of payment.
Ebba I have it all here. Their terms of delivery are DPU buyer's premises in Frankfurt Incoterms 2020.
Anna Just let me get that all down ... DPU buyer's premises in Frankfurt Incoterms 2020 ... and the delivery period?
Ebba Two to three weeks, sometimes less.
Anna OK, but I'll mark that as two to three weeks. And their terms of payment?
Ebba A third with order, a third on delivery and a third 60 days after delivery.
Anna OK, so that's a third with order, a third on delivery and a third ... how many days was that?
Ebba 60. 60 days after delivery.

Anna Thanks, and that brings me to my last two points, advertising material and credit rating.

Ebba They offer free advertising material, brochures, display stands and QR codes.

Anna Very good. And their credit rating?

Ebba Well, they've only been on the market for eighteen months, so they're still classified as an average risk company, but I'm pretty sure they'll be upgraded to low risk soon.

Anna So that's average risk. OK, fine. I've got all the information I need, and I'll get back to you very soon. Bye for now.

Ebba Bye.

Track 24: Unit 9, Communication, exercise 2, page 113

Nasir A.P. Leather International. Good morning, Nasir Mahmood speaking. How can I help you?

Sven Good morning, Mr Mahmood. It's Sven Maier from Outlet Becker in Germany.

Nasir Good morning, Mr Maier! It's very nice to hear from you again. Are the leather garments selling well?

Sven Indeed they are, Mr Mahmood, and I would like to order some more.

Nasir That is excellent news, Mr Maier. How many would you like?

Sven Well, before we talk about that, I'd like to discuss our terms and prices.

Nasir I see, Mr Maier. Our prices are already very competitive.

Sven Yes, but so far we have only placed orders for 400 items and now we would like to order much larger quantities.

Nasir This sounds very good, Mr Maier.

Sven And we require delivery CIF Bremen instead of EXW Lahore for the same price.

Nasir The same price! We will go bankrupt, Mr Maier! That is impossible. I'm very sorry but we cannot afford that. Our ex works price is already very competitive.

Sven Now we wish to order 6,000 items.

Nasir 6,000 items!

Sven On a regular basis. I mean every three months. And for that we want open account terms with quarterly settlement.

Nasir 6,000 items every three months! That's 24,000 a year. Let me think …

Sven Well, don't think for too long, Mr Mahmood, because we have customers waiting over here.

Nasir Look, can we offer you FCA Lahore. That is much better for your driver when he comes to collect the goods here in Lahore because we will load them onto his lorry for him.

Sven I'm afraid that isn't enough, Mr Mahmood. We have other suppliers who offer much more.

Nasir All right, Mr Maier. We will accept all risks and pay the transport costs of the goods from Lahore to the Port of Karachi including loading and export clearance.

Sven So you're offering FOB Karachi … And your terms of payment?

Nasir Yes, FOB Karachi but please understand that to finance production of such large numbers of leather garments we will still need part of the payment in advance.

Sven We're already paying you 25% in advance, Mr Mahmood.

Nasir But for such big orders we need to make a much bigger investment here … Look, I can offer you ⅓ with order, ⅓ on delivery and ⅓ 30 days after delivery.

Sven All right, Mr Mahmood. To get you started, we'll accept FOB Karachi but then the terms of payment must be ⅓ with order, ⅓ on delivery and ⅓ 90 days after delivery.

Nasir 90 days …

Sven Yes, and we'll accept those terms for one year only starting today. After that we'll expect open account terms.

Nasir No problem, Mr Maier.

Sven But I want a guarantee in writing, Mr Mahmood.

Nasir All right, it's a deal, Mr Maier.

Sven Good. Please send me an email confirming the new terms and I'll email you our order straight away.

Nasir You'll get my email in a few minutes, Mr Maier …

Track 25: Unit 10, Part A, exercise 4A, page 120

Gunner Dansk Electrics, you're through to Gunner Kristoffersen in exports. How can I help?

Tamara Hello, it's Tamara Meier from Outlet Becker in Germany.

Gunner Ah yes, Outlet Becker in Germany. I believe you recently placed an order with us.

Tamara Yes, we did. We ordered a number of items and the reason I'm calling is to tell you that we're extremely dissatisfied with the air conditioners you sent us. Some of the air conditioners are faulty, meaning that they cut out after a few minutes. Others are discoloured, and in some of them parts are missing.

Gunner Oh dear, faulty, discoloured and also missing parts! I'm very sorry to hear that, Ms Meier. Could I have the order number, please?

Tamara Yes, it's order number AC999 dated the twelfth of last month.

Gunner Let me just check. Yes, I've got it here. An order for 500 AC2000 mobile air conditioners.

Tamara Yes, and let me point out that the air conditioners are still under guarantee and we sell them to our customers in Germany with both the mandatory 24-month legal guarantee and an extra three years' commercial guarantee on our part, meaning they must last at least five years.

Gunner We're extremely sorry to hear that, Ms Meier. We take customers' complaints very seriously and I assure you we'll find a solution as soon as possible.

Tamara The weather is hot, people want mobile air conditioners but we have had to take yours off our shelves, Mr Kristoffersen, because we can't sell poor quality goods. We're losing customers and this has to stop.

Gunner I fully understand, Ms Meier. I'll contact the manufacturer immediately and get back to you.

Tamara We expect you to replace the whole consignment free of charge. And we won't be paying for the air conditioners until we are perfectly satisfied.

Gunner I see … Well, the terms of payment are 10 days 2%, 30 days net, so we still have some time.

Tamara	And just so you know, if we don't get replacements, we'll return the whole consignment carriage with you paying for the carriage.
Gunner	I'm sure that won't be necessary, Ms Meier.
Tamara	We're prepared to give you one week to send us replacements but no longer, Mr Kristoffersen.
Gunner	Please let me apologize for the inconvenience this has caused you, Ms Meier. You'll be hearing from us again very soon and I'm sure we'll find a solution.
Tamara	I very much hope so. Goodbye.
Gunner	Thanks for calling, Ms Meier. Goodbye.

Track 26: Unit 10, Part B, exercise 3A, page 123

Lina	Outlet Becker, Service-Abteilung. Sie sprechen mit Lina Braun. Was kann ich für Sie tun?
Eric	Good morning, it's Eric Paige here. Is it all right if we speak English?
Lina	No problem, Mr Paige. How can I help?
Eric	Well, I'm calling about a trampoline I bought three days ago at your shop. There's a bit missing.
Lina	Oh, dear! Do you have the receipt?
Eric	Yes, I've got it here.
Lina	Could I have the order number, please? It's in the top left-hand corner.
Eric	Yes, I've found it. It's 200 – dot – 191 – dot – TMP399.
Lina	So that's order number 200 – dot – 191 – dot – TMP399 … OK, I see you have an account with us and I've got your purchase on my screen now – a *Funtime* trampoline for children aged 3 – 12 and you bought it three days ago. You say there's a bit missing?
Eric	Yes, it should have six legs but it's only got five.
Lina	Just let me check … I see you bought it using 'click and collect', so you have 14 days to bring it back for a full refund if you wish.
Eric	I don't want a refund. I want the missing leg, that's all. The trampoline's a surprise birthday present for my grandson's seventh birthday. He and five of his schoolfriends are coming to our house the day after tomorrow for a party in the garden, so it has to be ready by then. I just need the missing part.
Lina	In that case, I think it's easiest if we exchange it for another one. We're open until 8 o'clock this evening, so if you'd like to bring back the trampoline, we'll exchange it for you immediately.
Eric	Look, it took me two hours to put up the trampoline and it'll take another hour to take it down and then two more hours to put up the new one. That's a lot of work for me at my age and I've done enough for today. All I want is the missing leg.
Lina	I see what you mean, Mr Paige, and I think I have the answer. If we get another trampoline ready for you to collect tomorrow, you can pick it up, take it home and then just take out one of the legs to complete the trampoline in your garden. We can sort the rest out later.
Eric	That sounds better.
Lina	Great! I'll tell our warehouse to have another trampoline ready for collection as from 7 a.m. tomorrow morning. All you'll need to do is sign for it.
Eric	OK, thanks. I'll bring back the original trampoline next week when I take it down and put up the new one in my daughter's garden. That's where we want to install it permanently. It's only in my garden to make sure it's a surprise.
Lina	Well, I'm sure it'll all work out now and if we get the original trampoline back next week, that's fine by us.
Eric	Good. I'll call by tomorrow morning and pick up the replacement.
Lina	It'll be waiting for you, Mr Paige, and in the meantime, I'll send you an email confirming this arrangement and we'll also double check that no parts are missing.
Eric	Good. Thanks.
Lina	Thanks for calling, Mr Paige. Bye for now and have a nice day and a nice party!
Eric	Thanks. Bye.

Track 27: Unit 10, Communication, exercise 2A, page 125

Assistant	Can I help you, sir?
Customer	Yes, I bought a bike here last week and there's a problem with the brakes.
Assistant	I'm sorrry to hear that, sir. Could you describe the problem?
Customer	Yes, every time it rains, the brakes don't grip at first, so I brake harder and then they're much too sharp. I think it's because the brake blocks are too hard. I think they need to be of a different material that grips better when it's wet.
Assistant	So just let me get that right. When it's wet, the brakes don't grip at first, then when you brake harder they're too sharp and you think they need to be made of a different material.
Customer	Yes, that's right.
Assistant	And you bought the bike here last month, right?
Customer	Yes, here's the receipt.
Assistant	Thanks. Could you leave the bike with us sir, so we can phone you back when our workshop has taken a look at it?
Customer	Yes, that's fine. When do you think you'll phone me?
Assistant	Is tomorrow all right?
Customer	Yes, fine. My phone number is …

Track 28: Unit 11, Foundation, exercise 1A, page 128

Franz	Good morning everyone. I'm Franz Haverkamp, the CEO of Outlet Becker, and today our guest is international retail expert Julie Fernandez. She's going to be talking about the future of retail over the next five years. Over to you, Julie.
Julie	Thanks, Franz and good morning, everyone. Now, the data that my team and I have collected shows that in five years' time, physical shops will still be a very important part of the retail landscape, and consumers will be spending 78% of their money in them. At the moment, it's about 86% but the changes we expect mean good news for some retailers and bad for others. We have identified four retail formats and I'm going to talk about how their market shares will change. As

you can see from this chart, one of them will shrink by about 8%. Does anyone have any idea which one this could be?

Voice 1 Department stores?

Julie Any other guesses?

Voice 2 Corner shops?

Julie Well, you could both be right, because the shops in danger of shrinking are purely physical shops, shops with no e-commerce at all. The days of physical only shops are numbered. On the other hand, there are two retail formats that are expected to expand, one by about nine per cent and the other by about eight. Any ideas which ones they could be?

Voice 1 How about click and collect? I think that has become very popular.

Julie And I agree with you, but click and collect is part of a bigger picture and that is omnichannel retailing. Omnichannel is the retail format that we believe will grow by about 9% over the next five years.

Franz Could you explain to us what omnichannel is, Julie?

Julie Yes, certainly. Omnichannel means that a retailer makes it possible for a customer to get information on a product and buy it through a number of channels, for example physical shops, click and collect, website, social media, live chats, in-store digital kiosks, scannable barcodes and QR codes and so on. Customers must be able to buy seamlessly wherever they are and whenever they please.

Voice 1 I'm sorry but I'm still not quite sure I've understood what you mean by buying seamlessly.

Julie No problem. Some customers start looking at an item online, view it in a store, click on a QR code for information, talk to an assistant, go home and order it from the company's website and then go back to the store to collect it. This is seamless retailing and we must offer customers this because it's the future.

Voice 1 Thanks.

Julie You're welcome. And it also means, for example, that you never say to a customer: 'I'm sorry but we don't have the product you want at this branch. Try our branch in the city centre.' Don't send the customer away! In such cases, the customer must be able to get what they want by ordering it online at the shop where they are right now.

Franz Yes, I see what you mean, Julie. The customer is at the centre of a network of sales outlets. What about the retail format that is expected to grow by 8%?

Julie We all know it and use it, Franz. It's online marketplaces. Here in the West there's one giant American online marketplace but there are others that are bigger, for example in China. Online marketplaces are third-party sellers, meaning they sell goods not in their own name but for other companies and take a commission for each sale. They are expected to grow and grow.

Franz Good, so there's one retail format left and on your chart it says zero growth.

Julie Yes, and it may even shrink. The retail format that will not grow is internet-only retailing with no physical outlets. Customers want more. They want what we call retail theatre and retail therapy. They want contact with people, beautiful displays and scenery, nice music, the smell of fresh coffee, in-store events, product demonstrations and so on. Some online only retailers are now starting to open physical shops to win their customers back.

Franz That's really interesting, Julie. What I suggest ...

Track 29: Unit 11, Part A, exercise 2C, page 131

Reporter Thank you for finding the time to give this interview about your predictions for the retail trade. Kate, could you start by describing your vision of how consumers will shop in the future?

Kate Yes, certainly. In future, consumers will snack on retail. They'll shop for anything and everything online several times a day using their smartphones, while they're doing something else. They won't go on shopping trips to their favourite shops any more. Their shopping will be seamlessly integrated into their day. Delivery will be same-day or even within one or two hours to a location of their choice, for example to their home, office or car boot by drone or robot.

Reporter That's amazing! What will make all that happen?

Kate Well, one of the major factors is speed. Younger people, I mean Millennials and Generation Z, want speed and convenience. They don't want to waste time counting out cash at the till. They often go out without cash and wear clothes with no room for a bulky wallet or a purse. But they always take their smartphone. Their phone is their link to the world and is also how they pay. They use their mobile wallet for all purchases.

Reporter Could you give us a typical scenario?

Kate Yes, but first we need to understand the idea of open banking and how retailers can use it. Open banking means that consumers give third parties permission to access their financial data.

Reporter That sounds very scary!

Kate That's what older people say, but younger ones aren't so worried nowadays. They share their data with their friends on social media all the time. Remember that you as a consumer own your financial data. Your financial data belongs to you. Open banking means you give someone you trust the right to access it. That person or company can look at it, analyse it, predict what you are looking for and help you find it. The big online marketplaces do this already.

Reporter Can you give me an example?

Kate Well, let's say you've agreed to share your financial data with a sports chain and a fast-food chain. You and a friend walk into a mall and when you're near the sports shop, they pick up your geo-location on your smartphone, register you have never been to that branch before, see from your purchases at their other branches that you like skateboarding and send you an instant personalized offer for a new skateboard with a discount of 20%. You walk in, check out the skateboard, like it and pay for it by scanning a QR code at the till with your phone. Payment takes less than ten seconds. You walk outside and the fast-food chain detects your phone. It registers that you always eat at one of its outlets

	on Saturdays but today is Tuesday, so it offers you and your friend a two-for-the-price-of-one lunch deal, and you take it and pay by face ID. That makes for a great day!
Reporter	Payment by face ID? My phone has face ID but I don't think my bank offers that service. Do banks now offer accounts that can do all this?
Kate	The traditional banks are slow to do this. They want to keep your data to themselves, but the EU has had a law in place since 2019 that makes them share your data with trusted third parties if you give your permission. But now there are new banks. We call them 'challenger banks' because they are challenging the traditional banking world. These banks are online, they have no physical branches, and they offer these new services automatically, including payment in crypto currencies.
Reporter	Crypto currencies! This is incredible! What do people buy with crypto currencies?
Kate	Well, if your avatar is going to an event in the metaverse and needs to wear something special, you can pay for a new outfit in crypto.
Reporter	This is truly unbelievable, but is this the end of cash?
Kate	Sooner or later cash will disappear. In some countries, like Sweden or China, this has already happened. In China, for example, even the beggars have barcodes for passers-by to scan when they give them money. You can't pay in cash in shops now.
Reporter	But how likely is it that this will happen in Germany?
Kate	Well, payment by QR code is already here at some airports and supermarket chains, and in the not-too-distant future I'm sure we'll be paying by face ID, too and then cash will go.
Reporter	Thanks for these insights, Kate.
Kate	You're welcome.

Track 30: Unit 11, Part B, exercise 2A, page 133

Karsten	Hi everyone and welcome to this evening's webinar on the future of retail. My name's Karsten Schmidt and today's topic is 'Creating a digital village'. Our guest speaker is Lisa Lehmann and she's going to tell us about the work she has been doing in her local community. Over to you, Lisa.
Lisa	Thanks, Karsten and good evening, everyone. As Karsten said, my talk this evening is about creating a digital village. Now, as we all know, villages are rural communities out in the countryside. They sound like nice, relaxing places to be, but unlike towns and cities, rural communities are dying. I'm talking about places with between 500 and 2,500 inhabitants. There are about 4,500 such communities in Germany, and the people there often have to travel ten kilometres or more to get to the nearest shop. Some are too old, or disabled, or can't afford to do so, and younger people are leaving these villages as soon as they can. I come from one of these small villages and when our local supermarket closed down due to lack of business, we thought our local community was dead. We talked to the big retail chains, but they said a bigger customer base was needed before they could operate a supermarket with full-time or even part-time staff. We were desperate to save our community, so, to cut a long story short, we got help from a smart retailing start-up, formed a co-operative and opened a smart store. This means that the store is owned by the community and not by a big retail chain. But before I talk about our smart store, let me explain that our suppliers are now the big retail chains and also local producers, bakers and farmers and so on. They're happy to sell their goods in our store! So what is a smart store? Well, the first thing people notice about our type of smart store is that it's open 24 hours a day, seven days a week. The second thing is that our store isn't staffed. The shelves are filled up regularly by our suppliers and the store is cleaned every day, but there are no sales staff. As it's the only shop in the village, it has a wide range of goods, approximately twelve hundred articles, including fresh fruit and vegetables, packaged food and household products. This means that just about everything you need is sold there. So how does it work? Well, as I said, it's a co-operative, so you need to join it. When you join, you're given a membership card and this opens the door to the shop. Everyone knows each other in my village, so people see each other at the entrance and inside and we all know what's going on. The shop is monitored by indoor and outdoor cameras and the data is used for a number of things: counting footfall, stock levels and security. Footfall data is needed to help us get an overview of customer numbers, the big picture, and local fresh food suppliers, the baker and the farmers, can check their shelves via their camera feed and see if they need to call by and re-fill them. Payment can be a big problem. If you have one of those stores where you walk in, pick up what you want, walk out and get billed later, you need a lot of expensive technology, lots of overhead cameras for customer tracking, weight-sensitive shelves with more cameras and sensors. All this high tech is linked to a big server room that takes up space, gets hot and costs big money. We can't afford that, so we have self-scanning. The goods are scanned by the customers themselves and then paid for by membership card, credit or debit card, or smartphone. But that isn't everything! Our smart store with its digital technology has created a digital village and saved our community. The shop has an important social function as a place for people to meet. There are benches outside for people to sit and chat; a box with bicycle repair tools; digital signage with community news, events, sports results, births, marriages, deaths and so on, and we even have a dog shelter to keep customers' dogs dry when it rains. There's a charging point for customers with electric vehicles, free internet, parcels can be collected at our store, you can post your letters there too and, perhaps most importantly, we have a self-service coffee machine, a must in every community. So, in a

	nutshell, the good news is that thanks to our smart store, our village is feeling a lot more optimistic about the future.
Karsten	Thanks for that, Lisa. I'm sure there are a lot of questions, so if you'd like to use the chat box to ask them, please go ahead …

Track 31: Unit 11, Communication, exercise 2, page 135

Lea	Good morning everybody and welcome to today's meeting. I'm Lea Schmidt, the sales director at Outlet Becker, and since we don't all know each other, the first item on today's agenda is introductions. Would you like to start, Danuta?
Danuta	Yes, certainly. I'm Danuta Kozlowski from Outlet Becker's Polish division in Warsaw.
Lea	Thanks, Danuta. Marc?
Marc	Hi. I'm Marc Vogel from Head Office in Frankfurt.
Lea	Thanks, Marc. Liam?
Liam	Good morning. My name is Liam O'Reilly. I head the Irish division here in Dublin.
Lea	Many thanks, Liam. Our next item is Liam's presentation, so would you go ahead, please, Liam?
Liam	Certainly, Lea. My presentation is called 'Digitization in Ireland' …
	… To conclude, I would say that we've made a lot of progress.
Lea	Many thanks, Liam. Would anyone like to comment or ask a question?
Marc	I'd just like to say that Liam's done a great job!
Lea	Yes, I agree. Well done, Liam! Let's move on to the next item, which is unstaffed walk-in stores. Can you give us a brief update, Danuta?
Danuta	Yes, we've found suppliers for the technology and we're still comparing offers. We'll update you as soon as we have made a decision.
Lea	Thanks, Danuta. Let's move on to the next item, which is digital vending machines. How are things going here, Liam? Are there any issues?
Liam	The big issue is choosing the right locations. We have lots of requests from places with low footfall – senior citizens' residences, office blocks and so on but we need more data. We should have it by next month.
Lea	Good. Anything else on digital vending machines? No? In that case, the next item is roll-out. Do we have a dates for the roll-out in Poland, Germany and Ireland? How about Poland, Danuta?
Danuta	If all goes well, it should be this year and not next, but could I just say that it mustn't be *too* soon because we are still missing some key information.
Lea	All right. Marc?
Marc	We're on track in Germany. We've chosen sites for unstaffed walk-in stores in locations all over Germany and roll-out should start in nine months' time.
Lea	So late?
Marc	I'm afraid so.
Liam	Can I come in on that, Lea?
Lea	Go ahead, Liam.
Liam	I thoroughly agree with Marc and Danuta. Roll-out mustn't be too soon because things can go wrong and that's bad for our image.
Lea	I'll make sure everyone at Head Office knows. So when is roll-out in Ireland, Liam?
Liam	Not until next year but early next year.
Lea	All right, Liam. Anything else on roll-out? No? So, we've covered item no. 4, digital vending machines, and item no. 5, roll-out, and I've decided to postpone the topic of security and shoplifting until tomorrow. Right, so we've covered all five items on today's agenda. Let's wrap up the meeting with AOB, shall we? I just have the one final point here from Liam – travel expenses. I've checked with Finance and they'll get back to you next week, Liam. Is that all right?
Liam	That's fine, Lea.
Lea	Well, that would seem to be it. You'll be getting the minutes by email after the conference. The next item on your programme for this morning is workshops, so would you all like to go to …

Track 32: Unit 12, Communication, exercise 3A, page 147

Interview 1: Arne Sohn

Arne	Hallo?
Jennifer	Good evening. Am I speaking to Arne Sohn?
Arne	Wer ist das? Ich versteh' nichts. Bist du das, Kati?
Jennifer	This is Jennifer Winters. I'm the Recruitment Manager at Outlet Becker UK. Am I speaking to Mr Arne Sohn?
Arne	Oh! Oh yes! Outlet Becker UK. Yes, I understand. Yes, my name is Arne Sohn. Please wait a moment. I must go outside …
Jennifer	Is this a good time to call you, Mr Sohn?
Arne	Yes! It's very good! No problem, Mrs Winter. We can talk in a moment. Just let me go outside with my mobile …
Jennifer	I can't hear you very …
Arne	Thank you for calling me, Miss Winters! I am very happy to answer your questions!
Jennifer	Could you tell me what job you're doing at the moment, Mr Sohn?
Arne	Yes, I'm an Azubi – I mean an apprentice, but I've finished now, so I'm not, but I was … but I'm still at Mercury Electronics in Frankfurt!
Jennifer	I see … I think we … problem … signal strength.
Arne	Strength? Yes, I have strengths, Mrs Winter. I am very good at work and at school and at football because I am a team player.
Jennifer	I see … And what about your weaknesses?
Arne	Weaknesses? I sometimes forget important things … but I now use the reminder function on my mobile. That helps.
Jennifer	And why do you want a job at Outlet Becker UK, Mr Sohn?
Arne	I've always wanted to work in Manchester. It has a famous football team and very nice people.
Jennifer	We are in London, Mr Sohn, but that doesn't really matter now. Could you tell me something about your plans for the future?
Arne	Well, I want a well-paid job so I can be independent and free.

Jennifer	I see. Are there any questions you would like to ask about the job, Mr Sohn?
Arne	I'm sorry. I didn't hear what you said, Miss Winter. The signal is very bad and the battery of my mobile is almost …

Interview 2: Laura Schulz

Laura	Schulz?
Jennifer	Good morning. Am I speaking to Laura Schulz?
Laura	Yes, that's right.
Jennifer	This is Jennifer Winters. I'm the Recruitment Manager at Outlet Becker UK. Is this a good time to talk to you for a few minutes about your application for the post of an English- and German-speaking sales adviser?
Laura	Yes, I'm at work but I have permission to use the office phone because it's my father's company – Schulz Trading in Dortmund.
Jennifer	Oh I see. Now I've studied your CV and would like to know a little more about you. Would you like to take me through your CV?
Laura	Well, I think the CV says everything, really. I haven't got a copy in front of me now, but it lists my skills and abilities. I went to the States for a year, so my English is very good.
Jennifer	And what other strengths do you have?
Laura	Other strengths? That's a standard question, isn't it? Anyway, I would say I have all the usual strengths – I'm punctual, so I'm reliable, honest, hard-working and so on.
Jennifer	I see. And weaknesses?
Laura	That's a very good question. Weaknesses … Well, perhaps I expect too much from other people. My own standards are very high, and I suppose it's unfair to want everyone to be perfect.
Jennifer	And why do you want this job in particular?
Laura	Why this job? Well, I think I'm probably best qualified for it. My grades at school were very good and I'd like to work abroad for a few years.
Jennifer	I see. What are your future plans, Miss Schulz? Where do you see yourself in five years' time?
Laura	I really can't say. It depends whether I like the job or not. If I like it, I'll stay on for a few years. It depends on the people, really.
Jennifer	Do you have any questions you wish to ask?
Laura	That's another standard question, isn't it? Actually, I do have one question. Would you help me to find a good flat? I want something comfortable and not too far from the company.
Jennifer	I'll pass the question on, Miss Schulz. Is there anything else you'd like to know?
Laura	No, that's all, thanks. When will I hear from you?
Jennifer	Within the next 48 hours. Thanks for answering my questions. Goodbye.
Laura	Bye.

Interview 3: Artur Kaminski

Artur	Kaminski?
Jennifer	Good evening. Am I speaking to Artur Kaminski?
Artur	Yes, that's right.
Jennifer	This is Jennifer Winters. I'm the Recruitment Manager at Outlet Becker UK. Is this a good time to talk to you for a few minutes about your application for the post of an English- and German-speaking sales adviser?
Artur	Yes, it's fine.
Jennifer	Good. What company are you working for at the moment, Mr Kaminski?
Artur	I'm at MegaKauf Shopping in Cologne.
Jennifer	Right, now I've studied your CV and would like to know a little more about you. Would you like to take me through it?
Artur	Yes, certainly. I chose to do an apprenticeship at MegaKauf Shopping in Cologne because I did a placement there and liked it, but now I want to move on. I would say one of my skills is the ability to work in a team and get the best out of myself with the help of others. That's one of the reasons why my team won the 'Welcome to Germany' competition to attract tourists in Cologne because we offered them the products they were looking for. I also organized a programme for some Norwegian visitors to the company last year. It was great fun and they've invited me back to Norway next summer.
Jennifer	So, in a nutshell, what would you say your strengths are?
Artur	Teamwork, taking the initiative, working independently and understanding what the customer wants.
Jennifer	And what about your weaknesses?
Artur	I'm sure I have many but I would say a lack of experience. That's why I want to start work abroad.
Jennifer	What made you apply for this job?
Artur	The skills listed are exactly what I have learned in my apprenticeship. There is also a link with Germany, so I feel I can make a special contribution. And I would like to work in the UK, so I see it as the perfect opportunity.
Jennifer	What are your plans for the future?
Artur	I hope to develop in the job. I want to gain experience and then perhaps study for higher qualifications in the evening. London is a good place for that.
Jennifer	Would you like to ask any questions yourself?
Artur	Yes, on your website it says you sometimes transfer employees to your branches in Scotland and Northern Ireland, for example. Would this be an option for me?
Jennifer	Not in the first year, but if you stay longer, you can apply for an internal transfer to a different branch. Many young people do this. Any other questions?
Artur	That was the most important one, thanks.
Jennifer	In that case we'll be in touch again within 48 hours and thank you for answering my questions.
Artur	My pleasure and thanks for calling. Goodbye.
Jennifer	Goodbye, Mr Kaminski.

Track 33: KMK Stufe II, Mock Exam, Rezeption I: Hörverstehen, page 149

Receptionist	Good morning and thank you for calling the Mandarin Hotel. How may I help you?
You	Good morning. It's Tim Hartmann from Outlet Becker in Germany calling about a reservation made for our CEO, Ms Lea Schmidt.

Receptionist	May I have the reservation number please, Mr Hartmann?
You	Yes, certainly. It's GBT42243.
Receptionist	Thanks. I have it here on my screen, one room for three nights from Friday to Monday next week. How can I help?
You	Ms Schmidt wants to bring her husband with her, so she would like a double room.
Receptionist	Just let me check ... The hotel's very full next week because of the Seamless Trade Fair ... but you're in luck because we have two double rooms left due to a cancellation.
You	Good. Could you describe them for me, please?
Receptionist	Yes, we have a deluxe room with a king size bed on the twenty-fifth floor and a premium room with twin beds on the third floor.
You	I see. Could you give me some more details, please?
Receptionist	Yes, certainly. The deluxe room is 40 square metres and has a king size bed measuring 183 by 203 centimetres. As I said, it's on the 25th floor and has a panoramic view of the city.
You	So that's the 25th floor, 40 square metres, panoramic view and how big is the bed?
Receptionist	183 by 203 centimetres, which is our biggest bed. And the room has a bathroom with a bathtub and a separate shower.
You	... Bathtub and separate shower. And the price?
Receptionist	€990 without breakfast.
You	€990 without breakfast. OK, I've got that. How about the other room?
Receptionist	The premium room with twin beds is on the third floor and it's 33 square metres.
You	OK, so it's on the third floor and it's 33 square metres. And the view?
Receptionist	The view is good but not panoramic. The view from the 25th floor is panoramic.
You	Yes, of course, and how about the bathroom? Does it have a bathtub and a shower?
Receptionist	Only a shower but it's a rainforest shower. All our showers are rainforest showers.
You	... Rainforest shower. And the price?
Receptionist	€750 without breakfast.
You	... €750 without breakfast.
Receptionist	I can give you an option on the two rooms for 24 hours, Mr Hartmann. Does that give you enough time?
You	Yes, we'll get back to you very soon to let you know which room Ms Schmidt and her husband want. Thanks for your help. Bye for now.
Receptionist	Goodbye Mr Hartmann and have a nice day.

UP Useful phrases

Describing apprenticeships	Unit 1
– I work at … *(name of shop)* in … *(place)*.	– *Ich arbeite bei …* (Name des Geschäfts) *in …* (Ort).
– I'm in the first/second/third/last year of my apprenticeship.	– *Ich befinde mich im ersten/zweiten/dritten/letzten Jahr meiner Ausbildung.*
– I go to vocational training college on day release every … *(e.g. Monday and Tuesday)*.	– *Ich gehe jeden …* (z. B. Montag und Dienstag) *in die Berufsschule zum berufsbegleitenden Unterricht.*
– … on block release for six weeks / three months twice/three times a year.	– *… habe sechs Wochen / drei Monate / zwei-/dreimal im Jahr Blockunterricht.*
– I decided to train as a retail sales adviser/assistant because I like …	– *Ich habe mich entschieden, eine Ausbildung zum/zur Verkäufer/-in / Kaufmann/-frau im Einzelhandel zu machen, weil ich gerne … .*
– My apprenticeship lasts/takes three years / is three years long.	– *Meine Ausbildung dauert drei Jahre / geht drei Jahre lang.*

Making introductions	Unit 1
Greeting people you do not know	
– Good morning/afternoon/evening. I'm …	– *Guten Morgen/Tag/Abend. Ich bin …*
– How do you do? My name is …	– *Freut mich. Mein Name ist …*
– Nice/Pleased to meet you.	– *Es freut mich, Sie kennenzulernen.*
– Nice to meet you, too.	– *Ganz meinerseits.*
– Excuse me. Are you …?	– *Entschuldigung. Sind Sie …?*
– Yes, I am. / No, I'm not. I'm …	– *Ja, das bin ich. / Nein, das bin ich nicht. Ich heiße …*
– Welcome to …	– *Herzlich willkommen bei/in …*
– Thank you. It's nice to be here.	– *Danke schön. Es ist schön, hier zu sein.*
– What do you do?	– *Was machen Sie / machst du beruflich?*
– What apprenticeship are you doing?	– *Welche Ausbildung machen Sie / machst du?*
– I'm interested in training as a …	– *Ich interessiere mich für eine Ausbildung zum / zur … .*
Introducing people	
– This is … . / These are my colleagues, John and Mary.	– *Das ist … . / Das sind meine Kollegen, John und Mary.*
– I'd like to introduce … from the … department.	– *Darf ich Ihnen … aus der …-Abteilung vorstellen?*
Making small talk	
– I hope you're well.	– *Ich hoffe, es geht dir/Ihnen gut.*
– … is such a beautiful city!	– *… ist so eine schöne Stadt!*
– The weather is so good today!	– *Das Wetter ist heute so schön.*
– Did you have a good trip/flight?	– *Hattest du / Hatten Sie eine gute Reise / einen guten Flug?*

Talking about my shop	Unit 2
– We (mostly/mainly/normally) sell …	– *Wir verkaufen (hauptsächlich/vorwiegend/gewöhnlich) …*
– At the moment, … *(product)* is selling well.	– *Im Moment verkauft sich …* (Produkt) *gut.*
– In spring/summer/autumn/winter we sell a lot of … *(product)*.	– *Im Frühling/Sommer/Herbst/Winter verkaufen wir viel/e …* (Produkt).
– There's high demand for … *(product)* at the moment.	– *Es gibt momentan eine große Nachfrage nach …* (Produkt).
– As it's spring/summer/autumn/winter, our customers are buying a lot of … *(product)*.	– *Da gerade Frühling/Sommer/Herbst/Winter ist, kaufen unsere Kunden und Kundinnen viel/e …* (Produkt).

– We (also) provide a … *(e.g. home delivery, click-and-collect)* service	– Wir bieten (auch) eine … *(z. B. Hauszustellung-, Click-and-Collect-)*Service an.
– Our shop is in … *(location, e.g. a mall).*	– *Unser Geschäft befindet sich* … (Standort, z. B. in einem Einkaufszentrum).
– We open from … *(time)* to … *(time)* 6 days a week.	– *Wir haben sechs Tage die Woche von* … (Uhrzeit) *bis* … (Uhrzeit) *Uhr geöffnet.*
– We have late-night shopping on … *(day)* and … *(day).*	– *Wir haben am* … (Tag) *und* … (Tag) *Late-Night-Shopping.*
– Our latest promotion is … *(product).* It (only) costs … *(price)* and a lot of … *(type of customer, e.g. young families, teenagers, senior citizens)* are buying it.	– *Unsere neueste Verkaufsaktion ist* … (Produkt). *Es kostet (nur)* … (Preis) *und viele* … (Kundentyp, z. B. junge Familien, Teenager, Senioren/Seniorinnen) *kaufen es.*

Giving directions **Unit 2**

Giving directions in a mall

– There's a … / There are two/three/several …	– *Es gibt ein/e / zwei/drei/mehrere …*
– upstairs/downstairs	– *oben/unten*
– on the ground floor/first floor	– *im Erdgeschoss / ersten Stock*
– in the basement	– *im Untergeschoss*
– You can take the escalator, the lift or the stairs.	– *Sie können die Rolltreppe, den Aufzug oder die Treppen nehmen.*
– The lift and the stairs are in the corner over there.	– *Der Aufzug und die Treppen befinden sich in der Ecke dort drüben.*
– When you get to the first floor / basement, turn left/ right, go straight ahead …	– *Wenn Sie in den ersten Stock / in das Untergeschoss kommen, biegen Sie nach links/rechts ab, gehen immer geradeaus …*
– When you come out of the lift, …	– *Wenn Sie aus dem Aufzug kommen, …*
– It's on your right/left / in front of you.	– *Es ist rechts/links / vor Ihnen.*
– just before / just after / next to / near / between …	– *kurz vor / kurz nach / neben / in der Nähe von / zwischen …*
– Here's a store guide to help you.	– *Hier ist ein Lageplan.*

Giving directions in a shop

– It's/They're at the back/front of the shop.	– *Es befindet sich / Sie befinden sich hinten/vorne im Laden.*
– Go to the first/second/third aisle …	– *Gehen Sie zum ersten/zweiten/dritten Gang …*
– Walk straight ahead down the first aisle …	– *Gehen Sie geradeaus den ersten Gang entlang.*
– Turn left/right half way/at the end.	– *Biegen Sie am Ende nach links/rechts ab.*
– It's/They're at the beginning/end of the third aisle.	– *Es ist / Sie sind am Anfang/Ende des dritten Ganges.*
– before/after/near/next to …	– *vor/nach/bei/neben …*
– opposite …	– *gegenüber …*
– between … and …	– *zwischen … und …*
– on the left/right	– *links/rechts*
– in the corner	– *in der Ecke*

Giving presentations	Unit 3
Introduction	
– My name is … and this is my partner, …	– *Mein Name ist … und das ist meine/e Partner/-in, …*
– We are apprentices at … in Germany.	– *Wir sind Auszubildende bei … in Deutschland.*
– This morning, I'm / we're going to talk about …	– *Heute spreche ich / sprechen wir über …*
– Our topic today is …	– *Das heutige Thema lautet …*
Structure	
– I've divided my presentation into three main parts, as follows: …	– *Ich habe meine Präsentation in drei (Haupt-)Teile gegliedert, und zwar …*
– First/Firstly, … ; Second/Secondly, … ; After that / Then …	– *Erstens, … ; Zweitens, … ; Anschließend/Dann …*
Signposts	
– To begin with, …; Next, …; Now …	– *Zuerst, …; Als Nächstes, …; Jetzt …*
– The next topic I'm going to talk about is …	– *Das nächste Thema, das ich behandeln möchte, lautet …*
– Now I'd like to move on to …	– *Jetzt möchte ich zum Thema … übergehen.*
Handouts	
– I've prepared a few things/handouts for you to take away.	– *Ich habe etwas/Handouts für Sie zum Mitnehmen vorbereitet.*
– I hope you'll find these copies of the graphs useful.	– *Ich hoffe, dass Ihnen diese Kopien der Grafiken weiterhelfen.*
Conclusion	
– Before I finish my presentation, I'd just like to mention …	– *Bevor ich meinen Vortrag beende, möchte ich … kurz erwähnen.*
– I'd like to go over the main points again.	– *Ich möchte die Hauptpunkte/Hauptargumente nochmals kurz darlegen.*
– Finally, …; In conclusion, …; In summary, …	– *Zum Schluss …; Abschließend …; Zusammenfassend …*
Questions / Thanking the audience	
– Are there any questions?	– *Gibt es / Haben Sie noch Fragen?*
– We have time for a few questions / one last question.	– *Wir haben noch Zeit für ein paar Fragen / eine letzte Frage.*
– Well, that's the end of my presentation.	– *Damit bin ich am Ende meiner Präsentation angelangt.*
– Thank you for your attention / for listening.	– *Vielen Dank für Ihre Aufmerksamkeit / fürs Zuhören.*

Describing events and times	Unit 4
– In 20.. / In August 20..	– *20.. / Im August 20…*
– After I left school, I …	– *Nachdem ich von der Schule ging, … ich …*
– I did 2-year (commercial) course at a vocational training college in …	– *Ich habe einen zweijährigen (Wirtschafts-) Kurs an der Fachhochschule in … absolviert.*
– I did a (2-week) work placement at … (company) when I was 15.	– *Mit 15 Jahren absolvierte ich ein (zweiwochiges) Praktikum bei …* (Firma).
– 6 months / 2 years later I started my apprenticeship at … (company)	– *Sechs 6 Monate / Zwei Jahre später begann ich meine Ausbildung bei …* (Firma).
– The course I'm doing takes 2 years.	– *Der Kurs, den ich gerade mache, dauert zwei Jahre.*
– When I finish my apprenticeship, I hope to …	– *Wenn ich mit meiner Ausbildung fertig bin, hoffe ich …*

Discussing graphs — Unit 4

– The graph/chart shows/presents …	– *Die Grafik / Das Diagramm zeigt … / stellt … dar.*
– The horizontal/vertical axis has a scale from … to …	– *Die waagerechte/senkrechte Achse hat eine Skala von … bis …*
– The x-axis / The y-axis is divided into … units/sections each representing …	– *Die x-Achse / Die y-Achse ist unterteilt in Einheiten/ Abschnitte, die … darstellen.*
– The sales of these products decreased slightly last month.	– *Der Verkauf dieser Produkte ging im letzten Monat leicht zurück.*
– The number of requests jumped sharply in June.	– *Die Zahl der Anfragen nahm im Juni stark zu.*
– They reached their peak in August, then levelled off towards the end of the year.	– *Sie erreichte ihren Höhepunkt im August und blieb dann bis zum Ende des Jahres gleich.*
– New customers accounted for about/roughly/ approximately one third of all the complaints.	– *Bei etwa/annähernd/ungefähr einem Drittel aller Beschwerden handelte es sich um Neukundschaft.*
– Purchases with direct debit made up just over/under one tenth of all purchases.	– *Bei etwas über/unter einem Zehntel der Einkäufe handelte es sich um Lastschriftverfahren.*

Sales talk — Unit 6

Greeting

– Please feel free to just look around.	– *Schauen Sie sich gerne um.*
– Hi, just let me know if I can help.	– *Hallo. Sagen Sie mir Bescheid, wenn Sie Hilfe brauchen.*
– Can I help (you), sir/madam?	– *Kann ich Ihnen helfen?*
– Would you like some help, sir/madam?	– *Benötigen Sie Hilfe?*
– Are you looking for anything in particular?	– *Suchen Sie etwas Bestimmtes?*

Customer's needs

– I need (a new) …	– *Ich brauche (einen neuen) …*
– I'm looking for …	– *Ich suche …*
– Do you have …?	– *Hätten Sie …?*
– Do you have it in … (e.g. black/white)?	– *Hätten Sie es in … (z.B. schwarz/weiß)?*
– It's for… (e.g. work, school, everyday use, a special occasion)	– *Ich brauche es für … (z.B. Arbeit, Schule, den täglichen Gebrauch, eine besondere Gelegenheit)*
– I want something … (e.g. modern/attractive/ practical)	– *Ich hätte gern etwas … (z.B. Modernes/Attraktives/ Praktisches)*

Presentation of product(s)

– How about … / What about … (product)?	– *Was halten Sie von …? Wie wäre es mit … (Produkt)?*
– Here's a(n) … Is this the sort of thing you're looking for?	– *Ich könnten Ihnen … anbieten. Geht das in die Richtung, wonach Sie suchen?*
– What do you think of this?	– *Wie finden Sie dies?*
– Would you like to try/open/look inside it?	– *Möchten Sie es probieren/öffnen/hineinschauen?*
– It comes with … (e.g. a case, cover, bag), in different … (e.g. sizes/versions)	– *Mit dabei ist … (z.B. einem Etui, einem Behälter, einer Tasche) / in verschiedenen … (z.B. Größen/Fassungen)*
– Feel how light/strong/comfortable etc. it is.	– *Sehen Sie, wie leicht/stark/bequem es ist.*
– It's practical/fashionable/stylish/popular/easy to use/understand.	– *Es ist sehr praktisch/modisch/elegant/einfach zu benutzen/verstehen.*
– It's on offer at the moment / this week/month / until …	– *Wir haben es derzeit / diese Woche / diesen Monat / bis zum … im Angebot.*
– It (only) costs …	– *Es kostet nur …*
– You (only) need to pay… now/up front and … later/per month.	– *Sie müssen jetzt bloß / im Voraus zahlen und … später / jeden Monat.*

Selling the product	
– How would you like to pay? Cash or card?	– *Wie möchten Sie zahlen? Bargeld oder Karte?*
– Do you have a loyalty card?	– *Haben Sie eine Kundenkarte?*
– Please sign here.	– *Bitte unterschreiben Sie hier.*
– Here's your change.	– *Ihr Wechselgeld, bitte.*
– Here's your receipt.	– *Ihr Kassenbon, bitte.*
Finishing the conversation	
– You've made a good choice, sir/madam!	– *Sie haben eine gute Wahl getroffen.*
– Have nice day.	– *Einen schönen Tag wünsche ich Ihnen.*
– Thanks for shopping with us.	– *Vielen Dank für Ihren Besuch.*

Telephoning	**Unit 8**
Identifying yourself	
– Good morning. My name's …	– *Guten Morgen, ich heiße …*
– Good afternoon. This is … from … *(company)*.	– *Guten Tag, hier spricht … von …* (Firma).
– Good evening. I work for …	– *Guten Abend, ich arbeite bei …*
Explaining the reason for your call	
– I'm enquiring about …	– *Ich wollte mich nach … erkundigen.*
– I'd like some information on …	– *Ich hätte gern nähere Informationen zu …*
Asking for a person/department	
– I'd like to speak to Mr/Ms …	– *Ich würde gerne (mit) Herrn/Frau … sprechen.*
– Could you put me through to the … department, please?	– *Könnten Sie mich bitte zur …-Abteilung durchstellen/weiterleiten?*
Saying what you want to do	
– Can I leave a message?	– *Kann ich eine Nachricht hinterlassen?*
– I'll call again later.	– *Ich rufe später noch einmal an.*
– Could you ask Mr/Ms … to call me back?	– *Könnten Sie Herrn/Frau … bitten, mich zurückzurufen?*
Ending the call	
– Thank you for your help/assistance.	– *Vielen Dank für Ihre Hilfe/Unterstützung.*
– You're welcome.	– *Gern geschehen. / Bitte sehr.*
– Goodbye.	– *Auf Wiederhören.*
– Have a nice day/evening.	– *Einen schönen Tag/Abend noch.*
Taking telephone calls	
– Who's calling, please?	– *Wie ist Ihr Name bitte?*
– Could you spell your name, please?	– *Könnten Sie bitte Ihren Namen buchstabieren?*
– I'm sorry, I didn't understand. Could you repeat that, please?	– *Es tut mir leid, ich habe das nicht verstanden. Könnten Sie es bitte wiederholen?*
– I'll put you through.	– *Ich stelle Sie durch.*
– I'm trying to connect you.	– *Ich versuche, Sie zu verbinden.*
– Please hold the line.	– *Bleiben Sie bitte dran.*
– I'm afraid the line is engaged.	– *Der Anschluss ist leider besetzt.*
– I'm sorry, … *(name)* is unavailable at the moment.	– *Es tut mir leid, aber …* (Name) *ist im Moment nicht da.*
– Would you like to speak to someone else?	– *Möchten Sie mit jemand anderem sprechen?*
– Would you like to leave a message?	– *Möchten Sie eine Nachricht hinterlassen?*

Writing offers	Unit 9
Reference to enquiry	
– As agreed in our telephone conversation of this morning (of today) ...	– *Wie heute (Morgen) in unserem Telefonat vereinbart ...*
– We were delighted to receive your enquiry dated ... about our ... (product[s]).	– *Wir freuen uns sehr über Ihre Anfrage vom ... über unser(e) ...* (Produkt[e]) *zu erhalten.*
– Many thanks for the above-mentioned enquiry / your enquiry dated ...	– *Herzlichen Dank für die oben genannte Anfrage / Ihre Anfrage vom ...*
– ... and feel sure we can supply you with all the goods you need.	– *... und versichern Ihnen, die gewünschten Waren zu liefern.*
– I am pleased let you have details of our offer in writing.	– *Es freut mich, Ihnen ein schriftliches Angebot zukommen zu lassen.*
Description of your company/goods/services	
– We are a major distributor of ... *(products, e.g. household products)*	– *Wir sind ein bedeutender Großhändler für ...* (Produkte, z. B. Haushaltswaren).
– ... with an excellent reputation both at home and abroad.	– *... mit einem hervorragenden Ruf im In- und Ausland.*
– Our company manufactures a wide range of high-quality products.	– *Unser Unternehmen stellt eine breite Palette hochwertiger Produkten her.*
– ... and already has many satisfied customers throughout Western Europe and North America.	– *... und hat bereits viele zufriedene Kunden und Kundinnen überall in Westeuropa und Nordamerika.*
Sales material	
– Please refer to the attached brochure for further information.	– *Weitere Informationen können dem beigefügten Prospekt entnommen werden.*
– A brochure on ... / Our current catalogue and price list is/are attached/enclosed for your information.	– *Zu Ihrer Information haben wir ein Prospekt über ... / sind unser aktueller Katalog und eine aktuelle Preisliste beigefügt.*
– To download details of our entire range together with our export price list, please visit our website at ...	– *Um Einzelheiten über Details zu unserer gesamten Produktpalette sowie unsere Exportpreisliste herunterzuladen, besuchen Sie bitte unsere Homepage: ...*
– Samples are available on request.	– *Muster sind auf Wunsch erhältlich.*
Price	
– As regards the goods requested, we are pleased to submit the following quotation:	– *Was die gewünschten Waren betrifft, freuen wir uns, Ihnen folgendes Angebot zu unterbreiten:*
– ... and will be pleased to supply you with ... *(product[s])* at ... *(price)* each	– *... und liefern Ihnen gerne ...* (Produkt/e) *zu je ...* (Preis)
– at ... *(price, e.g. €10)* per unit	– *zu ...* (Preis, *z.B. 10 €) pro Stück*
Terms and discounts	
– Our price is quoted FOB Hamburg.	– *Unser Preis versteht sich FOB Hamburg.*
– Delivery will be made CIP Dublin Airport.	– *Die Lieferung erfolgt CIP Flughafen Dublin.*
– Wholesalers are granted a trade discount of ... %.	– *Großhändlern wird ein Händlerrabatt von ...% eingeräumt.*
– A quantity discount of ...% is granted on orders for 10 or more ... *(e.g. items).*	– *Bei Abnahme von 10 oder mehr...* (z.B. Artikeln) *wird ein Mengenrabatt von ...% gewährt.*
– A discount of ...% is granted on initial orders.	– *Bei einem Erstauftrag wird ein Rabatt von ...% gewährt.*
– Our terms of payment for an initial order are CWO.	– *Unsere Zahlungsbedingungen für einen Erstauftrag sind Zahlung bei Auftragserteilung.*
– Our (usual) terms of payment are CWO by bank transfer.	– *Unsere (üblichen) Zahlungsbedingungen sind Zahlung bei Auftragserteilung per Überweisung.*
– ... or, with favourable references, 10 days 2%, 30 days net (for regular orders).	– *... oder, gute Referenzen vorausgesetzt, 2 % Skonto bei Zahlung innerhalb von 10 Tagen, netto bei Zahlung innerhalb von 30 Tagen (bei regelmäßiger Auftragserteilung)*

- Regular customers may be granted preferential terms.
- If regular orders are placed with our company, open account terms may be granted.

- *Stammkundinnen und -kunden können Vorzugsbedingungen gewährt werden.*
- *Bei regelmäßiger Auftragserteilung kann ein offenes Zahlungsziel gewährt werden.*

Delivery

- Delivery will be made within ... (e.g. 14/30 days) days after receipt of order.
- Delivery is made within approx. 30 days after receipt of order.
- Delivery can be made immediately from stock.
- ... while stocks last.

- *Die Lieferung erfolgt innerhalb von ...* (z. B. 14/30 Tagen) *nach Auftragseingang.*
- *Die Lieferung erfolgt spätestens 30 Tage nach Auftragseingang.*
- *Sofortige Lieferung kann ab Lager erfolgen.*
- *... solange der Vorrat reicht.*

Polite ending

- We hope our offer is to your liking.
- We look forward to receiving your order.
- We feel sure that a trial order will convince you of the quality of our products.
- ... and look forward to doing business with you.
- Please do not hesitate to contact us if you require further details.

- *Wir hoffen, dass unser Angebot Ihnen zusagt.*
- *Wir freuen uns, Ihren Auftrag zu erhalten.*
- *Wir sind sicher, dass ein Probeauftrag Sie von der Qualität unserer Produkte überzeugen wird.*
- *... und freuen uns, mit Ihnen in Geschäftsbeziehung zu treten.*
- *Bitte zögern Sie nicht, mit uns Kontakt aufzunehmen, wenn Sie weitere Informationen benötigen.*

Writing orders — Unit 9

Reference to offer

- Many thanks for your offer dated...
- Having seen your offer on the internet and spoken to you on the telephone...
- We have seen your offer for ... on the internet
- On the basis of the terms stated in your offer dated ...

- *Vielen Dank für Ihr Angebot vom...*
- *Nachdem wir Ihr Angebot im Internet gesehen und mit Ihnen gesprochen haben, ...*
- *Wir haben Ihr Angebot über ... im Internet gesehen*
- *Aufgrund der in Ihrem Angebot vom ...* (Datum) *aufgeführten Konditionen ...*

Details of goods / services ordered

- We now wish to place an (a further) order / a trial order for the following goods:
- [*Headings*] Quantity / Description / Size / Article no.

- *Wir möchten einen (weiteren) Auftrag / Probeauftrag über folgende Waren erteilen:*
- [Überschriften] *Menge / Beschreibung / Größe / Artikel-Nr.*

Price(s) and discount(s)

- We are pleased to note that you grant a quantity / trade / introductory / special discount of ...%.
- [*Headings*] Unit Price / List Price / Catalogue Price / Total
- 30% trade discount
- 10% quantity discount
- Subtotal / Total price
- ...% VAT *(value added tax)*

- *Erfreut nehmen wir zur Kenntnis, dass Sie einen Mengen-/ Händler-/ Einführungs-/ Sonderrabatt von ... % gewähren.*
- [Überschriften] *Stückpreis / Listenpreis / Katalogpreis / Gesamt*
- *Händlerrabatt 30 %*
- *Mengenrabatt 10 %*
- *Zwischensumme/ Gesamtpreis*
- *... % USt* (Umsatzsteuer/Mehrwertsteuer)

Delivery

- within 10 days after receipt of order
- by 30 June 20..
- Transport and insurance of the goods from ... to ... via ... will be arranged by us/you.
- in sturdy cartons / on pallets
- Insurance will be arranged by us / you.

- *innerhalb von 10 Tagen nach Auftragserhalt*
- *bis zum 30. Juni 20..*
- *Versand und Versicherung der Ware von ... nach ... über... wird von uns/ Ihnen übernommen.*
- *in festen Kartons / auf Paletten*
- *Die Versicherung wird von uns/ Ihnen übernommen.*

Payment	
– 30% in advance, 70% after completion	– *30 % im Voraus, 70 % bei Fertigstellung*
– by transfer to your a/c at ... *(name of bank)*	– *per Überweisung auf Ihr Konto bei ...* (Geldinstitut)
– by bank transfer	– *per Banküberweisung*
– 2% 10 days, 30 days net after receipt of invoice	– *2 % Skonto bei Zahlung innerhalb von 10 Tagen, netto bei Zahlung innerhalb von 30 Tagen nach Rechnungserhalt*
Acknowledgement	
– We look forward to receiving your advice of dispatch.	– *Wir freuen uns auf Ihre Versandanzeige.*
– Please send us your confirmation of order and advice of dispatch in the near future.	– *Bitte schicken Sie uns Ihre Auftragsbestätigung und Versandanzeige in den nächsten Tagen zu.*
Polite ending	
– We trust the goods will arrive punctually and in good condition...	– *Wir vertrauen darauf, dass die Ware pünktlich und in gutem Zustand ankommt...*
– ... and will place further / regular orders if they sell well.	– *... und werden weitere/regelmäßige Aufträge erteilen, wenn sie sich gut verkauft.*

Negotiating	**Unit 9**
Direct approach	
– Are you prepared to ...?	– *Sind Sie bereit, ...?*
– Can you reduce the price by ... *(e.g. €20)?*	– *Können Sie den Preis um ...* (z. B. 20 €) *reduzieren?*
– Will you increase ... *(e.g. production)* by ...?	– *Werden Sie ...* (z. B. die Produktion) *um ... steigern?*
– Are you able to guarantee ... *(e.g. delivery)?*	– *Können Sie ...* (z. B. die Auslieferung) *garantieren?*
– Do you accept these terms?	– *Akzeptieren Sie diese Konditionen?*
Indirect approach	
– We need to talk about ...	– *Wir müssen über ... sprechen.*
– ... is a problem for us.	– *Wir haben ein Problem mit ...*
– ... *(e.g. our competitors)* are ...% cheaper.	– ... (z. B. unsere Konkurrenz) *ist/sind ... % günstiger.*
– We're thinking of ordering more/less ...	– *Wir denken darüber nach, mehr/weniger ... zu bestellen*
– We need a maximum/minimum of ...	– *Wir benötigen ein Maximum/Minimum von ...*
– How much more ... can you produce?	– *Wie viel mehr ... können Sie produzieren?*
Refusing what the client asks for	
– I'm sorry, but the price that I quoted you is the best I can do.	– *Es tut mir leid, aber dies ist unser letztes Angebot. Mehr/Weniger kann ich Ihnen nicht anbieten.*
– No. I'm afraid I can't do that.	– *Nein, das geht leider nicht.*
Making concessions	
– OK. I'm prepared to offer you that.	– *In Ordnung. Das kann ich Ihnen gern anbieten.*
– Yes, I think we can do that for you.	– *Ja, ich denke, dass ist machbar.*
– Well, I can't offer you ... But what I can do is ...	– *Ich kann Ihnen kein/e ... anbieten. Ich kann Ihnen jedoch ...*

Dealing with customer complaints	**Unit 10**
Asking for proof of purchase	
– May I see the receipt, please?	– *Dürfte ich bitte den Kassenbon sehen?*
– I'm afraid we need the receipt before we can help you, sir/madam.	– *Leider brauchen wir den Kassenbon, bevor wir Ihnen helfen können.*
– We need to see proof that you bought it here.	– *Wir benötigen einen Nachweis, dass Sie es hier gekauft haben.*
–	
– Can you remember when you bought the ...?	– *Können Sie sich daran erinnern, wann sie ... gekauft haben?*

Solving the problem	
– If a product breaks down within the first six months we will normally replace it.	– *Wenn ein Produkt innerhalb den ersten sechs Monate kaputtgeht, werden wir es in der Regel ersetzen.*
– I can offer you a replacement or a refund.	– *Ich kann es umtauschen oder Ihnen eine Rückerstattung anbieten.*
– I'm afraid, I can't give you your money back but I can give you a voucher.	– *Es tut mir leid, ich kann Ihnen das Geld nicht erstatten, aber ich kann Ihnen einen Gutschein anbieten.*
– I'm sorry about the mistake, sir/madam. Here's the right change.	– *Bitte entschuldigen Sie, mein Fehler. Hier der richtige Wechselgeldbetrag.*

Taking part in meetings	**Unit 11**
Starting the meeting	
– Good morning everybody and welcome to …	– *Guten Tag zusammen und willkommen zu …*
– The first item on today's agenda is …	– *Der Tagesordnungspunkt heute lautet …*
Asking someone to speak	
– Would you go ahead, please?	– *Würden Sie / Würdest du bitte fortfahren?*
– Can you give us a brief update?	– *Könnten Sie / Könntest du uns einen kurzen Zwischenstand geben?*
Asking for reactions	
– Would anyone like to comment or ask a question?	– *Möchte jemand einen Kommentar abgeben oder eine Frage stellen?*
– Are there any issues?	– *Gibt es Probleme?*
Asking for opinions	
– What do you think about …?	– *Wie denken Sie / denkst du über …?*
– What's your opinion of / view on …?	– *Was ist Ihre/deine Meinung zu …?*
Expressing a point of view	
– It seems to me (that) …	– *Mir kommt es so vor, als ob …*
– In my opinion, …	– *Meiner Meinung nach …*
– From what I can see, …	– *Soweit ich das beurteilen kann, …*
Asking to speak	
– Could I just say that …?	– *Darf ich kurz anmerken, dass …?*
– Can I come in on that?	– *Darf ich dazu etwas sagen?*
Agreeing	
– Yes, I agree.	– *Ja, ich stimme zu / ich bin (damit) einverstanden.*
– I thoroughly agree with … *(name).*	– *Ich stimme …* (Name) *voll und ganz zu.*
Disagreeing politely	
– (I'm afraid) I don't agree with … *(name).*	– *Ich stimme …* (Name) *nicht zu. / Ich kann …* (Name) *(leider) nicht zustimmen.*
– I agree up to a point, but …	– *Ich stimme bis zu einem gewissen Punkt zu, aber …*
– Actually, / In fact, I think (that) …	– *Eigentlich/Vielmehr denke ich, dass …*
Starting a new topic	
– Let's move on to the next topic, which is …	– *Lassen Sie uns / Lass uns mit dem nächsten Thema fortfahren, es handelt sich um …*
– The next point is …	– *Der nächste Punkt lautet …*
Promising action	
– I'll pass that on to …	– *Ich werde das an … weiterleiten.*
– We'll get back to you.	– *Wir werden auf Sie/dich zurückkommen.*
Finishing the meeting	
– Let's wrap up the meeting with …	– *Lassen Sie uns / Lass uns das Treffen damit zum Abschluss bringen.*
– Well, that would seem to be it.	– *Gut, dann wären wir damit durch.*

TV Thematic vocabulary

Training and apprenticeships — Unit 1

A levels *pl*	Abitur, Abiturfächer
apprentice	Auszubildende/-r, Lehrling
apprenticeship	Lehre, Ausbildung
block release	Blockunterricht (an der Berufsschule)
certificate	Zeugnis, Diplom
course	Studiengang
coursework	schriftliche Arbeit(en)
day release	tageweise Freistellung zur beruflichen Weiterbildung
degree	Abschluss
diploma	Abschlusszeugnis
final grade	Abschlussnote
grade	Note
internship	Praktikum
job experience	Berufserfahrung, praktische Erfahrung
living expenses *pl*	Lebenshaltungskosten
part-time	Teilzeit
to qualify	einen/den Abschluss machen
qualification	Qualifikation, Abschluss
salary	Gehalt
school-leaving certificate	Schulabschluss
school qualification	Schulabschluss
theoretical	theoretisch
to train (to be a ...)	eine Ausbildung (zum/zur ...) machen
trainee	Auszubildende/-r
training shop	Ausbildungsbetrieb
training course	Ausbildung
training supervisor	Ausbildungsleiter/-in
vocational college/school	Berufsschule, Berufsfachschule
vocational training	Berufsausbildung
work experience	Praktikum
workplace	Arbeitsplatz

Shops — Unit 1

bakery	Bäckerei
big box store	Fachmarkt, (großflächiges) Kaufhaus
boutique	Boutique
chain store	Filiale (einer Handelskette)
chemist's	Apotheke
discounter	Discounter
DIY store	Heimwerkermarkt
drugstore	Drogerie
gardening centre	Gartencenter
pharmacy	Apotheke
supermarket	Supermarkt

Goods/Products — Units 1 and 2

accessories *pl*	Accessoires
alcoholic beverages *pl*	alkoholische Getränke
bedding	Bettwäsche
building materials *pl*	Baumaterial
cleaning agents *pl*	Reinigungsmittel
confectionery	Süßwaren
consumer electronics *pl*	Unterhaltungselektronik
cosmetics *pl*	Kosmetika
crockery	Geschirr
cutlery	Essbesteck
dairy products *pl*	Milchprodukte
disinfectant	Desinfektionsmittel
fresh food	frische Lebensmittel
frozen food	Tiefkühlkost
furniture	Möbel
groceries *pl*	Lebensmittel
home decorations *pl*	Wohnaccessoires, Einrichtungsgegenstände
household items *pl*	Haushaltsartikel
jewellery	Schmuck
kitchen appliance	Küchengerät
lighting	Beleuchtung
packaged food	verpackte Lebensmittel
paint	Farbe
plants	Pflanzen
preserves *pl*	Konserven
soft furnishings *pl*	Heimtextilien
timber	Holz
toiletries *pl*	Hygieneartikel
toys *pl*	Spielzeug

Responsibilities — Unit 2

to be in charge of sth	für etwas zuständig/verantwortlich sein
to report to sb	jdm unterstehen
to be responsible for sth	für etw zuständig/verantwortlich sein
to supervise sb	jdn betreuen, jdm vorgesetzt sein

Retail jobs — Unit 2

assistant manager	stellvertretende/r Filialleiter/-in
district manager	Bezirksleiter/-in
employee	Arbeitnehmer/-in
employer	Arbeitgeber/-in
franchisee	Franchisenehmer/-in
manager	Filialleiter/-in
owner	Eigentümer/-in
regional manager	Regionalleiter/-in
sales adviser	Einzelhandelskaufmann/-frau
sales assistant	Verkäufer/-in
sole trader	Einzelunternehmer/-in
supermarket manager	Marktleiter/-in
work placement student	Praktikant/-in

Types of companies — Unit 2

general partnership	offene Handelsgesellschaft (OHG)
limited partnership	Kommanditgesellschaft (KG)
cooperative	Genossenschaft
private limited company (Ltd)	Gesellschaft mit beschränkter Haftung (GmbH)

public limited company (plc)	Aktiensgesellschaft (AG)
registered merchant	eingetragene(r) Kaufmann/-frau (e. K.)

Services — Unit 2

bottle return machine	Leergutautomat
car park	Parkplatz
cash machine	Geldautomat
charging station	Ladesäule, E-Tankstelle
click and collect	Click & Collect
contactless payment	kontaktloses Bezahlen
delivery	Lieferung
refunds *pl*	Rückerstattung

Working conditions — Units 3 and 4

accident prevention	Unfallverhütung
availability	Verfügbarkeit
benefits *pl*	Zusatzleistungen, Sozialleistungen
company car	Firmenwagen
condition	Bedingung, Kondition
contract	Vertrag
dress code	Kleiderordnung
to be entitled to sth	auf etwas Anspruch haben
equal opportunities *pl*	Chancengleichheit
equal pay	gleicher Lohn
facilities *pl*	Einrichtungen, Anlagen
to fire sb.	jdn entlassen
flexitime	Gleitzeit
job prospects *pl*	berufliche Perspektiven
lunch break	Mittagspause
minimum wage	Unfallverhütung
notice period	Kündigungsfrist
opening hours *pl*	Verfügbarkeit
overtime	Überstunden
paid annual leave	bezahlter Jahresurlaub
permanent	unbefristet
salary	Gehalt
shift work	Schichtdienst
shopping hours *pl*	Ladenöffnungszeiten
Sunday trading	Sonntagsöffnung
well-being	Wohlbefinden
working conditions *pl*	Arbeitsbedingungen
working hours *pl*	Arbeitszeit(en)

Work clothes — Unit 3

apron	Schürze
blouse	Bluse
cap	Mütze, Kappe
cloth trousers *pl*	Stoffhosen
dress	Kleid
gloves *pl*	Handschuhe
jacket	Jacke, Sakko
jewellery	Schmuck
long-sleeved shirt	langärmliges Hemd
name tag	Namensschild
overalls *pl*	Latzhose
polo shirt	Polohemd
short-sleeved shirt	kurzärmliges Hemd
shirt and tie	Hemd und Krawatte
suit	Anzug
trouser suit	Hosenanzug

Charts and graphs — Unit 4

bar chart	Säulendiagramm
chart	Diagramm
decrease	Abnahme, Rückgang
to decrease	abnehmen, zurückgehen
drastic(ally)	drastisch
drop	Fall, Rückgang
to drop	fallen, zurückgehen
figures *pl*	Zahlen
graph	Diagramm, Kurve
increase	Zunahme, Anstieg
to increase	zunehmen, ansteigen
to level off	sich einpendeln
line graph	Liniendiagramm
minimum	Tiefstwert, Tiefstand
pie chart	Tortendiagramm
to rise	steigen, ansteigen
x-axis	x-Achse
y-axis	y-Achse

Returns — Unit 7

apology	Entschuldigung
to be entitled to	ein Recht auf etw haben
to be obliged to	verpflichtet sein, etw zu tun
broken	zerbrochen
compensation	Entschädigung
credit note	Gutschrift
damaged	beschädigt
dented	verbeult
dirty	verschmutzt
discoloured	verfärbt
dissatisfied	unzufrieden
exchange	Umtausch
faulty	fehlerhaft
free of charge	unentgeltlich, kostenlos
legal guarantee	gesetzliche Gewährleistung
non-returnable	nicht umtauschbar
original packaging	Originalverpackung
proof of purchase	Kaufbeleg
to receive a refund	eine Erstattung erhalten
to rectify a defect	einen Mangel beseitigen
refund	Erstattung
to refund the purchase price	den Kaufpreis erstatten
to reimburse sb	jdm Geld zurückzahlen
reimbursement	Rückerstattung
to repair sth	etw reparieren
to replace sth	etw ersetzen
replacement	Ersatz

return postage	Rückporto
scratched	verkratzt
signs of use *pl*	Gebrauchsspuren
soiled	beschmutzt
statutory	gesetzlich vorgeschrieben
warranty period	Gewährleistungszeit

Business correspondence — Unit 8

address	Adresse
addressee	Empfänger/-in
to attach sth	anhängen (E-Mail)
attachment	Anhang
attention (attn)	zu Händen
(Best) Regards	Viele Grüße, Mit freundlichen Grüßen
Best wishes	Mit freundlichen Grüßen
body	Haupttext
complimentary close	Schlussformel
date	Datum
Dear Sir or Madam	Sehr geehrte Damen und Herren,
to enclose	beifügen (Brief)
enclosure (enc)	Anlage
inside address	Innenadresse
letterhead	Briefkopf
paragraph	Absatz
reference (ref)	Zeichen
registered mail/post	Einschreiben
salutation	Anrede
sender	Absender/-in
signature	Unterschrift
subject (line)	Betreff(zeile)
Yours faithfully	Mit freundlichen Grüßen
Yours sincerely	Mit freundlichen Grüßen

Discounts — Unit 9

cash discount / early payment discount	Skonto / Barzahlungsrabatt
initial order discount	Erstauftragsrabatt
introductory offer discount	Einführungsrabatt
loyalty discount	Treuerabatt
quantity discount	Mengenrabatt
seasonal discount	Saisonrabatt
special discount	Sonderrabatt
trade discount	Händlerrabatt

Meetings — Unit 11

absence	Abwesenheit
absentee	Abwesende/r
agenda	Tagesordnung
any other business (AOB)	Verschiedenes
audience	Publikum
to call a meeting	eine Sitzung einberufen
conference	Tagung, Konferenz
conference room	Besprechungsraum, Sitzungssaal
contact details *pl*	Kontaktdaten
to cover	(Thema) behandeln
date	Termin
feedback	Reaktion(en), Rückmeldung(en)
graphic	Grafik
handout	Arbeitsblatt, Broschüre
to highlight sth	etw hervorheben
index card	Karteikarte
invitation	Einladung
item on the agenda	Tagesordnungspunkt
minutes *pl*	Protokoll
to participate in sth	an etw teilnehmen
participant	Teilnehmer/-in
presenter	Redner/-in, Vortragende/r,
report	Bericht
screen	Leinwand, Bildschirm
to take place	stattfinden
to take the chair	die Sitzung leiten

Travelling — Unit 12

accommodation	Unterkunft, Unterbringung
air-conditioned	klimatisiert
air conditioning	Klimaanlage, Klimatisierung
appointment	Termin
arrival	Ankunft
to attend sth	etw besuchen, an etw teilnehmen
to cancel	absagen, stornieren
to check in	sich anmelden, einchecken
to check out	sich abmelden, auschecken
conference centre	Tagungszentrum, Kongresszentrum
connecting flight	Anschlussflug
departure	Abreise, Abflug
front desk	Rezeption
insurance cover	Versicherungsschutz
one-way flight	einfacher Flug
passenger	Passagier/in
to postpone sth	etw verschieben
reception	Empfang, Rezeption
receptionist	Empfangsmitarbeiter/-in
request	Bitte, Anfrage
requirement	Anforderung
reservation	Reservierung, Buchung
return flight	Hin- und Rückflug
shuttle	Zubringer
smoke-free	rauchfrei
trade fair	Messe
travel expenses *pl*	Reisekosten, Reisespesen

A–Z word list

Dieses Wörterverzeichnis enthält alle neuen Wörter aus Shopping Matters 4th Edition in alphabetischer Reihenfolge. Nicht angeführt sind Wörter, die zum Grundwortschatz gehören. Die Zahl nach dem Stichwort bezieht sich auf die Seite, auf der das Wort zum ersten Mal erscheint. Wörter aus den Hörverständnisübungen sind zusätzlich mit einem T (Transkript) und Wörter aus den Partner Files mit einem P gekennzeichnet.

24/7 *22* rund um die Uhr

A

A-line *89* A-Linie, Trapezschnitt
abandonment, basket ~ *74* abgebrochener Online-Einkauf
ability *138* Fähigkeit
able, to **be ~ to do sth** *12T* etw tun können; in der Lage sein, etw zu tun
above-average pay rates *pl 142P* überdurchschnittliche Bezahlung
abroad *41* im/ins Ausland; **from ~** *50* aus dem Ausland
abstract *9* abstrakt
acceptable reason *47T* angemessener (Kündigungs-)Grund
access (to sth) *50* Zugriff (auf etw), Zugang (zu etw)
to **access: ~ sth** *10* etw *(Ort usw.)* erreichen; *131T* auf etw zugreifen; **sth can be ~ed by car** *10* etw ist mit dem Auto (gut) zu erreichen
accessories *pl 10* Accessoires; *62* Zubehör
accommodation *145* Unterkunft
to **accompany sth** *149* etw begleiten
according to *16* entsprechend; *56* zufolge, gemäß, (je) nach
account *12T* Konto; **open ~ terms** *pl 103* offenes Zahlungsziel, laufende Rechnung
accounting *141* Buchhaltung, Rechnungswesen
to **achieve sth** *140* etw erreichen
achievement *140* Leistung, Errungenschaft, Erfolg
acknowledgement *103* Auftragsbestätigung
to **acquaint oneself with sth** *119* sich mit etw vertraut machen
to **act responsibly** *84* verantwortungsvoll handeln
acting *9* Schauspielerei, Schauspielern
action *119* Maßnahmen; to **take ~** *122* Maßnahmen ergreifen, Schritte unternehmen; **unfinished ~** *22* noch nicht abgeschlossene Handlung; **routine ~s** *pl 11* wiederkehrende Handlungen
to **activate sth** *73T* etw aktivieren
to **adapt: ~ sth** *149* etw anpassen, etw bearbeiten; **~ to sth** *128* sich an etw anpassen
to **add sth to sth** *20* etw zu etw hinzufügen
additional commercial guarantee *82* erweiterte Herstellergarantie
address, inside ~ *93* Innenadresse
addressee *88* Addressat/in
adjustable *24* verstellbar
administration, business ~ *42* Betriebswirtschaft
advance, in ~ *83* im Voraus; **payment in ~** *105* Vorauszahlung, Vorkasse
advantage *44* Vorteil
to **advertise** *10* annoncieren, werben, Werbung machen; **~ a job** *138* eine Stelle ausschreiben; **as ~ed** *82* wie beschrieben, wie beworben
advertisement *23* Anzeige, Werbung; **job ~** *137* Stellenanzeige
advice *75* Beratung; *89* Ratschläge, (guter) Rat; **face-to-face ~** *80* persönliche Beratung; **~ of dispatch** *110* Versandanzeige; to **give ~ (to sb)** *57* (jdn) beraten
to **advise: ~ sb** *65* jdn beraten; **~ sb to do sth** *63T* jdm raten, etw zu tun
adviser, sales ~ *7* Kaufmann/-frau im Einzelhandel
to **affect sth** *90* sich auf etw auswirken, etw beeinflussen
to **afford sth** *132T* sich etw leisten
afraid: I'm ~ ... *47T* Leider ...
aftershave *147* Rasierwasser
afterwards *91* danach, anschließend
aged ... *8* im Alter von ... Jahren
agency, federal environment ~ *143* Umweltbundesamt; **recruitment ~** *138* Personalvermittlung, Personalagentur; **travel ~** *26* Reisebüro
agenda *47T* Tagesordnung; **item on the ~** *134* Tagesordnungspunkt
agent *132* Handelnde/r, Akteur/in; **buying ~** *109* Einkäufer/in; **cleaning ~** *10* Reinigungsmittel; **robotic ~** *74* Roboter
to **agree** *15* zustimmen, einer Meinung sein; **~ sth** *105* etw vereinbaren; **~ strongly** *34* nachdrücklich zustimmen; **~ thoroughly** *134T* voll und ganz zustimmen
agreed, unless otherwise ~ *99* sofern nicht anders vereinbart
agreement, collective labour ~ *41* Tarifvertrag; **wage ~** *33T* Tarifvertrag
ahead, straight ~ *27* geradeaus
aid, first ~ *26* Erste Hilfe
aids *pl*, **visual ~** *39* visuelle Hilfsmittel
air conditioning *70T* Klimaanlage, Klimatisierung; **~ unit** *75* Klimaanlage, Klimagerät
aisle *27* Gang; **end of ~** *59* Gondelkopf
alarm, smoke ~ *118* Rauchmelder
alcoholic beverage *11* alkoholisches Getränk
all, at ~ *57* überhaupt; **no ... at ~** *22* überhaupt kein/e ...; **~ day (long)** *12T* den ganzen Tag (lang)
allowance, to **make ~s for sb** *34* auf jdn Rücksicht nehmen
allowed *10* gestattet; to **be ~ to do sth** *31* etw (nicht) tun dürfen
amazed *88* erstaunt, verblüfft
amazing *15* erstaunlich, toll
ambulance service *9* Rettungsdienst
among other things *55T* unter anderem
to **amount to sth** *49* sich auf etw belaufen
to **analyse sth** *53* etw analysieren
to **anger:** to **be quick to ~** *78* jähzornig sein
anger *124* Ärger, Wut
angle, camera ~ *147* Kameraperspektive; **wide-~ lens** *65* Weitwinkelobjektiv
angry *65* verärgert, wütend
animal, not tested on ~s *25* tierversuchsfrei
ankle chain *81* Fußkettchen
announcement *88* Benachrichtigung, Ankündigung
annual, paid ~ leave *47T* bezahlter Jahresurlaub
another *12T* ein/e weitere/r/s
antique furniture *37* antike Möbel, Antiquitäten
any other business (AOB) *134* *(Tagesordnung:)* Verschiedenes
apart from *44* außer, abgesehen von
to **apologize** *120T* sich entschuldigen
apology *122* Entschuldigung
appearance *12* Erscheinungsbild, Auftreten, äußerer Eindruck

appliance, electrical ~ *54* Elektrogerät; **kitchen ~** *10* Küchengerät
applicant *16* Bewerber/in
application *140* Bewerbung
to **apply: ~ to sb/sth for sth** *16* sich bei jdm/etw um/auf/für etw bewerben; **~ for sth** *109T* etw beantragen
to **appreciate sth** *118* für etw Verständnis haben
apprentice *8* Auszubldende/r, Lehrling
apprenticeship *7* Ausbildung, Lehre
approach *113* Herangehensweise, Ansatz
appropriate(ly) *76* angemessen
to **approve sth** *86* etw genehmigen
approximately (approx.) *107* ungefähr, circa
apron *35* Schürze
area, market ~ *81T* Absatzgebiet; **sales ~** *11* Verkaufsfläche, -bereich
arithmetic, mental ~ *139* Kopfrechnen
around the clock *22* rund um die Uhr
to **arrange sth** *56* etw herrichten, etw arrangieren; *97* etw organisieren, etw abwickeln
arrangement *33* Vereinbarung
arrangement *58* Anordnung, Verteilung, Arrangement
arrival *115* Ankunft, Eintreffen; Anreise
to **arrive** *10* eintreffen, ankommen
art *56* Kunst
artificial intelligence (AI) *88* künstliche Intelligenz (KI)
artistic *140* künstlerisch begabt/veranlagt
as *10* da, weil; **as follows** *38* wie folgt; **as regards …** *49* was … betrifft
asap (= as soon as possible) *48* baldmöglichst
Asian *26* asiatisch
to **ask sb to do sth** *17* jdn bitten, etw zu tun
aspect *16* Gesichtspunkt, Aspekt
to **assemble sth** *10* etw montieren, etw zusammenbauen
assembly, self-~ *87* Selbstmontage
assessment *68* Beurteilung, Bewertung, Test
assistance *34* Hilfe, Unterstützung, Beratung
assistant, sales ~ *7* Verkäufer/in; **~ manager** *14* stellvertretende/r Filialleiter/in
associate, sales ~ *AE 42* Verkäufer/in
association *146* Verband
to **assure sb sth** *120T* jdm etw zusichern, jdm etw versichern
at: ~ all *57* überhaupt; **~ least** *67* mindestens
at-will employment *47T* jederzeit kündbare(s) Arbeitsverhältnis(se)
athletics *9* Leichtathletik
atmosphere *15* Atmosphäre
to **attach sth** *106* *(E-Mail:)* etw anhängen
to **attend sth** *8* an etw teilnehmen
attendee *133* Teilnehmer/in
attention *40* Aufmerksamkeit; to **attract sb's ~** *60T* jds Aufmerksamkeit wecken; to **bring sth to sb's ~** *31* jdn auf etw aufmerksam machen; to **catch sb's ~** *16* jds Aufmerksamkeit erregen/fesseln; **~ line** *93* Zeile "zu Händen"
attire *39* Kleidung, Tracht
to **attract: ~ sb** *75* jdn anziehen, jdn anlocken; **~ sb's attention** *60T* jds Aufmerksamkeit wecken
audience *38* Publikum, Zuhörer/innen; **target ~** *16* Zielgruppe
authority, with ~ *70* mit Bestimmtheit, kompetent
automatic(ally) *49* automatisch
available *23* erhältlich, verfügbar
average, on ~ *47T* im Durchschnitt; **above-~ pay rates** *pl 142P* überdurchschnittliche Bezahlung
to **avoid sth** *89* etw vermeiden
to **awaken sth** *88T* etw wecken
aware, to **be ~ of sth** *52* über etw Bescheid wissen; **environmentally ~** *109T* umweltbewusst
axis, x-~ *50* X-Achse; **y-~** *50* Y-Achse

B

back, at the ~ *27* hinten
background *7* Vorgeschichte, Berufserfahrung, (bisherige) Ausbildung; *34* Herkunft, Hintergrund; **~ music** *10* Hintergrundmusik
backwards *140* rückwärts
bag, sleeping ~ *61* Schlafsack
baked goods *pl 53* Backwaren
baker *44* Bäcker/in
bakery *11* Bäckerei
baking ingredients *pl 53* Backzutaten
balance, work-life ~ *34* *Gleichgewicht zwischen Berufs- und Privatleben*
to **ban sth** *44* etw verbieten
to **bandage sth** *36* etw *(Wunde usw.)* verbinden, etw bandagieren
bank, food ~ *9* Tafel; **~ statement** *87* Kontoauszug; **~ transfer** *86* Überweisung
banking *131T* Bankgeschäfte
bankrupt, to **go ~** *51* in Konkurs gehen, bankrott gehen
bar chart *50* Säulendiagramm
barbecue (BBQ) *24* Grill
bare *36* *(Hände, Füße usw.:)* nackt, bloß
barrier, to **break the ~** *51* die (Schall-) Mauer durchbrechen
base, customer ~ *88T* Kundenstamm
basement *26* Untergeschoss, Keller
basic *12* einfach, grundlegend; **~ price** *143* Grundpreis
basically *10* hauptsächlich, im Wesentlichen
the basics *pl 23T* das Wesentliche, die Grundlagen
basis, on a flexible ~ *32* flexibel
basket *23* Korb, Warenkorb; **~ abandonment** *74* abgebrochener Online-Einkauf
bathroom, shared ~ *145* Gemeinschaftsbad
battery *23T* Akku, Batterie; **~ hens** *pl 25* Hennen in Legebatterien
Bavaria *44* Bayern
beach wear *36* Bademode
bean *62* Bohne
to **bear: ~ sth** *97* etw *(Risiko, Kosten usw.)* tragen; **~ the risk** *18T* das Risiko tragen
bear, polar ~ *15* Eisbär
beauty *10* Schönheit
to **become sb/sth** *8* jd/etw werden
bed, bunk ~ *145* Etagenbett, Stockbett; **double ~** *145* Doppelbett; **single ~** *145* Einzelbett; **twin ~s** *pl 145* zwei Einzelbetten; **upholstered ~** *70T* Polsterbett; **~ linen** *146* Bettwäsche
bedding *10* Bettwäsche
beer mug *60T* Bierkrug, Bierseidel
beggar *131T* Bettler/in
to **behave** *58* sich verhalten
behaviour *70* Verhalten; **customer ~** *58* Kundenverhalten
to **belong to sb** *33T* jdm gehören
belt *58* Gürtel
bench *132T* Bank
benefits *pl 40* Zusatzleistungen
best: B~ regards *49* Mit freundlichen Grüßen; **B~ wishes** *48* Mit freundlichen Grüßen, Viele Grüße
best-before date *55* (Mindest-) Haltbarkeitsdatum
best-selling *38* meistverkauft, umsatzstark
beverage, alcoholic ~ *11* alkoholisches Getränk
beyond, and ~ *106* und darüber hinaus
big: ~ box store *10* Fachmarkt, (großflächiges) Kaufhaus; **the ~ picture** *128T* das große Ganze
bike, to **take the ~ out for a spin** *63T* eine Runde mit dem Fahrrad drehen
bill *134P* Rechnung

to **bill sb for sth** *132* jdm etw in Rechnung stellen
bin, dump ~ *56* Wühltisch, Wühlkorb
binding *116* verbindlich, bindend
biscuit *53* Keks
bit, to **do one's ~** *84T* seinen Beitrag leisten
blade, razor ~ *81T* Rasierklinge
blender *75* Mixer
block, brake ~ *125T* Bremsklotz
blouse *37* Bluse
board, full ~ *134* Vollpension; **on ~ a ship** *97* an Bord eines Schiffs
body *93* *(Text usw.:)* Hauptteil, Haupttext; **~ language** *39* Körpersprache
bolt *57* Schraube *(für Mutter)*
bonus *41* Prämie, Zulage; **Christmas ~** *32* Weihnachtsgeld; **holiday ~** *32* Urlaubsgeld; **performance ~** *142P* Leistungsprämie; **~ scheme** *138* Prämiensystem
bookseller *56* Buchhändler/in
bookshop *58* Buchhandlung
to **boom** *81T* *(Wirtschaft usw.:)* boomen, brummen
to **boost sth** *23* etw ankurbeln, etw steigern
boot, car ~ *131T* Kofferraum
booth *7* (Messe-)Stand
boots *pl*, **trekking ~** *23T* Wanderstiefel
bored, to **be ~** *12T* sich langweilen
boring *12* langweilig
to **borrow sth** *88* sich etw (aus)leihen
boss *12T* Chef/in
both … and *57* sowohl … als auch
to **bother: I can't be ~ed.** *72* Ich habe keine Lust. Ist mir zu blöd.
bottle return machine *20* Leergutautomat
bottled *53* in Flaschen abgefüllt
bracelet *81* Armband
to **brainstorm** *12* (Ideen) sammeln
to **brake** *125T* bremsen
brake *125* Bremse; **~ block** *125T* Bremsklotz
branch *10* Filiale
brand *10* Marke; **~ new** *87* nagelneu, brandneu
to **break: ~ sth** *124* etw kaputtmachen; **~ down** *116* kapputgehen; **~ the barrier** *51* die (Schall-)Mauer durchbrechen; to **make or ~ sth** *23T* über das Gelingen oder Scheitern von etw entscheiden
break, lunch ~ *125* Mittagspause
breakable *139* zerbrechlich
breaker, flow ~ *59* Stopper *(Aufsteller, Tische usw.)*
bridal: ~ gown *89* Brautkleid; **~ wear** *37* Brautmoden
bride *89* Braut
brief *28* knapp, kurz
bright *58* hell
to **bring sth to sb's attention** *31* jdn auf etw aufmerksam machen
brochure *7* Prospekt, Broschüre
broken *119* kaputt
to **browse** *22* sich *(im Laden)* umsehen, *(im Laden)* stöbern
bruised *57* *(Obst:)* angestoßen, mit Druckstellen
Brussels sprouts *pl* *24* Rosenkohl
to **build trust** *69* Vertrauen aufbauen
building: ~ materials *pl* *11* Baumaterial; **~ site** *66* Baustelle
built-in *67T* eingebaut
bubble, speech ~ *46* Sprechblase
buddy, work ~ *31* *erfahrene/r Kollege/-in, der/die einen gleichrangigen Neuzugang einarbeitet*
bulb, light ~ *23T* Glühlampe, Leuchtmittel
bulky *11* sperrig; *131T* unhandlich, dick
bullet point *16* Stichpunkt
bunk bed *145* Etagenbett, Stockbett
bus link *145* Busverbindung, Busanbindung
business, family ~ *81T* Familienbetrieb; **any other ~ (AOB)** *134* *(Tagesordnung:)* Verschiedenes; **~ administration** *42* Betriebswirtschaft; **~ correspondence** *91* Geschäftskorrespondenz; **~ course** *42* Wirtschaftsstudium; **~ customer** *91* Geschäftskunde/-kundin; **lack of ~** *132T* mangelndes Geschäftsaufkommen; **~ letter** *92* Geschäftsbrief; **~ organization** *19* Unternehmensform; **~ processes** *pl* *141* Geschäftsabläufe; **~ studies** *pl* *141* Betriebswirtschaft; **volume of ~** *103* Geschäftsvolumen; to **drive sb out of ~** *81T* jdn in den Bankrott treiben; to **run a ~** *18T* ein Unternehmen führen
busy *10* belebt, betriebsam, voll; *22* hektisch, geschäftig
butcher *56* Metzger/in, Fleischer/in
button *67T* Knopf
to **button sth up** *35* etw zuknöpfen
buy, impulse ~ *59* Impulskauf
buyer *82* Käufer/in
buying agent *109* Einkäufer/in
by the way *63T* übrigens

C

café *10* Café
to **calculate sth** *49* etw berechnen
to **call by** *132T* vorbeikommen
called, to **be ~** *8* heißen
to **calm: ~ down** *124* sich beruhigen; **~ sb down** *124* jdn beruhigen
calories *pl* *55* Kalorien
camera, overhead ~ *132T* Überkopfkamera; **~ angle** *147* Kameraperspektive; **~ feed** *132T* Kamerabilder, Livestream
can *40* Problem
to **cancel sth** *72* etw kündigen; *83* etw *(Bestellung usw.)* widerrufen, etw stornieren
cancellation *145* Stornierung, Absage; **~ right** *82* Widerrufsrecht, Rücktrittsrecht
candidate *139* Bewerber/in, Kandidat/in
canned goods *pl* *53* Konserven(dosen)
cap *35* Mütze, Kappe
cape, cycling ~ *63T* Fahrradponcho
capital letter *93* Großbuchstabe
car, company ~ *32* Firmenwagen; **~ boot** *131T* Kofferraum; **~ dealer** *46* Autohändler/in, Autohaus; **~ park** *10* Parkplatz, Parkhaus, Tiefgarage
carbohydrate *55* Kohlenhydrate
carbon dioxide (CO_2) *84T* Kohlendioxid
carbon: ~ emissions *pl* *143* CO_2-Emissionen; **~ footprint** *25* CO_2-Fußabdruck
card, debit ~ *86* Bankkarte, Geldkarte; **index ~** *38* Karteikarte; **loyalty ~** *67T* Kundenkarte, Bonuskarte; **membership ~** *132T* Mitgliedskarte; **prompt ~** *38* Moderationskarte
care, personal ~ *86* Körperpflege; **nursing ~ insurance** *32* Pflegeversicherung; **~ home** *9* Pflegeheim
career *7* Laufbahn, Beruf, Karriere; **~ goal** *142* Berufsziel; **~ ladder** *42* Karriereleiter; **~ path** *41* Berufsweg
careful(ly) *58* sorgfältig
caring *69* fürsorglich, sozial
carpet *81* Teppichboden
carriage *99* Transport, Beförderung; **main ~** *91* Hauptlauf, Haupttransport; **post-~** *97* Nachlauf, Nachlauftransport; **pre-~** *97* Vorlauf, Vorlauftransport; **contract of ~** *97* Frachtvertrag, Beförderungsvertrag; **~ forward** *120T* unfrei, auf Kosten des Empfängers
carrier *97* Frachtführer
carrot *55* Karotte, Möhre
carton, delivery ~ *10* Versandkarton, Lieferkarton

case *31* Fall; **glass ~** *56* Vitrine; **whatever the ~ may be** *118* wie auch immer, wie dem auch sei

cash *73T* Bargeld; **~ desk** *12T* Kasse; **~ machine** *20* Geldautomat; **~ register** *58* Registrierkasse, Kasse; **~ with order (CWO)** *103* Zahlung/Kasse bei Auftragserteilung; to **pay ~** *86T* bar zahlen

cashier *11* Kassierer/in

cashless *130* bargeldlos

catalogue *80* Katalog

to **catch: ~ a train** *22* einen Zug bekommen/erwischen; **~ sb's attention** *16* jds Aufmerksamkeit erregen/fesseln

to **categorize sth** *88* etw einstufen, etw einteilen

category *23T* Kategorie, Warengruppe; **sub-~** *23T* Unterkategorie, Untergruppe

to **cater for sb** *11* sich an jdn *(Kunden usw.)* wenden, sich auf jds Bedürfnisse ausrichten

catering, self-~ *146* Selbstversorgung

cause, (good) ~ *72* (gute) Sache

to **cause sth** *84T* etw verursachen

to **celebrate** *47T* feiern

celebrity *15* Prominente/r

cent, per ~ *33T* Prozent

central station *10* Hauptbahnhof

cereal *61* Müsli, Getreideflocken

certificate, school-leaving ~ *138* Schulabschluss

certification mark *55* Gütesiegel, Prüfzeichen

chain *10* Kette; **ankle ~** *81* Fußkettchen; **retail ~** *41* Einzelhandelskette; **supply ~** *25* Lieferkette, Versorgungskette; **~ store** *10* Filiale *(einer Handelskette)*

challenge *88T* (schwierige) Aufgabe, Herausforderung

to **challenge sb/sth** *131T* jdn/etw herausfordern

challenging *12* schwierig, (heraus-)fordernd

chamber of commerce *42* Handelskammer

champagne *59* Sekt, Champagner

to **change** *12T* sich verändern; **~ sth** *18* etw (ver)ändern

change, to **make ~s to sth** *46* Änderungen an etw vornehmen, etw verändern

changing room *57* Umkleidekabine

channel, distribution ~ *21* Vertriebskanal, Vertriebsweg; **sales ~** *81* Vertriebskanal, Vertriebsweg

chappy *24* Kerlchen

character *140* Charakter

characteristic *82* Merkmal, Eigenschaft

charcoal grill *24* Holzkohlengrill

charge *75* Gebühr; **extra ~** *82* Aufpreis, Zusatzgebühr; **free of ~** *84* gebührenfrei, kostenlos; to **be in ~ of sth** *19* für etw zuständig sein, für etw verantwortlich sein

to **charge: ~ sth** *67* etw laden, etw aufladen; **~ sb sth** *83* etw *(Preis usw.)* von jdm verlangen, jdm etw berechnen

charger *67* Ladegerät

charging: ~ point *132T* Ladesäule; **~ station** *20* Ladesäule, E-Tankstelle

charity *72* Wohltätigkeit

charity work *9* ehrenamtliche Arbeit

charmeuse *89* Charmeuse

chart, bar ~ *50* Säulendiagramm; **organization ~** *18* Organigramm; **pie ~** *50* Tortendiagramm

to **chat** *132T* sich unterhalten, miteinander plaudern

to **check: ~ sth (for sth)** *25* etw (auf etw) überprüfen; **~ sth out** *55T* sich etw (genauer) ansehen; **~ out** *134* *(Hotel etc.:)* auschecken

check, to **run a ~ on sb** *109T* jdn überprüfen, jdn durchleuchten

checkout *27* Kasse; **self-~** *53* Selbstbedienungskasse

cheeky *24* frech

cheerful *142P* heiter, gut gelaunt

chess *9* Schach

chest of drawers *54* Kommode

Chief Executive Officer (CEO) *128T* Vorstandsvorsitzende/r

chiffon *89* Chiffon

child, only ~ *8* Einzelkind; **supervised ~ren's play area** *10* betreuter Spielbereich für Kinder; **~ labour** *25* Kinderarbeit

chlorine *86T* Chlor

choice *12* Entscheidung, Wahl

to **choose: ~ sth** *12* etw wählen, sich etw aussuchen; **~ to do sth** *12* sich entscheiden, etw zu tun

chop, pork ~ *54* Schweinekotelett

Christmas: ~ bonus *32* Weihnachtsgeld; **~ Day** *44* Erster Weihnachtstag; **~ Eve** *44* Heiligabend

church *9* Kirche; **~ tax** *32* Kirchensteuer

circumstances *pl* *91* Umstände

citizen *50* (Staats-)Bürger/in

city centre *10* Innenstadt, Stadtzentrum

clarity *38* Klarheit

to **classify sth** *109T* etw einstufen, etw klassifizieren

vacuum ~ *75* Staubsauger

cleaning agent *10* Reinigungsmittel

clearance, export ~ *97* Ausfuhrabfertigung; **import ~** *91* Einfuhrabfertigung; **~ sale** *24* Ausverkauf

cleared for export *99* zur Ausfuhr freigemacht, verzollt

to **clock in/out** *30* ein-/ausstempeln

clock, around the ~ *22* rund um die Uhr

close, complimentary ~ *93* *(Brief usw.:)* Schlussformel

close: ~ to *21* nahe bei, in der Nähe von; **on ~er examination** *91* bei näherem Hinsehen; to **take a ~er look at sth** *55T* sich etw genauer ansehen

closing time *69* Ladenschluss, Feierabend

closure *79* Schließung

cloth *37* Tuch

clothes hanger *30* Kleiderbügel

clothing *23* Kleidung; **made-to-measure ~** *86* Maßkonfektion

cloud *12* Wolke

coach *143* Reisebus

code, dress ~ *35* Kleiderordnung

coffee: ~ maker *145* Kaffeemaschine; **~ table** *86T* Couchtisch

collar *87* Kragen; **~ size** *67T* Kragenweite

colleague *20* Kollege/-in

to **collect: ~ sb/sth** *20* jdn/etw abholen; **~ sth** *29* etw sammeln; **~ data** *29* Daten erheben; **~ one's thoughts** *147* seine Gedanken ordnen, sich sammeln

collection *123T* Abholung

collective labour agreement *41* Tarifvertrag

college, community ~ *AE* *42* *Art Fachhochschule in den USA;* **vocational training ~** *8* Berufsschule

Cologne *14T* Köln

colour-coded *68* farbkodiert

coloured hair *37* gefärbte Haare

column *88T* *(Text:)* Spalte

comb *54* Kamm

to **combine sth** *64* etw kombinieren

to **come: ~ in** *60T* ins Spiel kommen; **~ in on sth** *134T* etw zu etw sagen

comfort *144* Komfort

comfortable *58* bequem

command (of sth) *141* Beherrschung (von etw)

commerce, chamber of ~ *42* Handelskammer

commercial, additional ~ guarantee *82* erweiterte Herstellergarantie; **~ English**

141 Handelsenglisch, Wirtschaftsenglisch
commission 81T Provision, Kommission; **sales ~** 12 Verkaufsprovision
commitment (to sth) 25 Engagement (für etw), Verpflichtung (zu etw)
committed, to **be ~ to sth** 25 sich einer Sache verschrieben haben
common 19 üblich, verbreitet, häufig
communicator, to **be a good ~** 139 (sehr) kommunikativ sein
community 12 Gemeinde, Gemeinschaft; **~ college** *AE* 42 *Art Fachhochschule in den USA*
company 7 Unternehmen, Firma; **construction ~** 66 Bauunternehmen; **parent ~** 29 Muttergesellschaft, Dachgesellschaft; **private limited ~ (Ltd)** 18T Gesellschaft mit beschränkter Haftung (GmbH); **public limited ~ (plc)** 19 Aktiengesellschaft (AG); **~ car** 32 Firmenwagen; **~ pension scheme** 138 betriebliche Altersvorsorge
to **compare sth** 12 etw vergleichen
comparison 109 Vergleich
compartment 132 (Ablage-)Fach
compensation 116 Entschädigung, Schadenersatz
competition 38 Konkurrenz, Wettbewerb
competitive 113T konkurrenzfähig, *(Preis usw.:)* günstig, attraktiv
to **complain (to sb)** 65 sich (bei jdm) beschweren
complaint 116 Beschwerde, Reklamation; **letter of ~** 120 (formelle/schriftliche) Beschwerde
complicated 67T kompliziert
complimentary close 93 *(Brief usw.:)* Schlussformel
comprehensive (school) 9 Gesamtschule
compromise 114 Kompromiss
concerning 34 betreffend, bezüglich
concerns *pl* 84 Bedenken
concession 65 Nachlass
to **conclude:** to **~** 134T abschließend
conclusion 38 Schluss, Fazit
concrete 67 Beton
condiment 53 Würzmittel
condition 110 Zustand; **terms and ~s** *pl* 85 Allgemeine Geschäftsbedingungen; **working ~s** *pl* 25 Arbeitsbedingungen
to **conduct sth** 148 etw durchführen
confectionery 20 Süßwaren
conference 133 Tagung, Konferenz
confident 142P selbstsicher, selbstbewusst
confidential, private and ~ 93 streng vertraulich
to **confirm sth** 88 etw bestätigen
confirmation 83 Bestätigung; **~ of order** 110 Auftragsbestätigung
conflict 69 Streit, Streitigkeiten, Konflikt(e)
confusing 46 verwirrend
confusion 93 Verwirrung
connectivity 67T Anschluss, Anschlüsse
conscientiousness 68 Gewissenhaftigkeit
consecutive 144 aufeinanderfolgend
consequence 119 Folge, Konsequenz
to **consider sth** 12 über etw nachdenken; 33 etw beachten, etw berücksichtigen
consideration 25 Überlegung, Prüfung; to **take sth into ~** 34 etw berücksichtigen, etw beachten
consignment 118 Sendung
construction company 66 Bauunternehmen
to **consult sb** 47 jdn zu Rate ziehen, jdn um Rat fragen
consultancy (firm) 17 Unternehmensberatung
consultant 23 Berater/in
consultation 88T Beratung
to **consume sth** 55T etw verbrauchen
consumer 22 Verbraucher/in; **~ electronics** *pl* 20 Unterhaltungselektronik; **~ preferences** *pl* 80 Verbrauchergewohnheiten; **~ rights** *pl* 115 Verbraucherrechte
contact 48 Ansprechpartner/in; **eye ~** 39 Blickkontakt; **~ details** *pl* 16 Kontaktdaten
to **contact sb** 12T sich mit jdm in Verbindung setzen, zu jdm Kontakt aufnehmen
contactless payment 20 kontaktloses Bezahlen
to **contain sth** 28 etw enthalten
content 36 Inhalt
contract: ~ of carriage 97 Frachtvertrag, Beförderungsvertrag; **~ of employment** 33 Arbeitsvertrag; **sales ~** 82 Kaufvertrag
to **contrast sth with sth** 52 etw einander gegenüberstellen, etw miteinander vergleichen
contribution 32 Beitrag; to **make a ~** 148T einen Beitrag leisten
to **control sth** 129 etw steuern
control, quality ~ 122 Qualitätskontrolle; **remote ~** 67T Fernbedienung; to **be in ~** 68 das Sagen haben
convenience 131T Komfort, Nutzerfreundlichkeit; **~ store** 22 Minimarkt, Spätkauf; **at sb's earliest ~** 142 sobald es jdm möglich ist
convenient 97 günstig gelegen
conventional 80 herkömmlich, konventionell
to **convince sb (of sth)** 78 jdn (von etw) überzeugen
cooker, electric ~ 119 Elektroherd
cooperation 68 Zusammenarbeit, Kooperation
cooperative 19 Genossenschaft
copy 83 Exemplar
corner 23T Ecke
correctness 38 Richtigkeit
to **correspond with sb** 43 mit jdm korrespondieren
correspondence, business ~ 91 Geschäftskorrespondenz
cosmetics *pl* 10 Kosmetika
costs, to **cut ~** 10 Kosten senken
costume, swimming ~ 86T Badeanzug
cosy 46 behaglich, gemütlich
cotton 69 Baumwolle
council, works ~ *BE* 29 Betriebsrat
to **countersign sth** 85 etw gegenzeichnen
country of destination 93 Bestimmungsland
countryside, in the ~ 9 auf dem Land
course, business ~ 42 Wirtschaftsstudium; **distance-learning ~** 42 Fernstudium; **higher education ~** 42 Hochschulstudium; **training ~** 7 Ausbildung(sgang); 34 Schulung, Lehrgang
court, food ~ 22 Gastronomiebereich
cover letter 140 Anschreiben, Begleitschreiben
to **cover sth** 23T etw abdecken, etw erfassen; 28 etw *(Thema usw.)* behandeln, sich mit etw befassen; 49 etw decken, etw *(Kosten usw.)* übernehmen; 88T etw bedecken
covered shoes *pl* 36 geschlossene Schuhe
covering letter 137 Anschreiben, Begleitschreiben
to **crash** 95 abstürzen
crate 55 (Getränke-)Kiste
cream, shaving ~ 81T Rasiercreme
to **create sth** 7 etw erstellen; 15 etw schaffen
creative 12 kreativ
credit: ~ note 85 Gutschrift; **~ period** 105 Zahlungsfrist; **~ rating** 109T Bonitätseinstufung

creditworthiness *109T* Bonität, Kreditwürdigkeit
crisps *BE* *53* Chips
to **criticize sb/sth** *68* jdn/etw kritisieren
crockery *10* Geschirr
cross-sample *54* Querschnitt, Querschnittsprobe
to **cross-sell sth** *63* Querverkäufe zu etw machen
cross-selling *62* Querverkauf, Ergänzungsverkäufe, Cross-Selling
crypto currency *131T* Kryptowährung
cultural *39* kulturell, Kultur-
culture *15* Kultur
curling tongs *pl* *75* Lockenstab
currency, crypto ~ *131T* Kryptowährung; ~ **sign** *104* Währungssymbol
current *135* aktuell
currently *47T* aktuell, gerade
custody *99* Obhut, Gewahrsam
customer *10* Kunde/Kundin; **business** ~ *91* Geschäftskunde/-kundin; **long-standing** ~ *94* langjährige/r Kunde/Kundin; **regular** ~ *65* Stammkunde/-kundin; **walk-in ~s** *pl* *81T* Laufkundschaft; ~ **base** *88T* Kundenstamm; ~ **behaviour** *58* Kundenverhalten; ~ **flow** *58* Kundenlauf; ~ **journey** *74* Kontakthistorie, Customer Journey; ~ **loyalty** *72* Kundentreue, Kundenbindung; ~ **services** *pl* *53* Kundendienst; ~ **traffic** *59* Kundenstrom, -verkehr, -aufkommen; to **retain ~s** *135* Kunden binden
customs duty *97* Zoll, Zollgebühren
to **cut:** ~ **down on sth** *129* etw reduzieren; ~ **out** *120T* sich ausschalten, ausgehen; ~ **costs** *10* Kosten senken; **to ~ a long story short** *132T* um etw kurz zu machen; lange Rede, kurzer Sinn
cut, low ~ *37* tief ausgeschnitten
cutlery *10* Besteck, Essbesteck
CV (curriculum vitae) *BE* *137* Lebenslauf
cycling cape *63T* Fahrradponcho
cyclist *74* Radfahrer/in

D

daily routine *29* Tagesablauf, Alltagsroutine
dairy products *pl* *11* Milchprodukte
to **damage sth** *119* etw beschädigen
dangerous *55T* gefährlich
Danish *120* dänisch
dark store *22* Dark Store *(Distributionszentrum für den Onlinehandel)*
data *pl* *29* Daten; to **collect** ~ *29* Daten erheben; to **recover** ~ *117* Daten wiederherstellen, Daten retten
date, best-before ~ *55* (Mindest-) Haltbarkeitsdatum
dated … *118* (mit Datum) vom …
day, the ~ before yesterday *86T* vorgestern; **Christmas D~** *44* Erster Weihnachtstag; **all ~ (long)** *12T* den ganzen Tag (lang); **sb's ~s are numbered** *128T* jds Tage sind gezählt; ~ **release** *8* tagweise Freistellung, ausbildungsbegleitender Unterricht; **~'s takings** *pl* *30* Tageseinnahmen
dead *58* tot; ~ **end** *59* Sackgasse
deadline *73T* Frist
deal *23* Angebot; **special** ~ *23* (Sonder-)Angebot; **It's a ~!** *63T* Abgemacht!
to **deal:** ~ **with sb** *65* mit jdm umgehen, sich um jdn kümmern; ~ **with sth** *39* sich mit etw befassen, sich um etw kümmern; ~ **with a matter** *118* eine Angelegenheit regeln, sich um eine Angelegenheit kümmern
dealer, car ~ *46* Autohändler/in, Autohaus
death *132T* Sterbefall
debit card *86* Bankkarte, Geldkarte
decent *25* anständig, angemessen
decision, to **make a** ~ *18T* eine Entscheidung fällen, einen Beschluss fassen
decorations *pl*, **home** ~ *10* Wohnaccessoires, Einrichtungsgegenstände
decorative *56* dekorativ
to **decrease** *79* abnehmen, zurückgehen
deduction, to **make a** ~ *82* einen Abzug geltend machen
deductions *pl* *32* Abzüge
to **de-escalate** *125* deeskalieren
defect, technical ~ *116* technischer Mangel; to **rectify a** ~ *82* einen Mangel beseitigen
defective *116* fehlerhaft, defekt
to **define sth** *97* etw bestimmen, etw festlegen
to **delete sth** *73* etw löschen
delicatessen *53* Feinkost(theke)
delighted, to **be** ~ *47T* sich (sehr) freuen, erfreut sein
delivery *12T* Lieferung; **registered/recorded** ~ *93* Einschreiben; **same-day** ~ *79* Lieferung/Zustellung am selben Tag; ~ **carton** *10* Versandkarton, Lieferkarton; ~ **period** *100T* Lieferfrist, Lieferzeit; **terms** *pl* **of** ~ *83* Lieferbedingungen; to **take ~ of sth** *110* etw in Empfang nehmen
demand, to **satisfy** ~ *91* die Nachfrage befriedigen
to **demand sth** *25* etw fordern
demographics *74* Altersstruktur
to **demonstrate sth** *30* etw *(Produkt usw.)* vorführen
demonstration, product ~ *128T* Produktvorführung
denim *37* Jeansstoff, Denim
department *23T* Abteilung; **payroll** ~ *48* Lohnbuchhaltung; **purchasing** ~ *92* Einkauf(sabteilung); **head of** ~ *42* Abteilungsleiter/in
departure *146* Abreise
to **depend on sth** *118* von etw abhängen
deposit *55* Pfand; *145* Anzahlung
depressed *108* niedergeschlagen, deprimiert
depth *67* Tiefe; **~-sensor** *132* Tiefensensor
to **describe sth** *10* etw beschreiben
design *16* Gestaltung
to **design sth** *58* etw gestalten, etw entwerfen
designed, to **be ~ for sb/sth** *59* für jdn/etw gedacht sein
desire *142P* Wunsch, Verlangen
desk *12T* Schreibtisch; **cash** ~ *12T* Kasse; **information** ~ *26* Informationsschalter, Auskunft
desperate, to **be ~ to do sth** *132T* etw unbedingt tun wollen; verzweifelt versuchen, etw zu tun
destination *97* Bestimmungsort, Ziel; **country of** ~ *93* Bestimmungsland; ~ **goods** *pl* *58* Waren/Güter des täglichen Bedarfs
to **detail sth** *103* etw genau angeben, etw präzisieren
detail *23T* Einzelheit, Detail
details *pl* *18* Angaben, Daten; **contact** ~ *16* Kontaktdaten
to **detect sth** *131T* etw erkennen
detective story *80* Krimi
to **develop** *148T* (sich) entwickeln
development *80* Entwicklung
to **devise sth** *89* etw konzipieren, etw entwickeln
diagram *25* Schema, Schaubild, Diagramm
to **dictate sth** *93* etw diktieren
dietary requirements *pl* *133* Ernährungsbedürfnisse, -anforderungen

difference *12* Unterschied; to **make a ~** *81T* etw bewirken, etw ausmachen; to **make all the ~** *63T* entscheidend sein, enorm viel ausmachen
digital signage *132T* digitale Außenwerbung
digitization *134T* Digitalisierung
dimensions *pl* *85* Abmessungen
diploma, high school ~ *AE* *42* *US-Schulabschluss*
to **direct sb somewhere** *73T* jdn irgendwohin leiten
directions *pl*, to **give ~** *26* den Weg beschreiben
director, export sales ~ *120* Exportleiter/in; **marketing ~** *23T* Marketingleiter/in; **purchasing ~** *93* Einkaufsleiter/in; **sales ~** *15* Vertriebsleiter/in
disability *47T* Behinderung
disabled *132T* behindert
disadvantage *44* Nachteil
to **disagree** *15* widersprechen, streiten; **~ strongly** *34* überhaupt nicht zustimmen
to **disappear** *131T* verschwinden
discoloured *118* verfärbt
discount *12* Rabatt, Nachlass; **employee ~** *32* Mitarbeiterrabatt; **quantity ~** *106* Mengenrabatt; **trade ~** *107* Händlerrabatt
discounted *28* preisreduziert
to **discover sth** *53* etw entdecken, etw herausfinden
to **discuss sth** *12* etw besprechen, etw diskutieren
dish, satellite ~ *75* Satellitenschüssel
dishwasher *11* Geschirrspüler
disinfectant *24* Desinfektionsmittel
dislikes *pl* *9* Abneigungen
to **dismantle sth** *87* etw auseinanderbauen, etw demontieren
dismissal, reason for ~ *41* Kündigungsgrund
dispatch, advice of ~ *110* Versandanzeige
display *59* Aufsteller, Display; *60T* Auslage, Präsentation, Dekoration; *67* Bildschirm; **product ~** *58* Produktpräsentation; **~ stand** *12T* Präsentationsständer, Aufsteller, Infoständer; **~ table** *57* Präsentationstisch, Ausstellungstisch; to **be on ~** *58* *(Ware:)* ausliegen, zu sehen sein
to **display sth** *55T* etw anzeigen, etw ausweisen; *56* etw *(Waren usw.)* präsentieren, etw auslegen
dissatisfied *58* unzufrieden
distance *145* Entfernung; **~ sales** *pl* *82* Fernverkäufe, Fernabsatz; **~ selling** *82* Fernverkauf, Fernabsatz; **~-learning course** *42* Fernstudium; **~ channel** *21* Vertriebskanal, Vertriebsweg; **~ network** *17* Vertriebsnetz; **~ outlet** *28* Vertriebsstelle, Vertriebsstätte
distant, in the not-too-~ future *131T* in nicht allzu ferner Zukunft
distributor *25* Vertriebshändler/in, Zwischenhändler/in
district manager *15* Bezirksleiter/in
to **disturb** *147* stören
to **divide sth** *12T* etw aufteilen
division *134T* Sparte, Abteilung
DIY *9* Heimwerken; **~ store** *11* Heimwerkermarkt, Baumarkt
to **do: ~ one's bit** *84T* seinen Beitrag leisten; **~ sth about sth** *124* etw in einer Sache unternehmen/tun; **~ well** *18T* *(Geschäft usw.:)* gut laufen
documentation *97* Unterlagen, Papiere, Dokumente
dog, guide ~ *77* Blindenhund
domestic problems *pl* *34* Probleme zu Hause
dominance *68* Dominanz
to **donate sth to sb** *72* jdm etw spenden
dormitory *146* Schlafsaal, Mehrbettzimmer
dossier *41* Akte, Bericht, Dossier
dot *100T* Punkt
to **double** *103* sich verdoppeln
double bed *145* Doppelbett
to **double-check sth** *123T* etw nochmal überprüfen
to **download sth** *66* etw herunterladen
to **draft sth** *107* etw entwerfen, etw formulieren
to **draw** *43* zeichnen; **~ sth up** *37* etw erstellen, etw verfassen; to **be ~n to sth** *74* von etw angezogen werden
drawer, chest of ~s *54* Kommode
to **dream: I wouldn't ~ of …** *81* Ich würde nicht im Traum daran denken, …
to **dress** *35* sich kleiden
dress, fit-and-flare ~ *89* Godet-Kleid; **sheath ~** *89* Etuikleid; **~ code** *35* Kleiderordnung; **~ dummy** *30* Schaufensterpuppe
dresser, window ~ *12T* Schaufensterdekorateur/in
dressing, window ~ *12T* Schaufensterdekoration
drill, electric ~ *71* Bohrmaschine
drive, hard ~ *117* Festplatte
to **drive sb out of business** *81T* jdn in den Bankrott treiben
driving licence *140* Führerschein
drone *131T* Drohne
drop-down menu *23* Auswahlmenü, Ausklappmenü
drug *11* Arzneimittel
drugstore *11* Drogerie
drums *pl* *9* Schlagzeug
dry goods *pl* *132* Trockenware(n)
due to *91* aufgrund von, wegen
dummy, dress ~ *30* Schaufensterpuppe
dump bin *56* Wühltisch, Wühlkorb
during *34* während
duty *40* Aufgabe, Pflicht; **customs ~** *97* Zoll, Zollgebühren; **import ~ies** *pl* *99* Einfuhrabgaben, Einfuhrzölle; **heavy-~** *63T* robust

E

e.g. *8* z.B.
early: ~ reply *95* baldige Antwort; **~ shift** *12T* Frühschicht; **at sb's ~iest convenience** *142* sobald es jdm möglich ist
to **earn sth** *12T* etw verdienen
earring *15* Ohrring
Easter *44* Ostern
easy on the eye *58* wohltuend für die Augen
to **eat out** *140* essen gehen
economic(ally) *144* kostengünstig, wirtschaftlich
edge *10* Rand
to **edit sth** *129* etw *(Bild usw.)* bearbeiten
educated, to **make an ~ guess** *40* eine fundierte Vermutung anstellen
education *9* Schulbildung; **higher ~ course** *42* Hochschulstudium; **higher ~ entrance qualification** *141* Hochschulreife
educational leave *34* Bildungsurlaub
effect, with immediate ~ *103* ab sofort, mit sofortiger Wirkung
effective(ly) *91* effektiv
efficiency, energy ~ *55* Engergieeffizienz
efficient *50* effizient
Egypt *50* Ägypten
either: ~ … or *11* entweder … oder; **not … ~** *47T* ebenfalls nicht, auch nicht
electric: ~ cooker *119* Elektroherd; **~ drill** *71* Bohrmaschine; **~ kettle** *75* Wasserkocher; **~ razor** *81T* (elektrischer) Rasierapparat; **~ vehicle** *132T* Elektrofahrzeug
electrical *23T* *(Warengruppe:)* Elektro; **~ appliance** *54* Elektrogerät; **~ retailer** *72* Elektrofachmarkt; **~ shop** *62* Elektrogeschäft

electricity *55T* Strom
electronics *pl* **, consumer ~** *20* Unterhaltungselektronik
element, heating ~ *119* Heizspirale
to **eliminate sth** *59* etw beseitigen, etw eliminieren
elsewhere *65* woandershin
to **email sth** *88* etw mailen
emergency, technical ~ service *9* Technisches Hilfswerk
emissions *pl*, **carbon ~** *143* CO_2-Emissionen
to **employ sb** *17* jdn beschäftigen, jdn engagieren; *148* jdn einstellen
employee *16* Angestellte/r, Mitarbeiter/in; **~ discount** *32* Mitarbeiterrabatt
employer *7* Arbeitgeber/in
employment, at-will ~ *47T* jederzeit kündbare(s) Arbeitsverhältnis(se); **contract of ~** *33* Arbeitsvertrag
empty *12T* leer
to **enable sb to do sth** *129* jdn in die Lage versetzen, etw zu tun; jdn befähigen, etw zu tun
to **enclose sth** *93* *(Brief:)* etw beifügen
enclosure *93* *(Brief:)* Anlage
to **encourage sb to do sth** *16* jdn ermuntern, etw zu tun
end, dead ~ *59* Sackgasse; **~ of aisle** *59* Gondelkopf
to **end up somewhere** *88T* irgendwo landen
energy, green ~ *25* Ökostrom; **~ efficiency** *55* Engergieeffizienz; **~ value** *55T* Brennwert
engaging *141* *(Persönlichkeit:)* einnehmend, gewinnend
engine, search ~ *74* Suchmaschine
to **enjoy: ~ doing sth** *9* etw gern tun; **~ sth** *12T* etw genießen; **sb ~s sth** *12T* jdm gefällt etw, jdm macht etw Spaß
enquiry *91* (geschäftliche) Anfrage
to **enrol in sth** *42* sich für etw anmelden
en-suite room *133* Zimmer mit eigenem Bad und WC
to **enter: ~ sth** *58* etw betreten; **~ a (new) market** *47* in einen (neuen) Markt Fuß fassen, in einen (neuen) Markt eindringen
to **entertain sb** *73T* jdn unterhalten
entertainment *15* Unterhaltung
enthusiastic *142P* begeisterungsfähig
entire *58* gesamt, ganz
entitled, to **be ~ to sth** *47T* ein Recht auf etw haben, einen Anspruch auf etw haben
entitlement, holiday ~ *41* Urlaubsanspruch
entrance *11* Eingang; **higher education ~ qualification** *141* Hochschulreife
entry *86* Eintrag; *132* Zugang; **~-level salary** *138* Einstiegsgehalt; **~-level staff** *142P* Berufseinsteiger/innen
envelope *93* Briefumschlag
environment *25* Umwelt; *141* Umfeld; **federal ~ agency** *143* Umweltbundesamt
environmental *25* Umwelt-, die Umwelt betreffend
environmentally aware *109T* umweltbewusst
equal opportunities *pl* *34* Chancengleichheit
equality *29* Gleichberechtigung, Gleichstellung
equipment *22* Ausrüstung, Ausstattung, Geräte
equivalent *11* Entsprechung, Übersetzung
escalator *26* Rolltreppe
essential *44* unentbehrlich, unverzichtbar
estimate *75* Kostenvoranschlag
ethical *17* ethisch (handelnd)
ethics *pl* *17* Ethik, Moral
ethnic *34* ethnisch
ethnicity *47T* ethnische Zugehörigkeit
EU law *82* EU-Recht
to **evaluate sth** *71* etw auswerten, etw beurteilen
eve, Christmas E~ *44* Heiligabend; **New Year's E~** *59* Silvester
even *33T* sogar
event *73T* Veranstaltung
ever *31* je, jemals
examination, on closer ~ *91* bei näherem Hinsehen
to **examine sth** *24* etw untersuchen
excellent *106* hervorragend, ausgezeichnet
exception *44* Ausnahme
excessive *37* übermäßig, zu viel
exchange *75* Umtausch
to **exchange: ~ sth** *43* etw austauschen; **~ sth (for sth)** *77P* etw (gegen etw) umtauschen
exciting *138* spannend, interessant
to **exclude: sth ~s sth** *146* etw ist in etw nicht inbegriffen
excluded *116* ausgeschlossen, nicht inbegriffen
exclusive *37* exklusiv
to **execute an order** *118* einen Auftrag / eine Bestellung ausführen
to **exist** *131* existieren
existing *61* vorhanden, bestehend
exit *53* Ausgang
to **expand** *128T* wachsen, expandieren; **~ into a (new) market** *41* sich einen (neuen) Markt erschließen, in einen (neuen) Markt expandieren; **~ sth** *37* etw erweitern
to **expect sth of sb** *34* etw von jdm erwarten
expectation *34* Erwartung; to **manage ~s** *116* Erwartungen steuern, mit Erwartungen umgehen
expected, sb is ~ to do sth *35* von jdm wird erwartet, etw zu tun
expense, at sb's own ~ *99* auf eigene Kosten
expenses *pl* *82* (entstandene) Kosten, Unkosten; **travel ~** *134T* Reisekosten
expensive *10* teuer
experience *32* Erfahrung; to **get ~** *42* Erfahrung(en) sammeln
to **experience sth** *87* etw erleben
to **experiment** *58* experimentieren
to **explain sth (to sth)** *10* (jdm) etw erläutern, (jdm) etw erklären
export: ~ clearance *97* Ausfuhrabfertigung; **~ licence** *97* Ausfuhrgenehmigung; **~ sales director** *120* Exportleiter/in; **cleared for ~** *99* zur Ausfuhr freigemacht, verzollt
exporter *97* Exporteur
to **express sth** *122* etw ausdrücken
expression *10* Ausdruck
extra: ~ charge *82* Aufpreis, Zusatzgebühr; **~ guarantee** *75* Garantieverlängerung; **~ pay** *32* Zuschlag
eye: ~ contact *39* Blickkontakt; **~ level** *59* Augenhöhe; **easy on the ~** *58* wohltuend für die Augen

F

fabric *81T* Stoff
to **face: ~ sb** *39* sich jdm zuwenden, jdn anschauen; **~ sth** *79* mit etw konfrontiert werden, vor etw stehen; **Let's ~ it.** *23T* Seien wir ehrlich.
face ID *131T* Gesichtserkennung
face-to-face: ~ advice *80* persönliche Beratung; **~ teaching** *42* Präsenzunterricht
facilities *pl* *146* sanitäre Anlagen, Bad und WC
fact, nutrition ~s *pl* *55T* Nährwertangaben; **in ~** *27* sogar, eigentlich, im Grunde
factory *33T* Fabrik; **~ farming** *25* Intensivlandwirtschaft, Massentierhaltung

to **fail** *18* pleitegehen, in Konkurs gehen; *117* ausfallen, kaputtgehen
fair *25* gerecht, fair; **job ~** *7* Jobbörse, Jobmesse; **trade ~** *7* Messe
faithfully, Yours ~ *93* Mit freundlichen Grüßen
to **fall apart** *70T* auseinanderfallen
family: ~ business *81T* Familienbetrieb; **~ tree** *8* Stammbaum
far: So ~, so good. *18T* So weit, so gut.
fare *133* Fahrpreis, Flugpreis
farmer *55T* Bauer/Bäuerin, Landwirt/in
farming, factory ~ *25* Intensivlandwirtschaft, Massentierhaltung
fascinating *15* faszinierend
fashion *12T* Mode; **high-street ~** *26* aktuelle Mode, (preisgünstige) Massenmode
fashionable *26* modisch
fashionwear *100* Mode
fast moving goods *pl* *56* Schnelldreher
fat *55* Fett; *129* dick; **saturated ~** *55* gesättigte Fettsäuren
fault, sth is sb's ~ *124* jd ist schuld an etw
faulty *82* defekt, fehlerhaft
favour, in sb's ~ *112* zu jds Gunsten, zu jds Vorteil
favourable *91* günstig, gut
favourably *140* wohlwollend, positiv
favourite *9* Lieblings-
fear (of sth) *69* Angst (vor etw)
federal *48* Bundes-; **~ environment agency** *143* Umweltbundesamt
feed, camera ~ *132T* Kamerabilder, Livestream
feedback *39* Rückmeldung
to **feel: ~ free to do sth** *66* etw ruhig tun; nicht zögern, etw zu tun; **~ misunderstood** *78* sich missverstanden fühlen; **~ uncomfortable** *59* sich unwohl fühlen
female *37* weiblich
fibre *55T* Ballaststoffe
figure *18T* Zahl; **sales ~s** *pl* *42* Verkaufszahlen, Umsatzzahlen
to **fill: ~ sth up** *12T* etw auffüllen; **~ in a form** *77* ein Formular ausfüllen; **~ shelves** *42* Regale auffüllen
final *8* letzte/r/s; **~ price** *55T* Endpreis
finally *12T* schließlich
to **finance sth** *113T* etw finanzieren
financial services *pl* *73T* Finanzdienstleistungen
findings *pl* *34* Ergebnisse
fingerprint *132* Fingerabdruck
to **fire sb** *41* jdn rausschmeißen, jdn entlassen
firm *17* Firma, Unternehmen; *57* fest; **training ~** *17* Ausbildungsbetrieb
first: ~ aid *26* Erste Hilfe; **~ name** *8* Vorname
to **fit** *11* passen; **one-size-~s-all** *88T* Einheits-
fit-and-flare dress *89* Godet-Kleid
fitting room *58* Umkleidekabine, Anprobe
to **fix sth** *12T* etw in Ordnung bringen
fizzy water *147* Wasser mit Kohlensäure
flare, fit-and-~ dress *89* Godet-Kleid
flat *37* flach; *BE* *9* Wohnung
flat-pack furniture *10* Selbstaufbaumöbel, Mitnahmemöbel
flat-share *9* Wohngemeinschaft
flexible *12* flexibel; **on a ~ basis** *32* flexibel
floor, ground ~ *26* Erdgeschoss
to **flop** *74* versagen
Florence *100T* Florenz
flow, customer ~ *58* Kundenlauf; **~ breaker** *59* Stopper *(Aufsteller, Tische usw.)*
fluent *141* *(Sprache:)* fließend
fly *58* Fliege
the following *16* das Folgende
food, frozen ~ *20* Tiefkühlkost; **pet ~** *18T* Tierfutter; **~ bank** *9* Tafel; **~ court** *22* Gastronomiebereich; **~ handler** *36* *Ladenmitarbeiter/in, der/die mit Lebensmitteln in Kontakt kommt;* **non-~ item** *20* Non-Food-Artikel; to **handle ~** *36* mit Lebensmitteln umgehen
foot, on ~ *8* zu Fuß
footboard *70T* *(Bett:)* Fußteil
footfall *132T* Kundenfrequenz
footprint, carbon ~ *25* CO_2-Fußabdruck
footwear *24* Schuhe
force, task ~ *41* Arbeitsgruppe
foreign language *43* Fremdsprache
form, registration ~ *72* Anmeldeformular; to **fill in a ~** *77* ein Formular ausfüllen
formal *14* formell
formula *76* Formel
to **formulate sth** *103* etw formulieren
to **forward sth to sb** *118* etw an jdn weiterleiten
forward, carriage ~ *120T* unfrei, auf Kosten des Empfängers; to **look ~ to sth** *23T* sich auf etw freuen; to **look ~ to doing sth** *94* sich darauf freuen, etw zu tun
fountain, water ~ *26* Brunnen
frame *63T* Rahmen; **picture ~** *71* Bilderrahmen
franchise *18T* Konzession, Franchise
franchisee *18T* Franchisenehmer/in
franchisor *18T* Franchisegeber/in
free *10* kostenlos, gratis; **~ of charge** *84* gebührenfrei, kostenlos; to **be ~** *46* Zeit haben, frei haben; to **be ~ to do sth** *18T* etw tun dürfen; to **feel ~ to do sth** *66* etw ruhig tun; nicht zögern, etw zu tun; **sb is ~ to do sth** *117* jdm ist es freigestellt, etw zu tun
free-standing *59* freistehend
freedom *18T* Freiheit
to **freeze sth** *81T* etw einfrieren
freezer, fridge ~ *75* Kühl-Gefrier-Kombination
freight *98* Fracht
frequency *84* Häufigkeit
frequent(ly) *105* häufig
fresh *11* frisch
frictionless *132* reibungslos
fridge freezer *75* Kühl-Gefrier-Kombination
front, at the ~ *27* vorne
frozen food *20* Tiefkühlkost
frying pan *61* Bratpfanne
fuel *32* Treibstoff, Benzin, Sprit
full board *134* Vollpension
full-time *32* (in) Vollzeit(-)
fully *120T* völlig, voll und ganz; **~ qualified** *32* ausgebildet, voll qualifiziert
fun, to **be ~** *22* Spaß machen
function *67T* Funktion
fungible, non-~ token *129* Non-Fungible Token *(nicht austauschbares digitales Objekt)*
furnishings *pl*, **soft ~** *10* Heimtextilien
furniture *10* Möbel; **antique ~** *37* antike Möbel, Antiquitäten; **flat-pack ~** *10* Selbstaufbaumöbel, Mitnahmemöbel
future *34* künftig, zukünftig; **in the not-too-distant ~** *131T* in nicht allzu ferner Zukunft
future-ready *128* zukunftsfähig

G

gap, gender pay ~ *33T* geschlechtsspezifisches Lohngefälle
gardener, market ~ *134P* Gemüsebauer/-bäuerin
gardening centre *11* Gartencenter
garlic *61* Knoblauch
garment *10* Kleidungsstück, Bekleidungsartikel
gatekeeper *88T* Pförtner/in, Gatekeeper
gear *22* Ausrüstung; *63T* Gang

geared, to be ~ to sb 74 auf jdn ausgerichtet sein
gender 33T Geschlecht; ~ pay gap 33T geschlechtsspezifisches Lohngefälle
general 23T allgemein; ~ partner 18 Komplementär/in; ~ partnership 18 offene Handelsgesellschaft (OHG); ~ public 74 Allgemeinheit, die breite Öffentlichkeit
generous 138 großzügig
genetically modified (GM) 25 genmanipuliert
geo-location 131T Ortung, Lokalisierung
gesture 39 Geste; as a ~ of good will 86T aus Kulanz
to get: ~ somewhere 10 wohin gelangen/kommen; ~ on with sb 142P mit jdm zurechtkommen, mit jdm auskommen; ~ past sb/sth 88T an jdm/etw vorbeikommen; ~ in touch with sb 49 sich bei jdm melden, sich mit jdm in Verbindung setzen
to give sth away 73T etw verschenken
glad, to be ~ 47T sich freuen
glass case 56 Vitrine
global warming 84T Erderwärmung
gloves pl 35 Handschuhe
to go: ~ off 55T schlecht werden; ~ wrong 18T schieflaufen; ~ the extra mile 142P sich besonders anstrengen, sich ins Zeug legen
goal 15 (Sport:) Tor; 42 Ziel; career ~ 142 Berufsziel
good, to be ~ at sth 138 etw gut können; So far, so ~. 18T So weit, so gut.
goods pl 10 Waren, Güter; baked ~ 53 Backwaren; canned ~ 53 Konserven(dosen); destination ~ 58 Waren/Güter des täglichen Bedarfs; dry ~ 132 Trockenware(n); fast moving ~ 56 Schnelldreher; refrigerated ~ 132 Kühlware(n); seasonal ~ 22 Saisonartikel, Saisonware; staple ~ 10 Waren des täglichen Bedarfs
gown, bridal ~ 89 Brautkleid
to grab sth 132 sich etw greifen, sich etw schnappen
grade 42 Note
grammar school 9 Gymnasium
to grant sth 94 etw gewähren, etw einräumen
graph 39 Diagramm, Schaubild, Kurve
grass 115 Rasen, Gras
green energy 25 Ökostrom
greetings pl 66 Begrüßung
grill, charcoal ~ 24 Holzkohlengrill
to grip 125T greifen
groceries pl 24 Lebensmittel
grocery store 11 Lebensmittelgeschäft
gross 32 brutto, Brutto-
ground floor 26 Erdgeschoss
group, product ~ 54 Warengruppe; target ~ 74 Zielgruppe
to group sth 61 etw gruppieren, etw kombinieren
growth 128T Wachstum, Zunahme
guarantee 82 Garantie, Gewährleistung; additional commercial ~ 82 erweiterte Herstellergarantie; extra ~ 75 Garantieverlängerung; legal ~ 82 gesetzliche Gewährleistung; legal ~ period 83 Gewährleistungsfrist
to guarantee sth 70T etw garantieren
guard, security ~ 46 Sicherheitskraft, -mitarbeiter/in
to guess 60 raten, erraten, vermuten
guess 128T Vermutung; to make an educated ~ 40 eine fundierte Vermutung anstellen
guest house 146 Pension
guest speaker 132 Gastredner/in
guide, store ~ 27 *(Einkaufszentrum:)* Lageplan; ~ dog 77 Blindenhund
guideline 18T Richtlinie, Vorschrift
guitar 9 Gitarre
gun, tagging ~ 30 Etikettierpistole
gym 9 Fitness-Studio

H

habit 80 Gewohnheit
hairdresser 26 Friseur/in
hairdryer 87 Föhn
half board 133 Halbpension
to hand: ~ sth out 7 etw verteilen, etw ausgeben; ~ sth over 97 etw übergeben; ~ over to sb 23T an jdn übergeben
hand, on the other ~ 128T andererseits; show of ~s 23T Handzeichen; ~ tool 11 Handwerkzeug
handbag 10 Handtasche
to handle: ~ sb/sth 139 mit jdm/etw umgehen; ~ sth 86 etw bearbeiten, etw erledigen; ~ food 36 mit Lebensmitteln umgehen
handler, food ~ 36 *Ladenmitarbeiter/in, der/die mit Lebensmitteln in Kontakt kommt*
handling, rough ~ 119 grobe/unsachgemäße Handhabung
handout 39 Arbeitsblatt
to hang sth up 56 etw aufhängen
hanger, clothes ~ 30 Kleiderbügel
to happen: ~ to do sth 86T etw (zufällig) tun; to make sth ~ 131T etw möglich machen
hard drive 117 Festplatte
hard-working 138 fleißig
harmony 69 Harmonie
to hate sth 9 etw überhaupt nicht mögen, etw hassen
to have: to let sb ~ sth 49 jdm etw zukommen lassen
head: ~ of department 42 Abteilungsleiter/in; ~ office 53 Zentrale, Hauptsitz
to head up sth 23T etw leiten
headboard 70T *(Bett:)* Kopfteil
heading 8 Überschrift
headline 16 Überschrift
headquarters pl 42 Zentrale, Hauptsitz
health 10 Gesundheit; ~ insurance 32 Krankenversicherung
healthcare 48 Gesundheitsfürsorge, Krankenversicherung; ~ system 50 Gesundheitssystem
heating 145 Heizung; ~ element 119 Heizspirale
heavy 31 schwer, stark
heavy-duty 63T robust
heel 37 (Schuh-)Absatz
height 50 Höhe
helmet 63 Helm
helpful 64 nützlich, hilfreich; 140 hilfsbereit
hen, battery ~s pl 25 Hennen in Legebatterien
here, to be ~ to stay 132 Einzug halten, von Dauer sein
to hesitate 49 zögern
high street BE 22 Hauptstraße, Hauptgeschäftsstraße, Innenstadt
high-street fashion 26 aktuelle Mode, (preisgünstige) Massenmode
higher education: ~ course 42 Hochschulstudium; ~ entrance qualification 141 Hochschulreife
to highlight sth 16 etw hervorheben
highly 132 ausgesprochen, sehr
hiking, to go ~ 121 wandern gehen
to hire sb 41 jdn einstellen
history 9 Geschichte; 103 bisherige Praxis, Vorgeschichte
hob, induction ~ 75 Induktionsherd
holiday, national ~ 41 landesweiter Feiertag; paid ~ 32 bezahlter Urlaub; public ~ 41 gesetzlicher Feiertag; ~ bonus 32 Urlaubsgeld; ~ entitlement 41 Urlaubsanspruch
home, care ~ 9 Pflegeheim; old people's ~ 134T Altenheim; take-~ pay 32 Nettolohn, Nettogehalt; ~ decorations pl 10 Wohnaccessoires, Einrichtungsgegenstände
homeowner 74 Hausbesitzer/in

homeware *54* Haushaltswaren
honest *68* ehrlich, aufrichtig; to **be ~** *84T* ehrlich gesagt
hook *56* Haken
horizontal(ly) *50* waagrecht
hourly rate *34* Stundensatz, Stundenlohn
hours *pl*, **opening ~** *22* Öffnungszeiten; **shopping ~** *41* Ladenöffnungszeiten; **working ~** *12* Arbeitszeit(en); to **work long ~** *32* lange arbeiten, Überstunden machen
horse riding *9* Reiten
hostel, youth ~ *145* Jugendherberge
house, guest ~ *146* Pension
household *10* Haushalt; to **be a ~ name** *142P* ein Begriff sein
housewife *27* Hausfrau
huge *81T* riesig, riesengroß
human: H~ Resources (HR) *pl 42* Personalwesen; **~ rights** *pl 25* Menschenrechte
to **hurry** *22* eilen
hurry, to **be in a ~** *70* es eilig haben, in Eile sein
husband *32* (Ehe-)Mann
hygiene, personal ~ *36* Körperpflege, persönliche Hygiene
hyphen *100T* Bindestrich

I

ideally *105* idealerweise; to **be ~ suited for sth** *142* für etw hervorragend geeignet sein
identical *59* identisch, gleich, der-/die-/dasselbe
to **identify: ~ sth** *41* etw bestimmen, etw ermitteln, etw benennen; **~ oneself** *132* sich ausweisen
identity *83* Identität; **~ theft** *72* Identitätsdiebstahl
illness *15* Krankheit
to **illustrate sth** *98* etw veranschaulichen, etw illustrieren
illustration *36* Abbildung, Bild, Illustration
image *74* Bild
to **imagine sth** *62* sich etw vorstellen
immediate *116* sofortig; **with ~ effect** *103* ab sofort, mit sofortiger Wirkung
immediately *58* unverzüglich, sofort
impolite *77* unhöflich
import: ~ clearance *91* Einfuhrabfertigung; **~ duties** *pl 99* Einfuhrabgaben, Einfuhrzölle; **~ licence** *97* Einfuhrgenehmigung
importance *12* Wichtigkeit, Bedeutung
importer *97* Importeur
impossible *63T* unmöglich
impressed (by sth) *95* (von etw) beeindruckt
impression *38* Eindruck; to **make a bad ~ (on sb)** *38* einen schlechten Eindruck (bei jdm) hinterlassen
to **improve sth** *8* etw verbessern
to **improvise** *67* improvisieren
impulse, on ~ *59* spontan, im Affekt; **~ buy** *59* Impulskauf
in-house *34* betriebsintern
in-service *34* berufsbegleitend, betriebsintern
inbox *88* Posteingang
incentive *78* Anreiz
inch *67T* Zoll *(= 2,54 cm)*
to **include sth** *16* etw einbeziehen, etw beifügen; *70T* etw einschließen
including *11* einschließlich, mit
income *48* Einkommen; **~ tax** *32* Einkommensteuer
incoming *88T* eingehend
incomplete *118* unvollständig
inconvenience *120T* Unannehmlichkeit(en)
inconvenient *132* umständlich, unpraktisch
to **incorporate sth into sth** *25* etw in etw einbeziehen, etw in etw aufnehmen
incorrect(ly) *125* falsch
Incoterms rule *91* Internationale Handelsklausel
to **increase** *51* zunehmen, (an)steigen
increasing(ly) *103* zunehmend
incredible *131T* unglaublich
indeed *67T* in der Tat, tatsächlich
independent *79* unabhängig
index card *38* Karteikarte
to **index sth** *74* etw erschließen, etw indizieren
India *69* Indien
individual *40* einzeln, individuell
individual *141* (Einzel-)Person
induction hob *75* Induktionsherd
industry *127* Branche, Sparte
influence *68* Einfluss
to **inform sb** *119* jdn in Kenntnis setzen, jdn informieren
informal *14* zwanglos, informell; *110 (Kleidung:)* leger
information desk *26* Informationsschalter, Auskunft
informative *49* informativ
ingredients *pl*, **baking ~** *53* Backzutaten
to **inhabit sth** *129* etw bewohnen
inhabitant *132T* Einwohner/in, Bewohner/in
initial order *106* Erstauftrag, Erstbestellung
initials *pl 93* Initialien; **reference ~** *93* Zeichen, Kürzel
initiative, to **take the ~** *148T* die Initiative ergreifen
inquiry *66* Frage, Anfrage, Anliegen
to **insert sth into sth** *108* etw in etw einfügen
inside address *93* Innenadresse
insight *131T* Einblick
to **install sth** *11* etw installieren
to **install sth** *67T* etw einrichten, etw installieren
instant *131T* sofortig, Sofort-
instantly *129* sofort
instead *32* stattdessen
instructor *140* Lehrer/in
insurance, health ~ *32* Krankenversicherung; **nursing care ~** *32* Pflegeversicherung; **unemployment ~** *32* Arbeitslosenversicherung
to **insure sth** *97* etw versichern
to **integrate sth** *131T* etw einbinden, etw integrieren
intelligence, artificial ~ (AI) *88* künstliche Intelligenz (KI)
to **intend to do sth** *65* beabsichtigen, etw zu tun; vorhaben, etw zu tun
to **interact** *74* kommunizieren, interagieren
interested, to **be ~ in sth** *7* an etw interessiert sein
interior, shop ~ *56* Ladeneinrichtung, Ladenausstattung
internal *86* intern
international trade *97* Außenhandel
to **interrupt sb/sth** *31* jdn unterbrechen, jdn stören
interview *137* Vorstellungsgespräch
to **introduce: ~ sb to sb** *14* jdm jdn vorstellen; **~ sth** *55T* etw einführen, etw auf den Markt bringen
introductions *pl 14* Vorstellung, Begrüßung
intuitive *74* intuitiv
to **invent sth** *15* etw erfinden, sich etw ausdenken
inventory, to **do the ~** *30* Inventur machen
invitation *72* Einladung
to **invite sth from sb** *38* jdn um etw bitten, jdn zu etw auffordern
invoice *105* Rechnung
Irishman *27* Ire
irresponsible *140* verantwortungslos
item *10* Artikel; **~ on the agenda** *134* Tagesordnungspunkt; **~ for sale** *63* angebotener Artikel; **non-food ~** *20* Non-Food-Artikel
itinerary *143* Reiseplan

J

jam 54 Marmelade
jar 53 (Konserven-)Glas
jeweller 56 Juwelier/in
jeweller's 26 Juweliergeschäft
jewellery 10 Schmuck
job: ~ advert(isement) 137 Stellenanzeige; ~ application 140 Bewerbung; ~ fair 7 Jobbörse, Jobmesse; ~ interview 137 Vorstellungsgespräch; ~ profile 33 Stellenprofil, Tätigkeitsprofil; ~ title 140 Stellenbezeichnung; to advertise a ~ 138 eine Stelle ausschreiben
to join 79 beitreten, mitmachen; ~ sb 47T dabei sein, (zu jdm) kommen
journey 74 Weg, Reise; customer ~ 74 Kontakthistorie, Customer Journey
just so you know 120T damit das klar ist; damit wir uns richtig verstehen

K

to keep: ~ sth 18T etw behalten; ~ to sth 18T sich an etw halten, einer Sache folgen, etw einhalten; ~ up 142P auf dem Laufenden bleiben
kettle, electric ~ 75 Wasserkocher
key 57 Schlüssel; ~ word 39 Stichwort
kick-off 133 Auftakt
kind 23T liebenswürdig, freundlich, nett
kiosk 128T Verkaufsstand, Kiosk
kitchen appliance 10 Küchengerät
knee level 59 Kniehöhe
knitting 9 Stricken; ~ supplies *pl* 81T Strickbedarf
to know: just so you ~ 120T damit das klar ist; damit wir uns richtig verstehen
knowledge 42 Wissen, Kenntnisse

L

label 54 Etikett, Kennzeichnung; 55 Siegel; return ~ 122 Retourenaufkleber
to label sth 12T etw *(Ware usw.)* auszeichnen, etw auspreisen; 20 etw beschriften, etw kennzeichnen
labelling regulations *pl* 54 Etikettierungsvorschriften, Kennzeichnungsverordnung
labour, child ~ 25 Kinderarbeit; ~ market 47T Arbeitsmarkt; collective ~ agreement 41 Tarifvertrag
lack: ~ (of sth) 148T Mangel (an etw); ~ of business 132T mangelndes Geschäftsaufkommen
ladder, career ~ 42 Karriereleiter
laid out 53 angelegt
lampshade 81 Lampenschirm
landscape 22 Landschaft
language, body ~ 39 Körpersprache; foreign ~ 43 Fremdsprache
to last 42 dauern; 67T halten
late: ~ shift 32 Spätschicht; at the ~est 70T spätestens
to launch sth 132 etw *(Produkt usw.)* auf den Markt bringen, etw *(Geschäft usw.)* eröffnen
law 44 Gesetz(e), Recht; EU ~ 82 EU-Recht; by ~ 86T von Rechts wegen, nach dem Gesetz; under German ~ 116 nach deutschem Recht; the EU has had a ~ in place since … 131T in der EU ist seit … ein Gesetz in Kraft
to lay sth on sth 67 etw auf etw legen
layer 23T Schicht, Lage
layout 23 Gestaltung, Aufbau, Layout; 27 Anlage, Gestaltung, Flächenkonzept
to lead 58 führen
lead 70T (Hunde-)Leine
leader, seminar ~ 8 Seminarleiter/in
to leak 115 undicht werden/sein, auslaufen
least, at ~ 67 mindestens
leather 37 Leder
leave, educational ~ 34 Bildungsurlaub; paid annual ~ 47T bezahlter Jahresurlaub
to leave school 42 von der Schule abgehen
left, to be ~ to sb to do sth 84 es bleibt jdm überlassen, etw zu tun
legal 81T rechtmäßig, legal; ~ guarantee 82 gesetzliche Gewährleistung; ~ guarantee period 83 Gewährleistungsfrist; ~ minimum 79 gesetzliche Mindestanforderung(en); ~ position 47T Rechtslage, Gesetzeslage
length 50 Länge
lens, wide-angle ~ 65 Weitwinkelobjektiv
to let sb have sth 49 jdm etw zukommen lassen
letter, business ~ 92 Geschäftsbrief; capital ~ 93 Großbuchstabe; cover ~ 140 Anschreiben, Begleitschreiben; covering ~ 137 Anschreiben, Begleitschreiben; ~ of complaint 120 (formelle/schriftliche) Beschwerde; to post a ~ 132T einen Brief einwerfen
letterhead 93 Briefkopf
level 23T Ebene; eye ~ 59 Augenhöhe; knee ~ 59 Kniehöhe; pay ~ 40 Gehaltsstufe, Gehaltsniveau; stock ~ 132T (Lager-)Bestand; entry-~ salary 138 Einstiegsgehalt; entry-~ staff 142P Berufseinsteiger/innen
licence, driving ~ 140 Führerschein; export ~ 97 Ausfuhrgenehmigung; import ~ 97 Einfuhrgenehmigung
light 63T leicht; 67T hell; reading ~ 146 Leselampe; ~ bulb 23T Glühlampe, Leuchtmittel; ~ rail 143 Stadtbahn; traffic ~ system 55T Ampelsystem
light-coloured 147 hell
lighting 10 Beleuchtung
likes *pl* 9 Vorlieben
liking, to be to sb's ~ 107 jdm zusagen, jds Vorstellungen entsprechen
to limit sth (to sth) 46 etw (auf etw) begrenzen, etw (auf etw) beschränken
limited 10 begrenzt, beschränkt; ~ mobility 134P eingeschränkte Mobilität, Gehbehinderung; ~ partnership 19 Kommanditgesellschaft (KG); private ~ company (Ltd) 18T Gesellschaft mit beschränkter Haftung (GmbH); public ~ company (plc) 19 Aktiengesellschaft (AG)
line, A-~ 89 A-Linie, Trapezschnitt; attention ~ 93 Zeile "zu Händen"; reporting ~ 19 Unterstellung; subject ~ 88T Betreffzeile; ~ manager 106 (direkte/r) Vorgesetzte/r; main ~ train 143 Fernzug
lined, to be ~ with sth 56 mit etw gesäumt sein
linen, bed ~ 146 Bettwäsche
link 131T Verbindung; bus ~ 145 Busverbindung, Busanbindung; public transport ~s *pl* 22 Anbindung an den öffentlichen Nahverkehr
linked, to be ~ with sth 93 mit etw verknüpft sein
lipstick 24 Lippenstift
liquid, washing-up ~ 11 Spülmittel
liquor *AE* 44 Spirituosen; ~ store *AE* 44 (konzessioniertes) Wein- und Spirituosengeschäft
to list sth 12 etw aufführen, etw aufzählen
listener 124 Zuhörer/in
to load 74 laden; 97 verladen
load, a ~ of washing 55T eine Ladung Wäsche
to locate sth 26 etw ausfindig machen, etw orten
located, to be ~ 58 sich befinden; to be ~ in … 10 in … liegen/sein
location 10 Standort, Lage, Platz
locator, store ~ 23 Filialsuche, Filialfinder
lock 63 Schloss
lockable 146 abschließbar
locked 56 verschlossen, abgeschlossen

long, to cut a ~ story short *132T* um etw kurz zu machen; lange Rede, kurzer Sinn; no ~er *25* nicht mehr; in the ~er term *103* längerfristig, auf längere Sicht
long-sleeved *35* langärmlig
long-standing customer *94* langjährige/r Kunde/Kundin
to look: ~ forward to sth *23T* sich auf etw freuen; ~ forward to doing sth *94* sich darauf freuen, etw zu tun
look, to take a closer ~ at sth *55T* sich etw genauer ansehen
loose *36* *(Haar:)* offen; *67T* *(Kleidung:)* weit
to lose *18T* verlieren
loss *34* Verlust
lottery *73T* Verlosung
low cut *37* tief ausgeschnitten
lowercase *100* kleingeschrieben
loyalty, customer ~ *72* Kundentreue, Kundenbindung; ~ card *67T* Kundenkarte, Bonuskarte; ~ programme *65* Treueprogramm, Kundenbindungsprogramm
luggage *26* Reisegepäck; ~ rack *63T* Gepäckträger
lunch break *125* Mittagspause
lunchtime *51T* Mittag(szeit)

M

machine, bottle return ~ *20* Leergutautomat; cash ~ *20* Geldautomat; vending ~ *132* (Verkaufs-)Automat; washing ~ *54* Waschmaschine
machinery *11* Geräte
madam *27* *(Anrede:)* gnädige Frau
made up, to be ~ of sth *48* aus etw bestehen
made-to-measure clothing *86* Maßkonfektion
magic, to work one's ~ on sth *23T* zeigen, was man kann; sich einer Sache annehmen
mail order *82* Direktversand, Versandbestellung
main *38* Haupt-; ~ carriage *91* Hauptlauf, Haupttransport; ~ line train *143* Fernzug
mainly *66* hauptsächlich
major *11* bedeutend, groß
make *85* Fabrikat, Marke
to make: ~ it *88* es schaffen; ~ sth happen *131T* etw möglich machen; ~ sense *67* einleuchten; *75* sinnvoll sein, vernünftig sein; ~ sure *59* gewährleisten, dafür sorgen, sicherstellen; ~ or break sth *23T* über das Gelingen oder Scheitern von etw entscheiden
makeover *23T* komplette Umgestaltung, Imagewechsel
mall, shopping ~ *10* (überdachtes) Einkaufszentrum
to manage: ~ sth *58* etw *(Unternehmen usw.)* führen, etw leiten; ~ expectations *116* Erwartungen steuern, mit Erwartungen umgehen
management *29* Geschäftsführung, Geschäftsleitung
manager, assistant ~ *14* stellvertretende/r Filialleiter/in; district ~ *15* Bezirksleiter/in; line ~ *106* (direkte/r) Vorgesetzte/r; regional ~ *19* Regionalleiter/in; shop ~ *12T* Filialleiter/in; supermarket ~ *18T* Martkleiter/in
mandatory *55* obligatorisch, verpflichtend
mannequin *60T* Schaufensterpuppe
manner *39* Art (und Weise); *141* Auftreten, Verhalten
to manufacture sth *108* etw herstellen, etw fertigen
manufacturer *25* Hersteller
manufacturing *94* Fertigung, Produktion
market, labour ~ *47T* Arbeitsmarkt; ~ area *81T* Absatzgebiet; ~ gardener *134P* Gemüsebauer/-bäuerin; ~ share *128T* Marktanteil; to enter a (new) ~ *47* in einen (neuen) Markt Fuß fassen, in einen (neuen) Markt eindringen; to expand into a (new) ~ *41* sich einen (neuen) Markt erschließen, in einen (neuen) Markt expandieren; up-~ *142P* exklusiv
marketing director *23T* Marketingleiter/in
marketplace *128T* Marktplatz, Markt
marking *93* Kennzeichnung, Beschriftung
marriage *132T* Eheschließung
married *8* verheiratet; to get ~ *67T* heiraten
marvellous *67T* großartig
mascara *26* Wimperntusche
matching *67T* passend
material, building ~s *pl* *11* Baumaterial; raw ~ *25* Rohstoff(e)
maths *pl* *9* Mathe(matik)
matter *34* Angelegenheit; no ~ how *81* (ganz) egal wie; no ~ what *89* egal was; to deal with a ~ *118* eine Angelegenheit regeln, sich um eine Angelegenheit kümmern
to matter: sth doesn't ~ *148T* etw ist egal, etw ist unwichtig
mattress *70T* Matratze
maximum, for a ~ of *45* höchstens
mayor *134P* Bürgermeister
mayoress *134P* Bürgermeisterin
meal, ready-made ~ *53* Fertiggericht
to mean *25* bedeuten, heißen; ~ sth *12T* etw meinen
meaning *33T* das heißt
means: ~ of payment *130* Zahlungsmittel; ~ of transport *143* Transportmittel
meantime, in the ~ *122* unterdessen, bis dahin
measure, made-to-~ clothing *86* Maßkonfektion
measurement *71* Maß
meat *11* Fleisch
mechanic *18T* Mechaniker/in
to mediate *20* vermitteln
Medicare *AE* *48* *Gesundheitsdienst für Ältere in den USA*
medicine *11* Medikament(e)
to meet: ~ sth *25* etw *(Anforderungen usw.)* erfüllen; Pleased to ~ you. *14* Schön, Sie kennenzulernen! Angenehm!
meeting *32* Sitzung, Besprechung
melon *57* Melone
member *17* Mitglied
membership *33* Mitgliedschaft; ~ card *132T* Mitgliedskarte
memo *99* Notiz, Kurzmitteilung
men's outfitters *pl* *37* Herrenausstatter
men's wear *26* Herrenbekleidung
mental arithmetic *139* Kopfrechnen
mentor *31* Mentor/in
menu, drop-down ~ *23* Auswahlmenü, Ausklappmenü
merchandising *60* Verkaufsförderung, Absatzförderung
merchant, registered ~ *19* eingetragene/r Kaufmann/-frau (e.K.)
mess, to make a ~ of everything *115* alles dreckig machen, alles vollkleckern
message *55T* Botschaft, Aussage; to pass on a ~ to sb *100T* jdm etw ausrichten
method of payment *83* Zahlungsart, Zahlungsweise
microwave oven *75* Mikrowellenherd
midday *44* Mittag
midnight *44* Mitternacht
Milan *109T* Mailand
to mind *76* etw dagegen haben
mind, with this in ~ *58* in diesem Sinne, unter Beachtung dessen; to have peace of ~ *22* unbesorgt sein;

to **have sth in ~** *70T* sich etw vorstellen, an etw denken
minimum, legal ~ *79* gesetzliche Mindestanforderung(en); **~ wage** *33T* MIndestlohn
minutes *pl* *133* Protokoll
to **mirror** *70* spiegeln
misinterpretation *114* Missverständnis, Fehlinterpretation
missing, to **be ~** *123T* fehlen
misunderstanding *77P* Missverständnis
misunderstood, to **feel ~** *78* sich missverstanden fühlen
to **mix sth up** *57* etw durcheinanderbringen
mixed up, to **get ~** *95* durcheinander geraten
mixture (of sth) *52* Mischung (aus etw)
mobile device *74* Mobilgerät
mobility, limited ~ *134P* eingeschränkte Mobilität, Gehbehinderung
money, to **spend ~ on sth** *43* Geld für etw ausgeben
to **monitor sb/sth** *132T* jdn/etw beobachten, jdn/etw überwachen
monthly *32* monatlich, Monats-
mosque *9* Moschee
mother-in-law *89* Schwiegermutter
mounting screw *118* Befestigungsschraube
move, to **be on the ~** *66* unterwegs sein
moveable *59* beweglich
movement *129* Bewegung
Ms *47T* *(Anrede:)* Frau
mud *115* Schlamm
mug, beer ~ *60T* Bierkrug, Bierseidel
multi-store *73T* händlerübergreifend
multiple *58* mehrere
Munich *8* München
music, background ~ *10* Hintergrundmusik

N

nail salon *26* Nagelstudio
name, first ~ *8* Vorname; to **be a household ~** *142P* ein Begriff sein
to **name sth** *20* etw nennen, etw benennen
named *93* benannt, namentlich bekannt
name tag *30* Namensschild
Naples *98* Neapel
narrow *10* eng
national holiday *41* landesweiter Feiertag
nationality *140* Staatsangehörigkeit
natural resources *pl* *28* Rohstoffquellen
to **navigate sth** *60T* sich in etw zurechtfinden, durch etw durchkommen
necklace *36* Halskette
need, sb in ~ *72* Bedürftige/r
needs *pl* *66* Bedürfnisse
to **negotiate sth** *112* etw verhandeln, etw aushandeln
net *32* netto, Netto-
network, distribution ~ *17* Vertriebsnetz
New Year's Eve *59* Silvester
nightmare *57* Albtraum
nightwear *24* Nachtwäsche
no: That's a ~-no. *58* Das geht gar nicht.
noise *68* Lärm
noisy *68* laut, lärmend
non-food item *20* Non-Food-Artikel
non-fungible token *129* Non-Fungible Token *(nicht austauschbares digitales Objekt)*
normally *8* normalerweise
North Rhine-Westphalia *44* Nordrhein-Westfalen
Norway *98* Norwegen
Norwegian *98* norwegisch
not tested on animals *25* tierversuchsfrei
to **note sth** *94* etw feststellen, etw zur Kenntnis nehmen
note, credit ~ *85* Gutschrift
notice, at short ~ *142P* kurzfristig; **at a week's ~** *142* innerhalb einer Woche, mit einer Woche Vorankündigung; **~ period** *41* Kündigungsfrist
to **notice sth** *12T* etw bemerken, etw wahrnehmen
noticeboard *31* Schwarzes Brett
novel *9* Roman
nowadays *23T* heute, heutzutage
numbered *38* nummeriert; **sb's days are ~** *128T* jds Tage sind gezählt
nursery *59* Kita, Kindergarten
nursing care insurance *32* Pflegeversicherung
nut *57* Mutter, Schraubenmutter
nutrition facts *pl* *55T* Nährwertangaben
nutritional value *55* Nährwert
nutshell, in a ~ *132T* mit einem Wort, kurz gesagt

O

oak *70T* Eiche
object *31* Gegenstand, Sache
objective *81* objektiv
obligation, rights and ~s *pl* *82* Rechte und Pflichten
obliged, to **be ~ to do sth** *83* verpflichtet sein, etw zu tun
to **obtain sth** *141* etw erhalten, etw erwerben
obvious(ly) *132* klar (erkennbar), offensichtlich
occasion, special ~ *66* besonderer Anlass
off, 25% ~ *24* um 25% reduziert; **time ~** *32* Freizeit, Freizeitausgleich; to **take time ~** *47T* sich freinehmen
offensive *37* anstößig, beleidigend
to **offer sth** *10* etw anbieten, etw bieten
offer *55* Angebot; **special ~** *24* Sonderangebot; to **be on ~** *22* (zum Kauf) angeboten werden; *63T* im Angebot sein
office, head ~ *53* Zentrale, Hauptsitz
off-licence *BE* *56* (konzessioniertes) Wein- und Spirituosengeschäft
offline retailer *83* stationäre/r Händler/in
old people's home *134T* Altenheim
old-age pension *32* Altersvorsorge
omnichannel *21* Omnichannel(-) *(alle Vertriebskanäle nutzend)*
once *10* einmal
one-size-fits-all *88T* Einheits-
online presence *17* Online-Auftritt, Onlinepräsenz
only child *8* Einzelkind
open account terms *pl* *103* offenes Zahlungsziel, laufende Rechnung
opening hours *pl* *22* Öffnungszeiten
to **operate** *80* (geschäftlich) tätig sein, arbeiten; **~ sth** *73T* etw betreiben; *129* etw *(Gerät usw.)* bedienen, etw steuern
operating system *141* Betriebssystem
opinion, strong ~ *34* klare Meinung
opportunity *148T* Gelegenheit, Chance; **equal ~ies** *pl* *34* Chancengleichheit
opposite *27* gegenüber
to **optimize sth** *23* etw optimieren
option *33* Möglichkeit
to **order** *10* bestellen
order *12* Reihenfolge; *83* Bestellung, Auftrag; **initial ~** *106* Erstauftrag, Erstbestellung; **mail ~** *82* Direktversand, Versandbestellung; **trial ~** *106* Probeauftrag, Probebestellung; **~ acknowledgement** *103* Auftragsbestätigung; **cash with ~ (CWO)** *103* Zahlung/Kasse bei Auftragserteilung; **confirmation of ~** *110* Auftragsbestätigung; **receipt of ~** *110* Auftragserhalt, Auftragseingang; to **execute an ~** *118* einen Auftrag / eine Bestellung ausführen; to **place an ~** *91* einen Auftrag erteilen, eine Bestellung aufgeben; **in ~ to** *43* um … zu
orderly *68* geordnet, aufgeräumt
organic *24* Bio-, Öko-

organization, retail ~ *66* Einzelhandelsunternehmen; **(form of) business ~** *19* Unternehmensform; **~ chart** *18* Organigramm
organza *89* Organza
orientation, sexual ~ *138* sexuelle Orientierung
original *85* ursprünglich, original
originally *14T* ursprünglich
other, on the ~ hand *128T* andererseits
otherwise *44* ansonsten; **unless ~ agreed** *99* sofern nicht anders vereinbart
outer pocket *36* Außentasche
outfit *35* *(Kleidung:)* Anzug, Kombination; *67T* Ausstattung
outfitters *pl*, **men's ~** *37* Herrenausstatter
outlet, distribution ~ *28* Vertriebsstelle, Vertriebsstätte; **retail ~** *116* Einzelhandelsgeschäft; **sales ~** *17* Verkaufsstelle, Geschäft
to **outline sth** *25* etw umreißen, etw skizzieren
outrageous *125* unerhört, unfassbar
outside Cologne *14T* außerhalb von Köln
oven *75* Herd; **microwave ~** *75* Mikrowellenherd
overalls *pl* *35* Latzhose
overhead camera *132T* Überkopfkamera
overloaded *74* überladen
overnight stay *145* Übernachtung
overtime *31* Überstunden; to **do/work ~** *32* Überstunden machen
own *8* eigene/r/s
to **own: sb ~s sth** *18* jdm gehört etw, jd besitzt etw
owned, privately ~ *10* in Privatbesitz; to **be ~ by sb** *18T* jdm gehören, in jds Besitz sein
owner *19* Eigentümer/in, Inhaber/in; **pet ~** *18T* Tierhalter/in
ownership *132* Besitz, Eigentum, Inhaberschaft

P

to **pack sth** *81T* etw verpacken
package *84T* Paket
packaged *11* abgepackt; **ready ~** *53* regalfertig verpackt
packaging *25* Verpackung
packed with sth *22* voller ..., vollgepackt mit etw
packet, pay ~ *43* Gehalt, Lohntüte
paddling pool *115* Planschbecken
paid: ~ annual leave *47T* bezahlter Jahresurlaub; **~ holiday** *32* bezahlter Urlaub
painkiller *27* Schmerzmittel
paint *11* Farbe
pallet *56* Palette; **~ truck** *30* Hubwagen
palletized *110* auf Paletten
palm print *132* Handabdruck
pan, frying ~ *61* Bratpfanne
panel *149* Gremium, Kommission
paragraph *38* *(Text:)* Absatz
parent company *29* Muttergesellschaft, Dachgesellschaft
park, car ~ *10* Parkplatz, Parkhaus, Tiefgarage; **retail ~** *10* Einkaufszentrum, Fachmarktzentrum
part, spare ~ *81T* Ersatzteil; to **take ~ in sth** *42* an etw teilnehmen; **on our ~** *120T* unsererseits
part-time *12T* (in) Teilzeit(-)
particular *12* bestimmt, speziell; to **be ~ to sb/sth** *149* speziell auf jdn/etw zutreffen; **in ~** *53* insbesondere, besonders; **sth in ~** *66* etw Bestimmtes
particularly *94* besonders, insbesondere
partner, general ~ *18* Komplementär/in; **perfect ~s** *pl* *58* Ergänzungsartikel, Zusatzartikel; **trading ~** *104* Handelspartner/in
partnership, general ~ *18* offene Handelsgesellschaft (OHG); **limited ~** *19* Kommanditgesellschaft (KG)
party, third ~ *131T* Dritte/r; **third-~ seller** *81T* Fremdverkäufer/in; *128T* Drittanbieter
to **pass: ~ one another** *59* aneinander vorbeigehen; **~ to sb** *97* auf jdn übergehen; **~ sth** *27* an etw vorbeikommen; *42* etw *(Prüfung usw.)* bestehen; *55* etw *(Frist usw.)* überschreiten; **~ sth on** *88T* etw weiterleiten; **~ on a message to sb** *100T* jdm etw ausrichten
pass, rail ~ *144* Zeitkarte *(für die Bahn)*
passer-by *131T* Passant/in
passion *12T* Leidenschaft
passionate, to **be ~ about sth** *138* sich (leidenschaftlich) für etw begeistern
past *9* Vergangenheit; to **get ~ sb/sth** *88T* an jdm/etw vorbeikommen
pastime *140* Zeitvertreib
path, career ~ *41* Berufsweg
patience *74* Geduld
patient(ly) *69* geduldig
patio *95* Terrasse, Innenhof
paving stone *88* Pflasterstein
to **pay cash** *86T* bar zahlen
pay *18T* Gehalt, Lohn, Bezahlung; **extra ~** *32* Zuschlag; **take-home ~** *32* Nettolohn, Nettogehalt; **above-average ~ rates** *pl* *142P* überdurchschnittliche Bezahlung; **gender ~ gap** *33T* geschlechtsspezifisches Lohngefälle; **~ level** *40* Gehaltsstufe, Gehaltsniveau; **~ packet** *43* Gehalt, Lohntüte
payment, contactless ~ *20* kontaktloses Bezahlen; **~ in advance** *105* Vorauszahlung, Vorkasse; **means of ~** *130* Zahlungsmittel; **method of ~** *83* Zahlungsart, Zahlungsweise; **terms** *pl* **of ~** *83* Zahlungsbedingungen, -konditionen, -modalitäten
payroll department *48* Lohnbuchhaltung
peace, to **have ~ of mind** *22* unbesorgt sein
peak period *51T* Spitzenzeit, Hauptgeschäftszeit
pear *57* Birne
pedestrian precinct *10* Fußgängerzone
peg *56* Kleiderhaken
pension, old-age ~ *32* Altersvorsorge; **company ~ scheme** *138* betriebliche Altersvorsorge
per *32* pro; **~ cent** *33T* Prozent
percentage *49* Prozentsatz, Anteil
perfect partners *pl* *58* Ergänzungsartikel, Zusatzartikel
to **perform sth** *63* etw aufführen, etw spielen
performance, work ~ *140* Arbeitsleistung; **~ bonus** *142P* Leistungsprämie
perfume *147* Parfüm
period: ~ (of time) *50* Zeitraum; **credit ~** *105* Zahlungsfrist; **delivery ~** *100T* Lieferfrist, Lieferzeit; **legal guarantee ~** *83* Gewährleistungsfrist; **notice ~** *41* Kündigungsfrist; **peak ~** *51T* Spitzenzeit, Hauptgeschäftszeit
perishable *55T* verderblich
permanent(ly) *75* dauerhaft, unbefristet
permission *131T* Erlaubnis, Genehmigung
person, in ~ *142P* persönlich
personal: ~ care *86* Körperpflege; **~ hygiene** *36* Körperpflege, persönliche Hygiene
personality *140* Persönlichkeit; **~ test** *68* Persönlichkeitstest; **~ type** *68* Persönlichkeitstyp
to **personalize sth** *86* etw individuell anfertigen
personalized *131T* individuell, persönlich

to **persuade sb** *62* jdn überreden, jdn überzeugen
pesticide *55T* Schädlingsbekämpfungs-mittel
pet *18T* Haustier; **~ food** *18T* Tierfutter; **~ owner** *18T* Tierhalter/in
petrol station *BE* *22* Tankstelle
pharmacy *26* Apotheke
physical(ly) *72* materiell, real, physisch
piano *9* Klavier
to **pick sth up** *57* sich etw nehmen, etw hochnehmen
picture, the big ~ *128T* das große Ganze; **~ frame** *71* Bilderrahmen
pie chart *50* Tortendiagramm
pill, vitamin ~ *10* Vitaminpille
pin *84* Nadel
to **pin sth** *67T* etw *(Hose usw.)* abstecken
pine *70T* Kiefer
to **place: ~ sth** *56* etw stellen/legen, etw platzieren; **~ an order** *91* einen Auftrag erteilen, eine Bestellung aufgeben
place, the EU has had a law in ~ since … *131T* in der EU ist seit … ein Gesetz in Kraft
placement, work ~ *9* Praktikum; **work ~ student** *19* Praktikant/in
plant *20* Pflanze
plaster *10* Pflaster
play *60T* Theaterstück; **supervised children's ~ area** *10* betreuter Spielbereich für Kinder
pleasant *15* angenehm
to **please: ~ sb** *142P* jdn zufriedenstellen; **any time sb ~es** *47T* wann (immer) jd will; **as sb ~es** *18T* wie es jdm gefällt, nach jds Vorstellungen
pleased, to **be ~** *47T* sich freuen; to **be ~ with sth** *7* mit etw zufrieden sein; **P~ to meet you.** *14* Schön, Sie kennenzulernen! Angenehm!
pleasure *23T* Vergnügen; **My ~.** *47T* Gern geschehen.
plenty of *63T* jede Menge, sehr viele
to **plot sth** *51* etw *(Kurve usw.)* zeichnen
pocket, outer ~ *36* Außentasche
point, bullet ~ *16* Stichpunkt; **charging ~** *132T* Ladesäule; **~ of view** *46* Perspektive, Blickwinkel, Standpunkt; **there is no ~ …** *58* es hat keinen Sinn/Zweck, …
to **point sth out** *65* auf etw hinweisen, auf etw aufmerksam machen
Poland *134T* Polen
polar bear *15* Eisbär
policy *25* Programm, Strategie, Politik; **~ (on sth)** *79* Verfahrensweise (bei etw); **returns ~** *84* Rücknahmebedingungen, Verfahrensweise bei Rückgaben
Polish *11* Polnisch; polnisch
polite(ly) *27* höflich
politeness *76* Höflichkeit
politics *15* Politik
poor(ly) *53* schlecht
poncho, rain ~ *56* Regencape, Regenponcho
pop-up shop *22* Pop-up-Store *(kurzfristiges und provisorisches Einzelhandelsgeschäft)*
to **populate sth** *129* etw bevölkern
population *74* Bevölkerung
pork chop *54* Schweinekotelett
port *97* Hafen; **~ of shipment** *97* Verladehafen
portrait *8* Porträt
Portuguese *70T* portugiesisch
position *43* Stelle, Stellung, Position; **legal ~** *47T* Rechtslage, Gesetzeslage
possibility *46* Möglichkeit
possibly *77* eventuell, womöglich
post *141* (Arbeits-)Stelle, Position
to **post a letter** *132T* einen Brief einwerfen
postage *83* Porto
post-carriage *97* Nachlauf, Nachlauftransport
postcode *77P* Postleitahl
poster *11* Plakat
to **postpone sth** *134T* etw aufschieben, etw verschieben
potential *34* potenziell
poultry *53* Geflügel
powder, washing ~ *10* Waschpulver
power *60T* Macht, Vermögen, Kraft; **~ tool** *11* Elektrowerkzeug
powerful *77P* leistungsstark
powerless *81T* machtlos
practice, in ~ *97* in der Praxis; to **put sth into ~** *71* etw in die Praxis umsetzen
to **practise sth** *9* etw proben, etw üben
to **praise sb** *67* jdn loben
pre-carriage *97* Vorlauf, Vorlauftransport
precinct, pedestrian ~ *10* Fußgängerzone
to **predict sth** *131T* etw voraussagen, etw vorhersagen
prediction *131T* Voraussage, Vorhersage
predictive text function *108* Eingabevervollständigung
to **prefer sth** *91* etw bevorzugen
preferably *70T* möglichst, am besten
preference *85* Wahl, Wunsch; **consumer ~es** *pl* *80* Verbrauchergewohnheiten
premises *pl* *97* Betriebsgelände, Geschäftsräume
premium *73T* Prämie
preparation *32* Vorbereitung
to **prepare sth** *38* etw erstellen
prepared, to **be ~ to do sth** *74* bereit sein, etw zu tun
prerequisites *pl* *130* Voraussetzungen
presence, online ~ *17* Online-Auftritt, Onlinepräsenz
present *140* Gegenwart; *148* aktuell, gegenwärtig
to **present sb/sth** *8* jdn/etw vorstellen
preserves *pl* *20* Konserven
pressed *58* gebügelt
pressure *69* Druck; **~ washer** *88* Hochdruckreiniger
pretty *66* ziemlich
price, basic ~ *143* Grundpreis; **final ~** *55T* Endpreis; **purchase ~** *65* Kaufpreis; **sales ~** *81T* Verkaufspreis; **total ~** *83* Gesamtpreis; **unit ~** *55T* Preis pro Einheit, Stückpreis; **~ concession** *65* Preisnachlass; **~ range** *63T* Preisklasse, Preissegment; **~ tag** *55T* Preisschild
pricemarker *30* Preisauszeichner
primary *88* primär, Haupt-; **~ product** *62* Ursprungsprodukt
primrose *24* Schlüsselblume
principle *58* Grundlage, Prinzip
print, palm ~ *132* Handabdruck; **in big ~** *55T* großgedruckt; **the small ~** *72* das Kleingedruckte
priority *12* Priorität, Schwerpunkt
privacy *72* Privatsphäre
private: ~ and confidential *93* streng vertraulich; **~ limited company (Ltd)** *18T* Gesellschaft mit beschränkter Haftung (GmbH)
privately owned *10* in Privatbesitz
probably *81T* wahrscheinlich
procedure *130* Verfahren, Ablauf
to **process sth** *85* etw bearbeiten, etw verarbeiten
process, business ~es *pl* *141* Geschäftsabläufe
to **produce sth** *41* etw produzieren, etw herstellen, etw erstellen
produce *134P* (landwirtschaftliche) Erzeugnisse, Lebensmittel
producer *55* Produzent/in, Hersteller/in
product, dairy ~s *pl* *11* Milchprodukte; **primary ~** *62* Ursprungsprodukt; **shaving ~s** *pl* *81T* Rasurbedarf; **~ demonstration** *128T*

Produktvorführung; ~ **display** 58 Produktpräsentation; ~ **group** 54 Warengruppe; ~ **range** 10 Angebot, Sortiment, Produktpalette
professional 74 Fachmann/-frau, Berufsangehörige/r; 88T professionell, Profi(-)
profile 14 Porträt, Profil; **job** ~ 33 Stellenprofil, Tätigkeitsprofil
profit 18T Gewinn
programme 67T (Radio-/TV-)Sendung; **loyalty** ~ 65 Treueprogramm, Kundenbindungsprogramm
to **programme sth** 67T etw programmieren
progress, to **make** ~ 134T vorankommen, Fortschritte machen
to **promote sth** 59 für etw werben, etw bewerben
promotion 12 Beförderung; 23T (Sonder-)Angebot, (Werbe-)Aktion; ~ **prospects** *pl* 12 Aufstiegschancen
prompt card 38 Moderationskarte
proof of purchase 85 Kaufbeleg, Kaufnachweis
prop 60T Requisite
pros and cons *pl* 19 Für und Wider, Vor- und Nachteile
prospects *pl*, **promotion** ~ 12 Aufstiegschancen
to **protect sth** 129 etw schützen
protection 82 Schutz
protein 55 Eiweiß
to **prove sth** 116 etw nachweisen, etw beweisen
to **provide sth** 48 etw zur Verfügung stellen, etw bieten, für etw sorgen; 116 etw *(Dokument usw.)* vorlegen
provider 79 Anbieter/in
pub 9 Kneipe, Pub
public, general ~ 74 Allgemeinheit, die breite Öffentlichkeit; ~ **holiday** 41 gesetzlicher Feiertag; ~ **limited company (plc)** 19 Aktiengesellschaft (AG); ~ **sector** 33T öffentliche Hand; ~ **transport** 8 öffentliche Verkehrsmittel; ~ **transport links** *pl* 22 Anbindung an den öffentlichen Nahverkehr
to **pull sth** 63T etw ziehen
punctual(ly) 103 pünktlich
purchase 58 Kauf; ~ **price** 65 Kaufpreis; **proof of** ~ 85 Kaufbeleg, Kaufnachweis
to **purchase sth** 91 etw kaufen, etw beziehen
purchasing 92 Einkauf(sabteilung); ~ **director** 93 Einkaufsleiter/in
purely 128T ausschließlich
purse 72 (Damen-)Portemonnaie
to **put:** ~ **sth aside** 66 etw zurücklegen; ~ **sb through (to sb)** 100T *(Telefon:)* jdn durchstellen, jdn mit jdm verbinden; ~ **sth into practice** 71 etw in die Praxis umsetzen
put simply 74 einfach gesagt/formuliert
pyjamas *pl* 24 Schlafanzug
pyramid 60T Pyramide

Q
qualification 33T Abschluss, Qualifikation; **higher education entrance** ~ 141 Hochschulreife; **school ~s** *pl* 12 Schulabschluss
qualified, fully ~ 32 ausgebildet, voll qualifiziert
to **qualify as …** 42 den Abschluss zum/zur … machen
quality 57 Qualität(sstufe); ~ **control** 122 Qualitätskontrolle
quantity 56 Menge; ~ **discount** 106 Mengenrabatt
quarter 103 Quartal
quarterly settlement 103 vierteljährliche Abrechnung
questionnaire 34 Fragebogen
queue 59 Warteschlange
to **queue up** 57 sich anstellen *(in einer Warteschlange)*
queuing 58 Warteschlangenbildung
quick, to **be** ~ **to anger** 78 jähzornig sein
quotation 94 (Preis-)Angebot; to **submit a** ~ 106 ein Angebot unterbreiten
to **quote sth** 91 etw *(Preis usw.)* angeben

R
race 47T Rasse
rack 57 Regal, Ständer; **luggage** ~ 63T Gepäckträger
rail 57 Schiene; **light** ~ 143 Stadtbahn; ~ **pass** 144 Zeitkarte *(für die Bahn)*; ~ **travel** 144 Bahnfahren, Bahnreisen
rain poncho 56 Regencape, Regenponcho
range, price ~ 63T Preisklasse, Preissegment; **product** ~ 10 Angebot, Sortiment, Produktpalette
rate, hourly ~ 34 Stundensatz, Stundenlohn; **above-average pay ~s** *pl* 142P überdurchschnittliche Bezahlung
rating 55T Bewertung, Einstufung, Prädikat; **credit** ~ 109T Bonitätseinstufung
raw material 25 Rohstoff(e)
razor, electric ~ 81T (elektrischer) Rasierapparat; **safety** ~ 81T (Nass-)Rasierer, Rasierhobel; ~ **blade** 81T Rasierklinge
reach, out of ~ 59 außer Reichweite
to **react (to sth)** 56 (auf etw) reagieren
reading light 146 Leselampe
ready-made meal 53 Fertiggericht
ready packaged 53 regalfertig verpackt
reality 32 Wirklichkeit
to **realize: sb ~s sth** 81T jdm wird/ist etw klar, jdm wird/ist etw bewusst
reason 7 Grund, Motiv; ~ **for dismissal** 41 Kündigungsgrund; **acceptable** ~ 47T angemessener (Kündigungs-)Grund; **for no** ~ 47T ohne Grund
reasonable 116 zumutbar
reasonably 34 vernünftigerweise, zumutbar
receipt 77 Quittung; 83 (Waren-)Erhalt; ~ **of order** 110 Auftragserhalt, Auftragseingang
to **receive sth** 82 etw erhalten, etw bekommen
recently 110 vor kurzem, kürzlich, in letzter Zeit
to **recharge** 66 *(Akku)* laden, wiederaufladen
recommendation 70 Empfehlung
record, track ~ 141 Erfolgsbilanz; **stock ~s** *pl* 86T (Lager-)Bestand
recorded delivery 93 Einschreiben
to **recover data** 117 Daten wiederherstellen, Daten retten
to **recruit sb** 7 jdn anwerben, jdn einstellen
recruiter 140 Personalreferent/in, Personalvermittler/in
recruitment agency 138 Personalvermittlung, Personalagentur
to **rectify a defect** 82 einen Mangel beseitigen
recyclable 25 recyclebar
Red Cross 9 Rotes Kreuz
to **redesign sth** 53 etw umgestalten, etw neu konzipieren
to **reduce sth** 25 etw verringern, etw reduzieren
reduced 24 reduziert
reduction 78 (Preis-)Nachlass
reference 74 Auskunft, Nachschlagen; 94 Referenz; 138 Kennziffer; ~ **(to sth)** 107 Bezugnahme (auf etw); ~ **initials** *pl* 93 Zeichen, Kürzel
reflection, to **be a** ~ **on sth** 114 ein schlechtes Licht auf etw werfen, etw infrage stellen
refrigerated: ~ **goods** *pl* 132 Kühlware(n); ~ **unit** 56 Kühlregal, Kühltheke
refrigerator 56 Kühlraum

refund *20* Rückerstattung, Erstattung
to **refund sth** *65* etw (rück)erstatten
to **refuse: ~ sth** *82* etw ablehnen, etw verweigern; **~ to do sth** *83* sich weigern, etw zu tun
regarding *103* hinsichtlich, bezüglich, betreffend
regardless of sth *34* ungeachtet einer Sache, ohne Rücksicht auf etw
regard: R~s *49* Mit freundlichen Grüßen; **Best ~s** *49* Mit freundlichen Grüßen
regional manager *19* Regionalleiter/in
to **register** *72* sich anmelden; **~ sth** *131T* etw erkennen, etw registrieren
register, cash ~ *58* Registrierkasse, Kasse
registered: ~ merchant *19* eingetragene/r Kaufmann/-frau (e.K.); **~ delivery** *93* Einschreiben
registration form *72* Anmeldeformular
regret *122* Bedauern
regular customer *65* Stammkunde/-kundin
to **regulate sth** *35* etw regeln, etw vorschreiben
regulation *36* Vorschrift, Regelung; **labelling ~s** *pl* *54* Etikettierungsvorschriften, Kennzeichnungsverordnung
to **reject sth** *114* etw ablehnen, etw zurückweisen
rejection *114* Ablehnung, Zurückweisung
related to *25* bezüglich, in Zusammenhang mit
relationship *15* Beziehung
to **relax** *22* sich erholen, sich entspannen
release, day ~ *8* tagweise Freistellung, ausbildungsbegleitender Unterricht
relevant (to sb/sth) *39* wichtig (für jdn/etw), von Bedeutung (für jdn/etw)
religious *44* religiös
relocation *142P* Umzug
to **remind sb** *15* jdn (an etw) erinnern
reminder *148T* Erinnerung
remote control *67T* Fernbedienung
remotely *132* ferngesteuert
to **remove sth** *84* etw entfernen
repair *75* Reparatur
repetition *60T* Wiederholung
to **replace sth** *55T* etw ersetzen
replacement *86* Austausch, Ersatz
reply *88* Antwort; **early ~** *95* baldige Antwort
to **report to sb** *19* jdm unterstellt sein, jdm unterstehen
reporting line *19* Unterstellung
to **represent sb/sth** *7* jdn/etw vertreten, jdn/etw repräsentieren
representative *95* Vertreter/in
reputation *106* Ruf
request: ~ (for sth) *49* Anfrage (nach etw), Bitte (um etw); to **make a ~** *76* einen Wunsch äußern, um etw bitten; **on ~** *94* auf Wunsch, auf Anfrage
to **request sth** *87* um etw bitten, etw wünschen
to **require sth** *94* etw benötigen, etw wünschen
required *145* nötig, erforderlich; to **be (legally) ~ to do sth** *86T* (gesetzlich) verpflichtet sein, etw zu tun
requirements *pl* *95* Bedarf, Wünsche; **dietary ~** *133* Ernährungsbedürfnisse, -anforderungen
to **reroute sth** *88T* etw umleiten
research *88* Recherche, Nachforschungen
to **research sth** *25* etw recherchieren, Nachforschungen über etw anstellen
resolution *67T* Auflösung
resources *pl*, **Human R~ (HR)** *42* Personalwesen; **natural ~** *28* Rohstoffquellen
respectful *86* respektvoll
to **respond to sth** *88T* auf etw reagieren
responsibility *12* Verantwortung; *40* Aufgabe, Zuständigkeit; to **take ~** *84* Verantwortung übernehmen
responsible *144* verantwortungsbewusst, verantwortungsvoll; to **be ~ for sth** *19* für etw zuständig sein, für etw verantwortlich sein
rest *46* Erholung, Ruhepause
restless *58* unruhig
restriction *44* Beschränkung, Auflage
résumé *AE* *140* Lebenslauf
retail *7* Einzelhandel; **~ chain** *41* Einzelhandelskette; **~ organization** *66* Einzelhandelsunternehmen; **~ outlet** *116* Einzelhandelsgeschäft; **~ park** *10* Einkaufszentrum, Fachmarktzentrum; **~ sector** *54* Warenbereich; **~ theatre** *128T* *Inszenierung des Einkaufserlebnisses im stationären Handel;* **~ therapy** *128T* Shopping-Therapie *(Einkaufen zur Stimmungsaufhellung);* **~ trade** *7* Einzelhandel
retailer, electrical ~ *72* Elektrofachmarkt; **offline ~** *83* stationäre/r Händler/in
retailing *18* Einzelhandel
to **retain customers** *135* Kunden binden
to **re-think sth** *17* etw überdenken
to **retire** *42* in den Ruhestand gehen, in Rente gehen
return *79* Rückgabe, Retoure; **right of ~** *79* Rückgaberecht; **~ label** *122* Retourenaufkleber; **bottle ~ machine** *20* Leergutautomat
returns policy *84* Rücknahmebedingungen, Verfahrensweise bei Rückgaben
reunification *49* Wiedervereinigung
review *81* Kritik, Besprechung, Bewertung
to **review sth** *35* etw prüfen, etw überprüfen; *50* etw nochmals betrachten, etw durcharbeiten
to **reward sb** *142P* jdn entlohnen
to **ride** *63T* fahren; to **test ~ sth** *63T* etw probefahren
riding, horse ~ *9* Reiten
right: ~s *pl* **and obligations** *82* Rechte und Pflichten; **cancellation ~** *82* Widerrufsrecht, Rücktrittsrecht; **consumer ~s** *pl* *115* Verbraucherrechte; **human ~s** *pl* *25* Menschenrechte; **~ of return** *79* Rückgaberecht; **workers' ~s** *pl* *41* Arbeitnehmerrechte
right-handed, to **be ~** *58* Rechtshänder sein
to **ring true** *69* glaubhaft klingen
to **rise** *51* (an)steigen
risk, to **be at ~ of sth** *81* von etw bedroht sein; to **bear the ~** *18T* das Risiko tragen; **at sb's own ~** *99* auf eigenes Risiko
roadmap *74* Fahrplan,
robot *131T* Roboter
robotic agent *74* Roboter
role, to **swap ~s** *13* die Rollen tauschen
roll-out *134T* (Markt-)Einführung, Rollout
Romania *113P* Rumänien
room, changing ~ *57* Umkleidekabine; **en-suite ~** *133* Zimmer mit eigenem Bad und WC; **fitting ~** *58* Umkleidekabine, Anprobe; **twin ~** *145* Doppelzimmer mit zwei Einzelbetten
rotten *87* faul
rough handling *119* grobe/unsachgemäße Handhabung
round trip *143* Hin- und Rückfahrt/-flug
routine, daily ~ *29* Tagesablauf, Alltagsroutine; **work ~** *30* Arbeitsablauf, Routinearbeiten; **~ actions** *pl* *11* wiederkehrende Handlungen
rug *81* Teppich

rule *36* Regel, Vorschrift; **Incoterms ~** *91* Internationale Handelsklausel; **as a ~** *116* in der Regel, normalerweise
to **run: ~ sth** *79* etw *(Unternehmen usw.)* betreiben, etw führen; **~ out** *66* zur Neige gehen; **~ a business** *18T* ein Unternehmen führen; **~ a check on sb** *109T* jdn überprüfen, jdn durchleuchten
rural *127* ländlich

S

to **sack sb** *31* jdn rausschmeißen, jdn entlassen
safe *15* unbedenklich, sicher
safety: ~ razor *81T* (Nass-)Rasierer, Rasierhobel; **~ shoes** *pl* *36* Sicherheitsschuhe
salary *29* Gehalt; **entry-level ~** *138* Einstiegsgehalt; **thirteenth ~** *41* 13. Monatsgehalt
sale, clearance ~ *24* Ausverkauf; **item for ~** *63* angebotener Artikel; **on ~** *23T* im Angebot
sales *pl* *7* Verkauf, Vertrieb; *23* Umsatz, Verkäufe; **distance ~** *82* Fernverkäufe, Fernabsatz; **~ adviser** *7* Kaufmann/-frau im Einzelhandel; **~ area** *11* Verkaufsfläche, -bereich; **~ assistant** *7* Verkäufer/in; **~ associate** *AE* *42* Verkäufer/in; **~ channel** *81* Vertriebskanal, Vertriebsweg; **~ commission** *12* Verkaufsprovision; **~ contract** *82* Kaufvertrag; **~ director** *15* Vertriebsleiter/in; **export ~ director** *120* Exportleiter/in; **~ figures** *pl* *42* Verkaufszahlen, Umsatzzahlen; **~ outlet** *17* Verkaufsstelle, Geschäft; **~ price** *81T* Verkaufspreis; **~ staff** *132T* Verkaufspersonal; **~ strategy** *80* Vertriebsstrategie; **~ talk** *66* Verkaufsgespräch
salon, nail ~ *26* Nagelstudio
salutation *93* *(Brief usw.:)* Anrede
same-day delivery *79* Lieferung/ Zustellung am selben Tag
sample *95* Muster, Probe; **cross-~** *54* Querschnitt, Querschnittsprobe
sandals *pl* *24* Sandalen
satellite dish *75* Satellitenschüssel
satisfaction, to sb's ~ *122* zu jds Zufriedenheit
satisfactory *118* zufriedenstellend, befriedigend
satisfied *106* zufrieden
to **satisfy demand** *91* die Nachfrage befriedigen
saturated fat *55* gesättigte Fettsäuren
saucepan *60T* Kochtopf
saucer *58* Untertasse
to **save: ~ sb/sth** *132T* jdn/etw retten; **~ sb/sth from sth** *81T* jdn/etw vor etw bewahren; **~ sth** *10* etw (ein) sparen; **~ sth up** *73T* etw ansparen
to **scan sth for sth** *74* etw nach etw absuchen
scannable *128T* maschinenlesbar, scannbar
scenery *128T* Kulisse, Szenerie
scheme, bonus ~ *138* Prämiensystem; **company pension ~** *138* betriebliche Altersvorsorge
school, comprehensive ~ *9* Gesamtschule; **grammar ~** *9* Gymnasium; **secondary ~** *9* weiterführende Schule; **selective secondary** *9* *weiterführende Schule mit Aufnahmebedingungen, z.B. Realschule, Gymnasium;* **high ~ diploma** *AE* *42* *US-Schulabschluss;* **~ qualifications** *pl* *12* Schulabschluss; to **leave ~** *42* von der Schule abgehen
school-leaver *7* Schulabgänger/in
school-leaving certificate *138* Schulabschluss
science *9* Naturwssenschaft
score *55T* Punktzahl, Bewertung; **total ~** *39* Gesamtpunktzahl
scratched *117* verkratzt, zerkratzt
screw *57* Schraube; **mounting ~** *118* Befestigungsschraube
to **scroll** *23T* scrollen
seal *85* Siegel, (luftdichte) Verpackung
sealed *83* eingeschweißt, versiegelt
seamless(ly) *128T* nahtlos
search engine *74* Suchmaschine
season *91* Saison
seasonal goods *pl* *22* Saisonartikel, Saisonware
secondary school *9* weiterführende Schule; **selective ~** *9* *weiterführende Schule mit Aufnahmebedingungen, z.B. Realschule, Gymnasium*
secret *88T* Geheimnis
secretary *93* Sekretär/in
section *11* Abteilung, Bereich
sector, public ~ *33T* öffentliche Hand; **retail ~** *54* Warenbereich
secure *12* sicher
security, social ~ *41* Sozialversicherung; **social ~ tax** *48* Sozialabgaben; **~ guard** *46* Sicherheitskraft, -mitarbeiter/in
to **seek sth** *141* etw suchen
to **segment sth** *88T* etw aufteilen, etw segmentieren
seldom *84T* selten
to **select sth** *28* etw auswählen
selection *22* Auswahl
selective secondary school *9* *weiterführende Schule mit Aufnahmebedingungen, z.B. Realschule, Gymnasium*
self-assembly *87* Selbstmontage
self-catering *146* Selbstversorgung
self-checkout *53* Selbstbedienungskas-se
self-service *10* Selbstbedienung
to **sell** *10* verkaufen
seller *55T* Verkäufer/in; **third-party ~** *81T* Fremdverkäufer/in; *128T* Drittanbieter
selling, distance ~ *82* Fernverkauf, Fernabsatz; **best-~** *38* meistverkauft, umsatzstark
seminar *8* Seminar; **~ leader** *8* Seminarleiter/in
to **send out sth** *89* etw verschicken
sense, five ~es *pl* *60T* fünf Sinne; to **make ~** *67* einleuchten; *75* sinnvoll sein, vernünftig sein
sensible *147* vernünftig, angemessen
sensor *132* Melder, Sensor; **depth-~** *132* Tiefensensor
to **separate sth** *52* etw trennen
separate(ly) *93* getrennt, separat
sequin *89* Paillette
series, TV ~ *9* Fernsehserie
seriously *81T* im Ernst; to **take sth ~** *68* etw ernst nehmen
to **serve sb** *12T* jdn bedienen
service *17* Dienstleistung, Bedienung, Service; **financial ~es** *pl* *73T* Finanzdienstleistungen; **customer ~es** *pl* *53* Kundendienst; **self-~** *10* Selbstbedienung; **technical emergency ~** *9* Technisches Hilfswerk; **~ station** *44* Tankstelle
set *140* fest, feststehend
to **set: ~ sth out** *135* etw darlegen; **~ sth up** *17* etw einrichten
to **settle sth** *122* etw regeln, etw *(Streit usw.)* beilegen
settlement, quarterly ~ *103* vierteljährliche Abrechnung
several *28* mehrere, einige
sewing *9* Nähen
sex *138* Geschlecht
sexual orientation *138* sexuelle Orientierung
to **share: ~ sth** *18T* (sich) etw teilen; **~ sth with sb** *81T* mit jdm über etw sprechen
share, market ~ *128T* Marktanteil
shared bathroom *145* Gemeinschaftsbad
sharp *125T* scharf

shaver *75* Rasierer
shaving: ~ cream *81T* Rasiercreme; **~ products** *pl* *81T* Rasurbedarf
sheath dress *89* Etuikleid
sheet *60T* *(Glas, Holz:)* Platte
shelf *12T* Regal; to **fill ~ves** *42* Regale auffüllen; to **stock ~ves** *57* Regale befüllen/bestücken
shelf-stacker *42* Regalauffüller/in, Warenverräumer/in
shelter *132T* Unterstand
shelving unit *87* Regalelement
shift *8* Schicht; **early ~** *12T* Frühschicht; **late ~** *32* Spätschicht; **~ work** *8* Schichtarbeit
ship, on board a ~ *97* an Bord eines Schiffs
to **ship sth** *81T* etw versenden, etw verschicken
shipment, port of ~ *97* Verladehafen
shipping *74* Versand
shoes *pl*, **covered ~** *36* geschlossene Schuhe; **safety ~** *36* Sicherheitsschuhe
to **shop** *22* einkaufen
shop, electrical ~ *62* Elektrogeschäft; **pop-up ~** *22* Pop-up-Store *(kurzfristiges und provisorisches Einzelhandelsgeschäft)*; **specialist ~** *65* Fachgeschäft; **training ~** *10* Ausbildungsgeschäft, -betrieb; **~ interior** *56* Ladeneinrichtung, Ladenausstattung; **~ manager** *12T* Filialleiter/in; **~ window** *58* Schaufenster
shoplifter *132* Ladendieb/in
shoplifting *134* Ladendiebstahl
shopper *25* Kunde/Kundin *(im Laden)*
shopping: ~ hours *pl* *41* Ladenöffnungszeiten; **~ mall** *10* (überdachtes) Einkaufszentrum; **~ trip** *131T* Einkaufstour, Einkaufsbummel
short, to cut a long story ~ *132T* um etw kurz zu machen; lange Rede, kurzer Sinn; **in the ~er term** *103* kurzfristig, auf kürzere Sicht
shortlisted, to **be ~** *143* in die engere Auswahl kommen
short-sleeved *35* kurzärmlig
show of hands *23T* Handzeichen
to **show off** *15* angeben
showroom *10* Ausstellung(sfläche)
to **shrink** *128T* schrumpfen
sight *60T* Gesichtssinn, Sehen; **at first ~** *91* auf den ersten Blick; **out of ~** *59* außer Sicht(weite)
sign, currency ~ *104* Währungssymbol
to **sign sth** *33* etw unterschreiben, etw unterzeichnen

signage, digital ~ *132T* digitale Außenwerbung
signal strength *147* Signalstärke
signatory *93* Unterzeichner/in, Unterzeichnete/r
signature *86* Unterschrift
signpost *38* *orientierender Hinweis in einer Präsentation*
signs *pl* **of use** *82* Gebrauchsspuren
similar *34* ähnlich
similarity *40* Ähnlichkeit, Gemeinsamkeit
simply, put ~ *74* einfach gesagt/formuliert
sincerely, Yours ~ *92* Mit freundlichen Grüßen
single *8* alleinstehend; **~ bed** *145* Einzelbett
sir *27* *(Anrede:)* mein Herr
to **sit back** *70T* sich zurücklehnen
site, building ~ *66* Baustelle
size, collar ~ *67T* Kragenweite; **one-~-fits-all** *88T* Einheits-
sketch *64* Skizze
to **sketch sth out** *61* etw skizzieren
skiing *9* Skifahren
skill *76* Fähigkeit, Fertigkeit, Kompetenz
to **skim (a text)** *32* (einen Text) überfliegen
skin *37* Haut
skirt *37* Rock
to **slash sth** *88T* etw *(Preis usw.)* senken
slats *pl* *70T* Lattenrost
sleeping bag *61* Schlafsack
to **sleep: ~s two** *145* *(Unterkunft:)* bietet Platz für zwei Personen
slide *39* Dia, Slide; **~ show** *11* Diavortrag, Bildschirmpräsentation
slightly *68* geringfügig, ein wenig
slogan *37* (Werbe-)Spruch, Parole
slot *88T* Platz, Platzhalter
small: ~ town *9* Kleinstadt; **the ~ print** *72* das Kleingedruckte
smart *12* elegant, schick; *75* intelligent
smell *58* Geruch
smoke alarm *118* Rauchmelder
smooth *63T* geschmeidig, ohne Schwierigkeiten
to **snack on sth** *131T* etw zwischendurch essen
to **snap** *63T* einrasten
to **sniff sth** *57* an etw riechen
soap *10* Seife
so-called *44* sogenannt
social: ~ security *41* Sozialversicherung; **~ security tax** *48* Sozialabgaben
soft, to **be ~ to the touch** *57* sich weich anfühlen; **~ furnishings** *pl* *10* Heimtextilien

sole trader *18* Einzelunternehmer/in
solid *81* *(Metall, Holz usw.:)* massiv
solidarity surcharge *32* Solidaritätszuschlag
solution *31* Lösung
to **solve sth** *31* etw *(Problem usw.)* lösen
sort *12T* Art
to **sort sth** *12T* etw sortieren
sound *60T* Gehör(sinn)
to **sound** *67T* klingen
source *28* Herkunft; *109* Bezugsquelle, Quelle
sourcing *25* Beschaffung
space, storage ~ *66* Speicherplatz; **waste of ~** *140* Platzverschwendung; to **take up ~** *132T* Raum benötigen/einnehmen
spare *63T* Reserve-; **~ part** *81T* Ersatzteil; **~ time** *140* Freizeit
speaker, guest ~ *132* Gastredner/in
special: ~ deal *23* (Sonder-)Angebot; **~ occasion** *66* besonderer Anlass; **~ offer** *24* Sonderangebot
specialist *62* Fachmann/-frau, Experte/-in; **~ shop** *65* Fachgeschäft
speciality *22* Spezialität
specific *23T* konkret, bestimmt
speech bubble *46* Sprechblase
speed *131T* Geschwindigkeit
to **spell sth** *100T* etw buchstabieren, etw schreiben
spelling *38* Rechtschreibung
to **spend: ~ money on sth** *43* Geld für etw ausgeben; **~ time** *57* Zeit verbringen
spice *53* Gewürz
spillage *58* Verschüttetes
spin, to **take the bike out for a ~** *63T* eine Runde mit dem Fahrrad drehen
spirits *pl BE* *44* Spirituosen
to **split sth into sth** *88T* etw in etw aufteilen
spoiled *116* verdorben
to **spot sth** *108* etw finden, etw erkennen
sprouts *pl*, **Brussels ~** *24* Rosenkohl
squeaky clean *58* blitzsauber
to **squeeze sth** *57* etw drücken, etw zusammenquetschen
stack *60T* Stapel
to **stack sth** *56* etw stapeln
stacker, shelf-~ *42* Regalauffüller/in, Warenverräumer/in
staff *7* Mitarbeiter *pl*, Personal; **entry-level ~** *142P* Berufseinsteiger/innen; **sales ~** *132T* Verkaufspersonal
staff, temporary ~ *142P* Aushilfen
stage *60T* Bühne; *66* Phase

stand *24* Ständer; *26* (Verkaufs-)Stand; **display ~** *12T* Präsentationsständer, Aufsteller, Infoständer
to **stand: ~ out** *59* auffallen, sich abheben; **~ still** *58* stillstehen
stand-alone *73T* eigenständig
standard *25* Norm, Standard; *148T* Maßstab, Anspruch; to **be up to sb's ~s** *113* jds Niveau entsprechen, jds Erwartungen erfüllen
staple goods *pl* *10* Waren des täglichen Bedarfs
state *45* Bundesland
to **state sth** *26* etw angeben, etw nennen
statement *32* Äußerung, Schilderung; *34* Aussage; **bank ~** *87* Kontoauszug
station, central ~ *10* Hauptbahnhof; **charging ~** *20* Ladesäule, E-Tankstelle; **petrol ~** *BE* *22* Tankstelle; **service ~** *44* Tankstelle
stationery *32* Schreibwaren, Büromaterial
statistics *pl* *50* Statistik(en)
status *34* Status
to **stay** *18T* bleiben; to **be here to ~** *132* Einzug halten, von Dauer sein
stay, overnight ~ *145* Übernachtung
steadiness *68* Stetigkeit
sticker *55T* Aufkleber
still, to **stand ~** *58* stillstehen; **~ water** *147* Wasser ohne Kohlensäure
stock: ~ level *132T* (Lager-)Bestand; **~ records** *pl* *86T* (Lager-)Bestand; **from ~** *106* ab Lager; **in ~** *86T* vorrätig, auf Lager; **out of ~** *57* ausverkauft
to **stock: ~ sth** *10* etw *(Ware usw.)* führen; **~ up** *94* Bestand aufbauen, sich eindecken; **~ shelves** *57* Regale befüllen/bestücken
stone, paving ~ *88* Pflasterstein
to **stop sb from doing sth** *59* jdn (daran) hindern, etw zu tun
storage *146* Aufbewahrung; **~ space** *66* Speicherplatz
to **store sth** *81T* etw lagern
store, big box ~ *10* Fachmarkt, (großflächiges) Kaufhaus; **chain ~** *10* Filiale *(einer Handelskette)*; **convenience ~** *22* Minimarkt, Spätkauf; **dark ~** *22* Dark Store *(Distributionszentrum für den Onlinehandel)*; **DIY ~** *11* Heimwerkermarkt, Baumarkt; **grocery ~** *11* Lebensmittelgeschäft; **liquor ~** *AE* *44* (konzessioniertes) Wein- und Spirituosengeschäft; **~ guide** *27* *(Einkaufszentrum:)* Lageplan; **~ locator** *23* Filialsuche, Filialfinder; **multi-~** *73T* händlerübergreifend
story, to cut a long ~ short *132T* um etw kurz zu machen; lange Rede, kurzer Sinn
straight *10* direkt, gleich; **~ ahead** *27* geradeaus
strategy, sales ~ *80* Vertriebsstrategie
straw *56* Stroh
to **stream sth** *9* etw streamen
street, high ~ *BE* *22* Hauptstraße, Hauptgeschäftsstraße, Innenstadt
strength *148* Stärke; **signal ~** *147* Signalstärke
strict *44* streng, strikt
strong opinion *34* klare Meinung
strongly, to **agree ~** *34* nachdrücklich zustimmen; to **disagree ~** *34* überhaupt nicht zustimmen
structure *23* Aufbau, Struktur
to **structure sth** *24* etw aufbauen, etw strukturieren
student, work placement ~ *19* Praktikant/in
studies *pl*, **business ~** *141* Betriebswirtschaft
to **study sth** *16* sich etw genau ansehen
stuff *74* Sachen, Zeug
sturdy *110* stabil
style *70T* Ausführung, Art
sub-category *23T* Unterkategorie, Untergruppe
subject *9* (Schul-)Fach; **~ line** *88T* Betreffzeile
to **submit a quotation** *106* ein Angebot unterbreiten
subscriber *88* Abonnennt/in
substandard *119* minderwertig
successful *41* erfolgreich
suddenly *22* plötzlich
to **suggest** *60* vorschlagen, nahelegen
suggestion *23T* Vorschlag
suit *36* Anzug; **trouser ~** *37* Hosenanzug
to **suit sb** *84T* *(Kleidung usw.:)* jdm stehen
suitable *50* passend, geeignet
suitcase *27* Koffer
suited, to **be ideally ~ for sth** *142* für etw hervorragend geeignet sein
sum *73T* Betrag, Summe
to **summarize** *39* zusammenfassen
sunbed *96* (Sonnen-, Garten-)Liege
Sunday trading *44* verkaufsoffener Sonntag, Sonntagsöffnung
supermarket manager *18T* Martkleiter/in
to **supervise sb** *19* jdm vorgesetzt sein
supervised children's play area *10* betreuter Spielbereich für Kinder
supervision *138* Aufsicht, Leitung, Betreuung
supervisor *42* Teamleiter/in, Abteilungsleiter/in
supplier *12T* Lieferant/in
supplies *pl* *91* Lieferungen, Nachschub; **knitting ~** *81T* Strickbedarf
supply chain *25* Lieferkette, Versorgungskette
to **supply sb with sth** *106* jdn mit etw beliefern, jdm etw liefern
support *34* Unterstützung, Hilfe
to **support sth** *39* etw *(Argument usw.)* untermauern
to **suppose: I ~ …** *148T* wohl, vermutlich
supposed, to **be ~ to do sth** *74* etw (eigentlich) tun sollen
surcharge, solidarity ~ *32* Solidaritätszuschlag
sure, to **make ~** *59* gewährleisten, dafür sorgen, sicherstellen
surely *31* gewiss, sicher(lich)
surprised *22* erstaunt, überrascht
surroundings *pl* *22* Umgebung
survey *130* Umfrage
to **survey sb** *130* jdn befragen
to **survive** *81* überleben
sustainability *25* Nachhaltigkeit
sustainable *25* nachhaltig
to **swap roles** *13* die Rollen tauschen
sweatshop *25* Ausbeuterbetrieb, Sweatshop
Swedish *100* schwedisch
swimming costume *86T* Badeanzug
swing *95* Schaukel
to **swipe** *74* wischen
switch *119* Schalter
to **switch sth on/off** *87* etw an-/ausschalten
switchboard *18* Schalttafel
sympathy *124* Mitgefühl
synthetic *77* Synthetik
Syria *14T* Syrien
system, healthcare ~ *50* Gesundheitssystem; **operating ~** *141* Betriebssystem; **traffic light ~** *55T* Ampelsystem

T

table, coffee ~ *86T* Couchtisch; **display ~** *57* Präsentationstisch, Ausstellungstisch
tabular, in ~ form *140* in Tabellenform
to **tag sth** *30* etw etikettieren
tag, price ~ *55T* Preisschild
tagging gun *30* Etikettierpistole

tail, to **wag one's ~** *70T* mit dem Schwanz wedeln
tailor-made to sth *140* auf etw (individuell) zugeschnitten
to **take: ~ in sth** *58* etw erfassen, etw (Eindrücke usw.) aufnehmen; **~ sth up** *66* etw *(Platz usw.)* beanspruchen; *67T* etw *(Hose usw.)* kürzen; **~ up space** *132T* Raum benötigen/einnehmen; **~ sth seriously** *68* etw ernst nehmen; **~ part in sth** *42* an etw teilnehmen; **~ one's time** *58* sich Zeit lassen
take-home pay *32* Nettolohn, Nettogehalt
takings *pl*, **day's ~** *30* Tageseinnahmen
talk *38* Vortrag; **sales ~** *66* Verkaufsgespräch
to **tap** *23T* tippen; **~ sth** *67* etw antippen, etw *(Karte usw.)* auflegen
target: ~ audience *16* Zielgruppe; **~ group** *74* Zielgruppe
task *10* Aufgabe; **~ force** *41* Arbeitsgruppe
tattoo *37* Tätowierung
tax *32* Steuer; **church ~** *32* Kirchensteuer; **income ~** *32* Einkommensteuer; **social security ~** *48* Sozialabgaben; **value added ~ (VAT)** *55T* Mehrwertsteuer (MwSt)
teaching, face-to-face ~ *42* Präsenzunterricht
teapot *58* Teekanne
technical: ~ defect *116* technischer Mangel; **~ emergency service** *9* Technisches Hilfswerk
technician *116* Techniker/in
technology *134P* Technik, Technologie
template *91* Vorlage, Muster
temporary *138* befristet, vorübergehend, auf Zeit; **~ staff** *142P* Aushilfen
term *97* Klausel; *122* Begriff; **in the longer ~** *103* längerfristig, auf längere Sicht; **in the shorter ~** *103* kurzfristig, auf kürzere Sicht
terms *pl*: **~ and conditions** *85* Allgemeine Geschäftsbedingungen; **~of delivery** *83* Lieferbedingungen; **~ of payment** *83* Zahlungsbedingungen, -konditionen, -modalitäten; **open account ~** *103* offenes Zahlungsziel, laufende Rechnung
to **terminate sb** *47T* jdm kündigen
to **test: ~ sth on sb** *74* etw an jdm erproben; **~ ride sth** *63T* etw probefahren; **not ~ed on animals** *25* tierversuchsfrei
test, personality ~ *68* Persönlichkeitstest; **waterproofing ~** *122* Dichtigkeitsprüfung
text *66* SMS, Textnachricht
textiles *pl* *55T* Textilien
thanks to *22* dank
that's why *22* deshalb
theatre, retail ~ *128T* *Inszenierung des Einkaufserlebnisses im stationären Handel*
theft, identity ~ *72* Identitätsdiebstahl
theoretical *9* theoretisch
therapy, retail ~ *128T* Shopping-Therapie *(Einkaufen zur Stimmungsaufhellung)*
thereafter *99* danach
therefore *29* deshalb, daher
thin *129* dünn
thing, among other ~s *55T* unter anderem
thinking *37* Überlegung(en)
third *33T* Drittel; **~ party** *131T* Dritte/r
third-party seller *81T* Fremdverkäufer/in; *128T* Drittanbieter
thirdly *12T* drittens
thirteenth salary *41* 13. Monatsgehalt
thoroughly, to **agree ~** *134T* voll und ganz zustimmen
thought, to **collect one's ~s** *147* seine Gedanken ordnen, sich sammeln
throughout the EU *106* in der ganzen EU
to **throw sth (away)** *55T* etw (weg) werfen
to **tick: ~ sth** *84T* etw ankreuzen; **~ sth off** *34* etw abhaken
tidy *68* sauber, ordentlich
tie *35* Krawatte
to **tie sth** *36* etw zusammenbinden
tight *67T* eng
tights *pl* *147* Strumpfhose
till *BE* *30* Kasse
timber *54* Holz, Bauholz
time, closing ~ *69* Ladenschluss, Feierabend; **~ off** *32* Freizeit, Freizeitausgleich; **full-~** *32* (in) Vollzeit(-); **part-~** *12T* (in) Teilzeit(-); **period of ~** *50* Zeitraum; **spare ~** *140* Freizeit; **travel ~** *144* Fahrtzeit; **any ~ sb pleases** *47T* wann (immer) jd will; to **spend ~** *57* Zeit verbringen; to **take ~ off** *47T* sich freinehmen; to **take ~ out** *22* eine Pause machen, (sich) eine Auszeit nehmen; to **take one's ~** *58* sich Zeit lassen
timeline *43* Zeitachse, Verlauf
times *73T* mal
title, job ~ *140* Stellenbezeichnung
toiletries *pl* *10* Hygieneartikel
token, non-fungible ~ *129* Non-Fungible Token *(nicht austauschbares digitales Objekt)*
tongs *pl*, **curling ~** *75* Lockenstab
tool *57* Werkzeug; **hand ~** *11* Handwerkzeug; **power ~** *11* Elektrowerkzeug
toothpaste *10* Zahnpasta
to **top sth up** *115* etw (wieder) auffüllen
top, on ~ *33T* zusätzlich; **on ~ of each other** *60T* aufeinander
topic *15* Thema
total *48* Summe, Gesamtbetrag, Gesamt-; **~ price** *83* Gesamtpreis; **~ score** *39* Gesamtpunktzahl
touch *60T* Tastsinn; to **be soft to the ~** *57* sich weich anfühlen; to **get in ~ with sb** *49* sich bei jdm melden, sich mit jdm in Verbindung setzen
to **touch sth** *36* etw anfassen, etw berühren
tough *67* robust
towel *53* Handtuch
town, small ~ *9* Kleinstadt
toy *20* Spielzeug
traces *pl* *87* Spuren
track, to **be on ~** *134T* gut in der Zeit liegen; **~ record** *141* Erfolgsbilanz
to **track sb/sth** *50* jdn/etw (nach) verfolgen
to **trade** *25* handeln, Handel treiben; **~ in sth** *100* mit etw handeln
trade, international ~ *97* Außenhandel; **retail ~** *7* Einzelhandel; **~ discount** *107* Händlerrabatt; **~ fair** *7* Messe; **~ union** *33T* Gewerkschaft
trader *44* Händler/in, Kaufmann/-frau; **sole ~** *18* Einzelunternehmer/in
trading, Sunday ~ *44* verkaufsoffener Sonntag, Sonntagsöffnung; **~ partner** *104* Handelspartner/in
traffic, customer ~ *59* Kundenstrom, -verkehr, -aufkommen; **~ light system** *55T* Ampelsystem
trailer *63T* Anhänger
train, main line ~ *143* Fernzug; to **catch a ~** *22* einen Zug bekommen/erwischen
to **train: ~ (as …)** *7* eine Ausbildung (zum/zur …) machen; **~ sb as sth** *42* jdn zu etw ausbilden
trained *31* ausgebildet, geschult
trainer *68* Ausbilder/in, Dozent/in
trainers *pl* *24* Turnschuhe, Sportschuhe

training *10* Ausbildung; **~ course** *7* Ausbildung(sgang); *34* Schulung, Lehrgang; **~ firm** *17* Ausbildungsbetrieb; **~ shop** *10* Ausbildungsgeschäft, -betrieb; **vocational ~ college** *8* Berufsschule
trampoline *123T* Trampolin
to **transfer sb** *148T* jdn versetzen
transfer, bank ~ *86* Überweisung
transit, in ~ *119* beim Transport
transition zone *58* Übergangsbereich
transparency *39* (Overhead-)Folie
to **transport sth** *75* etw befördern, etw transportieren
transport, public ~ *8* öffentliche Verkehrsmittel; **means of ~** *143* Transportmittel; **public ~ links** *pl* *22* Anbindung an den öffentlichen Nahverkehr
transportation *99* Transport
travel, rail ~ *144* Bahnfahren, Bahnreisen; **~ agency** *26* Reisebüro; **~ expenses** *pl* *134T* Reisekosten; **~ time** *144* Fahrtzeit
tray *56* Kiste, Korb, Schale, Tablett
to **treat sb** *78* jdn behandeln
trekking boots *pl* *23T* Wanderstiefel
trial order *106* Probeauftrage, Probebestellung
tricky *84T* kompliziert
trip, round ~ *143* Hin- und Rückfahrt/-flug; **shopping ~** *131T* Einkaufstour, Einkaufsbummel
trivial *140* banal, belanglos, trivial
trolley *76* Einkaufswagen
trouser suit *37* Hosenanzug
truck, pallet ~ *30* Hubwagen
true, to **ring ~** *69* glaubhaft klingen
truly *131T* wirklich
to **trust** *110* hoffen; **~ sb** *105* jdm vertrauen; **~ sb with sth** *109T* jdm etw anvertrauen
trust, to **build ~** *69* Vertrauen aufbauen

trusted *105* zuverlässig, vertrauenswürdig
to **try** *17* versuchen
to **tuck sth somewhere** *36* etw irgendwohin stecken
to **tune in** *81T* *(Radio usw.:)* einschalten
Turkey *69* Türkei
to **turn: ~ into sth** *115* zu etw werden; **~ to sb** *31* sich an jdn wenden; **~ left/right** *27* links/rechts abbiegen; **~ right** *58* sich nach rechts wenden
turn, to **be one's ~** *39* an der Reihe sein; to **take ~s doing sth** *148* etw abwechselnd tun; to **take it in ~s to do sth** *9* etw abwechselnd tun
TV series *9* Fernsehserie
twin: ~ beds *pl* *145* zwei Einzelbetten; **~ brother/sister** *8* Zwillingsbruder/-schwester; **~ room** *145* Doppelzimmer mit zwei Einzelbetten
type *12* Art; **personality ~** *68* Persönlichkeitstyp
typical *27* charakteristisch, typisch

U

umbrella *56* Regenschirm
uncomfortable, to **feel ~** *59* sich unwohl fühlen
to **undercut sb/sth** *81T* jdn/etw unterbieten
underscore *100* Unterstrich
unemployed *42* arbeitslos
unemployment insurance *32* Arbeitslosenversicherung
unexpected *91* unerwartet
unfair *33T* ungerecht, unfair
unfinished action *22* noch nicht abgeschlossene Handlung
unhappy *69* unzufrieden, unglücklich
unhygienic *57* unhygienisch
uniform *12* Arbeitskleidung, Dienstkleidung
unimportant *132* unbedeutend, unwichtig
union, trade ~ *33T* Gewerkschaft
unique, to **be ~** *129* ein Unikat sein
unironed *37* ungebügelt
unit *95* Stück, Einheit; **air conditioning ~** *75* Klimaanlage, Klimagerät; **refrigerated ~** *56* Kühlregal, Kühltheke; **shelving ~** *87* Regalelement; **~ price** *55T* Preis pro Einheit, Stückpreis
universal *140* allgemeingültig, universell
unjust(ly) *78* ungerecht
unless *83* außer wenn; es sei denn, dass; **~ otherwise agreed** *99* sofern nicht anders vereinbart
unlimited *144* unbegrenzt, unbeschränkt
to **unload** *97* entladen, abladen
to **unlock sth** *30* etw aufschließen
unmarried *48* unverheiratet
unnamed *93* unbenannt, nicht namentlich bekannt
unnatural *37* unnatürlich
unopened *77P* ungeöffnet
to **unpack sth** *12T* etw auspacken
unpleasant *108* unerfreulich
unsafe *125* nicht sicher, gefährlich
unsatisfactory *119* unzulänglich, unzureichend
unstaffed *132* unbesetzt, ohne Personal
to **unsubscribe from sth** *88* sich von etw abmelden, etw kündigen
unsuccessful *67* erfolglos, ergebnislos
untrained *32* unausgebildet, ungelernt
to **unwrap sth** *83* etw auspacken
up: ~ to *74* bis zu; to **be ~ to sb's standards** *113* jds Niveau entsprechen, jds Erwartungen erfüllen
update (on sth) *88* Neuigkeiten (über etw)
to **update sth** *18* etw auf den neuesten Stand bringen, etw aktualisieren
uphill *63T* bergauf
upholstered bed *70T* Polsterbett
to **upload sth** *22* etw hochladen
up-market *142P* exklusiv
uppercase *100* großgeschrieben
to **upsell sth** *63* eine höherwertige Variante von etw verkaufen
upselling *62* Upselling *(Verkauf einer höherwertigen Variante eines Produkts)*
upset *124* verärgert, aufgebracht
urgent(ly) *93* dringend
use, signs of ~ *82* Gebrauchsspuren
use-by date *30* Verbrauchsdatum, Verfallsdatum
user *74* Nutzer/in, Anwender/in
usual *106* üblich

V

vacancy *42* freie Stelle, Stellenangebot
vacation *47T* Urlaub
vacuum cleaner *75* Staubsauger
valid *113T* gültig, wirksam
valuable *114* wertvoll, (sehr) geschätzt
value *23* Wert; **energy ~** *55T* Brennwert; **nutritional ~** *55* Nährwert; **~ added tax (VAT)** *55T* Mehrwertsteuer (MwSt)
van *31* Lieferwagen
variety *12T* Vielfalt; **a ~ of** *74* unterschiedliche, verschiedene
various *40* verschiedene
to **vary** *37* unterschiedlich sein, variieren
vegetables *pl* *11* Gemüse
vehicle *10* Fahrzeug; **electric ~** *132T* Elektrofahrzeug
vending machine *132* (Verkaufs-) Automat
venue *133* Veranstaltungsort
to **verify sth** *132* etw überprüfen, etw bestätigen
version *18* Version
vertical(ly) *50* senkrecht

vessel *99* Schiff
to **vibrate** *147* vibrieren
view, point of ~ *46* Perspektive, Blickwinkel, Standpunkt; **in ~ of** *103* angesichts; **with a ~ to doing sth** *103* in/mit der Absicht, etw zu tun; to **give one's ~** *57* seine Meinung äußern, seine Ansicht darlegen
village *132* Dorf
villager *132* Dorfbewohner/in
virtual *74* virtuell
visible *37* sichtbar
visitor *7* Besucher/in, Gast
visual aids *pl* *39* visuelle Hilfsmittel
visual(ly) *60* visuell
vitamin pill *10* Vitaminpille
vocabulary *16* Vokablen, Wortschatz
vocational training college *8* Berufsschule
voicemail *115* Anrufbeantworter, Mailbox
volume *147* Lautstärke
volume of business *103* Geschäftsvolumen
voluntary *55* freiwillig
to **volunteer** *9* ehrenamtlich tätig sein
voucher *72* Gutschein

W
to **wag one's tail** *70T* mit dem Schwanz wedeln
wage, minimum ~ *33T* Mindestlohn; **~ agreement** *33T* Tarifvertrag
walk-in *132* begehbar, für Laufkundschaft; **~ customers** *pl* *81T* Laufkundschaft
wallet *131T* Brieftasche, (Herren-) Portemonnaie
wardrobe *71* Kleiderschrank
warehouse *22* Lager, Lagerhalle
to **warm up** *119* heiß werden
warming, global ~ *84T* Erderwärmung
to **warn sb about sth** *47T* jdn auf etw aufmerksam machen
warranty *75* Garantie, Gewährleistung
Warsaw *134T* Warschau
washbasin *146* Waschbecken
washer *57* Unterlegscheibe; **pressure ~** *88* Hochdruckreiniger
washing, a load of ~ *55T* eine Ladung Wäsche; **~ machine** *54* Waschmaschine; **~ powder** *10* Waschpulver
washing-up liquid *11* Spülmittel
waste *25* Abfall; **~ of space** *140* Platzverschwendung
water, fizzy ~ *147* Wasser mit Kohlensäure; **still ~** *147* Wasser ohne Kohlensäure; **~ fountain** *26* Brunnen
watered-down *74* abgeschwächt, verkürzt
waterproof *67* wasserdicht
waterproofing test *122* Dichtigkeitsprüfung
way, by the ~ *63T* übrigens
way, this ~ *67T* hier entlang
weakness *148* Schwäche, Schwachpunkt
wear, bridal ~ *37* Brautmoden; **men's ~** *26* Herrenbekleidung
wearables *pl* *129* Wearables (*tragbare bzw. in Kleidung integrierte Technologie*)
weather, whatever the ~ *22* bei jedem Wetter
wedding *67T* Hochzeit; **~ ring** *27* Ehering, Trauring
to **weigh** *63T* wiegen
weight-sensitive *132* mit Gewichtssensor
weightlifting *9* Gewichtheben
to **welcome sb** *38* jdn willkommen heißen, jdn begrüßen
welcome: You're ~. *27* Bitte (sehr). Gern geschehen.
wellbeing *59* Wohlbefinden
well-known *18T* (sehr) bekannt
well-mannered *141* mit guten Manieren, kultiviert
whatever: ~ the case may be *118* wie auch immer, wie dem auch sei; **~ the weather** *22* bei jedem Wetter
whereas *56* während
wherever *22* wo (auch) immer
whether *49* ob
while *35* während
wholesaler *107* Großhändler/in
why, that's ~ *22* deshalb
wide *10* breit
wide-angle lens *65* Weitwinkelobjektiv
width *71* Breite
will, as a gesture of good ~ *86T* aus Kulanz
willing, to **be ~ to do sth** *18T* bereit sein, etw zu tun
window, shop ~ *58* Schaufenster; **~ dresser** *12T* Schaufensterdekorateur/in; **~ dressing** *12T* Schaufensterdekoration
wireless *67* kabellos
wish: Best ~es *48* Mit freundlichen Grüßen, Viele Grüße
within *83* innerhalb von, binnen
wooden *61* Holz-, aus Holz
wool *81T* Wolle
word, key ~ *39* Stichwort
wordy *28* wortreich, weitschweifig
to **work: ~ out** *123T* funktionieren, klappen, gelingen; **~ out sth** *43* etw ausrechnen, etw herausfinden; **~ long hours** *32* lange arbeiten, Überstunden machen; **~ one's magic on sth** *23T* zeigen, was man kann; sich einer Sache annehmen
work, charity ~ *9* ehrenamtliche Arbeit; **shift ~** *8* Schichtarbeit; **~ buddy** *31* *erfahrene/r Kollege/-in, der/die einen gleichrangigen Neuzugang einarbeitet;* **~-life balance** *34* *Gleichgewicht zwischen Berufs- und Privatleben;* **~ performance** *140* Arbeitsleistung; **~ placement** *9* Praktikum; **~ placement student** *19* Praktikant/in; **~ routine** *30* Arbeitsablauf, Routinearbeiten
worker *31* Arbeiter/in; **~s' rights** *pl* *41* Arbeitnehmerrechte
working: ~ conditions *pl* *25* Arbeitsbedingungen; **~ hours** *pl* *12* Arbeitszeit(en)
workmanship *109T* Verarbeitung
workplace *7* Arbeitsplatz
works council *BE* *29* Betriebsrat
workshop *125* Werkstatt
workwear *29* Arbeitskleidung, Berufskleidung
worth *72* wert; *105* im Wert von
wound *36* Wunde
to **wrap sth up** *134T* etw abschließen, etw beenden
wrinkle-free *58* knitterfrei
wristwatch *26* Armbanduhr
writing, in ~ *83* schriftlich, in Schriftform

XYZ
x-axis *50* X-Achse
y-axis *50* Y-Achse
year, New Y~'s Eve *59* Silvester
yesterday, the day before ~ *86T* vorgestern
Yours sincerely/faithfully *92* Mit freundlichen Grüßen
youth hostel *145* Jugendherberge
zone, high-selling ~ *59* umsatzstarker Bereich; **transition ~** *58* Übergangsbereich

INCOTERMS® RULES 2020

As trade becomes more and more global, goods travel further and further, crossing geographical, cultural and language barriers on their way. For this reason it is essential that importers and exporters agree to use the same terms of reference.

In 1936 the International Chamber of Commerce in Paris formulated a set of International Commercial Terms (Incoterms® rules) to define importers' and exporters' rights and obligations, such as transport costs, risk, insurance, customs duty, documentation, loading and unloading. Since then the Incoterms® rules have been revised eight times to keep up with developments in the field of international trade and translated into many different languages. The last revision was in 2020. There are now eleven Incoterms® rules, seven of which can be used for any mode or combined modes of transport, e.g. truck, train, ship or rail. The other four are used for ship or inland waterway transport only.

Rules for any mode or modes of transport

1
EXW (EX WORKS)
Ab Werk
The seller makes the goods available at his premises. The buyer bears all the costs and risks of transporting the goods to their destination.

2
FCA (FREE CARRIER)
Frei Frachtführer
The seller loads the goods on board the first carrier's vehicle. The buyer bears all the costs and risks of transporting the goods to their destination.

3
CPT (CARRIAGE PAID TO)
Frachtfrei bis
The seller bears all the costs and risks until the goods are handed over to the first carrier. He pays the transport costs, without insurance, for the main carriage to the named destination. The buyer insures the goods for the main carriage and bears all other costs.

4
CIP (CARRIAGE AND INSURANCE PAID TO)
Frachtfrei versichert bis
The seller bears all the costs and risks until the goods are handed over to the first carrier. He pays the transport costs, including all-risk insurance, for the main carriage to the named destination. The buyer bears all other costs.

5
DAP (DELIVERED AT PLACE)
Geliefert benannter Ort
The seller bears all the costs and risks until the goods have reached their destination. The buyer is responsible for import duties and unloading the goods.

6
DPU (DELIVERED NAMED PLACE UNLOADED)
Geliefert benannter Ort entladen
The seller bears all the costs and risks until the goods have reached the named place and is also responsible for unloading them. The buyer bears all other costs.

7
DDP (DELIVERED DUTY PAID)
Geliefert Zoll bezahlt
The seller bears all the costs and risks until the goods have reached their destination, including import duties. The buyer is responsible for unloading the goods.

Rules for sea and inland waterway transport

8
FAS (FREE ALONGSIDE SHIP)
Frei Längsseite Schiff
The seller delivers the goods alongside the ship at the port of shipment. The buyer bears all the costs and risks of transporting the goods to their destination.

9
FOB (FREE ON BOARD)
Frei an Bord
The seller delivers the goods on board the ship at the port of shipment. The buyer bears all the costs and risks of transporting the goods to their destination.

10
CFR (COST AND FREIGHT)
Kosten und Fracht
The seller delivers the goods on board the ship at the port of shipment. He pays the transport costs, without insurance, for the main carriage to the port of destination. The buyer insures the goods for the main carriage and bears all other costs.

11
CIF (COST, INSURANCE AND FREIGHT
Kosten, Versicherung und Fracht
The seller bears all the costs and risks until the goods are delivered on board the ship at the port of shipment. He pays the transport costs, including basic insurance, to the named port of destination. The buyer bears all other costs.

TERMS OF PAYMENT

Here is a list of the most common terms of payment in international trade.

payment in advance	*Vorauszahlung/Vorkasse*
cash with order (CWO)	*Kasse bei Auftragserteilung*
payment by irrevocable and confirmed documentary (letter of) credit	*Zahlung durch unwiderrufliches und bestätigtes Dokumentenakkreditiv*
documents against payment (D/P) / cash against documents (CAD)	*Kasse gegen Dokumente*
cash on delivery (COD)	*gegen Nachnahme*
30% with order, 70% on completion	*30% bei Auftragserteilung, 70% bei Fertigstellung*
⅓ with order, ⅓ on delivery, ⅓ within 30 days after delivery	*⅓ bei Auftragserteilung, ⅓ bei Lieferung, ⅓ innerhalb von 30 Tagen nach Lieferung*
payment within 30/60/90 days from date of invoice	*Zahlung innerhalb von 30/60/90 Tagen nach Rechnungsdatum*
10 days 2%, 30 days net	*Zahlung innerhalb 10 Tagen abzüglich 2% Skonto oder innerhalb 30 Tagen netto*
payment on receipt of goods	*Zahlung bei Erhalt der Waren*
payment on receipt of invoice	*Zahlung bei Rechnungserhalt*
documents against (three months') acceptance (D/A)	*Dokumente gegen (Dreimonats)akzept*
open account terms with monthly/ quarterly settlement	*offenes Zahlungsziel mit monatlicher/vierteljährlicher Abrechnung*

N Talking about numbers

Cardinal numbers / Ordinal numbers

Cardinal		Ordinal	
0	oh/nought/null (*AE*) zero		
1	one	1st	first
2	two	2nd	second
3	three	3rd	third
4	four	4th	fourth
5	five	5th	fifth
6	six	6th	sixth
7	seven	7th	seventh
8	eight	8th	eighth
9	nine	9th	ninth
10	ten	10th	tenth
11	eleven	11th	eleventh
12	twelve	12th	twelfth
13	thirteen	13th	thirteenth
14	fourteen	14th	fourteenth
15	fifteen	15th	fifteenth
16	sixteen	16th	sixteenth
17	seventeen	17th	seventeenth
18	eighteen	18th	eighteenth
19	nineteen	19th	nineteenth
20	twenty	20th	twentieth
21	twenty-one	21st	twenty-first
22	twenty-two	22nd	twenty-second
23	twenty-three	23rd	twenty-third
24	twenty-four	24th	twenty-fourth
30	thirty	30th	thirtieth
40	forty	40th	fortieth
50	fifty	50th	fiftieth
60	sixty	60th	sixtieth
70	seventy	70th	seventieth
80	eighty	80th	eightieth
90	ninety	90th	ninetieth
100	one hundred	100th	one hundredth

In English you say:

101	one hundred **and** one
235	two hundred **and** thirty-five
1,563,765 1 563 765	one million, five hundred **and** sixty-three thousand, seven hundred **and** sixty-five

You use commas or spaces (and not a point) after the thousands (or millions) in large numbers.

Decimals

In English, you write decimals with a point, not a comma.

0.25	oh/nought point two five (*BE*) zero point two five (*AE*)
3.76	three point seven six
55.37	fifty-five point three seven
1.585	one point five eight five

Fractions

¼	a/one quarter
⅓	a/one third
½	a/one half
⅔	two-thirds
¾	three-quarters
5/16	five sixteenths
1½	one and a half

1 m^2	one **square** metre
1 m^3	one **cubic** metre
5^2	five **squared**
10^4	ten **to the power of** four

Symbols

+	plus/and
–	minus
±	plus or minus
×	multiplied by / times; by (e.g. 6 mm × 2 mm)
÷	divided by
=	is equal to / equals
≠	isn't equal to / doesn't equal
≈	is approximately equal to
<	is less than
>	is greater / more than
%	per cent (*also:* percent)
°	degree

IR

Irregular verbs

be – was/were – been	sein
become – became – become	werden
begin – began – begun	anfangen, beginnen
break – broke – broken	brechen
bring – brought – brought	bringen
build – built – built	bauen
burn – burnt/burned – burnt/burned	(ver)brennen
buy – bought – bought	kaufen
catch – caught – caught	fangen
choose – chose – chosen	wählen
come – came – come	kommen
cost – cost – cost	kosten
cut – cut – cut	schneiden
do – did – done	tun, machen, erledigen
draw – drew – drawn	zeichnen
dream – dreamt – dreamt	träumen
drink – drank – drunk	trinken
drive – drove – driven	fahren
eat – ate – eaten	essen
fall – fell – fallen	fallen
feed – fed – fed	füttern, ernähren
feel – felt – felt	(sich) fühlen, empfinden
fight – fought – fought	kämpfen
find – found – found	finden
fit – fit/fitted – fit/fitted	passen
fly – flew – flown	fliegen
forget – forgot – for- gotten	vergessen
get – got – got (*AE* gotten)	bekommen, erhalten
give – gave – given	geben
go – went – gone	gehen, fahren
grow – grew – grown	wachsen
hang – hung – hung	hängen
have – had – had	haben
hear – heard – heard	hören
hide – hid – hidden	(sich) verstecken
hit – hit – hit	schlagen, aufprallen auf
hold – held – held	halten, festhalten
keep – kept – kept	behalten
know – knew – known	kennen, wissen
lay – laid – laid	legen
lead – led – led	führen, leiten
learn – learnt/learned – learnt/learned	lernen
leave – left – left	abfahren, verlassen, weggehen
let – let – let	lassen
lose – lost – lost	verlieren
make – made – made	machen
mean – meant – meant	meinen, bedeuten
meet – met – met	treffen
pay – paid – paid	bezahlen
put – put – put	setzen, stellen, legen
read – read – read	lesen
ride – rode – ridden	reiten, fahren
ring – rang – rung	klingeln, anrufen
rise – rose – risen	(an)steigen
run – ran – run	laufen, rennen
say – said – said	sagen
see – saw – seen	sehen
sell – sold – sold	verkaufen
send – sent – sent	senden, schicken
shake – shook – shaken	schütteln
set – set – set	setzen, stellen
show – showed – shown	zeigen
shut – shut – shut	schließen
sing – sang – sung	singen
sit – sat – sat	sitzen
sleep – slept – slept	schlafen
smell – smelt/smelled – smelt/smelled	riechen
speak – spoke – spoken	sprechen
spell – spelt/spelled – spelt/spelled	buchstabieren
spend – spent – spent	ausgeben, verbringen
stand – stood – stood	stehen
steal – stole – stolen	stehlen
swim – swam – swum	schwimmen
take – took – taken	nehmen
teach – taught – taught	unterrichten, beibringen
tear – tore – torn	(zer)reißen
tell – told – told	sagen, erzählen
think – thought – thought	denken
throw – threw – thrown	werfen
understand – understood – understood	verstehen
wake – woke – woken	wecken
wear – wore – worn	tragen (Kleidung)
win – won – won	gewinnen
write – wrote – written	schreiben

The World

Canada
United States of America
Mexico
Greenland
Iceland
Norway
Finland
Sweden
United Kingdom
Ireland
Ger-many
France
Portugal
Spain
Italy
Ukraine
Russia
Kazakhstan
Mongolia
China
Japan
North Korea
South Korea
Taiwan
Philippines
Uzbekistan
Kyrgyzstan
Turkmenistan
Tajikistan
Afghanistan
Pakistan
Nepal
India
Bangla-desh
Myan-mar
Thai-land
Laos
Vietnam
Cam-bodia
Malaysia
Indonesia
East Timor
Papua New Guinea
Australia
New Zealand
Sri Lanka
Georgia
Turkey
Greece
Iraq
Iran
Kuwait
Saudi Arabia
UAE
Oman
Yemen
Morocco
Western Sahara
Algeria
Tunisia
Libya
Egypt
Mauritania
Mali
Niger
Chad
Sudan
Eritrea
Ethiopia
Somalia
Senegal
Guinea
Sierra Leone
Liberia
Côte d'Ivoire
Ghana
Burkina Faso
Nigeria
Cameroon
Central African Rep.
South Sudan
Uganda
Kenya
Gabon
Congo
Dem. Rep. of Congo
Tanzania
Angola
Zambia
Malawi
Zim-babwe
Mo-zam-bique
Madagascar
Namibia
Bots-wana
South Africa
Eswatini
Lesotho
Cuba
Bahamas
Jamaica
Haiti
Dominican Rep.
Puerto Rico
Guatemala
El Salvador
Honduras
Nicaragua
Costa Rica
Panama
Venezuela
Guyana
Surinam
Fr. Guiana
Colombia
Ecuador
Peru
Brazil
Bolivia
Paraguay
Chile
Argentina
Uruguay
Los Angeles
Chicago
Toronto
New York
Washington D.C.
Mexico City
Lima
São Paulo
London
Moscow
Istanbul
Lagos
Kinshasa
Cape Town
Karachi
Mumbai
Dhaka
Beijing
Tianjin
Shanghai
Hong Kong
Tokyo
Manila
Sydney
Pacific Ocean
Atlantic Ocean
Indian Ocean
Pacific Ocean

European Union

A Acknowledgements

Cover: Cornelsen/shutterstock.com/zhu difeng; **S. 7:** Shutterstock.com/Dmitry Kalinovsky; **S. 8.1:** Shutterstock.com/Rido; **S. 8.2:** Shutterstock.com/SeventyFour; **S. 8.3:** Shutterstock.com/Odua Images; **S. 9:** Shutterstock.com/Helenshi; **S. 10.1:** Shutterstock.com/Ian Law; **S. 10.2:** Shutterstock.com/hxdbzxy; **S. 10.3:** Shutterstock.com/Helen Hotson; **S. 10.4:** Shutterstock.com/jax10289: **S. 11.1:** Shutterstock.com/Creative Lab; **S. 11.2:** Shutterstock.com/Deman; **S. 11.3:** Shutterstock.com/Fascinadora; **S. 11.4:** Shutterstock.com/Sorbis; **S. 11.5:** Shutterstock.com/tuu sitt; **S. 11.6:** Shutterstock.com/Degimages; **S. 12:** Shutterstock.com/Larina Marina; **S. 13:** Shutterstock.com/metamorworks; **S. 14.1:** Shutterstock.com/ViDI Studio; **S. 14.2:** Shutterstock.com/F8 studio; **S. 14.3:** Shutterstock.com/stockyimages; **S. 14.4:** Shutterstock.com/Standby Pictures; **S. 16:** Shutterstock.com/garagestock; **S. 17:** Shutterstock.com/ronstik; **S. 18:** Shutterstock.com/Marlon Lopez MMG1 Design; **S. 20.1:** Shutterstock.com/Ysami; **S. 20.2:** Shutterstock.com/cve iv; **S. 20.3:** Shutterstock.com/Anna.zabella; **S. 20.4.1:** Shutterstock.com/CastecoDesign; **S. 20.4.2:** Shutterstock.com/Anna Rassadnikova; **S. 20.5:** Shutterstock.com/Africa Studio; **S. 20.6:** Shutterstock.com/Oleksiy Mark; **S. 20.7:** Shutterstock.com/Oleksiy Mark; **S. 20.8:** Shutterstock.com/Paket; **S. 20.9:** Shutterstock.com/Irfan Muslimin; **S. 20.10:** Shutterstock.com/VectorV; **S. 20.11:** Shutterstock.com/graphego; **S. 20.12:** Shutterstock.com/Sudowoodo; **S. 20.13:** Shutterstock.com/linear_design; **S. 20.14:** Shutterstock.com/nexusby; **S. 20.15:** Shutterstock.com/Happy Illustrator; **S. 20.16:** Shutterstock.com/bioraven; **S. 20.17:** Shutterstock.com/Martial Red; **S. 20.18:** Shutterstock.com/ecco; **S. 20.19:** Shutterstock.com/Gearstd; **S. 20.20:** Shutterstock.com/Fotaro1965; **S. 20.21:** Shutterstock.com/Lia Li; **S. 20.22:** Shutterstock.com/Valentina Razumova; **S. 20.23:** Shutterstock.com/PICTWORKS; **S. 20.24:** Shutterstock.com/Vlad Kochelaevskiy; **S. 20.25:** Shutterstock.com/Janis Abolins; **S. 20.26:** Shutterstock.com/Macrovector; **S. 20.27:** Shutterstock.com/WarmWorld; **S. 20.28:** Shutterstock.com/koya979; **S. 20.29:** Shutterstock.com/LOVIN; **S. 20.30:** Shutterstock.com/Marharyta Kovalenko; **S. 21.1:** Shutterstock.com/Sentavio: **S. 21.2:** Shutterstock.com/Rvector; **S. 21.3:** Shutterstock.com/Kite_rin; **S. 21.4:** Shutterstock.com/tele52; **S. 21.5:** Shutterstock.com/AAYDESIGN; **S. 21.6:** Shutterstock.com/tele52; **S. 22:** Shutterstock.com/Prostock-studio; **S. 23:** Cornelsen/D'Avila Illustration Agency; **S. 23.1:** Shutterstock/ariefpro; **S. 23.2:** Shutterstock.com/NaturalBox; **S. 23.3:** Shutterstock/leonori; **S. 24.1:** Cornelsen/D'Avila Illustration Agency; **S. 24.1.1:** Shutterstock/ariefpro; **S. 24.1.2:** Shutterstock.com/Monkey Business Images; **S. 24.2:** Cornelsen/D'Avila Illustration Agency; **S. 24.2.1:** Shutterstock/ariefpro; **S. 24.2.2:** Shutterstock.com/RimBar; **S. 24.3:** Cornelsen/ D'Avila Illustration Agency; **S. 24.3.1:** Shutterstock/ariefpro; **S. 24.3.2:** Shutterstock.com/Zzvet; **S. 25.1:** Shutterstock.com/Romolo Tavani; **S. 25.2:** Shutterstock.com/bsd; **S. 25.3:** Shutterstock.com/Avector; **S. 25.4:** Shutterstock.com/DmOK; **S. 26:** Cornelsen/Straive; **S. 28:** Shutterstock.com/Mila Supinskaya Glashchenko; **S. 29.1:** Shutterstock.com/Jan_S; **S. 29.2:** Shutterstock.com/Hyejin Kang; **S. 29.3:** Shutterstock.com/Sirichai Puangsuwan; **S. 29.4:** Shutterstock.com/Honigjp31; **S. 29.5:** Shutterstock.com/Oakland Images; **S. 29.6:** Shutterstock.com/supawat bursuk; **S. 30.1:** Shutterstock.com/Mega Pixel; **S. 30.2:** Shutterstock.com/3DMI; **S. 30.3:** Shutterstock.com/AlexLMX; **S. 30.4:** Shutterstock.com/modustollens; **S. 30.5:** Shutterstock.com/Dima Moroz; **S. 30.6:** Shutterstock.com/Zadiraka Evgenii; **S. 30.7:** Shutterstock.com/Andrey_Kuzmin; **S. 30.8:** Shutterstock.com/Simic Vojislav; **S. 31.1:** Shutterstock.com/Olivier Le Moal; **S. 31.2:** Shutterstock.com/Dusan Petkovic; **S. 32:** Shutterstock.com/smolaw; **S. 33:** Shutterstock.com/giggsy25; **S. 34:** Shutterstock.com/JivkoM; **S. 35.1:** Shutterstock.com/RossHelen; **S. 35.2:** Shutterstock.com/Pressmaster; **S. 35.3:** Shutterstock.com/Juice Flair; **S. 35.4:** Shutterstock.com/Juice Dash; **S. 35.5:** Shutterstock.com/michaeljung: **S. 35.6:** Shutterstock.com/Tyler Olson; **S. 35.7:** Shutterstock.com/Pixel-Shot; **S. 35.8:** Shutterstock.com/Dmitry Kalinovsky; **S. 36.1:** Cornelsen/D'Avila Illustration Agency; **S. 36.2:** Shutterstock.com/Butus; **S. 37:** Shutterstock.com/Vitalii Vodolazskyi; **S. 40:** Shutterstock.com/michaeljung; **S. 41.1:** Shutterstock.com/simbos; **S. 41.2:** Shutterstock.com/Tattoboo; **S. 41.3:** Shutterstock.com/Mila Duchinskaya; **S. 42.1:** Shutterstock.com/fizkes; **S. 42.2:** Shutterstock.com/Mangostar; **S. 43:** Shutterstock.com/sirtravelalot; **S. 44.1:** Shutterstock.com/Netfalls Remy Musser; **S. 44.2:** Shutterstock.com/Kzenon; **S. 44.3:** Shutterstock.com/Robert Kneschke; **S. 44.4:** Shutterstock.com/cunaplus; **S. 46.1:** Shutterstock.com/Mar1kOFF; **S. 46.2:** Shutterstock.com/Monkey Business Images; **S. 47.1:** Shutterstock.com/Victor Metelskiy; **S. 47.2:** Shutterstock.com/Maria Ferencova: **S. 48:** Shutterstock.com/Pcess609; **S. 50:** Cornelsen/Straive; **S. 51.1:** Shutterstock.com/Masson; **S. 51.2:** Shutterstock.com/blurAZ; **S. 52:** Shutterstock.com/xtock; **S. 53:** Cornelsen/D'Avila Illustration Agency; **S. 54.1:** Shutterstock.com/Serghei Starus; **S. 54.2:** Shutterstock.com/adike; **S. 54.3:** Shutterstock.com/Flamingo Images; **S. 54.4:** Shutterstock.com/AlenKadr; **S. 54.5:** Shutterstock.com/Michael Stein 121272; **S. 54.6:** Shutterstock.com/Africa Studio; **S. 54.7:** Shutterstock.com/Yeti studio; **S. 54.8:** Shutterstock.com/pornpawit; **S. 54.9:** Shutterstock.com/THERDSAK SUPAWONG; **S. 54.10:** Shutterstock.com/Africa Studio; **S. 54.11:** Shutterstock.com/SFIO CRACHO; **S. 54.12:** Shutterstock.com/chrisbrignell; **S. 55.1–4:** Cornelsen/D'Avila Illustration Agency; **S. 55.5:** stock.adobe.com/designua; **S. 55.6:** Bundesanstalt für Landwirtschaft und Ernährung, Bonn; **S. 55.7:** Shutterstock.com/KravOK; **S. 55.8:** TransFair e.V. (Fairtrade Deutschland), Köln; **S. 56.1:** Shutterstock.com/nupook538; **S. 56.2:** Shutterstock.com/sirtravelalot; **S. 56.3:** Shutterstock.com/Fascinadora; **S. 56.4:** Shutterstock.com/Aurum171; **S. 56.5:** Shutterstock.com/l i g h t p o e t; **S. 56.6:** Shutterstock.com/Aurelian Nedelcu; **S. 56.7:**

Shutterstock.com/fiphoto; **S. 56.8:** Shutterstock.com/Valentyn Volkov; **S. 56.9:** Shutterstock.com/RG-vc; **S. 57:** Shutterstock.com/Monkey Business Images; **S. 59.1:** Shutterstock.com/mbezvodinskikh; **S. 59.2:** Shutterstock.com/Teerapong Pothong; **S. 59.3:** Shutterstock.com/CHIARI VFX; **S. 59.4:** Shutterstock.com/cigdem; **S. 60.1.o:** Shutterstock.com/Deman; **S. 60.2.o:** Shutterstock.com/gabriel12; **S. 60.3.o:** Shutterstock.com/gpointstudio; **S. 60.4.o:** Shutterstock.com/Trong Nguyen; **S. 60.1.u:** Shutterstock.com/Lena Si; **S. 60.2.u:** Shutterstock.com/Creative Lab; **S. 60.3.u:** Shutterstock.com/Firma V; **S. 60.4.u:** Shutterstock.com/Sergey Ryzhov; **S. 60.5.u:** Shutterstock.com/oradige59; **S. 60.6.u:** Shutterstock.com/Natalya Erofeeva; **S. 60.7.u:** Shutterstock.com/hxdbzxy; **S. 60.8.u:** Shutterstock.com/fancy; **S. 61:** Shutterstock.com/Creative Lab; **S. 62.1:** Shutterstock.com/Yashkin Ilya; **S. 62.2:** Shutterstock.com/Jr images; **S. 62.3:** Shutterstock.com/GoncharukMaks; **S. 62.4:** Shutterstock.com/ApoGapo; **S. 62.5:** Shutterstock.com/AmaPhoto; **S. 63.1:** Shutterstock.com/EstudiosOMH; **S. 63.2:** Shutterstock.com/kreatorex; **S. 63.3:** Shutterstock.com/Gilang Prihardono; **S. 63.4:** Shutterstock.com/Kingkarn Mala; **S. 63.5:** Shutterstock.com/Volodymyr Hlukhovskyi; **S. 63.6:** Shutterstock.com/wk1003mike; **S. 63.7:** Shutterstock.com/Eshma; **S. 63.8:** Shutterstock.com/wk1003mike; S. 63.9: Shutterstock.com/Vladyslav Starozhylov; **S. 63.10:** Shutterstock.com/gopfaster; **S. 64:** Shutterstock.com/Syda Productions; **S. 65.1:** stock.adobe.com/bernardojbp; **S. 65.2:** stock.adobe.com/Bohdan Malitskiy; **S. 65.3:** Shutterstock.com/Eviart; **S. 65.4:** Shutterstock.com/Sergey Ryzhov; **S. 69.1:** Shutterstock.com/Roman Samborskyi; **S. 69.2:** Shutterstock.com/Dean Drobot; **S. 69.3:** Shutterstock.com/fizkes; **S. 69.4:** Shutterstock.com/Cookie Studio; **S. 69.5:** Shutterstock.com/Ranta Images; **S. 69.6:** Shutterstock.com/WAYHOME studio; **S. 69.7:** Shutterstock.com/Koldunov Alexey; **S. 69.8:** Shutterstock.com/Cookie Studio; **S. 71.1–2:** Cornelsen/D'Avila Illustration Agency; **S. 71.3:** Shutterstock.com/George Rudy; **S. 72.1:** Shutterstock.com/Aleksandra Gigowska; **S. 72.2:** Shutterstock.com/Tero Vesalainen; **S. 73.1:** Shutterstock.com/ViDI Studio; **S. 73.2:** Shutterstock.com/Geobor; **S. 74:** Shutterstock.com/rassco; **S. 75.1:** Shutterstock.com/P.S_2; **S. 75.2:** Shutterstock.com/ppart; **S. 75.3:** Shutterstock.com/gomolach; **S. 75.4:** Shutterstock.com/ApoGapo; **S. 75.5:** Shutterstock.com/Madele; **S. 75.6:** Shutterstock.com/AmaPhoto; **S. 75.7:** Shutterstock.com/IB Photography; **S. 75.8:** Shutterstock.com/Oleksiy Mark; **S. 75.9:** Shutterstock.com/AlexPhotoGo; **S. 75.10:** Shutterstock.com/Hurst Photo; **S. 75.11:** Shutterstock.com/New Africa; S. **75.12:** Shutterstock.com/Maxx-Studio; **S. 75.13:** Shutterstock.com/AnnaBabich; **S. 75.14:** Shutterstock.com/Sport08; **S. 75.15:** Shutterstock.com/Top Photo Engineer; **S. 76:** Shutterstock.com/G-Stock Studio; **S. 79.1:** Shutterstock.com/Kinga; **S. 79.2:** Shutterstock.com/Monkey Business Images; **S. 79.3:** Shutterstock.com/sirtravelalot; **S. 79.4:** Shutterstock.com/GoodStudio; **S. 79:** (pin) Shutterstock/Jan Engel; **S. 80:** Cornelsen/Straive; **S. 81:** Shutterstock.com; **S. 82.1:** Shutterstock.com/Ariwasabi; **S. 82.2:** Shutterstock.com/Surasak_Ch; **S. 83:** Shutterstock.com/Syda Productions; **S. 86:** Shutterstock.com/Onlyshaynestockphoto; **S. 87.1:** Shutterstock.com/Spantomoda; **S. 87.2:** Shutterstock.com/Janis Smits; **S. 87.3:** Shutterstock.com/elenovsky; **S. 87.4:** Shutterstock.com/Dima Moroz; **S. 87.5:** Shutterstock.com/Artur Szczybylo; **S. 88:** Shutterstock/Gater Images; **S. 89.1:** Shutterstock.com/Sofia Zhuravetc; **S. 89.2:** Shutterstock.com/md-pictures; **S. 89.3:** Shutterstock.com/Netkoff; **S. 90.1:** Shutterstock.com/Marish; **S. 90.2:** Shutterstock.com/TarikVision; **S. 91:** Shutterstock.com/Travel mania; **S. 94:** Shutterstock.com/Bignai; **S. 95:** Shutterstock.com/Sergey Spritnyuk; **S. 96:** Shutterstock.com/Chiyacat; **S. 98:** Cornelsen/D'Avila Illustration Agency; **S. 100:** Shutterstock.com/Elena Elisseeva; **S. 102:** Shutterstock.com/Siwakorn1933; **S. 105:** Shutterstock.com/tatianasun; **S. 107:** Shutterstock.com/New Africa; **S. 108:** Shutterstock.com/volodyar; **S. 111.1:** Shutterstock.com/Robie Online; **S. 111.2:** Shutterstock.com/Ansis Klucis; **S. 113:** Shutterstock.com/Avigator Fortuner; **S. 114:** Shutterstock.com/Andrii Yalanskyi; **S. 115:** Shutterstock.com/fotorawin; **S. 116:** Shutterstock.com/Cookie Studio; **S. 118:** Shutterstock.com/cigdem; **S. 120:** Shutterstock.com/stockphoto-graf; **S. 122:** Shutterstock.com/Mostovyi Sergii Igorevich; **S. 123:** Shutterstock.com/Afanasiev Andrii; **S. 124:** Shutterstock.com/linear_design; **S. 126:** Shutterstock.com/ALPA PROD; **S. 127.1:** Shutterstock.com/Syda Productions; **S. 127.2:** Shutterstock/AAYDESIGN **S. 127.3:** Shutterstock.com/antoniodiaz; **S. 127.4:** Shutterstock.com/Jacob Lund; **S. 127.5:** stock.adobe.com/tonktiti; **S. 127.6:** Shutterstock.com/Terri Francis; **S. 127.7:** stock.adobe.com/pressmaster; **S. 127.8:** stock.adobe.com/zhu difeng; **S. 127.9:** stock.adobe.com/Dangubic; **S. 128.1:** Shutterstock.com/Inara Prusakova; **S. 128.2:** Shutterstock.com/printstocker; **S. 128.3.1:** Shutterstock.com/khuruzero; **S. 128.3.2:** Shutterstock.com/Art Avanturin; **S. 130:** Cornelsen/Straive; **S. 131.1:** Shutterstock.com/mipan; **S. 131.2:** Shutterstock.com/zhu difeng; **S. 132:** Cornelsen/D'Avila Illustration Agency; **S. 133:** Shutterstock.com/panuwat phimpha; **S. 134:** Shutterstock.com/Matej Kastelic; **S. 136:** Shutterstock.com/wrangler; **S. 137.1:** Shutterstock.com/Jason Winter; **S. 137.2:** Shutterstock.com/Marta Design; **S. 137.3:** Shutterstock.com/Christopher Hall; **S. 137.4:** Shutterstock.com/Cagkan Sayin; **S. 137.5:** Shutterstock.com/Lucian Milasan; **S. 137.6:** Shutterstock.com/Jason Winter; **S. 137.7:** Shutterstock.com/Lucian Milasan; **S. 137.8:** Shutterstock.com/Minerva Studio; **S. 139:** Shutterstock.com/EtiAmmos; **S. 140:** Shutterstock/Kaspars Grinvalds; **S. 143.1:** Shutterstock/Caftor; **S. 143.2:** Shutterstock/Tommy Alven; **S. 143.3:** Shutterstock/pozitivo; **S. 144.1:** Shutterstock.com/Eviled; **S. 144.2:** Shutterstock.com/Diana Rui; **S. 144.3:** Shutterstock.com/Elnur; **S. 144.4:** Shutterstock.com/Alpay Erdem; **S. 148:** Shutterstock.com/wavebreakmedia; **S. 150:** Cornelsen/ D'Avila Illustration Agency